DDC Readymade

A treasury to 15,000 readymade DDC class numbers relating to Indian subjects, English language and literature

DDC Readymade

A treasury to 15,000 readymade DDC class numbers relating to Indian subjects, English language and literature

By

B K Sen

Ess Ess Publications

4837/24, Ansari Road, Darya Ganj,
New Delhi-110002
✆ : 23260807, 41563444
Fax : 011-41563334
E-mail: info@essessreference.com
url:http://www.essessreference.com

DDC READYMADE

A treasury to 15,000 readymade DDC class numbers relating to Indian subjects, English language and literature

ISBN: 978-81-7000-520-9

First Published 2008

Published by:
Ess Ess Publications
4831/24, Ansari Road,
Darya Ganj,
New Delhi-110 002.
INDIA
Phones: 23260807, 41563444
Fax: 41563334
E-mail: info@essessreference.com
www.essessreference.com

Cover Design by *Patch Creative Unit*

Printed and bound in India at Salasar Imaging Systems.

Dedicated to

My Beloved Mother

Whose eternal blessings
Provide me strength and courage
To look forward and move ahead

Introduction

Retro-conversion activities in Indian libraries has been going on for about two decades now. In this activity many libraries apart from converting their catalogue data in machine-readable form are also reclassifying their books mostly in Dewey Decimal Classification using the recent editions. In many cases, the number of books go beyond one hundred thousand, sometimes it touches one million or even more. The concerned library wants to get the work done as quickly as possible. The agency responsible for retro-conversion also intends to finish the job as fast as possible since finishing the job in one library helps it to take up similar job in another library.

In speeding up the operation, reclassification of books on Indian subjects especially religion and literature pose the formidable problem. For classifying books on literature, one has to consult the period table in one volume, the tables 3A, 3B and 3C in another volume. In almost all cases two tables, sometimes three or four tables are to be consulted from two or three different volumes. For example, Table 3C obliges the classifier to see Table 2 in the case of –32 Places; Table 7 in the case of –352 Specific kinds of persons; or class numbers such as 59 (in another volume) in the case of –362 Animals. Needless to say, this considerably brings down the efficiency of the classifier. Generally, a classifier classifies more than 60 books a day. However, in the case of Indic literature, religion and to a certain extent languages their speed registers a sharp decline. To overcome this difficulty, this volume has been prepared basing 21st edition of DDC, the numbers for Chhattisgarh, Jharkhand and Uttaranchal have been taken from 22nd edition as these states were non-existent when 21st edition came out. The publication is not only useful for reclassification of books for retro-conversion of catalogue data, but also useful for day-to-day classification work using DDC. English being the most predominant language of Indian as well as South Asian libraries, class numbers relating to English language and literature have also been provided.

This book is supposed to act as a useful aid for classifying Indian subjects according to DDC with ease. This will save time in classification, enhance the efficiency of the classifier, and above all make DDC a much more user-friendly classification scheme. It is hoped that this book will make DDC more popular not only in India but also in the South Asian region as a whole as languages and literature of those countries have also been covered.

Though the publication is based on DDC 21. Classifiers using recent earlier or latter editions may also use the publication as in most cases the class numbers remain the same.

It needs to be mentioned here that the book is not cent-percent exhaustive as far as Indian subjects are concerned even though it has provided enough numbers to satisfy most of the needs of the classifiers.

There has been every effort to make the publication error-free. However, to err is human. Some errors might still be there. The author will feel highly obliged if any error found in the book is brought to his notice.

Last but not the least, I must thank profoundly Mr. Devinder Punia, the architect of Udbhav Computers Pvt. Ltd and its employees. Needless to say, my association with this very concern and its employees engaged in library automation has generated in me the passionate urge to venture this volume initially for the employees of Udbhav Computers and finally for all.

Contents

Explanatory Note

SYMBOLS

In many cases the class number (CN) is followed by different types of symbols indicating that the CN can be subdivided further. The meanings of the symbols used are as follows:

*	Standard subdivision (SSD) 01-07 may be added.
**	Notations from Table 3C may be added.
@	The number is to be divided as Hindi diaries etc.
+	01-07 for SSD, 08 for Collections, and 09 for History, criticism, etc may be added.
++	Further subdivision as per the instruction in the schedule
CD	Chronological subdivision is to be used

LIST OF ABBREVIATIONS

CD	Chronological subdivision
CN	Class number
DDC 21	Dewey Decimal Classification, 21st ed.
Ex.	Example
SSD	Standard subdivision

The book has mostly covered the Indic religions, languages and literature, geography and history of India, apart from a few other subjects.

RELIGIONS

The religions covered are: Buddhism, Hinduism, Jainism, and Sikhism. Under each of these religions class numbers have been provided for more than two hundred subdivisions. For locating the CN of any aspect, concept, etc pertaining to a religion, the classifier is advised to use the following search expression:

Religion- Subdivision etc

Ex. Buddhism- Gurus 294.361

If the search is conducted with the term Gurus, even then he will find out the number. For locating the number for a sacred book, the classifier should straightway search the name of the book.

LANGUAGES

The class numbers for around fifty subdivisions of each of the important **South Asian languages** like Assamese, Bengali, English, Gujarati, Hindi, Kannada, Malayalam, Marathi, Nepali, Oriya, Punjabi, Sanskrit, Sindhi, Sinhalese, Tamil, Telugu and Urdu have been provided. The numbers for other South Asian languages noticed in DDC have also been given. In many cases numbers are available for their subdivisions as well. The following search expression is to be used for locating the class numbers.

Language – Subdivisions

Ex. Assamese language- Grammar 491.451 5

For the bilingual dictionaries of the aforementioned languages a general number has been provided in each language. Depending on the dictionary, the number is to be constructed.

The number for bilingual dictionaries of Assamese language has been given as 491.45132-39. Here, 491.4513 stands for Assamese dictionary. Now, if we add the number for English language, i.e. 21 (from Table 6) to this number, then we get the number for the Assamese-English dictionary. In this way, the class number for any bilingual dictionary can be constructed.

Literature

While classifying books on literature, classifiers in general are to spend a lot of time shuttling between one Table to another, and not infrequently, from one volume to another of DDC. For all classifiers this is a big botheration. This volume has attempted to lessen the botheration to a very great extent by providing readymade numbers for about 450 subdivisions etc of each important literature of the region. Before classifying books on literature, classifiers should better glance through the arrangements of the subdivisions etc of an important literature like Hindi in this volume. It has been seen from experience that just in a few days time classifiers gets well-accustomed to classify books on literature using this book with considerable ease.

WORKS OF SINGLE AUTHORS

It is to be noted that most books on literature are by single authors. For locating the class number of such books, the following type of search expression is to be used.

Literature Form (single author) – Period.

Ex. Urdu poetry (single author- 2000- 891.439 172

In case the collection is devoted to a particular theme such as nature, even then the number will be the same. When the period is not ascertainable, then the class number will simply be 891.4391.

WORKS OF MULTIPLE AUTHORS

To locate the class numbers for literary works by two or more authors (in this book termed as **multiple authors**), the classifier is to search the Table with such expressions as

i) **Literature Form (multiple authors) – Period**

Ex. Assamese drama (multiple authors)- 1940 – 891.45127+

ii) **Literature Form (multiple authors)– SSD, Collections, History etc**

Ex. Assamese drama (multiple authors)- Philosophy 891.45127001

iii) **Literature (collections of multiple forms)- Period**

Ex. Assamese literature (collections of multiple forms)- 19th century. 891.4510804

iv) **Literature (collections of multiple forms)- Theme**

Ex. Assamese literature (collections of multiple forms)- Allegory 891.45108015

v) **Literature (multiple forms)- Period**

Ex. Assamese literature (multiple forms)- 20th century 891.451090071

vi) **Literature (multiple forms)- Theme – History and criticism**

Ex. Assamese literature (multiple forms)-
Comedy- History and criticism 891.4510917

In the class number of literary works contributed by multiple authors greater depths can be achieved and apart from period the specific form as well as the theme of the work can be shown. See the following examples.

Ex. 1: Best Tamil narrative poems of the 20th century.

The book is a collection of poems by various authors. The class number for this topic given in this book is 894.81110308**. The symbol ** indicates that the number can be expanded further if the content of the book so demands. The number 894.81110308 indicates Tamil literature- 894.811; narrative poem- 103 and collection - 08. 'The 20th century' is missing in the number which can be provided using the number, i.e. 71 from the Period Table given in the main schedule. While attaching 71 to the aforementioned number 0 is to be added before 71 following the instruction in Table 3C. So, the final number for the book will be 894.81110308071.

Ex. 2: Tamil narrative poems devoted to love.

The number for Tamil narrative poem (by multiple authors) is 894.81110308 and the number for love is 3543 which can be straightway added to 894.81110308 and the resultant number for the aforesaid title will be 894.811103083543.

Ex. 3: Tamil narrative poems devoted to love – a criticism.

This book is not a collection of poems, but a criticism of narrative poems (by multiple authors) on love, hence the number 08 for collection is to be replaced by 09 for criticism. The ultimate number will be 894.811103093543.

In the above paragraph, the collection of literary works of a single form by multiple authors has been discussed. Now, let us discuss works of multiple forms by multiple authors. *A work containing poems, short stories, essays, letters and so on is termed as a work of multiple forms.* Obviously this type of work is a collection. The period and theme for this type of work can be shown in the class number.

Ex.: Bengali literature on birds: a collection of stories, poems, and essays.

The search expression to be used here is - *Literature (collections of multiple forms)- Theme.* If we use the term 'birds' for the theme, then we won't get the specific number as the number in this book is provided up to Animals which is 891.44080362++. The symbol ++ indicates that the number is to be expanded as per the instruction in the schedule. Table 3C of DDC 21 instructs that the number –362 Animals is to be expanded as 592-599 excluding 59. The number 598 stands for 'Birds'. Excluding 59 from the number 598, we get 8 which when added to 891.44080362 gives the complete CN for the aforesaid title as 891.440803628.

HISTORY

More than 250 class numbers have been provided under this heading including all the periods of Indian history and the Indian states and union territories. The search expression for this stands as:

History- India/State- Period

Ex. 1 History- India- British period. 954.035

Ex. 2 History- Bengal- British period 954.14

[It is to be noted that the number for historical periods has not been provided for Indian states and union territories]

OTHER SUBJECTS

Class numbers have also been provided for such subjects as Architecture, Conservation of resources, Cultural contact, Economic development, Economic geography, Elections, Elementary education, Fauna, Flora, Folk dancing, Folk literature, Food supply, General clubs, Geography, Geology, Higher education, Journalism, Local public debt, Local taxes, Museums, Newspapers, Organizations, Painting and paintings, Political situation, Postal organizations, Public administration, Public finance, Public policy on education, Revenue, Secondary education, Social problems/ social welfare, Social welfare problems and services, State taxes, Statistics, Strikes, and so on with more than 40 geographical subdivisions. In addition to this, more than a dozen class numbers have been provided for all the Indian states and union territories.

A

Abidharmapitaka.	294.382 4
Abuse within a family (Buddhism)	294.337 832 7
Abuse within a family (Hinduism)	294.517 832 7
Abuse within a family (Jainism)	294.417 832 7
Abuse within a family (Sikhism)	294.617 832 7
Addicts (Buddhism)	294.344 42
Addicts (Hinduism)	294.5442
Addicts (Jainism)	294.4 42
Addicts (Sikhism)	294.6 442
Adults – victims of abuse as children (Buddhism)	294.337 832 73
Adults – victims of abuse as children (Hinduism)	294.517 832 73
Adults – victims of abuse as children (Jainism)	294.417 832 73
Adults – victims of abuse as children (Sikhism)	294.617 832 73
Advaita philosophy.	181.482
Almanacs	030
Alms giving (Buddhism)	294.344 6

Alms giving (Hinduism)	294.544 6
Alms giving (Jainism)	294.444 6
Alms giving (Sikhism)	294.644 6
Ancestors as objects of worship and veneration (Buddhism)	294.342 13
Ancestors as objects of worship and veneration (Hinduism)	294.521 3
Ancestors as objects of worship and veneration (Jainism)	294.421 3
Ancestors as objects of worship and veneration (Sikhism)	294.6213
Ancient Indian architecture	722.44
Ancient Indian sculpture	732.44
Andaman and Nicobar Islands- Architecture	720.954 88
Andaman and Nicobar Islands- Budget	352.495 488
Andaman and Nicobar Islands- Economic development	338.954 88
Andaman and Nicobar Islands- Economic geography	330.954 88
Andaman and Nicobar Islands- Education	370.954 88
Andaman and Nicobar Islands- Fauna	591.954 88
Andaman and Nicobar Islands- Flora	581.954 88
Andaman and Nicobar Islands- Folk dancing	793.319 548 8
Andaman and Nicobar Islands- Geography	915.488
Andaman and Nicobar Islands- Geology	555.488
Andaman and Nicobar Islands- History	954.88
Andaman and Nicobar Islands- Public	

administration	351.548 8
Andaman and Nicobar Islands- Public finance	336.548 8
Andamanese (people)	305.899 11
Andamanese folk music	781.629 911
Andhra Pradesh- Architecture	720.954 84
Andhra Pradesh- Budget	352.495 484
Andhra Pradesh- Economic development	338.954 84
Andhra Pradesh- Economic geography	330.954 84
Andhra Pradesh- Education	370.954 84
Andhra Pradesh- Fauna	591.954 84
Andhra Pradesh- Flora	581.954 84
Andhra Pradesh- Folk dancing	793.319 548 4
Andhra Pradesh- Geography	915.484
Andhra Pradesh- Geology	555.484
Andhra Pradesh- History	954.84
Andhra Pradesh- Public administration	351.548 4
Andhra Pradesh- Public finance	336.548 4
Anglo-Indians	305.891 411
Animals	***See*** Fauna. Zoology
Animism (Buddhism)	294.3421
Animism (Hinduism)	294.521
Animism (Jainism)	294.421
Animism (Sikhism)	294.621

Architecture- Andaman and Nicobar Islands	720.954 88
Architecture- Andhra Pradesh	720.954 84
Architecture- Arunachal Pradesh	720.954 163
Architecture- Assam	720.954 162
Architecture- Bengal	720.954 14
Architecture- Bihar	720.954 12
Architecture- Bombay	720.954 792 3
Architecture- Calcutta	720.954 147
Architecture- Chandigarh	720.954 552
Architecture- Chhattisgarh	720.954 137
Architecture- Dadra and Nagar Haveli	720.954 796
Architecture- Delhi	720.954 56
Architecture- Goa, Daman and Diu	720.954 799
Architecture- Gujarat	720.954 75
Architecture- Haryana	720.954 558
Architecture- Himachal Pradesh	720.954 52
Architecture- Hyderabad state	720.954 84
Architecture- India	720.954
Architecture- Jammu and Kashmir	720.954 6
Architecture- Jharkhand	720.954 127
Architecture- Karnataka	720.954 87
Architecture- Kerala	720.954 83
Architecture- Madhya Pradesh	720.954 3
Architecture- Madras	720.954 82
Architecture- Maharashtra	720.954 792

Architecture- Manipur	720.954 17
Architecture- Meghalaya	720.954 164
Architecture- Mizoram	720.954 166
Architecture- Nagaland	720.954 165
Architecture- Northeast India	720.954 1
Architecture- Orissa	720.954 13
Architecture- Pondicherry	720.954 86
Architecture- Punjab	720.954 552
Architecture- Rajasthan	720.954 4
Architecture- Sikkim	720.954 167
Architecture- South Asia	720.954
Architecture- Southern India	720.954 8
Architecture- Tamil Nadu	720.954 82
Architecture- Tripura	720.954 15
Architecture- Uttar Pradesh	720.954 2
Architecture- Uttaranchal	720.954 51
Architecture- West Bengal	720.954 14
Architecture- Western India	720.954 7
Arunachal Pradesh- Architecture	720.954 163
Arunachal Pradesh- Budget	352.495 416 3
Arunachal Pradesh- Economic development	338.954 163
Arunachal Pradesh- Economic geography	330.954 163
Arunachal Pradesh- Education	370.954 163
Arunachal Pradesh- Fauna	591.954 163
Arunachal Pradesh -Flora	581.954 163

Arunachal Pradesh- Folk dancing	793.319 541 63
Arunachal Pradesh- Geography	915.4163
Arunachal Pradesh- Geology	555.416 3
Arunachal Pradesh- History	954.163
Arunachal Pradesh- Public administration	351.541 63
Arunachal Pradesh- Public finance	336.541 63
Arya Samaj	294.5563
Asceticism (Buddhism)	294.344 47
Asceticism (Hinduism)	294.544 7
Asceticism (Jainism)	294.444 7
Asceticism (Sikhism)	294.644 7
Assam- Architecture	720.954 162
Assam- Budget	352.495 416 2
Assam- Economic development	338.954 162
Assam- Economic geography	330.954 162
Assam- Education	370.954 162
Assam- Fauna	591.954 162
Assam- Flora	581.954 162
Assam- Folk dancing	793.319 541 62
Assam- Geography	915.4162
Assam- Geology	555.416 2
Assam- History	954.162
Assam- Public administration	351.541 62
Assam- Public finance	336.541 62
Assamese - English dictionary	491.451 321

Assamese - Hindi dictionary	491.451 391 31
Assamese adventure fiction (multiple authors)	891.451308 7*
Assamese adventure fiction (multiple authors) -Collections	891.451308 708**
Assamese adventure fiction (multiple authors)- History and criticism	891.451308 709**
Assamese anecdotes, epigrams, graffiti, jokes, quotations (multiple authors)	891.451 802
Assamese anecdotes, epigrams, graffiti, jokes, quotations (single author)	891.451 8+CD+02
Assamese as second language in elementary education	372.659 145 1
Assamese ballads (multiple authors)	891.451104 4*
Assamese ballads (multiple authors)- Collections	891.451104 408**
Assamese ballads (multiple authors)- History and criticism	891.451104 409**
Assamese comedy (multiple authors)	891.451205 23*
Assamese comedy (multiple authors) - Collections	891.451205 2308**
Assamese comedy (multiple authors) - History and criticism	891.451205230 9**
Assamese conversations (multiple authors)	891.451506*
Assamese conversations (multiple authors) - Collections	891.45150608**
Assamese conversations (multiple authors) - History and criticism	891.45150609**
Assamese debates and public discussions (multiple authors)	891.451503*

Assamese debates and public discussions (multiple authors)- Collections	891.45150308**
Assamese debates and public discussions (multiple authors)- History and criticism	891.45150309**
Assamese detective fiction (multiple authors)	891.45130872*
Assamese detective fiction (multiple authors) - Collections	891.4513087208**
Assamese detective fiction (multiple authors) - History and criticism	891.4513087209**
Assamese diaries, notebooks, reminiscences (multiple authors)	891.451803
Assamese diaries, notebooks, reminiscences (single author)	891.4518@
Assamese didactic poetry (multiple authors)	891.451105*
Assamese didactic poetry (multiple authors)- Collections	891.45110508**
Assamese didactic poetry (multiple authors)- History and criticism	891.45110509**
Assamese drama	891.451 2
Assamese drama (multiple authors) - to 1845	***See*** Main schedule
Assamese drama (multiple authors) - 1845-1895	891.45124+
Assamese drama (multiple authors) - 1895-1919	891.45125+
Assamese drama (multiple authors) - 1920-1939	891.45126+
Assamese drama (multiple authors) -	

1940-	891.45127+
Assamese drama (multiple authors) - 1940-1999	891.451271+
Assamese drama (multiple authors) - 19th century	891.45124+
Assamese drama (multiple authors) – 2000-	891.451272+
Assamese drama (multiple authors) - 20th century	891.451271+
Assamese drama (multiple authors) - Collections	891.4512008**
Assamese drama (multiple authors) - Dictionaries etc	891.4512003
Assamese drama (multiple authors) - History and criticism	891.4512009**
Assamese drama (multiple authors) - Periodicals	891.4512005
Assamese drama (multiple authors) - Philosophy and theory	891.4512001
Assamese drama (multiple authors) - Psychological aspects	891.45120019
Assamese drama (multiple authors) - Research	891.45120072
Assamese drama (multiple authors) - Study and teaching	891.4512007
Assamese drama (multiple authors) - Value	891.45120013
Assamese drama (single author) - to 1845	***See*** Main schedule
Assamese drama (single author)-1845 -1895	891.4512 4
Assamese drama (single author)- 1895-1919	891.4512 5

Assamese drama (single author)- 1920-1939	891.4512 6
Assamese drama (single author)- 1940 -	891.4512 7
Assamese drama (single author)- 1940-1999	891.4512 71
Assamese drama (single author)- 19th century	891.4512 4
Assamese drama (single author)- 2000-	891.4512 72
Assamese drama (single author)- 20th century	891.4512 71
Assamese drama for cinema (multiple authors)	891.451203*
Assamese drama for cinema (multiple authors) - Collections	891.45120308**
Assamese drama for cinema (multiple authors) - History and criticism	891.45120309**
Assamese drama for radio (multiple authors)	891.4512022*
Assamese drama for radio (multiple authors) - History and criticism	891.451202209**
Assamese drama for radio (multiple authors) - Collections	891.451202208**
Assamese drama for television (multiple authors)	891.4512025*
Assamese drama for television (multiple authors) - Collections	891.451202508**
Assamese drama for television (multiple authors) - History and criticism	891.451202509**
Assamese dramatic poetry (multiple authors)	891.451102*
Assamese dramatic poetry	

(multiple authors)- Collections	891.45110208**
Assamese dramatic poetry (multiple authors)- History and criticism	891.45110209**
Assamese encyclopaedias	039.91451
Assamese ephemeral and light verse (multiple authors)	891.451108*
Assamese ephemeral and light verse (multiple authors) - History and criticism	891.45110809**
Assamese ephemeral and light verse (multiple authors)- Collections	891.45110808**
Assamese epic poetry (multiple authors)	891.4511032*
Assamese epic poetry (multiple authors)- Collections	891.451103208**
Assamese epic poetry (multiple authors)- History and criticism	891.451103209**
Assamese epigrams	***See*** Assamese anecdotes...
Assamese essays	891.451 4
Assamese essays (multiple authors) - to 1845	***See*** Main schedule
Assamese essays (multiple authors) - 1845-1895	891.45144+
Assamese essays (multiple authors) - 1895-1919	891.45145+
Assamese essays (multiple authors) - 1920-1939	891.45146+
Assamese essays (multiple authors) -1940-	891.45147+
Assamese essays (multiple authors) - 1940-1999	891.451471+

Assamese essays (multiple authors) - 19th century	891.45144+
Assamese essays (multiple authors) – 2000-	891.451472+
Assamese essays (multiple authors) - 20th century	891.451471+
Assamese essays (multiple authors) - Collections	891.4514008**
Assamese essays (multiple authors) - Dictionaries etc	891.4514003
Assamese essays (multiple authors) - History and criticism	891.4514009**
Assamese essays (multiple authors) - Periodicals	891.4514005
Assamese essays (multiple authors) - Philosophy and theory	891.4514001
Assamese essays (multiple authors) - Psychological aspects	891.45140019
Assamese essays (multiple authors) - Research	891.45140072
Assamese essays (multiple authors) - Study and teaching	891.4514007
Assamese essays (multiple authors) - Value	891.45140013
Assamese essays (single author)- - to 1845	***See*** Main schedule
Assamese essays (single author)- 1845 -1895	891.4514 4
Assamese essays (single author)- 1895 - 1919	891.4514 5
Assamese essays (single author)-	

1920-1939	891.4514 6
Assamese essays (single author)- 1940 -	891.4514 7
Assamese essays (single author)- 1940-1999	891.4514 71
Assamese essays (single author)- 19th century	891.4514 4
Assamese essays (single author)- 2000-	891.4514 72
Assamese essays (single author)- 20th century	891.4514 71
Assamese experimental and non-formalized works (single author)	891.4518
Assamese experimental works (multiple authors)	891.451807
Assamese fantasy fiction (multiple authors)	891.451308766*
Assamese fantasy fiction (multiple authors)- Collections	891.45130876608**
Assamese fantasy fiction (multiple authors)- History and criticism	891.45130876609**
Assamese farce (multiple authors)	891.451205232*
Assamese farce (multiple authors)- Collections	891.45120523208**
Assamese farce (multiple authors) - History and criticism	891.45120523209**
Assamese fiction	891.4513
Assamese fiction (multiple authors) - to 1845	***See*** Main schedule
Assamese fiction (multiple authors) - 1845-1895	891.45134+
Assamese fiction (multiple authors) -	

1895-1919	891.45135+
Assamese fiction (multiple authors) - 1920-1939	891.45136+
Assamese fiction (multiple authors) - 1940-	891.45137+
Assamese fiction (multiple authors) - 1940-1999	891.451371+
Assamese fiction (multiple authors) - 19th century	891.45134+
Assamese fiction (multiple authors) – 2000-	891.451372+
Assamese fiction (multiple authors) - 20th century	891.451371+
Assamese fiction (multiple authors) - Collections	891.4513008**
Assamese fiction (multiple authors) - Dictionaries etc	891.4513003
Assamese fiction (multiple authors) - History and criticism	891.4513009**
Assamese fiction (multiple authors) - Periodicals	891.4513005
Assamese fiction (multiple authors) - Philosophy and theory	891.4513001
Assamese fiction (multiple authors) - Psychological aspects	891.45130019
Assamese fiction (multiple authors) - Research	891.45130072
Assamese fiction (multiple authors) - Study and teaching	891.4513007
Assamese fiction (multiple authors) -	

Value	891.45130013
Assamese fiction (single author)- to 1845	***See*** Main schedule
Assamese fiction (single author)- 1845 -1895	891.4513 4
Assamese fiction (single author)- 1895 - 1919	891.4513 5
Assamese fiction (single author)- 1919- 1939	891.4513 6
Assamese fiction (single author)- 1940 -	891.4513 7
Assamese fiction (single author)- 1940-1999	891.4513 71
Assamese fiction (single author)- 19th century	891.4513 4
Assamese fiction (single author)- 2000-	891.4513 72
Assamese fiction (single author)- 20th century	891.4513 71
Assamese folk music	781 629 145
Assamese ghost fiction (multiple authors)	891.451308733*
Assamese ghost fiction (multiple authors) - Collections	891.45130873308**
Assamese ghost fiction (multiple authors)- History and criticism	891.45130873309**
Assamese graffiti	***See*** Assamese anecdotes...
Assamese historical drama (multiple authors)	891.45120514*
Assamese historical drama (multiple authors)- Collections	891.4512051408**
Assamese historical drama (multiple	

authors)- History and criticism	891.4512051409**
Assamese historical fiction (multiple authors)	891.4513081*
Assamese historical fiction (multiple authors)- Collections	891.451308108**
Assamese historical fiction (multiple authors)- History and criticism	891.451308109**
Assamese horror fiction (multiple authors)	891.451308738*
Assamese horror fiction (multiple authors)- Collections	891.45130873808**
Assamese horror fiction (multiple authors)- History and criticism	891.45130873809**
Assamese humour and satire	891.4517
Assamese humour and satire (multiple authors) - to 1845	***See*** Main schedule
Assamese humour and satire (multiple authors) -1845-1895	891.45174+
Assamese humour and satire (multiple authors) -1895-1919	891.45175+
Assamese humour and satire (multiple authors) -1920-1939	891.45176+
Assamese humour and satire (multiple authors) -1940-	891.45177+
Assamese humour and satire (multiple authors) -1940-1999	891.451771+
Assamese humour and satire (multiple authors) -19th century	891.45174+
Assamese humour and satire (multiple authors) -2000-	891.451772+

Assamese humour and satire (multiple authors) -20th century	891.451771+
Assamese humour and satire (multiple authors) -Collections	891.4517008**
Assamese humour and satire (multiple authors) -Dictionaries etc	891.4517003
Assamese humour and satire (multiple authors) -History and criticism	891.4517009**
Assamese humour and satire (multiple authors) -Periodicals	891.4517005
Assamese humour and satire (multiple authors) -Philosophy and theory	891.4517001
Assamese humour and satire (multiple authors) -Psychological aspects	891.45170019
Assamese humour and satire (multiple authors) -Research	891.45170072
Assamese humour and satire (multiple authors) -Study and teaching	891.4517007
Assamese humour and satire (multiple authors) -Value	891.45170013
Assamese humourous and satirical poetry (multiple authors)	891.451107*
Assamese humourous and satirical poetry (multiple authors)- Collections	891.45110708**
Assamese humourous and satirical poetry (multiple authors)- History and criticism	891.45110709**
Assamese jokes	***See*** Assamese anecdotes...
Assamese language	491.451
Assamese language- Applied linguistics	491.451 8

Assamese language- Bilingual dictionaries	491.451 32-39
Assamese language- Bilingualism	491.451 042
Assamese language- Concordances	491.451 03
Assamese language- Content analysis	491.451 014 1
Assamese language- Dialects	491.451 7
Assamese language- Dictionaries	491.451 3
Assamese language- Discourse analysis	491.451 014 1
Assamese language- Education	491.451 071
Assamese language- Encyclopaedias	491.451 03
Assamese language- Etymology	491.451 2
Assamese language- Functionalism	491.451 018
Assamese language- Grammar	491.451 5
Assamese language- History, geography, persons	491.451 09
Assamese language- Intonation	491.451 16
Assamese language- Lexicography	491.451 302 8
Assamese language- Lexicology	491.451 014
Assamese language- Miscellany	491.451 02
Assamese language- Multilingualism	491.451 042
Assamese language- Organizations	491.451 06
Assamese language- Orthography	491.451 152
Assamese language- Pauses	491.451 16
Assamese language- Periodicals	491.451 05
Assamese language- Persons (men, women, etc)	491.451 08

Assamese language- Philosophy and theory	491.451 01
Assamese language- Phonetics	491.451 158
Assamese language- Phonology, etc	491.451 15
Assamese language- Pitch	491.451 16
Assamese language- Pronunciation	491.451 152
Assamese language- Readers	491.451 86
Assamese language- Research	491.451 072
Assamese language- Rhetoric	808.049 1451++
Assamese language- Schools and theories of linguistics	491.451 018
Assamese language- Semantics	491.451 014 3
Assamese language- Semiotics	491.451 014 1
Assamese language- Slang	491.451 7
Assamese language- Special topics	491.451 04
Assamese language- Specialized dictionaries	491.451 31
Assamese language- Spelling	491.451 152
Assamese language- Stress	491.451 16
Assamese language- Structural linguistics	491.451 018
Assamese language- Suprasegmental features	491.451 16
Assamese language- Terminology	491.451 014
Assamese language- Usage	491.451 8
Assamese language- Variations	491.451 7
Assamese language- Writing systems	491.451 11
Assamese letters	891.451 6

Assamese letters (multiple authors)	891.451 6
Assamese letters (multiple authors) - to 1845	***See*** Main schedule
Assamese letters (multiple authors) - 1845-1895	891.45164+
Assamese letters (multiple authors) - 1895-1919	891.45165+
Assamese letters (multiple authors) - 1920-1939	891.45166+
Assamese letters (multiple authors) - 1940-	891.45167+
Assamese letters (multiple authors) - 1940-1999	891.451671+
Assamese letters (multiple authors) - 19th century	891.45164+
Assamese letters (multiple authors) -2000-	891.451672+
Assamese letters (multiple authors) - 20th century	891.451671+
Assamese letters (multiple authors) - Collections	891.4516008**
Assamese letters (multiple authors) - Dictionaries etc	891.4516003
Assamese letters (multiple authors) - History and criticism	891.4516009**
Assamese letters (multiple authors) - Periodicals	891.4516005
Assamese letters (multiple authors) - Philosophy and theory	891.4516001
Assamese letters (multiple authors) - Psychological aspects	891.45160019

Assamese letters (multiple authors) - Research	891.45160072
Assamese letters (multiple authors) - Study and teaching	891.4516007
Assamese letters (multiple authors) -Value	891.45160013
Assamese letters (single author)	891.4516
Assamese letters (single author)- - to 1845	***See*** Main schedule
Assamese letters (single author)- 1845 -1895)	891.4516 4
Assamese letters (single author)- 1895 - 1919	891.4516 5
Assamese letters (single author)- 1920- 1939	891.4516 6
Assamese letters (single author)- 1940 -	891.4516 7
Assamese letters (single author)- 1940-1999	891.4516 71
Assamese letters (single author)- 19th century	891.4516 4
Assamese letters (single author)- 2000-	891.4516 72
Assamese letters (single author)- 20th century	891.4516 71
Assamese light verse	***See*** Assamese ephemeral and light verse
Assamese limericks (multiple authors)	891.4511075*
Assamese limericks (multiple authors)- Collections	891.451107508**
Assamese limericks (multiple authors)- History and criticism	891.451107509**
Assamese literature	891.451

Assamese literature (collections of multiple forms)	891.45108
Assamese literature (collections of multiple forms) - 19th century	891.4510804
Assamese literature (collections of multiple forms) - 20th century	891.45108071
Assamese literature (collections of multiple forms) - 21st century	891.45108072
Assamese literature (collections of multiple forms) - Allegory	891.45108015
Assamese literature (collections of multiple forms) - Animals	891.451080362++
Assamese literature (collections of multiple forms) - Artistic themes	891.451080357
Assamese literature (collections of multiple forms) - Atmosphere	891.45108032161
Assamese literature (collections of multiple forms) - Characters	891.45108027
Assamese literature (collections of multiple forms) - Comedy	891.45108017
Assamese literature (collections of multiple forms) - Evening	891.45108033
Assamese literature (collections of multiple forms) - Fantasy	891.45108015
Assamese literature (collections of multiple forms) - Forests	891.45108032152
Assamese literature (collections of multiple forms) - Historical themes	891.451080358
Assamese literature (collections of multiple forms) - Horror	891.451080164

Assamese literature (collections of multiple forms) - Human characteristics (Biological, moral, psychological)	891.451080353
Assamese literature (collections of multiple forms) - Legendary objects/themes	891.45108037
Assamese literature (collections of multiple forms) - Literary themes	891.451080357
Assamese literature (collections of multiple forms) - Love	891.4510803543
Assamese literature (collections of multiple forms) - Marriage	891.4510803543
Assamese literature (collections of multiple forms) - Morning	891.45108033
Assamese literature (collections of multiple forms) - Mountains	891.45108032143
Assamese literature (collections of multiple forms) - Myth	891.45108015
Assamese literature (collections of multiple forms) - Mythological objects/themes	891.45108037
Assamese literature (collections of multiple forms) - Philosophic themes	891.451080384
Assamese literature (collections of multiple forms) - Places	891.45108032++
Assamese literature (collections of multiple forms) - Plants	891.451080364
Assamese literature (collections of multiple forms) - Political themes	891.451080358
Assamese literature (collections of multiple forms) - Religious themes	891.451080382++
Assamese literature (collections of multiple	

forms) - Rivers	891.451080321693
Assamese literature (collections of multiple forms) - Romanticism	891.451080145
Assamese literature (collections of multiple forms) - Scientific themes	891.451080356
Assamese literature (collections of multiple forms) - Sea	891.45108032162
Assamese literature (collections of multiple forms) - Seasons	891.45108033
Assamese literature (collections of multiple forms) - Sex	891.4510803538
Assamese literature (collections of multiple forms) - Social themes	891.451080355
Assamese literature (collections of multiple forms) - Space	891.4510803219
Assamese literature (collections of multiple forms) - Specific kinds of persons, e.g. heroes	891.451080352++
Assamese literature (collections of multiple forms) - Specific persons (real or imaginary)	891.451080351
Assamese literature (collections of multiple forms) - Stream of consciousness	891.45108025
Assamese literature (collections of multiple forms) - Supernatural objects/themes	891.45108037
Assamese literature (collections of multiple forms) - Symbolism	891.45108015
Assamese literature (collections of multiple forms) - Technical themes	891.451080356
Assamese literature (collections of multiple forms) - Times (seasons, parts of day, etc)	891.45108033

Assamese literature (collections of multiple forms) - Towns	891.451080321732
Assamese literature (collections of multiple forms) - Tragedy	891.451080162
Assamese literature (collections of multiple forms) - Villages	891.451080321734
Assamese literature (collections of multiple forms) - Weather	891.45108036
Assamese literature (collections of multiple forms) emphasizing subjects	891.4510804++
Assamese literature (collections of multiple forms) for/by children	891.4510809282
Assamese literature (collections of multiple forms) for/by persons of racial, ethnic and national groups	891.4510808++
Assamese literature (collections of multiple forms) for/by persons of specific classes	891.45108092++
Assamese literature (collections of multiple forms) for/by persons resident in specific regions	891.45108091++
Assamese literature (collections of multiple forms) for/by women	891.4510809287
Assamese literature (multiple authors)	891.451
Assamese literature (multiple authors) - Concordances	891.45103
Assamese literature (multiple authors) - Dictionaries	891.45103
Assamese literature (multiple authors) - Education	891.451071
Assamese literature (multiple authors) -	

Encyclopaedias	891.45103
Assamese literature (multiple authors) - Organizations	891.45106
Assamese literature (multiple authors) - Periodicals	891.45105
Assamese literature (multiple authors) - Philosophy and theory	891.45101
Assamese literature (multiple authors) - Research	891.451072
Assamese literature (multiple authors) - Research in India	891.451072054
Assamese literature (multiple authors) - Study and teaching	891.45107
Assamese literature (multiple forms) - 19th century	891.45109004
Assamese literature (multiple forms) – 2000-	891.451090072
Assamese literature (multiple forms) - 20th century	891.451090071
Assamese literature (multiple forms) - Allegory – History and criticism	891.4510915
Assamese literature (multiple forms) - Animals - History and criticism	891.45109362++
Assamese literature (multiple forms) - Artistic themes - History and criticism	891.45109357
Assamese literature (multiple forms) - Atmosphere - History and criticism	891.4510932161
Assamese literature (multiple forms) - Characters - History and criticism	891.4510927
Assamese literature (multiple forms) -	

Comedy - History and criticism	891.4510917
Assamese literature (multiple forms) - Evening - History and criticism	891.4510933
Assamese literature (multiple forms) - Fantasy - History and criticism	891.4510915
Assamese literature (multiple forms) - Forests History and criticism	891.4510932152
Assamese literature (multiple forms) - Historical themes - History and criticism	891.45109358
Assamese literature (multiple forms) - History and criticism	891.45109
Assamese literature (multiple forms) - Horror - History and criticism	891.45109164
Assamese literature (multiple forms) - Human characteristics - Biological aspects - History and criticism	891.45109353
Assamese literature (multiple forms) - Human characteristics - Moral aspects - History and criticism	891.45109353
Assamese literature (multiple forms) - Human characteristics -Psychological aspects - History and criticism	891.45109353
Assamese literature (multiple forms) - Legendary objects/themes - History and criticism	891.4510937
Assamese literature (multiple forms) - Literary themes - History and criticism	891.45109357
Assamese literature (multiple forms) - Love - History and criticism	891.451093543
Assamese literature (multiple forms) - Marriage - History and criticism	891.451093543

Assamese literature (multiple forms) - Morning - History and criticism	891.4510933
Assamese literature (multiple forms) - Mountains - History and criticism	891.4510932143
Assamese literature (multiple forms) - Myth - History and criticism	891.4510915
Assamese literature (multiple forms) - Mythological objects/themes - History and criticism	891.4510937
Assamese literature (multiple forms) - Persons of racial, ethnic and national groups - History and criticism	891.451098++
Assamese literature (multiple forms) - Persons of specific classes - History and criticism	891.4510992++
Assamese literature (multiple forms) - Persons resident in specific regions - History and criticism	891.4510991++
Assamese literature (multiple forms) - Philosophic themes - History and criticism	891.45109384
Assamese literature (multiple forms) - Places - History and criticism	891.4510932++
Assamese literature (multiple forms) - Plants - History and criticism	891.45109364
Assamese literature (multiple forms) - Political themes - History and criticism	891.45109358
Assamese literature (multiple forms) - Religious themes - History and criticism	891.45109382++
Assamese literature (multiple forms) - Rivers - History and criticism	891.45109321693
Assamese literature (multiple forms) -	

Romanticism - History and criticism	891.45109145
Assamese literature (multiple forms) - Scientific themes - History and criticism	891.45109356
Assamese literature (multiple forms) - Sea - History and criticism	891.4510932162
Assamese literature (multiple forms) - Seasons - History and criticism	891.4510933
Assamese literature (multiple forms) - Sex - History and criticism	891.451093538
Assamese literature (multiple forms) - Social themes - History and criticism	891.45109355
Assamese literature (multiple forms) - Space - History and criticism	891.451093219
Assamese literature (multiple forms) - Specific kinds of persons, e.g. heroes, - History and criticism	891.45109352++
Assamese literature (multiple forms) - Specific persons - History and criticism	891.45109351
Assamese literature (multiple forms) - Stream of consciousness - History and criticism	891.4510925
Assamese literature (multiple forms) - Subjects - History and criticism	891.451094++
Assamese literature (multiple forms) - Supernatural objects/themes - History and criticism	891.4510937
Assamese literature (multiple forms) - Symbolism- History, description, criticism	891.4510915
Assamese literature (multiple forms) - Technical themes - History and criticism	891.45109356

Assamese literature (multiple forms) - Times - History and criticism	891.4510933
Assamese literature (multiple forms) - Towns - History and criticism	891.45109321732
Assamese literature (multiple forms) - Tragedy - History and criticism	891.45109162
Assamese literature (multiple forms) - Villages - History and criticism	891.45109321734
Assamese literature (multiple forms) - Weather - History and criticism	891.4510936
Assamese literature (single author)- - to 1845- Biography, collections, criticism	***See*** Main schedule
Assamese literature (single author)- 1845 - 1895- Biography, collections, criticism	891.4518 409
Assamese literature (single author)- 1895 - 1919 - Biography, collections, criticism	891.4518 509
Assamese literature (single author)- 1920- 1939 - Biography, collections, criticism	891.4518 609
Assamese literature (single author)- 1940 - Biography, collections, criticism	891.4518 709
Assamese literature (single author)- 1940- 1999 - Biography, collections, criticism	891.4518 7109
Assamese literature (single author)- 19th century- Biography, collections, criticism	891.4518 409
Assamese literature (single author)- 2000- Biography, collections, criticism	891.4518 7209

Assamese literature (single author)- 20th century - Biography, collections, criticism	891.4518 7109
Assamese literature for/by children - History and criticism	891.451099282
Assamese literature for/by women - History and criticism	891.451099287
Assamese love fiction (multiple authors)	891.4513085*
Assamese love fiction (multiple authors)- Collections	891.451308508**
Assamese love fiction (multiple authors)- History and criticism	891.451308509**
Assamese melodrama (multiple authors)	891.45120527*
Assamese melodrama (multiple authors)- Collections	891.4512052708**
Assamese melodrama (multiple authors)- History and criticism	891.4512052709**
Assamese miscellaneous writings (multiple authors)	891.4518
Assamese miscellaneous writings (multiple authors) - to 1845	***See*** Main schedule
Assamese miscellaneous writings (multiple authors) -1845-1895	891.45184++
Assamese miscellaneous writings (multiple authors) -1895-1919	891.45185++
Assamese miscellaneous writings (multiple authors) -1920-1939	891.45186++
Assamese miscellaneous writings (multiple authors) -1940-	891.45187++
Assamese miscellaneous writings	

(multiple authors) -1940-1999	891.451871++
Assamese miscellaneous writings (multiple authors) -19th century	891.45184++
Assamese miscellaneous writings (multiple authors) –2000-	891.451872++
Assamese miscellaneous writings (multiple authors) -20th century	891.451871++
Assamese miscellaneous writings (multiple authors) -Collections	891.4518008**
Assamese miscellaneous writings (multiple authors) -Dictionaries etc	891.4518003
Assamese miscellaneous writings (multiple authors) -History and criticism	891.4518009**
Assamese miscellaneous writings (multiple authors) -Periodicals	891.4518005
Assamese miscellaneous writings (multiple authors) -Philosophy and theory	891.4518001
Assamese miscellaneous writings (multiple authors) -Psychological aspects	891.45180019
Assamese miscellaneous writings (multiple authors) -Research	891.45180072
Assamese miscellaneous writings (multiple authors) -Study and teaching	891.4518007
Assamese miscellaneous writings (multiple authors) -Value	891.45180013
Assamese miscellaneous writings (single author)	891.4518
Assamese miscellaneous writings (single author)- - to 1845	***See*** Main schedule
Assamese miscellaneous writings	

(single author)- 1845 -1895	891.4518 4
Assamese miscellaneous writings (single author)- 1895 - 1919	891.4518 5
Assamese miscellaneous writings (single author)- 1920- 1939	891.4518 6
Assamese miscellaneous writings (single author)- 1940 -	891.4518 7
Assamese miscellaneous writings (single author)- 1940-1999	891.4518 71
Assamese miscellaneous writings (single author)- 19th century	891.4518 4
Assamese miscellaneous writings (single author)- 2000-	891.4518 72
Assamese miscellaneous writings (single author)- 20th century	891.4518 71
Assamese monologues (multiple authors)	891.4512045*
Assamese monologues (multiple authors)- Collections	891.451204508**
Assamese monologues (multiple authors)- History and criticism	891.451204509**
Assamese morality plays	***See*** Assamese religious and morality plays
Assamese mystery fiction (multiple authors)	891.45130872*
Assamese mystery fiction (multiple authors)- Collections	891.4513087208**
Assamese mystery fiction (multiple authors)- History and criticism	891.4513087209**
Assamese narrative poetry (multiple authors)	891.451103*

Assamese narrative poetry (multiple authors)- Collections	891.45110308**
Assamese narrative poetry (multiple authors)- History and criticism	891.45110309**
Assamese notebooks	***See*** Assamese diaries ...
Assamese odes (multiple authors)	891.4511043*
Assamese odes (multiple authors)- Collections	891.451104308**
Assamese odes (multiple authors)- History and criticism	891.451104309**
Assamese one act plays (multiple authors)	891.4512041*
Assamese one act plays (multiple authors)- Collections	891.451 204 108**
Assamese one act plays (multiple authors)- History and criticism	891.451 204 109**
Assamese oratory (multiple authors)	***See*** Assamese public speeches
Assamese periodicals	059.91451
Assamese poetry	891.451 1
Assamese poetry (multiple authors) - to 1845	***See*** Main schedule
Assamese poetry (multiple authors) - 1845-1895	891.45114+
Assamese poetry (multiple authors) - 1895-1919	891.45115+
Assamese poetry (multiple authors) - 1920-1939	891.45116+
Assamese poetry (multiple authors) -	

1940-	891.45117+
Assamese poetry (multiple authors) - 1940-1999	891.451171+
Assamese poetry (multiple authors) - 19th century	891.45114+
Assamese poetry (multiple authors) – 2000-	891.451172+
Assamese poetry (multiple authors) - 20th century	891.451171+
Assamese poetry (multiple authors)- Collections	891.4511008**
Assamese poetry (multiple authors)- Dictionaries etc	891.4511003
Assamese poetry (multiple authors)- History and criticism	891.4511009**
Assamese poetry (multiple authors)- Periodicals	891.4511005
Assamese poetry (multiple authors)- Philosophy and theory	891.4511001
Assamese poetry (multiple authors)- Psychological aspects	891.45110019
Assamese poetry (multiple authors)- Research	891.45110072
Assamese poetry (multiple authors)- Study and teaching	891.4511007
Assamese poetry (multiple authors)- Value	891.45110013
Assamese poetry (single author)- - to 1845	***See*** Main schedule
Assamese poetry (single author)- 1845 -1895	891.4511 4

Assamese poetry (single author)- 1895 - 1919	891.4511 5
Assamese poetry (single author)- 1920-1939	891.4511 6
Assamese poetry (single author)- 1940 -	891.4511 7
Assamese poetry (single author)- 1940-1999	891.4511 71
Assamese poetry (single author)- 19th century	891.4511 4
Assamese poetry (single author)- 2000-	891.4511 72
Assamese poetry (single author)- 20th century	891.4511 71
Assamese prose (single author)- to 1845	***See*** Main schedule
Assamese prose (single author)- 1845 -1895	891.4518 408
Assamese prose (single author)- 1895 - 1919	891.4518 508
Assamese prose (single author)- 1920- 1939	891.4518 608
Assamese prose (single author)- 1940 -	891.4518 708
Assamese prose (single author)- 1940-1999	891.4518 7108
Assamese prose (single author)- 19th century	891.4518 408
Assamese prose (single author)- 2000-	891.4518 7208
Assamese prose (single author)- 20th century	891.4518 7108
Assamese prose literature (multiple authors)	891.451808
Assamese psychological, realistic, sociological fiction (multiple authors) - Collections	891.451308308**

Assamese psychological, realistic, sociological fiction (multiple authors)	891.4513083*
Assamese psychological, realistic, sociological fiction (multiple authors) - History and criticism	891.451308309**
Assamese public discussions	***See*** Assamese debates and public discussions
Assamese public speeches (multiple authors)	891.451501
Assamese public speeches (multiple authors)- Collections	891.45150108
Assamese public speeches (multiple authors)- History and criticism	891.45150109
Assamese quotations	***See*** Assamese anecdotes...
Assamese realistic fiction	***See*** Assamese psychological... fiction
Assamese recitations (multiple authors)	891.451504+
Assamese religious and morality plays (multiple authors)	891.45120516+
Assamese reminiscences ***See*** Assamese diaries ...	891.451803
Assamese romantic fiction (multiple authors)	891.4513085*
Assamese romantic fiction (multiple authors)- Collections	891.451308508**
Assamese romantic fiction (multiple authors)- History and criticism	891.451308509**

Assamese satire	***See*** Assamese humour and satire
Assamese satirical poetry	***See*** Assamese humourous and satirical poetry
Assamese science fiction (multiple authors)	891.451308762*
Assamese science fiction (multiple authors)- Collections	891.45130876208**
Assamese science fiction (multiple authors)- History and criticism	891.45130876209**
Assamese serious drama (multiple authors)	891.4512051+
Assamese short stories (multiple authors)	891.451301*
Assamese short stories (multiple authors)- Collections	891.45130108**
Assamese short stories (multiple authors)- History and criticism	891.45130109**
Assamese sociological fiction (multiple authors)	***See*** Assamese psychological... fiction
Assamese sonnets (multiple authors)	891.4511042*
Assamese sonnets (multiple authors)- Collections	891.451104208**
Assamese sonnets (multiple authors)- History and criticism	891.451104209**
Assamese speaking people	305.791 451
Assamese speeches	891.4515
Assamese speeches (multiple authors) — to 1845	***See*** Main schedule
Assamese speeches (multiple authors) -	

1845-1895	891.45154+
Assamese speeches (multiple authors) - 1895-1919	891.45155+
Assamese speeches (multiple authors) - 1920-1939	891.45156+
Assamese speeches (multiple authors) - 1940-	891.45157+
Assamese speeches (multiple authors) - 1940-1999	891.451571+
Assamese speeches (multiple authors) - 19th century	891.45154+
Assamese speeches (multiple authors) - 2000-	891.451572+
Assamese speeches (multiple authors) - 20th century	891.451571+
Assamese speeches (multiple authors) - Collections	891.4515008**
Assamese speeches (multiple authors) - Dictionaries etc	891.4515003
Assamese speeches (multiple authors) - History and criticism	891.4515009**
Assamese speeches (multiple authors) - Periodicals	891.4515005
Assamese speeches (multiple authors) - Philosophy and theory	891.4515001
Assamese speeches (multiple authors) - Psychological aspects	891.45150019
Assamese speeches (multiple authors) - Research	891.45150072
Assamese speeches (multiple authors) -	

Study and teaching	891.4515007
Assamese speeches (multiple authors) - Value	891.45150013
Assamese speeches (single author)	891.4515
Assamese speeches (single author)- 1845 -1895	891.4515 4
Assamese speeches (single author)- 1895 - 1919	891.4515 5
Assamese speeches (single author)- 1920- 1939	891.4515 6
Assamese speeches (single author)- 1940 -	891.4515 7
Assamese speeches (single author)- 1940-1999	891.4515 71
Assamese speeches (single author)- 19th century	891.4515 4
Assamese speeches (single author)- 2000-	891.4515 72
Assamese speeches (single author)- 20th century	891.4515 71
Assamese speeches (single author)- to 1845	***See*** Main schedule
Assamese suspense fiction (multiple authors)	891.45130872*
Assamese suspense fiction (multiple authors)- Collections	891.4513087208**
Assamese suspense fiction (multiple authors)- History and criticism	891.4513087209**
Assamese tragedy (multiple authors)	891.45120512*
Assamese tragedy (multiple authors)- Collections	891.4512051208**

Assamese tragedy (multiple authors)-History and criticism	891.4512051209**
Assamese variety drama (multiple authors)	891.4512057*
Assamese variety drama (multiple authors)-Collections	891.451205708**
Assamese variety drama (multiple authors)-History and criticism	891.451205709**
Associations (Buddhism)	294.365
Associations (Hinduism)	294.565
Associations (Jainism)	294.465
Associations (Sikhism)	294.665
Atharvaveda	294.59215++
Atonement (Buddhism)	294.342 2
Atonement (Hinduism)	294.522
Atonement (Jainism)	294.422
Atonement (Sikhism)	294.622
Attitude towards age groups (Buddhism)	294.33783 4++
Attitude towards age groups (Hinduism)	294.517 834++
Attitude towards age groups (Jainism)	294.417 834++
Attitude towards age groups (Sikhism)	294.617 834++
Attitude towards ethnic groups (Buddhism)	294.33783 4++
Attitude towards ethnic groups (Hinduism)	294.517 834++
Attitude towards ethnic groups (Jainism)	294.417 834++
Attitude towards ethnic groups (Sikhism)	294.617 834++
Attitude towards language groups (Buddhism)	294.33783 4++

Attitude towards language groups (Hinduism)	294.517 834++
Attitude towards language groups (Jainism)	294.417 834++
Attitude towards language groups (Sikhism)	294.617 834++
Attitude towards other religions (Buddhism)	294.337
Attitude towards other religions (Hinduism)	294.517
Attitude towards other religions (Jainism)	294.417
Attitude towards other religions (Sikhism)	294.617
Attitude towards social classes (Buddhism)	294.33783 4++
Attitude towards social classes (Hinduism)	294.517 834++
Attitude towards social classes (Jainism)	294.417 834++
Attitude towards social classes (Sikhism)	294.617 834++
Attitude towards the sexes (Buddhism)	294.33783 4++
Attitude towards the sexes (Hinduism)	294.517 834++
Attitude towards the sexes (Jainism)	294.417 834++
Attitude towards the sexes (Sikhism)	294.617 834++
Attributes of God (Buddhism)	294.342 112
Attributes of God (Hinduism)	294.521 12
Attributes of God (Jainism)	294.421 12
Attributes of God (Sikhism)	294.621 12
Attributes of the gods (Buddhism)	294.342 112
Attributes of the gods (Hinduism)	294.521 12
Attributes of the gods (Jainism)	294.421 12
Attributes of the gods (Sikhism)	294.621 12
Awadhi language	491.49
Awadhi literature	891.49
Ayurveda.	615.53

B

Bagheli language	491.49
Bagheli literature	891.49
Bengal	***See*** West Bengal
Bengali adventure fiction (multiple authors)	891.443087*
Bengali adventure fiction (multiple authors)- History and criticism	891.44308709**
Bengali adventure fiction (multiple authors)-Collections	891.44308708**
Bengali anecdotes, epigrams, graffiti, jokes, quotations (multiple authors)	891.44802
Bengali anecdotes, epigrams, graffiti, jokes, quotations (single author)	891.448+CD+02
Bengali as second language in elementary education	372.659 144
Bengali ballads (multiple authors)	891.441044*
Bengali ballads (multiple authors)-Collections	891.44104408**
Bengali ballads (multiple authors)- History and criticism	891.44104409**
Bengali comedy (multiple authors)	891.4420523*
Bengali comedy (multiple authors)-	

Collections	891.442052308**
Bengali comedy (multiple authors)- History and criticism	891.442052309**
Bengali conversations (multiple authors)	891.44506*
Bengali conversations (multiple authors)- Collections	891.4450608**
Bengali conversations (multiple authors)- History and criticism	891.4450609**
Bengali debates and public discussions (multiple authors)	891.44503*
Bengali debates and public discussions (multiple authors)- Collections	891.4450308**
Bengali debates and public discussions (multiple authors)- History and criticism	891.4450309**
Bengali detective fiction (multiple authors)	891.4430872*
Bengali detective fiction (multiple authors)- Collections	891.443087208**
Bengali detective fiction (multiple authors)- History and criticism	891.443087209**
Bengali diaries, notebooks, reminiscences (multiple authors)	891.44803
Bengali diaries, notebooks, reminiscences (single author)	891.448@
Bengali didactic poetry (multiple authors)	891.44105*
Bengali didactic poetry (multiple authors)- Collections	891.4410508**
Bengali didactic poetry (multiple authors)- History and criticism	891.4410509**
Bengali drama	891.442

Bengali drama (multiple authors)- - to 1845	***See*** Main schedule
Bengali drama (multiple authors)- 1845-1895	891.4424+
Bengali drama (multiple authors)- 1895-1919	891.4425+
Bengali drama (multiple authors)- 1920-1939	891.4426+
Bengali drama (multiple authors)- 1940-	891.4427+
Bengali drama (multiple authors)- 1940-1999	891.44271+
Bengali drama (multiple authors)- 19th century	891.4424+
Bengali drama (multiple authors)– 2000-	891.44272+
Bengali drama (multiple authors)- 20th century	891.44271+
Bengali drama (multiple authors)- Collections	891.442008**
Bengali drama (multiple authors)- Dictionaries etc	891.442003
Bengali drama (multiple authors)- History and criticism	891.442009**
Bengali drama (multiple authors)- Periodicals	891.442005
Bengali drama (multiple authors)- Philosophy and theory	891.442001
Bengali drama (multiple authors)- Psychological aspects	891.4420019
Bengali drama (multiple authors)- Research	891.4420072

Bengali drama (multiple authors)- Study and teaching	891.442007
Bengali drama (multiple authors)- Value	891.4420013
Bengali drama (single author)- - to 1845 schedule	***See*** Main
Bengali drama (single author)- 1845-1895	891.442 4
Bengali drama (single author)- 1895- 1919	891.442 5
Bengali drama (single author)- 1920- 1939	891.442 6
Bengali drama (single author)- 1940-	891.442 7
Bengali drama (single author)- 1940-1999	891.442 71
Bengali drama (single author)- 19th century	891.442 4
Bengali drama (single author)- 2000-	891.442 72
Bengali drama (single author)- 20th century	891.442 71
Bengali drama for cinema (multiple authors)	891.44203*
Bengali drama for cinema (multiple authors)- Collections	891.4420308**
Bengali drama for cinema (multiple authors)- History and criticism	891.4420309**
Bengali drama for radio (multiple authors)	891.442022*
Bengali drama for radio (multiple authors) - History and criticism	891.44202209**
Bengali drama for radio (multiple authors)- Collections	891.44202208**
Bengali drama for television (multiple authors)	891.442025*
Bengali drama for television (multiple authors)- Collections	891.44202508**
Bengali drama for television (multiple	

authors)- History and criticism	891.44202509**
Bengali dramatic poetry (multiple authors)	891.44102*
Bengali dramatic poetry (multiple authors)- Collections	891.4410208**
Bengali dramatic poetry (multiple authors)- History and criticism	891.4410209**
Bengali- English dictionary	491.443 21
Bengali ephemeral and light verse (multiple authors)	891.44108*
Bengali ephemeral and light verse (multiple authors)- Collections	891.4410808**
Bengali ephemeral and light verse (multiple authors)- History and criticism	891.4410809**
Bengali epic poetry (multiple authors)	891.441032*
Bengali epic poetry (multiple authors)- Collections	891.44103208**
Bengali epic poetry (multiple authors)- History and criticism	891.44103209**
Bengali epigrams	***See*** Bengali anecdotes ...
Bengali essays	891.444
Bengali essays (multiple authors)- - to 1845	***See*** Main schedule
Bengali essays (multiple authors)- 1845-1895	891.4444+
Bengali essays (multiple authors)- 1895-1919	891.4445+
Bengali essays (multiple authors)- 1920-1939	891.4446+

Bengali essays (multiple authors)-1940-	891.4447+
Bengali essays (multiple authors)-1940-1999	891.44471+
Bengali essays (multiple authors)-19th century	891.4444+
Bengali essays (multiple authors)–2000-	891.44472+
Bengali essays (multiple authors)-20th century	891.44471+
Bengali essays (multiple authors)-Collections	891·444008**
Bengali essays (multiple authors)-Dictionaries etc	891·444003
Bengali essays (multiple authors)-History and criticism	891·444009**
Bengali essays (multiple authors)-Periodicals	891·444005
Bengali essays (multiple authors)-Philosophy and theory	891·444001
Bengali essays (multiple authors)-Psychological aspects	891·4440019
Bengali essays (multiple authors)-Research	891·4440072
Bengali essays (multiple authors)-Study and teaching	891·444007
Bengali essays (multiple authors)-Value	891·4440013
Bengali essays (single author)- - to 1845	***See*** Main schedule
Bengali essays (single author)- 1845-1895	891.444 4
Bengali essays (single author)- 1895- 1919	891.444 5
Bengali essays (single author)- 1920- 1939	891.444 6

Bengali essays (single author)- 1940-	891.444 7
Bengali essays (single author)- 1940-1999	891.444 71
Bengali essays (single author)- 19th century	891.444 4
Bengali essays (single author)- 2000-	891.444 72
Bengali essays (single author)- 20th century	891.444 71
Bengali experimental and non-formalized works (single author)	891.448+CD+07
Bengali experimental and non-formalized works (multiple authors)	891.44807
Bengali fantasy fiction (multiple authors)	891.44308766*
Bengali fantasy fiction (multiple authors)- Collections	891.4430876608**
Bengali fantasy fiction (multiple authors)- History and criticism	891.4430876609**
Bengali farce (multiple authors)	891.44205232*
Bengali farce (multiple authors)- Collections	891.4420523208**
Bengali farce (multiple authors)- History and criticism	891.4420523209**
Bengali fiction	891.443
Bengali fiction (multiple authors)- - to 1845	***See*** Main schedule
Bengali fiction (multiple authors)- 1845-1895	891.4434+
Bengali fiction (multiple authors)- 1895-1919	891.4435+
Bengali fiction (multiple authors)- 1920-1939	891.4436+
Bengali fiction (multiple authors)- 1940-	891.4437+
Bengali fiction (multiple authors)- 1940-1999	891.44371+
Bengali fiction (multiple authors)-	

19th century	891.4434+
Bengali fiction (multiple authors)– 2000-	891.44372+
Bengali fiction (multiple authors)- 20th century	891.44371+
Bengali fiction (multiple authors)- Collections	891.443008**
Bengali fiction (multiple authors)- Dictionaries etc	891.443003
Bengali fiction (multiple authors)- History and criticism	891.443009**
Bengali fiction (multiple authors)- Periodicals	891.443005
Bengali fiction (multiple authors)- Philosophy and theory	891.443001
Bengali fiction (multiple authors)- Psychological aspects	891.4430019
Bengali fiction (multiple authors)- Research	891.4430072
Bengali fiction (multiple authors)- Study and teaching	891.443007
Bengali fiction (multiple authors)- Value	891.4430013
Bengali fiction (single author)- - to 1845	***See*** Main schedule
Bengali fiction (single author)- 1845-1895	891.443 4
Bengali fiction (single author)- 1895- 1919	891.443 5
Bengali fiction (single author)- 1920- 1939	891.443 6
Bengali fiction (single author)- 1940-	891.443 7
Bengali fiction (single author)- 1940-1999	891.443 71

Bengali fiction (single author)- 19th century	891.443 4
Bengali fiction (single author)- 2000-	891.443 72
Bengali fiction (single author)- 20th century	891.443 71
Bengali folk music	781 629 144
Bengali ghost fiction (multiple authors)	891.44308733*
Bengali ghost fiction (multiple authors)- Collections	891.4430873308**
Bengali ghost fiction (multiple authors)- History and criticism	891.4430873309**
Bengali graffiti	***See*** Bengali anecdotes ...
Bengali- Hindi dictionary	491.443 914 31
Bengali historical drama (multiple authors)	891.4420514*
Bengali historical drama (multiple authors)- Collections	891.442051408**
Bengali historical drama (multiple authors)- History and criticism	891.442051409**
Bengali historical fiction (multiple authors)	891.443081*
Bengali historical fiction (multiple authors)- Collections	891.44308108**
Bengali historical fiction (multiple authors)- History and criticism	891.44308109**
Bengali horror fiction (multiple authors)	891.44308738*
Bengali horror fiction (multiple authors)- Collections	891.4430873808**
Bengali horror fiction (multiple authors)- History and criticism	891.4430873809**
Bengali humour and satire	891.447

Bengali humour and satire (multiple authors)- to 1845	***See*** Main schedule
Bengali humour and satire (multiple authors)-1845-1895	891.4474+
Bengali humour and satire (multiple authors)-1895-1919	891.4475+
Bengali humour and satire (multiple authors)-1920-1939	891.4476+
Bengali humour and satire (multiple authors)-1940-	891.4477+
Bengali humour and satire (multiple authors)-1940-1999	891.44771+
Bengali humour and satire (multiple authors)-19th century	891.4474+
Bengali humour and satire (multiple authors)–2000-	891.44772+
Bengali humour and satire (multiple authors)-20th century	891.44771+
Bengali humour and satire (multiple authors)-Collections	891.447008**
Bengali humour and satire (multiple authors)-Dictionaries etc	891.447003
Bengali humour and satire (multiple authors)-History and criticism	891.447009**
Bengali humour and satire (multiple authors)-Periodicals	891.447005
Bengali humour and satire (multiple authors)-Philosophy and theory	891.447001
Bengali humour and satire (multiple authors)-Psychological aspects	891.4470019

Bengali humour and satire (multiple authors)-Research	891.4470072
Bengali humour and satire (multiple authors)-Study and teaching	891.447007
Bengali humour and satire (multiple authors)-Value	891.4470013
Bengali humourous and satirical poetry (multiple authors)	891.44107*
Bengali humourous and satirical poetry (multiple authors)- Collections	891.4410708**
Bengali humourous and satirical poetry (multiple authors)- History and criticism	891.4410709**
Bengali jokes	***See*** Bengali anecdotes ...
Bengali language	491.44
Bengali language- Applied linguistics	491.448
Bengali language- Bilingual dictionaries	491.443 2-39
Bengali language- Bilingualism	491.440 42
Bengali language- Concordances	491.440 3
Bengali language- Content analysis	491.440 141
Bengali language- Dialects	491.447
Bengali language- Dictionaries	491.443
Bengali language- Discourse analysis	491.440 141
Bengali language- Education	491.440 71
Bengali language- Encyclopaedias	491.440 3
Bengali language- Etymology	491.442
Bengali language- Functionalism	491.440 18

Bengali language- Grammar	491.445
Bengali language- History, geography, persons	491.440 9
Bengali language- Intonation	491.441 6
Bengali language- Lexicography	491.443 028
Bengali language- Lexicology	491.440 14
Bengali language- Miscellany	491.440 2
Bengali language- Multilingualism	491.440 42
Bengali language- Organizations	491.440 6
Bengali language- Orthography	491.441 52
Bengali language- Pauses	491.441 6
Bengali language- Periodicals	491.440 5
Bengali language- Persons (men, women, etc)	491.440 8
Bengali language- Philosophy and theory	491.440 1
Bengali language- Phonetics	491.441 58
Bengali language- Phonology, etc	491.441 5
Bengali language- Pitch	491.441 6
Bengali language- Pronunciation	491.441 52
Bengali language- Readers	491.448 6
Bengali language- Research	491.440 72
Bengali language- Rhetoric	808.049 144++
Bengali language- Schools and theories of linguistics	491.440 18
Bengali language- Semantics	491.440 143
Bengali language- Semiotics	491.440 141

Bengali language- Slang	491.447
Bengali language- Special topics	491.440 4
Bengali language- Specialized dictionaries	491.443 1
Bengali language- Spelling	491.441 52
Bengali language- Stress	491.441 6
Bengali language- Structural linguistics	491.440 18
Bengali language- Suprasegmental features	491.441 6
Bengali language- Terminology	491.440 14
Bengali language- Theory	491.440 1
Bengali language- Usage	491.448
Bengali language- Variations (Dialects etc).	491.447
Bengali language- Writing systems	491.441 1
Bengali letters	891.446
Bengali letters (multiple authors)- - to 1845	***See*** Main schedule
Bengali letters (multiple authors)-1845-1895	891.4464+
Bengali letters (multiple authors)-1895-1919	891.4465+
Bengali letters (multiple authors)-1920-1939	891.4466+
Bengali letters (multiple authors)-1940-	891.4467+
Bengali letters (multiple authors)-1940-1999	891.44671+
Bengali letters (multiple authors)-19th century	891.4464+
Bengali letters (multiple authors)–2000-	891.44672+
Bengali letters (multiple authors)-20thcentury	891.44671+
Bengali letters (multiple authors)-Collections	891.446008**
Bengali letters (multiple authors)-	

Dictionaries etc	891.446003
Bengali letters (multiple authors)-History and criticism	891.446009**
Bengali letters (multiple authors)-Periodicals	891.446005
Bengali letters (multiple authors)-Philosophy and theory	891.446001
Bengali letters (multiple authors)-Psychological aspects	891.4460019
Bengali letters (multiple authors)-Research	891.4460072
Bengali letters (multiple authors)-Study and teaching	891.446007
Bengali letters (multiple authors)-Value	891.4460013
Bengali letters (single author)- - to 1845	***See*** Main schedule
Bengali letters (single author)- 1845-1895	891.446 4
Bengali letters (single author)- 1895- 1919	891.446 5
Bengali letters (single author)- 1920- 1939	891.446 6
Bengali letters (single author)- 1940-	891.446 7
Bengali letters (single author)- 1940-1999	891.446 71
Bengali letters (single author)- 19th century	891.446 4
Bengali letters (single author)- 2000-	891.446 72
Bengali letters (single author)- 20th century	891.446 71
Bengali light verse	***See*** Bengali ephemeral and light verse
Bengali limericks (multiple authors)	891.441075*
Bengali limericks (multiple authors)-	

Collections	891.44107508**
Bengali limericks (multiple authors)- History and criticism	891.44107509**
Bengali literature	891.44
Bengali literature (collections of multiple forms)	891.4408
Bengali literature (collections of multiple forms)- 19th century	891.440804
Bengali literature (collections of multiple forms)- 20th century	891.4408071
Bengali literature (collections of multiple forms)– 21st century	891.4408072
Bengali literature (collections of multiple forms)- Allegory	891.4408015
Bengali literature (collections of multiple forms)- Animals	891.44080362++
Bengali literature (collections of multiple forms)- Artistic themes	891.44080357
Bengali literature (collections of multiple forms)- Atmosphere	891.4408032161
Bengali literature (collections of multiple forms)- Characters	891.4408027
Bengali literature (collections of multiple forms)- Comedy	891.4408017
Bengali literature (collections of multiple forms) emphasizing subjects	891.440804++
Bengali literature (collections of multiple forms)- Evening	891.4408033
Bengali literature (collections of multiple forms)- Fantasy	891.4408015

Bengali literature (collections of multiple forms) for/by children	891.440809282
Bengali literature (collections of multiple forms) for/by persons of racial, ethnic and national groups	891.440808++
Bengali literature (collections of multiple forms) for/by persons of specific classes	891.4408092++
Bengali literature (collections of multiple forms) for/by persons resident in specific regions	891.4408091++
Bengali literature (collections of multiple forms) for/by women	891.440809287
Bengali literature (collections of multiple forms)- Forests	891.4408032152
Bengali literature (collections of multiple forms)- Historical themes	891.44080358
Bengali literature (collections of multiple forms)- Horror	891.44080164
Bengali literature (collections of multiple forms)- Human characteristics (Biological, moral, psychological)	891.44080353
Bengali literature (collections of multiple forms)- Legendary objects/themes	891.4408037
Bengali literature (collections of multiple forms)- Literary themes	891.44080357
Bengali literature (collections of multiple forms)- Love	891.440803543
Bengali literature (collections of multiple forms)- Marriage	891.440803543
Bengali literature (collections of multiple forms)- Morning	891.4408033

Bengali literature (collections of multiple forms)- Mountains	891.4408032143
Bengali literature (collections of multiple forms)- Myth	891.4408015
Bengali literature (collections of multiple forms)- Mythological objects/themes	891.4408037
Bengali literature (collections of multiple forms)- Philosophic themes	891.44080384
Bengali literature (collections of multiple forms)- Places	891.4408032++
Bengali literature (collections of multiple forms)- Plants	891.44080364
Bengali literature (collections of multiple forms)- Political themes	891.44080358
Bengali literature (collections of multiple forms)- Religious themes	891.44080382
Bengali literature (collections of multiple forms)- Rivers	891.44080321693
Bengali literature (collections of multiple forms)- Romanticism	891.44080145
Bengali literature (collections of multiple forms)- Scientific themes	891.44080356
Bengali literature (collections of multiple forms)- Sea	891.4408032162
Bengali literature (collections of multiple forms)- Seasons	891.4408033
Bengali literature (collections of multiple forms)- Sex	891.440803538
Bengali literature (collections of multiple forms)- Social themes	891.44080355

Bengali literature (collections of multiple forms)- Space	891.440803219
Bengali literature (collections of multiple forms)- Specific kinds of persons, e.g. heroes	891.44080352++
Bengali literature (collections of multiple forms)- Specific persons (real or imaginary)	891.44080351
Bengali literature (collections of multiple forms)- Stream of consciousness	891.4408025
Bengali literature (collections of multiple forms)- Supernatural objects/themes	891.4408037
Bengali literature (collections of multiple forms)- Symbolism	891.4408015
Bengali literature (collections of multiple forms)- Technical themes	891.44080356
Bengali literature (collections of multiple forms)- Times (seasons, parts of day, etc)	891.4408033
Bengali literature (collections of multiple forms)- Towns	891.44080321732
Bengali literature (collections of multiple forms)- Tragedy	891.44080162
Bengali literature (collections of multiple forms)- Villages	891.44080321734
Bengali literature (collections of multiple forms)- Weather	891.4408036
Bengali literature (multiple authors)- Concordances	891.4403
Bengali literature (multiple authors)- Dictionaries etc	891.4403
Bengali literature (multiple authors)-	

Education	891.44071
Bengali literature (multiple authors)- Encyclopaedias	891.4403
Bengali literature (multiple authors)- Organizations	891.4406
Bengali literature (multiple authors)- Periodicals	891.4405
Bengali literature (multiple authors)- Philosophy and theory	891.4401
Bengali literature (multiple authors)- Research	891.44072
Bengali literature (multiple authors)- Research in India	891.44072054
Bengali literature (multiple authors)- Study and teaching	891.4407
Bengali literature (multiple forms)- 19th century	891.4409004
Bengali literature (multiple forms)– 2000-	891.44090072
Bengali literature (multiple forms)- 20th century	891.44090071
Bengali literature (multiple forms)- Allegory – History and criticism	891.440915
Bengali literature (multiple forms)- Animals - History and criticism	891.4409362++
Bengali literature (multiple forms)- Artistic themes - History and criticism	891.4409357
Bengali literature (multiple forms)- Atmosphere - History and criticism	891.440932161
Bengali literature (multiple forms)- Characters - History and criticism	891.440927

Bengali literature (multiple forms)- Comedy - History and criticism	891.440917
Bengali literature (multiple forms)- Evening- History and criticism	891.440933
Bengali literature (multiple forms)- Fantasy- History , description, criticism	891.440915
Bengali literature (multiple forms)- Forests - History and criticism	891.440932152
Bengali literature (multiple forms)- Historical themes - History and criticism	891.4409358
Bengali literature (multiple forms)- History and criticism	891.4409
Bengali literature (multiple forms)- Horror - History and criticism	891.4409164
Bengali literature (multiple forms)- Human characteristics (Biological, moral, psychological) - History and criticism	891.4409353
Bengali literature (multiple forms)- Legendary objects/themes - History and criticism	891.440937
Bengali literature (multiple forms)- Literary themes - History and criticism	891.4409357
Bengali literature (multiple forms)- Love- History and criticism	891.44093543
Bengali literature (multiple forms)- Marriage - History and criticism	891.44093543
Bengali literature (multiple forms)- Morning- History and criticism	891.440933
Bengali literature (multiple forms)- Mountains- History and criticism	891.440932143

Bengali literature (multiple forms)- Myth - History and criticism	891.440915
Bengali literature (multiple forms)- Mythological objects/themes - History and criticism	891.440937
Bengali literature (multiple forms)- Persons of racial, ethnic and national groups - History and criticism	891.44098++
Bengali literature (multiple forms)- Persons of specific classes - History and criticism	891.440992++
Bengali literature (multiple forms)- Persons resident in specific regions - History and criticism	891.440991++
Bengali literature (multiple forms)- Philosophic themes - History and criticism	891.4409384
Bengali literature (multiple forms)- Places - History and criticism	891.440932++
Bengali literature (multiple forms)- Plants - History and criticism	891.4409364
Bengali literature (multiple forms)- Political themes - History and criticism	891.4409358
Bengali literature (multiple forms)- Religious themes - History and criticism	891.4409382
Bengali literature (multiple forms)- Rivers - History and criticism	891.4409321693
Bengali literature (multiple forms)- Romanticism - History and criticism	891.4409145
Bengali literature (multiple forms)- Scientific themes - History and criticism	891.4409356
Bengali literature (multiple forms)-	

Sea - History and criticism	891.440932162
Bengali literature (multiple forms)- Seasons- History and criticism	891.440933
Bengali literature (multiple forms)- Sex - History and criticism	891.44093538
Bengali literature (multiple forms)- Social themes - History and criticism	891.4409355
Bengali literature (multiple forms)- Space - History and criticism	891.44093219
Bengali literature (multiple forms)- Specific kinds of persons (e.g. heroes)- History and criticism	891.4409352++
Bengali literature (multiple forms)- Specific persons - History and criticism	891.4409351
Bengali literature (multiple forms)- Stream of consciousness - History and criticism	891.440925
Bengali literature (multiple forms)- Subjects - History and criticism	891.44094++
Bengali literature (multiple forms)- Supernatural objects/themes - History and criticism	891.440937
Bengali literature (multiple forms)- Symbolism- History, description, criticism	891.440915
Bengali literature (multiple forms)- Technical themes - History and criticism	891.4409356
Bengali literature (multiple forms)- Times - History and criticism	891.440933
Bengali literature (multiple forms)- Towns - History and criticism	891.4409321732

Bengali literature (multiple forms)- Tragedy - History and criticism	891.4409162
Bengali literature (multiple forms)- Villages - History and criticism	891.4409321734
Bengali literature (multiple forms)- Weather - History and criticism	891.440936
Bengali literature (single author)- - to 1845- Biography, collections, criticism schedule	***See*** Main
Bengali literature (single author)- 1845- 1895- Biography, collected works, criticism	891.448 409
Bengali literature (single author)- 1895- 1919- Biography, collections, criticism	891.448 509
Bengali literature (single author)- 1920- 1939- Biography, collections, criticism	891.448 609
Bengali literature (single author)- 1940-1999- Biography, collections, criticism	891.448 7109
Bengali literature (single author)- 19th century- Biography, collected works, criticism	891.448 409
Bengali literature (single author)- 2000- Biography, collected works, criticism	891.448 7209
Bengali literature (single author)- 20th century- Biography, collections, criticism	891.448 7109
Bengali literature for/by children - History and criticism	891.44099282
Bengali literature for/by women - History and criticism	891.44099287
Bengali love fiction (multiple authors)	891.443085*

Bengali love fiction (multiple authors)-Collections	891.44308508**
Bengali love fiction (multiple authors)-History and criticism	891.44308509**
Bengali melodrama (multiple authors)	891.4420527*
Bengali melodrama (multiple authors)-Collections	891.442052708**
Bengali melodrama (multiple authors)-History and criticism	891.442052709**
Bengali miscellaneous writings	891.448
Bengali miscellaneous writings (multiple authors)	891.448
Bengali miscellaneous writings (multiple authors)- - to 1845	***See*** Main schedule
Bengali miscellaneous writings (multiple authors)-1845-1895	891.4484++
Bengali miscellaneous writings (multiple authors)-1895-1919	891.4485++
Bengali miscellaneous writings (multiple authors)-1920-1939	891.4486++
Bengali miscellaneous writings (multiple authors)-1940-	891.4487++
Bengali miscellaneous writings (multiple authors)-1940-1999	891.44871++
Bengali miscellaneous writings (multiple authors)-19th century	891.4484++
Bengali miscellaneous writings (multiple authors)–2000-	891.44872++
Bengali miscellaneous writings (multiple authors)-20th century	891.44871++

Bengali miscellaneous writings (multiple authors)-Collections	891.448008**
Bengali miscellaneous writings (multiple authors)-Dictionaries etc	891.448003
Bengali miscellaneous writings (multiple authors)-History and criticism	891.448009**
Bengali miscellaneous writings (multiple authors)-Periodicals	891.448005
Bengali miscellaneous writings (multiple authors)-Philosophy and theory	891.448001
Bengali miscellaneous writings (multiple authors)-Psychological aspects	891.4480019
Bengali miscellaneous writings (multiple authors)-Research	891.4480072
Bengali miscellaneous writings (multiple authors)-Study and teaching	891.448007
Bengali miscellaneous writings (multiple authors)-Value	891.4480013
Bengali miscellaneous writings (single author)- - to 1845	***See*** Main schedule
Bengali miscellaneous writings (single author)- 1845-1895	891.448 4
Bengali miscellaneous writings (single author)- 1895- 1919	891.448 5
Bengali miscellaneous writings (single author)- 1920- 1939	891.448 6
Bengali miscellaneous writings (single author)- 1940-	891.448 7
Bengali miscellaneous writings (single author)- 1940-1999	891.448 71

Bengali miscellaneous writings (single author)- 19th century	891.448 4
Bengali miscellaneous writings (single author)- 2000-	891.448 72
Bengali miscellaneous writings (single author)- 20th century	891.448 71
Bengali monologues (multiple authors)	891.442045*
Bengali monologues (multiple authors)- Collections	891.44204508**
Bengali monologues (multiple authors)- History and criticism	891.44204509**
Bengali morality plays	***See*** Bengali religious and morality plays
Bengali mystery fiction (multiple authors)	891.4430872*
Bengali mystery fiction (multiple authors)- Collections	891.443087208**
Bengali mystery fiction (multiple authors)- History and criticism	891.443087209**
Bengali narrative poetry (multiple authors)	891.44103*
Bengali narrative poetry (multiple authors)- Collections	891.4410308**
Bengali narrative poetry (multiple authors)- History and criticism	891.4410309**
Bengali non-formalized works	***See*** Bengali experimental and non-formalized works
Bengali notebooks	***See*** Bengali diaries ...

Bengali odes (multiple authors)	891.441043*
Bengali odes (multiple authors)- Collections	891.44104308**
Bengali odes (multiple authors)- History and criticism	891.44104309**
Bengali one act plays (multiple authors)	891.442 041*
Bengali one act plays (multiple authors)- Collections	891.442 041 08**
Bengali one act plays (multiple authors)- History and criticism	891.442 041 09**
Bengali oratory (multiple authors)	***See*** Bengali public speeches
Bengali periodicals	059.9144
Bengali poetry	891.441
Bengali poetry (multiple authors)- - to 1845	***See*** Main schedule
Bengali poetry (multiple authors)- 1845-1895	891.4414+
Bengali poetry (multiple authors)- 1895-1919	891.4415+
Bengali poetry (multiple authors)- 1920-1939	891.4416+
Bengali poetry (multiple authors)- 1940-	891.4417+
Bengali poetry (multiple authors)- 1940-1999	891.44171+
Bengali poetry (multiple authors)- 19th century	891.4414+
Bengali poetry (multiple authors)- 2000-	891.44172+
Bengali poetry (multiple authors)- 20th century	891.44171+

Bengali poetry (multiple authors)- Collections	891.441008**
Bengali poetry (multiple authors)- Dictionaries etc	891.441003
Bengali poetry (multiple authors)- History and criticism	891.441009**
Bengali poetry (multiple authors)- Periodicals	891.441005
Bengali poetry (multiple authors)- Philosophy and theory	891.441001
Bengali poetry (multiple authors)- Psychological aspects	891.4410019
Bengali poetry (multiple authors)-Research	891.4410072
Bengali poetry (multiple authors)- Study and teaching	891.441007
Bengali poetry (multiple authors)- Value	891.4410013
Bengali poetry (single author)- - to 1845	***See*** Main schedule
Bengali poetry (single author)- 1845-1895	891.441 4
Bengali poetry (single author)- 1895- 1919	891.441 5
Bengali poetry (single author)- 1920- 1939	891.441 6
Bengali poetry (single author)- 1940-	891.441 7
Bengali poetry (single author)- 1940-1999	891.441 71
Bengali poetry (single author)- 19th century	891.441 4
Bengali poetry (single author)- 2000-	891.441 72
Bengali poetry (single author)- 20th century	891.441 71
Bengali prose	891.448

Bengali prose (single author)- - to 1845	***See*** Main schedule
Bengali prose (single author)- 1845-1895	891.448 408
Bengali prose (single author)- 1895- 1919	891.448 508
Bengali prose (single author)- 1920- 1939	891.448 608
Bengali prose (single author)- 1940-	891.448 708
Bengali prose (single author)- 1940-1999	891.448 7108
Bengali prose (single author)- 19th century	891.448 408
Bengali prose (single author)- 2000-	891.448 7208
Bengali prose (single author)- 20th century	891.448 7108
Bengali prose literature (multiple authors)	891.44808
Bengali psychological, realistic, sociological fiction (multiple authors)	891.443083
Bengali psychological, realistic, sociological fiction (multiple authors)- History and criticism	891.44308309**
Bengali psychological, realistic, sociological fiction (multiple authors)- Collections	891.44308308**
Bengali public discussions	***See*** Bengali debates and public discussions
Bengali public speeches (multiple authors)	891.44501
Bengali public speeches (multiple authors)- Collections	891.4450108
Bengali public speeches (multiple authors)- History and criticism	891.4450109
Bengali quotations	***See*** Bengali anecdotes ...

Bengali realistic fiction	***See*** Bengali psychological... fiction
Bengali recitations (multiple authors)	891.44504
Bengali religious and morality plays (multiple authors)	891.4420516+
Bengali reminiscences ***See*** Bengali diaries ...	891.44803
Bengali romantic fiction (multiple authors)	891.443085*
Bengali romantic fiction (multiple authors)-Collections	891.44308508**
Bengali romantic fiction (multiple authors)-History and criticism	891.44308509**
Bengali satire	***See*** Bengali humour and satire
Bengali satirical poetry	***See*** Bengali humourous and satirical poetry
Bengali science fiction (multiple authors)	891.44308762*
Bengali science fiction (multiple authors)-Collections	891.4430876208**
Bengali science fiction (multiple authors)-History and criticism	891.4430876209**
Bengali serious drama (multiple authors)	891.442051*
Bengali serious drama (multiple authors)-Collections	891.44205108**
Bengali serious drama (multiple authors)-History and criticism	891.44205109**
Bengali short stories (multiple authors)	891.44301*
Bengali short stories (multiple authors)-	

Collections	891.4430108**
Bengali short stories (multiple authors)-History and criticism	891.4430109**
Bengali sociological fiction (multiple authors)	***See*** Bengali psychological... fiction
Bengali sonnets (multiple authors)	891.441042*
Bengali sonnets (multiple authors)-Collections	891.44104208**
Bengali sonnets (multiple authors)-History and criticism	891.44104209**
Bengali speaking people	305.791 44
Bengali speeches	891.445
Bengali speeches (multiple authors)-to 1845	***See*** Main schedule
Bengali speeches (multiple authors)-1845-1895	891.4454+
Bengali speeches (multiple authors)-1895-1919	891.4455+
Bengali speeches (multiple authors)-1920-1939	891.4456+
Bengali speeches (multiple authors)-1940-	891.4457+
Bengali speeches (multiple authors)-1940-1999	891.44571+
Bengali speeches (multiple authors)-19th century	891.4454+
Bengali speeches (multiple authors)–2000-	891.44572+
Bengali speeches (multiple authors)-20th century	891.44571+

Bengali speeches (multiple authors)-Collections	891.445008**
Bengali speeches (multiple authors)-Dictionaries etc	891.445003
Bengali speeches (multiple authors)-History and criticism	891.445009**
Bengali speeches (multiple authors)-Periodicals	891.445005
Bengali speeches (multiple authors)-Philosophy and theory	891.445001
Bengali speeches (multiple authors)-Psychological aspects	891.4450019
Bengali speeches (multiple authors)-Research	891.4450072
Bengali speeches (multiple authors)-Study and teaching	891.445007
Bengali speeches (single author)- - to 1845	***See*** Main schedule
Bengali speeches (single author)-1845-1895	891.445 4
Bengali speeches (single author)-1895- 1919	891.445 5
Bengali speeches (single author)-1920- 1939	891.445 6
Bengali speeches (single author)- 1940-	891.445 7
Bengali speeches (single author)-1940-1999	891.445 71
Bengali speeches (single author)-19th century	891.445 4
Bengali speeches (single author)- 2000-	891.445 72

Bengali speeches (single author)- 20th century	891.445 71
Bengali suspense fiction (multiple authors)	891.4430872*
Bengali suspense fiction (multiple authors)- Collections	891.443087208**
Bengali suspense fiction (multiple authors)- History and criticism	891.443087209**
Bengali tragedy (multiple authors)	891.4420512*
Bengali tragedy (multiple authors)- Collections	891.442051208**
Bengali tragedy (multiple authors)- History and criticism	891.442051209**
Bengali variety drama (multiple authors)	891.442057*
Bengali variety drama (multiple authors)- Collections	891.44205708**
Bengali variety drama (multiple authors)- History and criticism	891.44205709**
Bengalis	305.891 44
Bhagavad Gita	294.592 4++
Bhakh Yoga	294.543 6
Bhedabheda philosophy	181.484.2
Bhil (People)	305.891 47
Bhil folk music.	781 629 147
Bhili language	491.47
Bhili literature	891.47
Bhojpuri language	491.454 7
Bhojpuri literature	891.454

Bhojpuri speaking people	305.791 454
Bhopal- Architecture	720.954 3
Bhopal- Economic geography	330.954 3
Bhopal- Fauna	591.954 3
Bhopal- Flora	581.954 3
Bhopal- Folk dancing	793.319 543
Bhopal- Geography	915.43
Bhopal- History	954.3
Bhopal- Painting and paintings	759.954 3
Bhopal- Sculpture	730.954 3
Bibliography of books by Indian authors	013.954
Bihar- Architecture	720.954 12
Bihar- Botany	580.954 12
Bihar- Budget	352.495 412
Bihar- Economic development	338.954 12
Bihar- Economic geography	330.954 12
Bihar- Education	370.954 12
Bihar- Fauna	591.954 12
Bihar- Flora	581.954 12
Bihar- Folk dancing	793.319 5412
Bihar- Geography	915.412
Bihar- Geology	555.412
Bihar- History	954.12
Bihar- Painting and paintings	759.954 12
Bihar- Public administration	351.541 2

Bihar- Public finance	336.541 2
Bihar- Sculpture	730.954 12
Bihari drama	891.454 2
Bihari- English dictionary	491.454 321
Bihari essays	891.454 4
Bihari fiction	891.454 3
Bihari folk music.	781 629 145
Bihari language	491.454
Bihari language- Applied linguistics	491.454 8
Bihari language- Bilingual dictionaries	491.454 32-39
Bihari language- Dictionaries	491.454 3
Bihari language- Education	491.454 071
Bihari language- Grammar	491.454 5
Bihari language- History	491.454 09
Bihari language- Readers	491.454 86
Bihari language- Research	491.454 072
Bihari language- Rhetoric	808.049 145 4++
Bihari language- Usage	491.454 8
Bihari letters	891.454 6
Bihari literature	891.454
Bihari poetry	891.454 1
Bihari speaking people	305.791 454
Bihari speeches	891.454 5
Biography (Buddhism)	294.3092
Biography (Hinduism)	294.5092

Biography (Jainism)	294.4092
Biography (Sikhism)	294.6092
Bombay- Architecture	720.954 792 3
Bombay- Economic geography	330.954 792 3
Bombay- Education	370.954 792 3
Bombay- Fauna	591.954 792 3
Bombay- Flora	581.954 792 3
Bombay- Folk dancing	793.319 547923
Bombay- Geography	915.47923
Bombay- History	954.7923
Bombay- Painting and paintings	759.954 7923
Bombay- Sculpture	730.954 7923
Botany- India	580.954
Brahma Samaj	294.5562
Brahui (People)	305.894 83
Brahui folk music	781 629 483
Brahui language	494.83
Brahui language- Applied linguistics	494.838
Brahui language- Dictionaries	494.833
Brahui language- Education	494.830 71
Brahui language- Grammar	494.835
Brahui language- History	494.830 9
Brahui language- Readers	494.838 6
Brahui language- Research	494.830 72
Brahui language- Rhetoric	808.049 483++

Brahui language- Usage	494.838
Brahui literature	894.83
Brahui speaking people	305.794 83
Brahui-English dictionary	494.833 21
Brahui-Hindi dictionary	494.833 914 31
British educational aid to India	379.129 540 41
Buddha	294.363
Buddhism	294.3
Buddhism- Abuse within a family	294.33783 27
Buddhism- Addicts	294.344 42
Buddhism- Adults – victims of abuse as children	294.33783 273
Buddhism- Alms giving.	294.344 46
Buddhism- Ancestors as objects of worship and veneration	294.342 13
Buddhism and communication media	294.337 5
Buddhism and literature	294.337 5
Buddhism and medicine	294.337 5
Buddhism and political affairs	294.337 7
Buddhism and psychology	294.337 5
Buddhism and religious freedom	294.337 72
Buddhism and science	294.337 5
Buddhism and social problems	294.33783
Buddhism and socioeconomic problems	294.3378
Buddhism and technology	294.337 5

Buddhism- Animism	294.3421
Buddhism- Asceticism	294.3444 7
Buddhism- Associations	294.365
Buddhism- Atonement	294.342 2
Buddhism- Attitude towards age, ethnic and language groups	294.33783 4*
Buddhism- Attitude towards other religions	294.337
Buddhism- Attitude towards social classes	294.33783 4*
Buddhism- Attitude towards the sexes	294.33783 4*
Buddhism- Bereaved persons	294.344 42
Buddhism- Biography	294.3092
Buddhism- Branches	294.39
Buddhism- Ceremonial and ritual observances.	294.344 46
Buddhism- Ceremonies	294.3438
Buddhism- Child abuse and neglect	294.33783 271
Buddhism- Concordances	294.303
Buddhism- Congregations	294.365
Buddhism- Conscience	294.35
Buddhism- Contemplation	294.344 3
Buddhism- Conversion	294.344 2
Buddhism- Cosmology	294.342 4
Buddhism- Creation	294.342 4
Buddhism- Creation of humankind	294.342 2
Buddhism- Crime	294.33783 3*

Buddhism- Dead persons	294.342 13
Buddhism- Death (Eschatology)	294.342 3
Buddhism- Deities	294.342 11
Buddhism- Demons	294.342 16
Buddhism- Devotional literature	294.344 32
Buddhism- Dictionaries	294.303
Buddhism- Divination (omen, oracles, prophecies)	294.343 2
Buddhism- Divinities	294.342 11
Buddhism- Divorce	294.33783 5*
Buddhism- Doctrines	294.342
Buddhism- Doctrines and practices	294.34
Buddhism- Doctrines of specific branches, sects, reform movements	294.342 04
Buddhism- Ecology and population	294.33783 6*
Buddhism- Economic order	294.33785
Buddhism- Education	294.307 1
Buddhism- Education, research, related topics	294.307
Buddhism- Emblems	294.343 7
Buddhism- Encyclopaedias	294.303
Buddhism- End of the world (Eschatology)	294.342 3
Buddhism- Enlightenment	294.3442
Buddhism- Eschatology	294.342 3
Buddhism- Ethics	294.35
Buddhism- Ethics of communication	294.356 5*

Buddhism- Ethics of consumption	294.356 8*
Buddhism- Ethics of leisure	294.356 5*
Buddhism- Ethics of public performances	294.356 5*
Buddhism- Ethics of recreation	294.356 5*
Buddhism- Ethics of sex and reproduction	294.356 6*
Buddhism- Ethics of social relations	294.356 7*
Buddhism- Evil spirits	294.342 16
Buddhism- Exercise of religious authority	294.365
Buddhism- Family	294.33783 5*
Buddhism- Family ethics	294.356 3*
Buddhism- Family life	294.344 41
Buddhism- Fasts	294.3438
Buddhism- Fire	294.342 12
Buddhism- General classes of religions	294.334
Buddhism- Geography	294.3091
Buddhism- God, gods, goddesses, divinities, deities	294.342 11
Buddhism- Good spirits (angels)	294.342 15
Buddhism- Gurus	294.361
Buddhism- Heaven (Eschatology)	294.342 3
Buddhism- Hell (Eschatology)	294.342 3
Buddhism- Heroes	294.342 13
Buddhism- History	294.309
Buddhism- Holy days	294.343 6
Buddhism- Humankind	294.342 2

Buddhism- Hunger	294.33783 26
Buddhism- Images	294.342 18
Buddhism- Immortality (Eschatology)	294.342 3
Buddhism- Individual observances.	294.344 46
Buddhism- Institutions	294.365
Buddhism- International affairs	294.33787
Buddhism- Inter-religious relations and attitudes	294.337
Buddhism- Karma	294.342 2
Buddhism- Laws and decisions	294.384
Buddhism- Leaders and organization	294.36
Buddhism- Leaders and their work (duties, function, role)	294.361
Buddhism- Literature on meditation	294.344 32
Buddhism- Liturgical year	294.343 6
Buddhism- Mandalas	294.343 7
Buddhism- Mantras	294.343 7
Buddhism- Marriage	294.33783 5*
Buddhism- Marriage and family life	294.344 41
Buddhism- Meditation	294.344 35
Buddhism- Meditation literature	294.343 2
Buddhism- Miracles	294.342 117
Buddhism- Missions	294.372
Buddhism- Monarchs	294.342 13
Buddhism- Moral theology	294.35

Buddhism- Music	294.3438
Buddhism- Mysticism	294.344 22
Buddhism- Mythology and mythological foundations	294.333
Buddhism- Nature	294.342 12
Buddhism- Nuclear weapon and nuclear war	294.33787 32
Buddhism- Objects of worship and veneration	294.342 1
Buddhism- Observance of restrictions and limitations	294.344 46
Buddhism- Occupational ethics	294.356 4*
Buddhism- Offerings, sacrifices, penances	294.343 4
Buddhism- Omen	294.343 2
Buddhism- Oracles	294.343 2
Buddhism- Oral traditions	294.383
Buddhism- Orders	294.365
Buddhism- Organizations	294.365
Buddhism- Other worlds (Eschatology)	294.342 3
Buddhism- Parties	294.365
Buddhism- Peace	294.33787 3
Buddhism- Penances	294.343 4
Buddhism- Periodicals	294.305
Buddhism- Personified abstraction	294.342 14
Buddhism- Persons (ancestors, the dead, heroes, monarchs, saints)	294.342 13
Buddhism- Persons (male, female, etc)	294.308

Buddhism- Persons (sick, troubled, addicted, bereaved)	294.344 442
Buddhism- Persons experiencing illness, trouble, addiction, bereavement	294.344 2
Buddhism- Philosophy and theory	294.301
Buddhism- Pilgrimages	294.343 51
Buddhism- Pilgrimages and sacred places	294.343 5
Buddhism- Political ethics	294.356 2*
Buddhism- Politics	294.337 7
Buddhism- Population	294.33783 6*
Buddhism- Prayer	294.344 3
Buddhism- Prayer books	294.344 33
Buddhism- Priests	294.361
Buddhism- Processions	294.3438
Buddhism- Prophecies (Divination)	294.343 2
Buddhism- Prophecy (Relation to the world)	294.342 117
Buddhism- Providence	294.342 117
Buddhism- Public feasts	294.3438
Buddhism- Public prayer	394.3438
Buddhism- Public worship and other practices	294.343
Buddhism- Punishment (Eschatology)	294.342 3
Buddhism- Punishment and crime	294.33783 3++
Buddhism- Pure land sects	294.392 6
Buddhism- Reform movements	294.39
Buddhism- Refugees	294.33783 28

Buddhism- Reincarnation	294.342 37
Buddhism- Relationship with communication media	294.337 5
Buddhism- Relationship with irreligions	294.337 2
Buddhism- Relationship with literature	294.337 5
Buddhism- Relationship with medicine	294.337 5
Buddhism- Relationship with other religions	294.337 2
Buddhism- Relationship with psychology	294.337 5
Buddhism- Relationship with science	294.337 5
Buddhism- Relationship with secular disciplines	294.337 5
Buddhism- Relationship with technology	294.337 5
Buddhism- Religious calendar	294.343 6
Buddhism- Religious education	294.375
Buddhism- Religious experience	294.344 2
Buddhism- Religious festivals	294.343 6
Buddhism- Religious freedom	294.337 72
Buddhism- Religious healing	294.343 1
Buddhism- Religious life	294.344 4
Buddhism- Religious practice	294.344 4
Buddhism- Repentance	294.342 2
Buddhism- Revelation	294.342 117
Buddhism- Rewards (Eschatology)	294.342 3
Buddhism- Rites	294.3438
Buddhism- Role in society	294.337 1

Buddhism- Sacred books	294.382
Buddhism- Sacred places	294.343 5
Buddhism- Sacred times	294.343 6
Buddhism- Sacrifices	294.343 4
Buddhism- Saints	294.342 13
Buddhism- Salvation	294.342 2
Buddhism- Scriptures	294.382
Buddhism- Sects and reform movements	294.39
Buddhism- Sex	294.342 12
Buddhism- Sexual abuse	294.33783 272
Buddhism- Sexual relations	294.33783 5
Buddhism- Sick persons	294.344 42
Buddhism- Sin (Doctrines)	294.342 2
Buddhism- Sin (Moral theology)	294.35
Buddhism- Social problems	294.33783
Buddhism- Social theology	294.337
Buddhism- Social welfare	294.33783 2
Buddhism- Social welfare problems	294.33783 2
Buddhism- Social welfare services	294.33783 2
Buddhism- Society	294.337 1
Buddhism- Socioeconomic problems	294.3378
Buddhism- Soul	294.342 2
Buddhism- Sounds (Symbolism)	294.343 7
Buddhism- Sources	294.38
Buddhism- Sources of branches, sects,	

reform movements	294.385
Buddhism- Specific moral issues	294.356
Buddhism- Specific sins	294.356
Buddhism- Specific vices	294.356
Buddhism- Specific virtues	294.356
Buddhism- Spiritism	294.3421
Buddhism- Spirituality	294.344
Buddhism- Sun	294.342 12
Buddhism- Symbolic objects	294.343 7
Buddhism- Symbolism	294.343 7
Buddhism- Theocracy	294.337 73
Buddhism- Theodicy	294.342 118
Buddhism- Theory	294.301
Buddhism- Trees	294.342 12
Buddhism- Troubled persons	294.344 42
Buddhism- Vice	294.35
Buddhism- Victims of political oppression	294.33783 28
Buddhism- Virtue	294.35
Buddhism- War	294.33787 3
Buddhism- Water	294.342 12
Buddhism- Witchcraft	294.343 3
Buddhism- World (miracles, prophecy, providence, revelation)	294.342 117
Buddhism- Worship	294.344 3
Buddhism- Yoga	294.344 36

Budget-Maharashtra	352.495 479 2
Budget-Manipur	352.495 417
Budget-Meghalaya	352.495 416 4
Budget-Mizoram	352.495 416 6
Budget-Nagaland	352.495 416 5
Budget-Orissa	352.495 413
Budget-Pondicherry	352.495 486
Budget-Punjab	352.495 452 52
Budget-Rajasthan	352.495 44
Budget-Sikkim	352.495 416 7
Budget-South Asia	352.495 4
Budget-Southern India	352.495 48
Budget-Tamil Nadu	352.495 482
Budget-Tripura	352.495 415
Budget-Uttar Pradesh	352.495 42
Budget-Uttaranchal	352.495 451
Budget-West Bengal	352.495 414

C

Calcutta- Architecture	720.954 147
Calcutta- Economic geography	330.954 147
Calcutta- Flora	581.954 14 7
Calcutta- Geography	915.4147
Calcutta- Geology	555.414 7
Calcutta- History	954.147
Calcutta- Museums of fine and decorative arts	708.954 147
Calcutta- Painting and paintings	759.954 147
Calcutta- Sculpture	730.954 147
Caricatures- Collection	741.59
Carpets- India	746.754
Cartoons- Collection	741.59
Central Dravidians	305.894 82
Ceremonial and ritual observances (Buddhism)	294.344 46
Ceremonial and ritual observances (Hinduism)	294.544 6
Ceremonial and ritual observances (Jainism)	294.444 6

Commerce between India and European countries	382.095404
Commerce between India and Indonesia	382.09540598
Commerce between India and Japan	382.0954052
Commerce between India and Malaysia	382.09540595
Commerce between India and Maldives	382.095405495
Commerce between India and Middle East	382.0954056
Commerce between India and Myanmar	382.09540591
Commerce between India and Nepal	382.095405496
Commerce between India and Pakistan	382.095405491
Commerce between India and Russia	382.0954047
Commerce between India and Singapore	382.095405957
Commerce between India and Sri Lanka	382.095405493
Commerce between India and Thailand	382.09540593
Commerce between India and UK	382.0954041
Commerce between India and USA	382.0954073
Communication media and Buddhism	294.337 5
Communication media and Hinduism	294.5175
Communication media and Jainism	294.4175
Communication media and Sikhism	294.6175
Compensation -Andaman and Nicobar Islands	331.295 488
Compensation -Andhra Pradesh	331.295 484
Compensation -Arunachal Pradesh	331.295 416 3
Compensation -Assam	331.295 416 2

Compensation -Bengal	331.295 414
Compensation -Bihar	331.295 412
Compensation -Chandigarh	331.295 45 52
Compensation -Chhattisgarh	331.295 413 7
Compensation -Dadra and Nagar Haveli	331.295 479 6
Compensation -Delhi	331.295 45 6
Compensation -Goa, Daman and Diu	331.295 479 9
Compensation -Gujarat	331.295 475
Compensation -Haryana	331.295 45 58
Compensation -Himachal Pradesh	331.295 452
Compensation -India	331.295 4
Compensation -Jammu and Kashmir	331.295 46
Compensation -Jharkhand	331.295 412 7
Compensation -Karnataka	331.295 487
Compensation -Kerala	331.295 483
Compensation -Lakshwadweep	331.295 481
Compensation -Madhya Pradesh	331.295 43
Compensation -Madras	331.295 482
Compensation -Maharashtra	331.295 479 2
Compensation -Manipur	331.295 417
Compensation -Meghalaya	331.295 416 4
Compensation -Mizoram	331.295 416 6
Compensation -Nagaland	331.295 416 5
Compensation -Northeast India	331.295 41

Compensation -Orissa	331.295 413
Compensation -Pondicherry	331.295 486
Compensation -Punjab	331.295 45 52
Compensation -Rajasthan	331.295 44
Compensation -Sikkim	331.295 416 7
Compensation -South Asia	331.295 4
Compensation -Southern India	331.295 48
Compensation -Tamil Nadu	331.295 482
Compensation -Tripura	331.295 415
Compensation -Uttar Pradesh	331.295 42
Compensation -Uttaranchal	331.295 451
Compensation -West Bengal	331.295 414
Compensation -Western India	331.295 47
Concordances (Buddhism)	294.303
Concordances (Hinduism)	294.503
Concordances (Jainism)	294.403
Concordances (Sikhism)	294.603
Congregations (Buddhism)	294.365
Congregations (Hinduism)	294.565
Congregations (Jainism)	294.465
Congregations (Sikhism)	294.665
Conscience (Buddhism)	294.35
Conscience (Hinduism)	294.548
Conscience (Jainism)	294.45
Conscience (Sikhism)	294.65

Conservation of national resources	339.49
Conservation of resources - Andaman and Nicobar Islands	339.495 488
Conservation of resources - Andhra Pradesh	339.495 484
Conservation of resources - Arunachal Pradesh	339.495 416 3
Conservation of resources - Assam	339.495 416 2
Conservation of resources - Bengal	339.495 414
Conservation of resources - Bihar	339.495 412
Conservation of resources - Chandigarh	339.495 45 52
Conservation of resources - Chhattisgarh	339.495 413 7
Conservation of resources - Dadra and Nagar Haveli	339.495 479 6
Conservation of resources - Delhi	339.495 45 6
Conservation of resources - Goa, Daman and Diu	339.495 479 9
Conservation of resources - Gujarat	339.495 475
Conservation of resources - Haryana	339.495 45 58
Conservation of resources - Himachal Pradesh	339.495 452
Conservation of resources - India	339.495 4
Conservation of resources - Jammu and Kashmir	339.495 46
Conservation of resources - Jharkhand	339.495 412 7
Conservation of resources - Karnataka	339.495 487
Conservation of resources - Kerala	339.495 483

Conservation of resources - Lakshwadweep	339.495 481
Conservation of resources - Madhya Pradesh	339.495 43
Conservation of resources - Madras	339.495 482
Conservation of resources - Maharashtra	339.495 479 2
Conservation of resources - Manipur	339.495 417
Conservation of resources - Meghalaya	339.495 416 4
Conservation of resources - Mizoram	339.495 416 6
Conservation of resources - Nagaland	339.495 416 5
Conservation of resources - Northeast India	339.495 41
Conservation of resources - Orissa	339.495 413
Conservation of resources - Pondicherry	339.495 486
Conservation of resources - Punjab	339.495 45 52
Conservation of resources - Rajasthan	339.495 44
Conservation of resources - Sikkim	339.495 416 7
Conservation of resources - South Asia	339.495 4
Conservation of resources - Southern India	339.495 48
Conservation of resources - Tamil Nadu	339.495 482
Conservation of resources - Tripura	339.495 415
Conservation of resources - Uttar Pradesh	339.495 42
Conservation of resources - Uttaranchal	339.495 451
Conservation of resources - West Bengal	339.495 414
Conservation of resources - Western India	339.495 47
Constitutional and administrative law	342

Constitutional and administrative law- India	342.54
Contemplation (Buddhism)	294.344 3
Contemplation (Hinduism)	294.543
Contemplation (Jainism)	294.443
Contemplation (Sikhism)	294.643
Conversion (Buddhism)	294.344 2
Conversion (Hinduism)	294.542
Conversion (Jainism)	294.442
Conversion (Sikhism)	294.642
Cosmology (Buddhism)	294.342 4
Cosmology (Hinduism)	294.524
Cosmology (Jainism)	294.424
Cosmology (Sikhism)	294.624
Creation (Buddhism)	294.342 4
Creation (Hinduism)	294.524
Creation (Jainism)	294.424
Creation (Sikhism)	294.624
Creation of humankind (Buddhism)	294.342 2
Creation of humankind (Hinduism)	294.522
Creation of humankind (Jainism)	294.422
Creation of humankind (Sikhism)	294.622
Crime (Buddhism)	294.33783 3*
Crime (Hinduism)	294.517 833
Crime (Jainism)	294.417 833

Crime (Sikhism)	294.617 833
Criminal law	345
Criminal law- India	345. 54
Cultural contact- Haryana	303.482 545 258
Cultural contact- Andaman and Nicobar Islands	303.482 548 8
Cultural contact- Andhra Pradesh	303.482 548 4
Cultural contact- Arunachal Pradesh	303.482 541 63
Cultural contact- Assam	303.482 541 62
Cultural contact- Bengal	303.482 541 4
Cultural contact- Bihar	303.482 541 2
Cultural contact- Chandigarh	303.482 545 52
Cultural contact- Chhattisgarh	303.482 541 37
Cultural contact- Dadra and Nagar Haveli	303.482 547 96
Cultural contact- Delhi	303.482 545 6
Cultural contact- Goa, Daman and Diu	303.482 547 99
Cultural contact- Gujarat	303.482 547 5
Cultural contact- Haryana	303.482 54 558
Cultural contact- Himachal Pradesh	303.482 545 2
Cultural contact- India	303.482 54
Cultural contact- Jammu and Kashmir	303.482 546
Cultural contact- Jharkhand	303.482 541 27
Cultural contact- Karnataka	303.482 548 7
Cultural contact- Kerala	303.482 548 3
Cultural contact- Lakshwadweep	303.482 548 1

Cultural contact- Madhya Pradesh	303.482 543
Cultural contact- Madras	303.482 548 2
Cultural contact- Maharashtra	303.482 547 92
Cultural contact- Manipur	303.482 541 7
Cultural contact- Meghalaya	303.482 541 64
Cultural contact- Mizoram	303.482 541 66
Cultural contact- Nagaland	303.482 541 65
Cultural contact- Northeast India	303.482 541
Cultural contact- Orissa	303.482 541 3
Cultural contact- Pondicherry	303.482 548 6
Cultural contact- Punjab	303.482 545 52
Cultural contact- Rajasthan	303.482 544
Cultural contact- Sikkim	303.482 541 67
Cultural contact- South Asia	303.482 54
Cultural contact- Southern India	303.482 548
Cultural contact- Tamil Nadu	303.482 548 2
Cultural contact- Tripura	303.482 541 5
Cultural contact- Uttar Pradesh	303.482 542
Cultural contact- Uttaranchal	303. 482 545 1
Cultural contact- West Bengal	303.482 541 4
Cultural contact- Western India	303.482 547
Cultural law- India	344.54
Cultural relation between India and China	303.482 540 51

D

Dadra and Nagar Haveli- Architecture	720.954 796
Dadra and Nagar Haveli- Budget	352.495 479 6
Dadra and Nagar Haveli- Economic development	338.954 79 6
Dadra and Nagar Haveli- Economic geography	330.954 796
Dadra and Nagar Haveli- Education	370.954 79 6
Dadra and Nagar Haveli- Flora	581.954 796
Dadra and Nagar Haveli- Geography	915.4796
Dadra and Nagar Haveli- Geology	555.479 6
Dadra and Nagar Haveli- History	954.796
Dadra and Nagar Haveli- Public administration	351.547 96
Dadra and Nagar Haveli- Public finance	336.547 96
Dardic folk music	781 629 149 9
Dardic peoples	305.891 499
Dead persons as objects of worship and veneration (Buddhism)	294.342 13
Dead persons as objects of worship and veneration (Hinduism)	294.5213

Dead persons as objects of worship and veneration (Jainism)	294.4213
Dead persons as objects of worship and veneration (Sikhism)	294.6213
Death (Buddhism)	294.342 3
Death (Hinduism)	294.523
Death (Jainism)	294.423
Death (Sikhism)	294.623
Deities (Budhism)	294.342 11
Deities (Hinduism)	294.5211
Deities (Jainism)	294.4211
Deities (Sikhism)	294.6211
Delhi- Architecture	720.954 56
Delhi- Budget	352.495 45 6
Delhi- Economic development	338.954 5 6
Delhi- Economic geography	330.954 56
Delhi- Education	370.954 5 6
Delhi- Fauna	591.954 56
Delhi- Flora	581.954 56
Delhi- Geography	915.456
Delhi- Geology	555.456
Delhi- History	954.56
Delhi- Painting and paintings	759.954 56
Delhi- Public administration	351.545 6
Delhi- Public finance	336.545 6

Delhi- Sculpture	730.954 56
Demons (Buddhism)	294.342 16
Demons (Hinduism)	294.521 6
Demons (Sikhism)	294.621 6
Devotional literature - Buddhism	294.344 32
Devotional literature - Hinduism	294.543 2
Devotional literature - Jainism	294.443 2
Devotional literature - Sikhism	294.643 2
Dhammapada	294.382 322
Dharmasastras	294.592 6
Dictionaries- Buddhism	294.303
Dictionaries- Hinduism	294.503
Dictionaries- Jainism	294.403
Dictionaries- Sikhism	294.603
Digambara	294.493
Divehi language	491.487
Divehi literature	891.48
Divination (Buddhism)	294.343 2
Divination (Hinduism)	294.532
Divination (Jainism)	294.432
Divination (Sikhism)	294.632
Divine Light Mission	294
Divinities (Buddhism)	294.342 11
Divinities (Hinduism)	294.5211
Divinities (Jainism)	294.4211

Divinities (Sikhism)	294.6211
Divorce (Buddhism)	294.337 7835
Divorce (Hinduism)	294.517 835
Divorce (Jainism)	294.417 835
Doctrines (Buddhism)	294.342
Doctrines (Hinduism)	294.52
Doctrines (Jainism)	294.42
Doctrines (Sikhism)	294.62
Doctrines and practices (Buddhism)	294.34
Doctrines of specific branches, sects, reform movements (Buddhism)	294.342 04
Dravidian folk music	781 629 48
Dravidian language speaking people	305.794 8
Dravidian languages	494.81
Dravidian literatures	894.81
Dravidians	305.894 8
Dualistic school	181.484
Dvaita philosophy	181.484 1
Dvaitadvaita philosophy	181.484.3

E

East Indo-European and Celtic languages	491
Eastern Himalayan languages	495.49
Eastern Himalayan literatures	895.49
Eastern Hindi language	491.49
Eastern Hindi speaking people	305.791 49
Ecology (Buddhism)	294.33783 6++
Ecology (Hinduism)	294.517 836++
Ecology (Jainism)	294.417 836++
Ecology (Sikhism)	294.617 836++
Economic conditions	***See*** Economic geography
Economic development- Andaman and Nicobar Islands	338.954 88
Economic development- Andhra Pradesh	338.954 84
Economic development- Arunachal Pradesh	338.954 163
Economic development- Assam	338.954 162
Economic development- Bengal	338.954 14
Economic development- Bihar	338.954 12
Economic development- Chandigarh	338.954 55 2

Economic development- Chhattisgarh	338.954 137
Economic development- Dadra and Nagar Haveli	338.954 796
Economic development- Delhi	338.954 56
Economic development- Gujarat	338.954 75
Economic development- Haryana	338.954 55 8
Economic development- Himachal Pradesh	338.954 52
Economic development- India	338.954
Economic development- Jammu and Kashmir	338.954 6
Economic development- Jharkhand	338.954 127
Economic development- Karnataka	338.954 87
Economic development- Kerala	338.954 83
Economic development- Lakshwadweep	338.954 81
Economic development- Madhya Pradesh	338.954 3
Economic development- Madras	338.954 82
Economic development- Maharashtra	338.954 792
Economic development- Manipur	338.954 17
Economic development- Meghalaya	338.954 164
Economic development- Mizoram	338.954 166
Economic development- Nagaland	338.954 165
Economic development- Northeast India	338.954 1
Economic development- Orissa	338.954 13
Economic development- Pondicherry	338.954 86
Economic development- Punjab	338.954 55 2

Economic development- Rajasthan	338.954 4
Economic development- Sikkim	338.954 167
Economic development- South Asia	338.954
Economic development- Southern India	338.954 8
Economic development- Tamil Nadu	338.954 82
Economic development- Tripura	338.954 15
Economic development- Uttar Pradesh	338.954 2
Economic development- Uttaranchal	338.954 51
Economic development- West Bengal	338.954 14
Economic development- Western India	338.954 7
Economic geography	330.9
Economic geography- Andaman and Nicobar Islands	330.954 88
Economic geography- Andhra Pradesh	330.954 84
Economic geography- Arunachal Pradesh	330.954 163
Economic geography- Assam	330.954 162
Economic geography- Bengal	330.954 14
Economic geography- Bhopal	330.954 3
Economic geography- Bihar	330.954 12
Economic geography- Bombay	330.954 792 3
Economic geography- Calcutta	330.954 147
Economic geography- Chandigarh	330.954 55 2
Economic geography- Chhattisgarh	330.954 137
Economic geography- Dadra and Nagar Haveli	330.954 796

Economic geography- Delhi	330.954 56
Economic geography- Goa, Daman and Diu	330.954 799
Economic geography- Gujarat	330.954 75
Economic geography- Haryana	330.954 55 8
Economic geography- Himachal Pradesh	330.954 52
Economic geography- India	330.954
Economic geography- Jammu and Kashmir	330.954 6
Economic geography- Jharkhand	330.954 127
Economic geography- Karnataka	330.954 87
Economic geography- Kerala	330.954 83
Economic geography- Lakshwadweep	330.954 81
Economic geography- Madhya Pradesh	330.954 3
Economic geography- Madras	330.954 82
Economic geography- Maharashtra	330.954 792
Economic geography- Manipur	330.954 17
Economic geography- Meghalaya	330.954 164
Economic geography- Mizoram	330.954 166
Economic geography- Nagaland	330.954 165
Economic geography- Northeast India	330.954 1
Economic geography- Orissa	330.954 13
Economic geography- Pondicherry	330.954 86
Economic geography- Punjab	330.954 55 2
Economic geography- Rajasthan	330.954 4
Economic geography- Sikkim	330.954 167
Economic geography- South Asia	330.954

Economic geography- Southern India	330.954 8
Economic geography- Tamil Nadu	330.954 82
Economic geography- Tripura	330.954 15
Economic geography- Uttar Pradesh	330.954 2
Economic geography- Uttaranchal	330.954 51
Economic geography- West Bengal	330.954 14
Economic geography- Western India	330.954 7
Economic growth	***See*** Economic development
Economic order (Buddhism)	294.33785
Economic order (Hinduism)	294.517 85
Economic order (Jainism)	294.417 85
Economic order (Sikhism)	294.617 85
Economic policy- India	337.54
Economic relation between India and Australia	337.54094
Economic relation between India and Bangladesh	337.5405492
Economic relation between India and Bhutan	337.5405498
Economic relation between India and Canada	337.54071
Economic relation between India and China	337.54051
Economic relation between India and Developed countries	337.5401722
Economic relation between India and Developing countries	337.5401724
Economic relation between India and	

England	337.54042
Economic relation between India and European countries	337.5404
Economic relation between India and Indonesia	337.540598
Economic relation between India and Japan	337.54052
Economic relation between India and Malaysia	337.540595
Economic relation between India and Maldives	337.5405495
Economic relation between India and Middle East	337.54056
Economic relation between India and Myanmar	337.540591
Economic relation between India and Nepal	337.5405496
Economic relation between India and Pakistan	337.5405491
Economic relation between India and Russia	337.54047
Economic relation between India and Singapore	337.5405957
Economic relation between India and Sri Lanka	337.5405493
Economic relation between India and Thailand	337.540593
Economic relation between India and UK	337.54041
Economic relation between India and USA	337.54073
Economic situation	***See*** Economic geography

Education	370
Education- Andaman and Nicobar Islands	370.954 88
Education- Andhra Pradesh	370.954 84
Education- Arunachal Pradesh	370.954 163
Education- Assam	370.954 162
Education- Bengal	370.954 14
Education- Bhopal	370.954 3
Education- Bihar	370.954 12
Education- Bombay	370.954 792 3
Education- Calcutta	370.954 147
Education- Chandigarh	370.954 55 2
Education- Chhattisgarh	370.954 137
Education- Dadra and Nagar Haveli	370.954 796
Education- Delhi	370.954 56
Education- Goa, Daman and Diu	370.954 799
Education- Gujarat	370.954 75
Education- Haryana	370.954 55 8
Education- Himachal Pradesh	370.954 52
Education- India	370.954
Education- Jammu and Kashmir	370.954 6
Education- Jharkhand	370.954 127
Education- Karnataka	370.954 87
Education- Kerala	370.954 83
Education- Lakshwadweep	370.954 81

Education- Madhya Pradesh	370.954 3
Education- Madras	370.954 82
Education- Maharashtra	370.954 792
Education- Manipur	370.954 17
Education- Meghalaya	370.954 164
Education- Mizoram	370.954 166
Education- Nagaland	370.954 165
Education- Northeast India	370.954 1
Education- Orissa	370.954 13
Education- Pondicherry	370.954 86
Education- Punjab	370.954 55 2
Education- Rajasthan	370.954 4
Education- Sikkim	370.954 167
Education- South Asia	370.954
Education- Southern India	370.954 8
Education- Tamil Nadu	370.954 82
Education- Tripura	370.954 15
Education- Uttar Pradesh	370.954 2
Education- Uttaranchal	370.954 51
Education- West Bengal	370.954 14
Education- Western India	370.954 7
Education (Buddhism)	294.3071
Education (Hinduism)	294.5071
Education (Jainism)	294.4071
Education (Sikhism)	294.6071

Education law- India	344.54
Educational aid to India	379.129 54
Elections- Andaman and Nicobar Islands	324.954 88
Elections- Andhra Pradesh	324.954 84
Elections- Arunachal Pradesh	324.954 163
Elections- Assam	324.954 162
Elections- Bengal	324.954 14
Elections- Bhopal	324.954 3
Elections- Bihar	324.954 12
Elections- Bombay	324.954 792 3
Elections- Calcutta	324.954 147
Elections- Chandigarh	324.954 55 2
Elections- Chhattisgarh	324.954 137
Elections- Dadra and Nagar Haveli	324.954 796
Elections- Delhi	324.954 56
Elections- Goa, Daman and Diu	324.954 799
Elections- Gujarat	324.954 75
Elections- Haryana	324.954 55 8
Elections- Himachal Pradesh	324.954 52
Elections- India	324.954++
Elections- Jammu and Kashmir	324.954 6
Elections- Jharkhand	324.954 127
Elections- Karnataka	324.954 87
Elections- Kerala	324.954 83
Elections- Lakshwadweep	324.954 81

Elections- Madhya Pradesh	324.954 3
Elections- Madras	324.954 82
Elections- Maharashtra	324.954 792
Elections- Manipur	324.954 17
Elections- Meghalaya	324.954 164
Elections- Mizoram	324.954 166
Elections- Nagaland	324.954 165
Elections- Northeast India	324.954 1
Elections- Orissa	324.954 13
Elections- Pondicherry	324.954 86
Elections- Punjab	324.954 55 2
Elections- Rajasthan	324.954 4
Elections- Sikkim	324.954 167
Elections- South Asia	324.954++
Elections- Southern India	324.954 8
Elections- Tamil Nadu	324.954 82
Elections- Tripura	324.954 15
Elections- Uttar Pradesh	324.954 2
Elections- Uttaranchal	324.954 51
Elections- West Bengal	324.954 14
Elections- Western India	324.954 7
Elementary education	372
Elementary education- Andaman and Nicobar Islands	372.954 88
Elementary education- Andhra Pradesh	372.954 84

Elementary education- Arunachal Pradesh	372.954 163
Elementary education- Assam	372.954 162
Elementary education- Bengal	372.954 14
Elementary education- Bhopal	372.954 3
Elementary education- Bihar	372.954 12
Elementary education- Bombay	372.954 792 3
Elementary education- Calcutta	372.954 147
Elementary education- Chandigarh	372.954 55 2
Elementary education- Chhattisgarh	372.954 137
Elementary education- Dadra and Nagar Haveli	372.954 796
Elementary education- Delhi	372.954 56
Elementary education- Goa, Daman and Diu	372.954 799
Elementary education- Gujarat	372.954 75
Elementary education- Haryana	372.954 55 8
Elementary education- Himachal Pradesh	372.954 52
Elementary education- India	372.954
Elementary education- Jammu and Kashmir	372.954 6
Elementary education- Jharkhand	372.954 127
Elementary education- Karnataka	372.954 87
Elementary education- Kerala	372.954 83
Elementary education- Lakshwadweep	372.954 81
Elementary education- Madhya Pradesh	372.954 3
Elementary education- Madras	372.954 82

Elementary education- Maharashtra	372.954 792
Elementary education- Manipur	372.954 17
Elementary education- Meghalaya	372.954 164
Elementary education- Mizoram	372.954 166
Elementary education- Nagaland	372.954 165
Elementary education- Northeast India	372.954 1
Elementary education- Orissa	372.954 13
Elementary education- Pondicherry	372.954 86
Elementary education- Punjab	372.954 55 2
Elementary education- Rajasthan	372.954 4
Elementary education- Sikkim	372.954 167
Elementary education- South Asia	372.954
Elementary education- Southern India	372.954 8
Elementary education- Tamil Nadu	372.954 82
Elementary education- Tripura	372.954 15
Elementary education- Uttar Pradesh	372.954 2
Elementary education- Uttaranchal	372.954 51
Elementary education- West Bengal	372.954 14
Elementary education- Western India	372.954 7
Emblems (Buddhism)	294.343 7
Emblems (Hinduism)	294.537
Emblems (Jainism)	294.437
Emblems (Sikhism)	294.637
Emigration from India	325.254
Emigration from India to USA	325.2540973

Encyclopaedias - Buddhism	294.303
Encyclopaedias - Hinduism	294.503
Encyclopaedias - Jainism	294.403
Encyclopaedias - Sikhism	294.603
Encyclopedia yearbooks	030
End of the world (Buddhism)	294.342 3
End of the world (Hinduism)	294.523
End of the world (Jainism)	294.423
End of the world (Sikhism)	294.623
English adventure fiction (multiple authors)	823.087*
English adventure fiction (multiple authors) –Collections	823.08708**
English adventure fiction (multiple authors)- History and criticism	823.08709**
English anecdotes, epigrams, graffiti, jokes, quotations (multiple authors)	828.02
English anecdotes, epigrams, graffiti, jokes, quotations (single author)	828. +CD+02
English ballads (multiple authors)	821.044*
English ballads (multiple authors)- Collections	821.04408**
English ballads (multiple authors)- History and criticism	821.04409**
English comedy (multiple authors)	822.0523*
English comedy (multiple authors) – Collections	822.052308**
English comedy (multiple authors) – History and criticism	822.052309**

English conversations (multiple authors)	825.06*
English conversations (multiple authors) – Collections	825.0608**
English conversations (multiple authors) – History and criticism	825.0609**
English debates and public discussions (multiple authors)	825.03*
English debates and public discussions (multiple authors)- Collections	825.0308**
English debates and public discussions (multiple authors)- History and criticism	825.0309**
English detective fiction (multiple authors)	823.0872*
English detective fiction (multiple authors) – Collections	823.087208**
English detective fiction (multiple authors) – History and criticism	823.087209**
English diaries, notebooks, reminiscences (single author)–1066- 1400	828. 103
English diaries, notebooks, reminiscences (single author)–1400 – 1558	828. 203
English diaries, notebooks, reminiscences (single author)–1558 – 1625	828. 303
English diaries, notebooks, reminiscences (single author)–1625 – 1702	828. 403
English diaries, notebooks, reminiscences (single author)–16th century	828. 303
English diaries, notebooks, reminiscences (single author)–1702 – 1745	828. 503
English diaries, notebooks, reminiscences (single author)–1745 – 1799	828. 603

English diaries, notebooks, reminiscences (single author)–1800 – 1837	828. 703
English diaries, notebooks, reminiscences (single author)–1837-1899	828. 803
English diaries, notebooks, reminiscences (single author)–18th century	828. 503
English diaries, notebooks, reminiscences (single author)–1900-	828. 903
English diaries, notebooks, reminiscences (single author)–1900 – 1999	828. 9103
English diaries, notebooks, reminiscences (single author)–19th century	828. 803
English diaries, notebooks, reminiscences (single author)–2000-	828. 9203
English diaries, notebooks, reminiscences (single author)–20th century	828. 9103
English diaries, notebooks, reminiscences (single author)–Elizabethan period	828. 303
English diaries, notebooks, reminiscences (single author)-Medieval period	828. 103
English diaries, notebooks, reminiscences (single author)–Queen Anne period	828. 503
English diaries, notebooks, reminiscences (single author)–Renaissance period	828. 303
English diaries, notebooks, reminiscences (single author)–Romantic period	828. 703
English diaries, notebooks, reminiscences (multiple authors)	828.03
English didactic poetry (multiple authors)	821.05*
English didactic poetry (multiple authors)-	

Collections	821.0508**
English didactic poetry (multiple authors)-History and criticism	821.0509**
English drama	822
English drama (multiple authors) – 1066- 1400	822. 1+
English drama (multiple authors) – 1400 – 1558	822. 2+
English drama (multiple authors) – 1558 – 1625	822. 3+
English drama (multiple authors) – 1625 – 1702	822. 4+
English drama (multiple authors) – 16th century	822. 3+
English drama (multiple authors) – 1702 – 1745	822. 5+
English drama (multiple authors) – 1745 – 1799	822. 6+
English drama (multiple authors) – 1800 – 1837	822. 7+
English drama (multiple authors) – 1837-1899	822. 8+
English drama (multiple authors) – 18th century	822. 5+
English drama (multiple authors) –1900-	822. 9+
English drama (multiple authors) –1900 – 1999	822. 91+
English drama (multiple authors) – 19th century	822. 8+

English drama (multiple authors) –2000-	822. 92+
English drama (multiple authors) – 20th century	822. 91+
English drama (multiple authors) – Collections	822.008**
English drama (multiple authors) – Dictionaries etc	822.003
English drama (multiple authors) – Elizabethan period	822. 3+
English drama (multiple authors) – History and criticism	822.009**
English drama (multiple authors) – Medieval period	822. 1+
English drama (multiple authors) – Periodicals	822.005
English drama (multiple authors) – Philosophy and theory	822.001
English drama (multiple authors) – Psychological aspects	822.0019
English drama (multiple authors) – Queen Anne period	822. 5+
English drama (multiple authors) – Renaissance period	822. 3+
English drama (multiple authors) – Research	822.0072
English drama (multiple authors) – Romantic period	822. 7+
English drama (multiple authors) – Study and teaching	822.007
English drama (multiple authors) –Value	822.0013

English drama (single author) –1066- 1400	822. 1
English drama (single author) –1400 – 1558	822. 2
English drama (single author) –1558 – 1625	822. 3
English drama (single author) –1625 – 1702	822. 4
English drama (single author) –16th century	822. 3
English drama (single author) –1702 – 1745	822. 5
English drama (single author) –1745 – 1799	822. 6
English drama (single author) –1800 – 1837	822. 7
English drama (single author) –1837-1899	822. 8
English drama (single author) –18th century	822. 5
English drama (single author) –1900-	822. 9
English drama (single author) –1900 – 1999	822. 91
English drama (single author) –19th century	822. 8
English drama (single author) –2000-	822. 92
English drama (single author) –20th century	822. 91
English drama (single author) – Elizabethan period	822. 3
English drama (single author) – Medieval period	822. 1
English drama (single author) – Queen Anne period	822. 5
English drama (single author) – Renaissance period	822. 3
English drama (single author) – Romantic period	822. 7
English drama for cinema (multiple authors)	822.03*

English drama for cinema (multiple authors) – Collections	822.0308**
English drama for cinema (multiple authors) – History and criticism	822.0309**
English drama for radio (multiple authors)	822.022*
English drama for radio (multiple authors) - History and criticism	822.02209**
English drama for radio (multiple authors) – Collections	822.02208**
English drama for television (multiple authors)	822.025*
English drama for television (multiple authors) – Collections	822.02508**
English drama for television (multiple authors) – History and criticism	822.02509**
English dramatic poetry (multiple authors)	821.02*
English dramatic poetry (multiple authors)-Collections	821.0208**
English dramatic poetry (multiple authors)-History and criticism	821.0209**
English ephemeral and light verse (multiple authors)	821.08*
English ephemeral and light verse (multiple authors) – History and criticism	821.0809**
English ephemeral and light verse (multiple authors)- Collections	821.0808**
English epic poetry (multiple authors)	821.032*
English epic poetry (multiple authors)-Collections	821.03208**

English epic poetry (multiple authors)-History and criticism	821.03209**
English epigrams	***See*** English anecdotes...
English essays	824
English essays (multiple authors) – 1066- 1400	824. 1+
English essays (multiple authors) – 1400 – 1558	824. 2+
English essays (multiple authors) – 1558 – 1625	824. 3+
English essays (multiple authors) – 1625 – 1702	824. 4+
English essays (multiple authors) – 16th century	824. 3+
English essays (multiple authors) – 1702 – 1745	824. 5+
English essays (multiple authors) – 1745 – 1799	824. 6+
English essays (multiple authors) – 1800 – 1837	824. 7+
English essays (multiple authors) – 1837-1899	824. 8+
English essays (multiple authors) – 18th century	824. 5+
English essays (multiple authors) –1900-	824. 9+
English essays (multiple authors) – 1900 – 1999	824. 91+
English essays (multiple authors) – 19th century	824. 8+

English essays (multiple authors) –2000-	824. 92+
English essays (multiple authors) – 20th century	824. 91+
English essays (multiple authors) – Collections	824.008**
English essays (multiple authors) – Dictionaries etc	824.003
English essays (multiple authors) – Elizabethan period	824. 3+
English essays (multiple authors) – History and criticism	824.009**
English essays (multiple authors) – Medieval period	824. 1+
English essays (multiple authors) – Periodicals	824.005
English essays (multiple authors) – Philosophy and theory	824.001
English essays (multiple authors) – Psychological aspects	824.0019
English essays (multiple authors) – Queen Anne period	824. 5+
English essays (multiple authors) – Renaissance period	824. 3+
English essays (multiple authors) – Research	824.0072
English essays (multiple authors) – Romantic period	824. 7+
English essays (multiple authors) – Study and teaching	824.007
English essays (multiple authors) –Value	824.0013

English essays (single author) –1066- 1400	824. 1
English essays (single author) – 1400 – 1558	824. 2
English essays (single author) – 1558 – 1625	824. 3
English essays (single author) – 1625 – 1702	824. 4
English essays (single author) – 16th century	824. 3
English essays (single author) – 1702 – 1745	824. 5
English essays (single author) – 1745 – 1799	824. 6
English essays (single author) – 1800 – 1837	824. 7
English essays (single author) – 1837-1899	824. 8
English essays (single author) – 18th century	824. 5
English essays (single author) –1900-	824. 9
English essays (single author) – 1900 – 1999	824. 91
English essays (single author) –19th century	824. 8
English essays (single author) –2000-	824. 92
English essays (single author) –20th century	824. 91
English essays (single author) – Elizabethan period	824. 3
English essays (single author) – Medieval period	824. 1

English essays (single author) – Queen Anne period	824. 5
English essays (single author) – Renaissance period	824. 3
English essays (single author) – Romantic period	824. 7
English experimental and non-formalized works (single author)	828
English experimental works (multiple authors)	828.07
English fantasy fiction (multiple authors)	823.08766*
English fantasy fiction (multiple authors)- Collections	823.0876608**
English fantasy fiction (multiple authors)- History and criticism	823.0876609**
English farce (multiple authors)	822.05232*
English farce (multiple authors) – History and criticism	822.0523209**
English farce (multiple authors)- Collections	822.0523208**
English fiction	823
English fiction (multiple authors) – 1066- 1400	823. 1+
English fiction (multiple authors) – 1400 – 1558	823. 2+
English fiction (multiple authors) – 1558 – 1625	823. 3+
English fiction (multiple authors) – 1625 – 1702	823. 4+
English fiction (multiple authors) –	

16th century	823. 3+
English fiction (multiple authors) – 1702 – 1745	823. 5+
English fiction (multiple authors) – 1745 – 1799	823. 6+
English fiction (multiple authors) – 1800 – 1837	823. 7+
English fiction (multiple authors) – 1837-1899	823. 8+
English fiction (multiple authors) – 18th century	823. 5+
English fiction (multiple authors) –1900-	823. 9+
English fiction (multiple authors) – 1900 – 1999	823. 91+
English fiction (multiple authors) – 19th century	823. 8+
English fiction (multiple authors) –2000-	823. 92+
English fiction (multiple authors) –2000-	823. 92+
English fiction (multiple authors) – 20th century	823. 91+
English fiction (multiple authors) – Collections	823.008**
English fiction (multiple authors) – Dictionaries etc	823.003
English fiction (multiple authors) – Elizabethan period	823. 3+
English fiction (multiple authors) – History and criticism	823.009**
English fiction (multiple authors) –	

Medieval period	823. 1+
English fiction (multiple authors) – Periodicals	823.005
English fiction (multiple authors) – Philosophy and theory	823.001
English fiction (multiple authors) – Psychological aspects	823.0019
English fiction (multiple authors) – Queen Anne period	823. 5+
English fiction (multiple authors) – Renaissance period	823. 3+
English fiction (multiple authors) – Research	823.0072
English fiction (multiple authors) – Romantic period	823. 7+
English fiction (multiple authors) – Study and teaching	823.007
English fiction (multiple authors) –Value	823.0013
English fiction (single author) –1066- 1400	823. 1
English fiction (single author) –1400 – 1558	823. 2
English fiction (single author) –1558 – 1625	823. 3
English fiction (single author) –1625 – 1703	823. 4
English fiction (single author) –16th century	823. 3
English fiction (single author) –1703 – 1745	823. 5
English fiction (single author) –1745 – 1799	823. 6
English fiction (single author) –1800 – 1837	823. 7
English fiction (single author) –1837-1899	823. 8

English fiction (single author) –18th century	823. 5
English fiction (single author) –1900-	823. 9
English fiction (single author) –1900 – 1999	823. 91
English fiction (single author) –19th century	823. 8
English fiction (single author) –2000-	823. 92
English fiction (single author) –20th century	823. 91
English fiction (single author) – Elizabethan period	823. 3
English fiction (single author) – Medieval period	823. 1
English fiction (single author) – Queen Anne period	823. 5
English fiction (single author) – Renaissance period	823. 3
English fiction (single author) – Romantic period	823. 7
English ghost fiction (multiple authors)	823.08733*
English ghost fiction (multiple authors) – Collections	823.0873308**
English ghost fiction (multiple authors)- History and criticism	823.0873309**
English graffiti	***See*** English anecdotes…
English grammar	425
English historical drama (multiple authors)	822.0514*
English historical drama (multiple authors)- Collections	822.051408**
English historical drama (multiple authors)-	

History and criticism	822.051409**
English historical fiction (multiple authors)	823.081*
English historical fiction (multiple authors)-Collections	823.08108**
English historical fiction (multiple authors)-History and criticism	823.08109**
English horror fiction (multiple authors)	823.08738*
English horror fiction (multiple authors)-Collections	823.0873808**
English horror fiction (multiple authors)-History and criticism	823.0873809**
English humour and satire	827
English humour and satire (multiple authors) –1066- 1400	827. 1+
English humour and satire (multiple authors) –1400 – 1558	827. 2+
English humour and satire (multiple authors) –1558 – 1625	827. 3+
English humour and satire (multiple authors) –1625 – 1703	827. 4+
English humour and satire (multiple authors) –16th century	827. 3+
English humour and satire (multiple authors) –1703 – 1745	827. 5+
English humour and satire (multiple authors) –1745 – 1799	827. 6+
English humour and satire (multiple authors) –1800 – 1837	827. 7+
English humour and satire (multiple	

authors) –1837-1899	827. 8+
English humour and satire (multiple authors) –18th century	827. 5+
English humour and satire (multiple authors) –1900-	827. 9+
English humour and satire (multiple authors) –1900 – 1999	827. 91+
English humour and satire (multiple authors) –19th century	827. 8+
English humour and satire (multiple authors) –2000-	827. 92+
English humour and satire (multiple authors) –20th century	827. 91+
English humour and satire (multiple authors) –Collections	827.008**
English humour and satire (multiple authors) –Dictionaries etc	827.003
English humour and satire (multiple authors) –Elizabethan period	827. 3+
English humour and satire (multiple authors) –History and criticism	827.009**
English humour and satire (multiple authors) –Medieval period	827. 1+
English humour and satire (multiple authors) –Periodicals	827.005
English humour and satire (multiple authors) –Philosophy and theory	827.001
English humour and satire (multiple authors) –Psychological aspects	827.0019
English humour and satire (multiple	

authors) –Queen Anne period	827. 5+
English humour and satire (multiple authors) –Renaissance period	827. 3+
English humour and satire (multiple authors) –Research	827.0072
English humour and satire (multiple authors) –Romantic period	827. 7+
English humour and satire (multiple authors) –Study and teaching	827.007
English humour and satire (multiple authors) –Value	827.0013
English humourous and satirical poetry (multiple authors)	821.07
English humourous and satirical poetry (multiple authors)- Collections	821.0708**
English humourous and satirical poetry (multiple authors)- History and criticism	821.0709**
English jokes	***See*** English anecdotes…
English language	420
English language- Applied linguistics	428
English language- Bilingual dictionaries	423. 2-39
English language- Bilingualism	420. 42
English language- Concordances	420. 3
English language- Content analysis	420. 141
English language- Dialects	427
English language- Dictionaries	423
English language- Discourse analysis	420. 141

English language- Education	420. 71
English language- Encyclopaedias	420. 3
English language- Etymology	422
English language- Functionalism	420. 18
English language- Geographic variations in England	427.1 - .8
English language- Geographic variations in other places	427.9
English language- Grammar	425
English language- Historical and geographic variations	427
English language- History	420. 9
English language- Intonation	421. 6
English language- Lexicography	423. 028
English language- Lexicology	420. 14
English language- Miscellany	420. 2
English language- Modern non-geographic variations	427
English language- Multilingualism	420. 42
English language- Organizations	420. 6
English language- Orthography	421. 52
English language- Pauses	421. 6
English language- Periodicals	420. 5
English language- Persons (men, women, etc)	420. 8
English language- Philosophy and theory	420. 1

English language- Phonetics	421. 58
English language- Phonology, etc	421. 5
English language- Pitch	421. 6
English language- Pronunciation	421. 52
English language- Readers	428.6
English language- Research	420. 72
English language- Rhetoric	808.042
English language- Schools and theories of linguistics	420. 18
English language- Semantics	420. 143
English language- Semiotics	420. 141
English language- Slang	427
English language- Specialized dictionaries	423. 1
English language- Spelling, orthography	421.52
English language- Stress	421. 6
English language- Structural linguistics	420. 18
English language- Suprasegmental features	421. 6
English language- Terminology	420. 14
English language- Theory	420. 1
English language- Usage	428
English language- Variations (Dialects etc)	427
English language- Writing system, phonology, phonetics	421
English language- Writing systems	421 1
English letters	826

English letters (multiple authors) – 1066- 1400	826. 1+
English letters (multiple authors) – 1400 – 1558	826. 2+
English letters (multiple authors) – 1558 – 1625	826. 3+
English letters (multiple authors) – 1625 – 1702	826. 4+
English letters (multiple authors) – 16th century	826. 3+
English letters (multiple authors) – 1702 – 1745	826. 5+
English letters (multiple authors) – 1745 – 1799	826. 6+
English letters (multiple authors) – 1800 – 1837	826. 7+
English letters (multiple authors) – 1837-1899	826. 8+
English letters (multiple authors) – 18th century	826. 5+
English letters (multiple authors) –1900-	826. 9+
English letters (multiple authors) – 1900 – 1999	826. 91+
English letters (multiple authors) – 19th century	826. 8+
English letters (multiple authors) –2000-	826. 92+
English letters (multiple authors) – 20th century	826. 91+
English letters (multiple authors) – Collections	826.008**

English letters (multiple authors) – Dictionaries etc	826.003
English letters (multiple authors) – Elizabethan period	826. 3+
English letters (multiple authors) – History and criticism	826.009**
English letters (multiple authors) – Medieval period	826. 1+
English letters (multiple authors) – Periodicals	826.005
English letters (multiple authors) – Philosophy and theory	826.001
English letters (multiple authors) – Psychological aspects	826.0019
English letters (multiple authors) – Queen Anne period	826. 5+
English letters (multiple authors) – Renaissance period	826. 3+
English letters (multiple authors) –Research	826.0072
English letters (multiple authors) – Romantic period	826. 7+
English letters (multiple authors) – Study and teaching	826.007
English letters (multiple authors) –Value	826.0013
English letters (single author) –1066- 1400	826. 1
English letters (single author) –1400 – 1558	826. 2
English letters (single author) –1558 – 1625	826. 3
English letters (single author) –1625 – 1703	826. 4
English letters (single author) –16th century	826. 3

English letters (single author) –1703 – 1745	826. 5
English letters (single author) –1745 – 1799	826. 6
English letters (single author) –1800 – 1837	826. 7
English letters (single author) –1837-1899	826. 8
English letters (single author) –18th century	826. 5
English letters (single author) –1900-	826. 9
English letters (single author) –1900 – 1999	826. 91
English letters (single author) –19th century	826. 8
English letters (single author) –2000-	826. 92
English letters (single author) –20th century	826. 91
English letters (single author) – Elizabethan period	826. 3
English letters (single author) – Medieval period	826. 1
English letters (single author) - Queen Anne period	826. 5
English letters (single author) - Renaissance period	826. 3
English letters (single author) - Romantic period	826. 7
English light verse	***See*** English ephemeral and light verse
English limericks (multiple authors)	821.075*
English limericks(multiple authors)- Collections	821.07508**
English limericks(multiple authors)- History and criticism	821.07509**

English literature	820
English literature (collections of multiple forms)	820.8
English literature (collections of multiple forms) - 19th century	820.808
English literature (collections of multiple forms) - 20th century	820.8091
English literature (collections of multiple forms) - 21st century	820.8092
English literature (collections of multiple forms) - Allegory	820.8015
English literature (collections of multiple forms) - Animals	820.80362++
English literature (collections of multiple forms) - Artistic themes	820.80357
English literature (collections of multiple forms) - Atmosphere	820.8032161
English literature (collections of multiple forms) - Characters	820.8027
English literature (collections of multiple forms) - Comedy	820.8017
English literature (collections of multiple forms) - Evening	820.8033
English literature (collections of multiple forms) - Fantasy	820.8015
English literature (collections of multiple forms) - Forests	820.8032152
English literature (collections of multiple forms) - Historical themes	820.80358
English literature (collections of multiple	

forms) - Horror	820.80164
English literature (collections of multiple forms) - Human characteristics (Biological, moral, psychological)	820.80353
English literature (collections of multiple forms) - Legendary objects/themes	820.8037
English literature (collections of multiple forms) - Literary themes	820.80357
English literature (collections of multiple forms) - Love	820.803543
English literature (collections of multiple forms) - Marriage	820.803543
English literature (collections of multiple forms) - Morning	820.8033
English literature (collections of multiple forms) - Mountains	820.8032143
English literature (collections of multiple forms) - Myth	820.8015
English literature (collections of multiple forms) - Mythological objects/themes	820.8037
English literature (collections of multiple forms) - Philosophic themes	820.80384
English literature (collections of multiple forms) - Places	820.8032+
English literature (collections of multiple forms) - Plants	820.80364
English literature (collections of multiple forms) - Political themes	820.80358
English literature (collections of multiple forms) - Religious themes	820.80382++

English literature (collections of multiple forms) - Rivers	820.80321693
English literature (collections of multiple forms) - Romanticism	820.80145
English literature (collections of multiple forms) - Scientific themes	820.80356
English literature (collections of multiple forms) - Sea	820.8032162
English literature (collections of multiple forms) - Seasons	820.8033
English literature (collections of multiple forms) - Sex	820.803538
English literature (collections of multiple forms) - Social themes	820.80355
English literature (collections of multiple forms) - Space	820.803219
English literature (collections of multiple forms) - Specific kinds of persons, e.g. heroes	820.80352+
English literature (collections of multiple forms) - Specific persons (real or imaginary)	820.80351
English literature (collections of multiple forms) - Stream of consciousness	820.8025
English literature (collections of multiple forms) - Supernatural objects/themes	820.8037
English literature (collections of multiple forms) - Symbolism	820.8015
English literature (collections of multiple forms) - Technical themes	820.80356
English literature (collections of multiple	

forms) - Times (seasons, parts of day, etc)	820.8033
English literature (collections of multiple forms) - Towns	820.80321732
English literature (collections of multiple forms) - Tragedy	820.80162
English literature (collections of multiple forms) - Villages	820.80321734
English literature (collections of multiple forms) - Weather	820.8036
English literature (collections of multiple forms) emphasizing subjects	820.804++
English literature (collections of multiple forms) for/by children	820.809282
English literature (collections of multiple forms) for/by persons of racial, ethnic and national groups	820.808++
English literature (collections of multiple forms) for/by persons of specific classes	820.8092++
English literature (collections of multiple forms) for/by persons resident in specific regions	820.8091++
English literature (collections of multiple forms) for/by women	820.809287
English literature (multiple authors) - Concordances	820.3
English literature (multiple authors) - Dictionaries	820.3
English literature (multiple authors) - Education	820.71
English literature (multiple authors) -	

Encyclopaedias	820.3
English literature (multiple authors) - Organizations	820.6
English literature (multiple authors) - Periodicals	820.5
English literature (multiple authors) - Philosophy and theory	820.1
English literature (multiple authors) - Research	820.72
English literature (multiple authors) - Research in India	820.72054
English literature (multiple authors) - Study and teaching	820.7
English literature (multiple forms)- 19th century	820.9004
English literature (multiple forms)- 2000-	820.90072
English literature (multiple forms)- 20th century	820.90071
English literature (multiple forms)- Allegory – History and criticism	820.915
English literature (multiple forms)- Animals - History and criticism	820.9362++
English literature (multiple forms)- Artistic themes - History and criticism	820.9357
English literature (multiple forms)- Atmosphere - History and criticism	820.932161
English literature (multiple forms)- Characters - History and criticism	820.927
English literature (multiple forms)- Comedy - History and criticism	820.917

English literature (multiple forms)- Evening - History and criticism	820.933
English literature (multiple forms)- Fantasy – History and criticism	820.915
English literature (multiple forms)- Forests- History and criticism	820.932152
English literature (multiple forms)- Historical themes - History and criticism	820.9358
English literature (multiple forms)- History and criticism	820.9
English literature (multiple forms)- Horror - History and criticism	820.9164
English literature (multiple forms)- Human characteristics (Biological, moral and psychological) - History and criticism	820.9353
English literature (multiple forms)- Legendary objects/themes - History and criticism	820.937
English literature (multiple forms)- Literary themes - History and criticism	820.9357
English literature (multiple forms)- Love - History and criticism	820.93543
English literature (multiple forms)- Marriage - History and criticism	820.93543
English literature (multiple forms)- Morning - History and criticism	820.933
English literature (multiple forms)- Mountains - History and criticism	820.932143
English literature (multiple forms)- Myth - History and criticism	820.915

English literature (multiple forms)- Mythological objects/themes - History and criticism	820.937
English literature (multiple forms)- Persons of racial, ethnic and national groups - History and criticism	820.98++
English literature (multiple forms)- Persons of specific classes - History and criticism	820.992++
English literature (multiple forms)- Persons resident in specific regions - History and criticism	820.991++
English literature (multiple forms)- Philosophic themes - History and criticism	820.9384
English literature (multiple forms)- Places - History and criticism	820.932++
English literature (multiple forms)- Plants - History and criticism	820.9364
English literature (multiple forms)- Political themes - History and criticism	820.9358
English literature (multiple forms)- Religious themes - History and criticism	820.9382
English literature (multiple forms)- Rivers - History and criticism	820.9321693
English literature (multiple forms)- Romanticism - History and criticism	820.9145
English literature (multiple forms)- Scientific themes - History and criticism	820.9356
English literature (multiple forms)- Sea - History and criticism	820.932162
English literature (multiple forms)-	

Seasons - History and criticism	820.933
English literature (multiple forms)- Sex - History and criticism	820.93538
English literature (multiple forms)- Social themes - History and criticism	820.9355
English literature (multiple forms)- Space - History and criticism	820.93219
English literature (multiple forms)- Specific kinds of persons (e.g. heroes) - History and criticism	820.9352++
English literature (multiple forms)- Specific persons - History and criticism	820.9351
English literature (multiple forms)- Stream of consciousness - History and criticism	820.925
English literature (multiple forms)- Subjects - History and criticism	820.94++
English literature (multiple forms)- Supernatural objects/themes - History and criticism	820.937
English literature (multiple forms)- Symbolism- History, criticism	820.915
English literature (multiple forms)- Technical themes - History and criticism	820.9356
English literature (multiple forms)- Times - History and criticism	820.933
English literature (multiple forms)- Towns - History and criticism	820.9321732
English literature (multiple forms)- Tragedy - History and criticism	820.9162

English literature (multiple forms)- Villages - History and criticism	820.9321734
English literature (multiple forms)- Weather - History and criticism	820.936
English literature (single author) - 1066-1400 - Biography, collections, criticism	828. 109
English literature (single author) - 1400 – 1558 - Biography, collections, criticism	828. 209
English literature (single author) - 1558 - 1625 - Biography, collections, criticism	828. 309
English literature (single author) - 1625 - 1702 - Biography, collections, criticism	828. 409
English literature (single author) - 16th century - Biography, collections, criticism	828. 309
English literature (single author) - 1702 - 1745 - Biography, collections, criticism	828. 509
English literature (single author) - 1745 - 1799 -Biography, collections, criticism	828. 609
English literature (single author) - 1800 - 1837 - Biography, collections, criticism	828. 709
English literature (single author) - 1837-1899 - Biography, collections, criticism	828. 809
English literature (single author) - 18th century - Biography, collections, criticism	828. 509
English literature (single author) - 1900 - 1999 - Biography, collections, criticism	828. 9109
English literature (single author) - 1900- Biography, collections, criticism	828. 909

English literature (single author) - 19th century - Biography, collections, criticism	828. 809
English literature (single author) - 2000- Biography, collections, criticism	828. 9209
English literature (single author) - 20th century - Biography, collections, criticism	828. 9109
English literature (single author) - Elizabethan period - Biography, collections, criticism	828. 309
English literature (single author) - Medieval period - Biography, collections, criticism	828. 109
English literature (single author) - Queen Anne period - Biography, collections, criticism	828. 509
English literature (single author) - Renaissance period - Biography, collections, criticism	828. 309
English literature (single author) - Romantic period - Biography, collections, criticism	828. 709
English literature for/by children - History and criticism	820.99282
English literature for/by women - History and criticism	820.99287
English love fiction (multiple authors)	823.085*
English love fiction (multiple authors)- Collections	823.08508**
English love fiction (multiple authors)- History and criticism	823.08509**

English melodrama (multiple authors)	822.0527*
English melodrama (multiple authors)-Collections	822.052708**
English melodrama (multiple authors)-History and criticism	822.052709**
English miscellaneous writings (multiple authors) -Collections	828.008**
English miscellaneous writings (multiple authors) -Dictionaries etc	828.003
English miscellaneous writings (multiple authors) -History and criticism	828.009**
English miscellaneous writings (multiple authors) -Periodicals	828.005
English miscellaneous writings (multiple authors) -Philosophy and theory	828.001
English miscellaneous writings (multiple authors) -Psychological aspects	828.0019
English miscellaneous writings (multiple authors) -Research	828.0072
English miscellaneous writings (multiple authors) -Study and teaching	828.007
English miscellaneous writings (multiple authors) -Value	828.0013
English miscellaneous writings (multiple authors) -1066- 1400	828. 1+
English miscellaneous writings (multiple authors) -1400 – 1558	828. 2+
English miscellaneous writings (multiple authors) -1558 - 1625	828. 3+
English miscellaneous writings (multiple	

authors) -1625 - 1702	828. 4+
English miscellaneous writings (multiple authors) -16th century	828. 3+
English miscellaneous writings (multiple authors) -1702 - 1745	828. 5+
English miscellaneous writings (multiple authors) -1745 - 1799	828. 6+
English miscellaneous writings (multiple authors) -1800 – 1837	828. 7+
English miscellaneous writings (multiple authors) -1837-1899	828. 8+
English miscellaneous writings (multiple authors) -18th century	828. 5+
English miscellaneous writings (multiple authors) -1900-	828. 9+
English miscellaneous writings (multiple authors) -1900 - 1999	828. 91+
English miscellaneous writings (multiple authors) -19th century	828. 8+
English miscellaneous writings (multiple authors) -2000-	828. 92+
English miscellaneous writings (multiple authors) -20th century	828. 91+
English miscellaneous writings (multiple authors) -Elizabethan period	828. 3+
English miscellaneous writings (multiple authors) -Medieval period	828. 1+
English miscellaneous writings (multiple authors) -Queen Anne period	828. 5+
English miscellaneous writings	

(multiple authors) -Renaissance period	828. 3+
English miscellaneous writings (multiple authors) -Romantic period	828. 7+
English monologues (multiple authors)	822.045*
English monologues (multiple authors)- Collections	822.04508**
English monologues (multiple authors)- History and criticism	822.04509**
English morality plays	***See*** English religious and morality plays
English mystery fiction (multiple authors)	823.0872*
English mystery fiction (multiple authors)- Collections	823.087208**
English mystery fiction (multiple authors)- History and criticism	823.087209**
English narrative poetry (multiple authors)	821.03*
English narrative poetry (multiple authors)- Collections	821.0308**
English narrative poetry (multiple authors)- History and criticism	821.0309**
English notebooks	***See*** English diaries ...
English odes (multiple authors)	821.043*
English odes (multiple authors)- Collections	821.04308**
English odes (multiple authors)- History and criticism	821.04309**
English one act plays (multiple authors)	822.041*
English one act plays (multiple authors)-	

Collections	822.041 08**
English one act plays (multiple authors)-History and criticism	822.041 09**
English oratory (multiple authors)	***See*** English public speeches
English periodicals	052
English poetry	821
English poetry (multiple authors) - 1066- 1400	821. 1+
English poetry (multiple authors) - 1400 – 1558	821. 2+
English poetry (multiple authors) - 1558 - 1625	821. 3+
English poetry (multiple authors) - 1625 - 1702	821. 4+
English poetry (multiple authors) - 16th century	821. 3+
English poetry (multiple authors) - 1702 - 1745	821. 5+
English poetry (multiple authors) - 1745 - 1799	821. 6+
English poetry (multiple authors) - 1800 – 1837	821. 7+
English poetry (multiple authors) - 1837-1899	821. 8+
English poetry (multiple authors) - 18th century	821. 5+
English poetry (multiple authors) -1900-	821. 9+
English poetry (multiple authors) -	

1900 - 1999	821. 91+
English poetry (multiple authors) - 19th century	821. 8+
English poetry (multiple authors) -2000-	821. 92+
English poetry (multiple authors) - 20th century	821. 91+
English poetry (multiple authors) - Elizabethan period	821. 3+
English poetry (multiple authors) - Medieval period	821. 1+
English poetry (multiple authors) - Queen Anne period	821. 5+
English poetry (multiple authors) - Renaissance period	821. 3+
English poetry (multiple authors) - Romantic period	821. 7+
English poetry (multiple authors)- Collections	821.008**
English poetry (multiple authors)- Dictionaries etc	821.003
English poetry (multiple authors)- History and criticism	821.009**
English poetry (multiple authors)- Periodicals	821.005
English poetry (multiple authors)- Philosophy and theory	821.001
English poetry (multiple authors)- Psychological aspects	821.0019
English poetry (multiple authors)- Research	821.0072

English poetry (multiple authors)- Study and teaching	821.007
English poetry (multiple authors)- Value	821.0013
English poetry (single author) -1066- 1400	821. 1
English poetry (single author) -1400 – 1558	821. 2
English poetry (single author) -1558 - 1625	821. 3
English poetry (single author) -1625 - 1703	821. 4
English poetry (single author) -16th century	821. 3
English poetry (single author) -1703 - 1745	821. 5
English poetry (single author) -1745 - 1799	821. 6
English poetry (single author) -1800 – 1837	821. 7
English poetry (single author) -1837-1899	821. 8
English poetry (single author) -18th century	821. 5
English poetry (single author) -1900-	821. 9
English poetry (single author) -1900 - 1999	821. 91
English poetry (single author) -19th century	821. 8
English poetry (single author) -2000-	821. 92
English poetry (single author) -20th century	821. 91
English poetry (single author) - Elizabethan period	821. 3
English poetry (single author) - Medieval period	821. 1
English poetry (single author) - Queen Anne period	821. 5
English poetry (single author) - Renaissance period	821. 3

English poetry (single author) - Romantic period	821. 7
English prose (single author) -1066- 1400	828. 108
English prose (single author) -1400 – 1558	828. 208
English prose (single author) -1558 - 1625	828. 308
English prose (single author) -1625 - 1702	828. 408
English prose (single author) -16th century	828. 308
English prose (single author) -1702 - 1745	828. 508
English prose (single author) -1745 - 1799	828. 608
English prose (single author) -1800 – 1837	828. 708
English prose (single author) -1837-1899	828. 808
English prose (single author) -18th century	828. 508
English prose (single author) -1900-	828. 908
English prose (single author) -1900 - 1999	828. 9108
English prose (single author) -19th century	828. 808
English prose (single author) -2000-	828. 9208
English prose (single author) -20th century	828. 9108
English prose (single author) - Elizabethan period	828. 308
English prose (single author) - Medieval period	828. 108
English prose (single author) - Queen Anne period	828. 508
English prose (single author) - Renaissance period	828. 308
English prose (single author) - Romantic period	828. 708

English prose literature (multiple authors)	828.08
English psychological, realistic, sociological fiction (multiple authors)	823.083*
English psychological, realistic, sociological fiction (multiple authors) - Collections	823.08308**
English psychological, realistic, sociological fiction (multiple authors) - History and criticism	823.08309**
English public discussions	***See*** English debates and public discussions
English public speeches (multiple authors)	825.01
English public speeches (multiple authors)- Collections	825.0108**
English public speeches (multiple authors)- History and criticism	825.0109**
English quotations	***See*** English anecdotes...
English realistic fiction	***See*** English psychological... fiction
English recitations (multiple authors)	825.04
English religious and morality plays (multiple authors)	822.0516+
English reminiscences	***See*** English diaries...
English romantic fiction (multiple authors)	823.085*
English romantic fiction (multiple authors)- Collections	823.085 08**

English romantic fiction (multiple authors)-History and criticism	823.085 09**
English satire	***See*** English humour and satire
English satirical poetry	***See*** English humourous and satirical poetry
English science fiction (multiple authors)	823.087 62*
English science fiction (multiple authors)-Collections	823.087 620 8**
English science fiction (multiple authors)-History and criticism	823.087 620 9**
English serious drama (multiple authors)	822.051+
English short stories (multiple authors)	823.01*
English short stories (multiple authors)-Collections	823.0108**
English short stories (multiple authors)-History and criticism	823.0109**
English sociological fiction (multiple authors)	***See*** English psychological... fiction
English sonnets (multiple authors)	821.042*
English sonnets(multiple authors)-Collections	821.04208**
English sonnets(multiple authors)-History and criticism	821.04209**
English speeches	825
English speeches (multiple authors) - 1066- 1400	825. 1+

English speeches (multiple authors) - 1400 – 1558	825. 2+
English speeches (multiple authors) - 1558 - 1625	825. 3+
English speeches (multiple authors) - 1625 - 1702	825. 4+
English speeches (multiple authors) - 16th century	825. 3+
English speeches (multiple authors) - 1702 - 1745	825. 5+
English speeches (multiple authors) - 1745 - 1799	825. 6+
English speeches (multiple authors) - 1800 – 1837	825. 7+
English speeches (multiple authors) - 1837-1899	825. 8+
English speeches (multiple authors) - 18th century	825. 5+
English speeches (multiple authors) -1900-	825. 9+
English speeches (multiple authors) - 1900 - 1999	825. 91+
English speeches (multiple authors) - 19th century	825. 8+
English speeches (multiple authors) -2000-	825. 92+
English speeches (multiple authors) - 20th century	825. 91+
English speeches (multiple authors) - Collections	825.008**
English speeches (multiple authors) - Dictionaries etc	825.003

English speeches (multiple authors) - Elizabethan period	825. 3+
English speeches (multiple authors) - History and criticism	825.009**
English speeches (multiple authors) - Medieval period	825. 1+
English speeches (multiple authors) - Periodicals	825.005
English speeches (multiple authors) - Philosophy and theory	825.001
English speeches (multiple authors) - Psychological aspects	825.0019
English speeches (multiple authors) - Queen Anne period	825. 5+
English speeches (multiple authors) - Renaissance period	825. 3+
English speeches (multiple authors) - Research	825.0072
English speeches (multiple authors) - Romantic period	825. 7+
English speeches (multiple authors) - Study and teaching	825.007
English speeches (multiple authors) -Value	825.0013
English speeches (single author) - 1066- 1400	825. 1
English speeches (single author) - 1400 – 1558	825. 2
English speeches (single author) - 1558 - 1625	825. 3
English speeches (single author) -	

1625 - 1703	825. 4
English speeches (single author) - 16th century	825. 3
English speeches (single author) - 1703 - 1745	825. 5
English speeches (single author) - 1745 - 1799	825. 6
English speeches (single author) - 1800 – 1837	825. 7
English speeches (single author) -1837-1899	825. 8
English speeches (single author) - 18th century	825. 5
English speeches (single author) -1900-	825. 9
English speeches (single author) - 1900 - 1999	825. 91
English speeches (single author) - 19th century	825. 8
English speeches (single author) -2000-	825. 92
English speeches (single author) - 20th century	825. 91
English speeches (single author) - Elizabethan period	825. 3
English speeches (single author) - Medieval period	825. 1
English speeches (single author) - Queen Anne period	825. 5
English speeches (single author) - Renaissance period	825. 3
English speeches (single author) -	

Romantic period	825. 7
English suspense fiction (multiple authors)	823.0872*
English suspense fiction (multiple authors)-Collections	823.087208**
English suspense fiction (multiple authors)-History and criticism	823.087209**
English tragedy(multiple authors)	822.0512*
English tragedy(multiple authors)-Collections	822.051208**
English tragedy(multiple authors)-History and criticism	822.051209**
English variety drama (multiple authors)	822.057*
English variety drama (multiple authors)-Collections	822.05708**
English variety drama (multiple authors)-History and criticism	822.05709**
Enlightenment (Buddhism)	294.344 2
Enlightenment (Hinduism)	294.542
Enlightenment (Jainism)	294.442
Enlightenment (Sikhism)	294.642
Eschatology (Buddhism)	294.342 3
Eschatology (Hinduism)	294.523
Eschatology (Jainism)	294.423
Eschatology (Sikhism)	294.623
Espionage by India	327.125 4
Ethics (Buddhism)	294.35
Ethics (Hinduism)	294.548

Ethics (Jainism)	294.45
Ethics (Sikhism)	294.65
Ethics of communication (Buddhism)	294.3486 5
Ethics of communication (Hinduism)	294.556 5
Ethics of communication (Jainism)	294.456 5
Ethics of communication (Sikhism)	294.656 5
Ethics of consumption (Buddhism)	294.356 8
Ethics of consumption (Hinduism)	294.5486 8
Ethics of consumption (Jainism)	294.456 8
Ethics of consumption (Sikhism)	294.656 8
Ethics of leisure (Buddhism)	294.356 5
Ethics of leisure (Hinduism)	294.5486 5
Ethics of leisure (Jainism)	294.456 5
Ethics of leisure (Sikhism)	294.656 5
Ethics of public performances (Buddhism)	294.356 5
Ethics of public performances (Hinduism)	294.5486 5
Ethics of public performances (Jainism)	294.456 5
Ethics of public performances (Sikhism)	294.656 5
Ethics of recreation (Buddhism)	294.356 5
Ethics of recreation (Hinduism)	294.5486 5
Ethics of recreation (Jainism)	294.456 5
Ethics of recreation (Sikhism)	294.656 5
Ethics of reproduction (Buddhism)	294.356 6
Ethics of reproduction (Hinduism)	294.5486 6
Ethics of reproduction (Jainism)	294.456 6

Ethics of reproduction (Sikhism)	294.656 6
Ethics of sex (Buddhism)	294.356 6
Ethics of sex (Hinduism)	294.5486 6
Ethics of sex (Jainism)	294.456 6
Ethics of sex (Sikhism)	294.656 6
Ethics of sex and reproduction (Buddhism)	294.356 6
Ethics of sex and reproduction (Hinduism)	294.5486 6
Ethics of sex and reproduction (Jainism)	294.456 6
Ethics of sex and reproduction (Sikhism)	294.656 6
Ethics of social relations (Buddhism)	294.356 7
Ethics of social relations (Hinduism)	294.5486 7
Ethics of social relations (Jainism)	294.456 7
Ethics of social relations (Sikhism)	294.656 7
Evil spirits (Buddhism)	294.342 16
Evil spirits (Hinduism)	294.521 6
Evil spirits (Jainism)	294.421 6
Evil spirits (Sikhism)	294.621 6
Exercise of religious authority (Buddhism)	294.365
Exercise of religious authority (Hinduism)	294.565
Exercise of religious authority (Jainism)	294.465
Exercise of religious authority (Sikhism)	294.665
Experimental works in various literature	***See*** under specific literature

F

Family (Buddhism)	294.33783 5
Family (Hinduism)	294.517835
Family (Hinduism)	294.417835
Family (Hinduism)	294.617835
Family ethics (Buddhism)	294.356 3
Family ethics (Hinduism)	294.5486 3
Family ethics (Jainism)	294.456 3
Family ethics (Sikhism)	294.656 3
Family life (Buddhism)	294.344 41
Family life (Hinduism)	294.544 1
Family life (Jainism)	294.444 1
Family life (Sikhism)	294.644 1
Fauna- Andaman and Nicobar Islands	591.954 88
Fauna- Andhra Pradesh	591.954 84
Fauna- Arunachal Pradesh	591.954 163
Fauna- Assam	591.954 162
Fauna- Bengal	591.954 14
Fauna- Bhopal	591.954 3

Fauna- Bihar	591.954 12
Fauna- Bombay	591.954 792 3
Fauna- Calcutta	591.954 147
Fauna- Chandigarh	591.954 552
Fauna- Chhattisgarh	591.954 137
Fauna- Dadra and Nagar Haveli	591.954 796
Fauna- Delhi	591.954 56
Fauna- Goa, Daman and Diu	591.954 799
Fauna- Gujarat	591.954 75
Fauna- Haryana	591.954 558
Fauna- Himachal Pradesh	591.954 52
Fauna- Hyderabad state	591.954 84
Fauna- India	591.954
Fauna- Jammu and Kashmir	591.954 6
Fauna- Jharkhand	591.954 127
Fauna- Karnataka	591.954 87
Fauna- Kerala	591.954 83
Fauna- Lakshwadweep	591.954 81
Fauna- Madhya Pradesh	591.954 3
Fauna- Madras	591.954 82
Fauna- Maharashtra	591.954 792
Fauna- Manipur	591.954 17
Fauna- Meghalaya	591.954 164
Fauna- Mizoram	591.954 166
Fauna- Nagaland	591.954 165

Fauna- Northeast India	591.954 1
Fauna- Orissa	591.954 13
Fauna- Pondicherry	591.954 86
Fauna- Punjab	591.954 552
Fauna- Rajasthan	591.954 4
Fauna- Sikkim	591.954 167
Fauna- South Asia	591.954
Fauna- Southern India	591.954 8
Fauna- Tamil Nadu	591.954 82
Fauna- Tripura	591.954 15
Fauna- Uttar Pradesh	591.954 2
Fauna- Uttaranchal	591.954 51
Fauna- West Bengal	591.954 14
Fauna- Western India	591.954 7
Fine and decorative art galleries	***See*** Galleries of fine and decorative arts
Fine and decorative art museums	***See*** Museums of fine and decorative arts
Fine and decorative arts: Andaman and Nicobar Islands	709.5488
Fine and decorative arts: Andhra Pradesh	709.5484
Fine and decorative arts: Arunachal Pradesh	709.54163
Fine and decorative arts: Assam	709.54162
Fine and decorative arts: Bengal	709.5414

Fine and decorative arts: Bhopal	709.543
Fine and decorative arts: Bihar	709.5412
Fine and decorative arts: Bombay	709.547923
Fine and decorative arts: Calcutta	709.54147
Fine and decorative arts: Chandigarh	709.54552
Fine and decorative arts: Dadra and Nagar Haveli	709.54796
Fine and decorative arts: Delhi	709.5456
Fine and decorative arts: Goa, Daman and Diu	709.54799
Fine and decorative arts: Gujarat	709.5475
Fine and decorative arts: Haryana	709.54558
Fine and decorative arts: Himachal Pradesh	709.5452
Fine and decorative arts: India	709.54
Fine and decorative arts: Jammu and Kashmir	709.546
Fine and decorative arts: Karnataka	709.5487
Fine and decorative arts: Kerala	709.5483
Fine and decorative arts: Lakshwadweep	709.5481
Fine and decorative arts: Madhya Pradesh	709.543
Fine and decorative arts: Madras	709.5482
Fine and decorative arts: Maharashtra	709.54792
Fine and decorative arts: Manipur	709.5417
Fine and decorative arts: Meghalaya	709.54164
Fine and decorative arts: Mizoram	709.54166
Fine and decorative arts: Nagaland	709.54165

Fine and decorative arts: Northeast India	709.541
Fine and decorative arts: Orissa	709.5413
Fine and decorative arts: Pondicherry	709.5486
Fine and decorative arts: Punjab	709.54552
Fine and decorative arts: Rajasthan	709.544
Fine and decorative arts: Sikkim	709.54167
Fine and decorative arts: South Asia	709.54
Fine and decorative arts: Southern India	709.548
Fine and decorative arts: Tamil Nadu	709.5482
Fine and decorative arts: Tripura	709.5415
Fine and decorative arts: Uttar Pradesh	709.542
Fine and decorative arts: Uttaranchal	709.5451
Fine and decorative arts: West Bengal	709.5414
Fine and decorative arts: Western India	709.547
Fine arts	***See*** Fine and decorative arts
Fire (Buddhism)	294.342 12
Fire (Hinduism)	294.521 2
Fire (Jainism)	294.421 2
Fire (Sikhism)	294.621 2
Flora- Andaman and Nicobar Islands	581.954 88
Flora- Andhra Pradesh	581.954 84
Flora- Arunachal Pradesh	581.954 16 3
Flora- Assam	581.954 16 2
Flora- Bengal	581.954 14

Flora- Bhopal	581.954 3
Flora- Bihar	581.954 12
Flora- Bombay	581.954 792 3
Flora- Calcutta	581.954 14 7
Flora- Chandigarh	581.954 552
Flora- Dadra and Nagar Haveli	581.954 796
Flora- Delhi	581.954 56
Flora- Goa, Daman and Diu	581.954 799
Flora- Gujarat	581.954 75
Flora- Haryana	581.954 558
Flora- Himachal Pradesh	581.954 52
Flora- Hyderabad state	581.954 84
Flora- India	581.954
Flora- Jammu and Kashmir	581.954 6
Flora- Karnataka	581.954 87
Flora- Kerala	581.954 83
Flora- Lakshwadweep	581.954 81
Flora- Madhya Pradesh	581.954 3
Flora- Madras	581.954 82
Flora- Maharashtra	581.954 792
Flora- Manipur	581.954 17
Flora- Meghalaya	581.954 16 4
Flora- Mizoram	581.954 16 6
Flora- Nagaland	581.954 16 5
Flora- Northeast India	581.954 1

Flora- Orissa	581.954 13
Flora- Pondicherry	581.954 86
Flora- Punjab	581.954 552
Flora- Rajasthan	581.954 4
Flora- Sikkim	581.954 16 7
Flora- South Asia	581.954
Flora- Southern India	581.954 8
Flora- Tamil Nadu	581.954 82
Flora- Tripura	581.954 15
Flora- Uttar Pradesh	581.954 2
Flora- Uttaranchal	581.954 51
Flora- West Bengal	581.954 14
Flora- Western India	581.954 7
Folk dancing- Andaman and Nicobar Islands	793.319 5488
Folk dancing- Andhra Pradesh	793.319 5484
Folk dancing- Arunachal Pradesh	793.319 54163
Folk dancing- Assam	793.319 54162
Folk dancing- Bengal	793.319 5414
Folk dancing- Bhopal	793.319 543
Folk dancing- Bihar	793.319 5412
Folk dancing- Bombay	793.319 547923
Folk dancing- Dadra and Nagar Haveli	793.319 54796
Folk dancing- Goa, Daman and Diu	793.319 54799
Folk dancing- Gujarat	793.319 5475
Folk dancing- Haryana	793.319 54558

Folk dancing- Himachal Pradesh	793.319 5452
Folk dancing- India	793.319 54
Folk dancing- Jammu and Kashmir	793.319 546
Folk dancing- Karnataka	793.319 5487
Folk dancing- Kerala	793.319 5483
Folk dancing- Lakshwadweep	793.319 5481
Folk dancing- Madhya Pradesh	793.319 543
Folk dancing- Madras	793.319 5482
Folk dancing- Maharashtra	793.319 54792
Folk dancing- Manipur	793.319 5417
Folk dancing- Meghalaya	793.319 54164
Folk dancing- Mizoram	793.319 54166
Folk dancing- Nagaland	793.319 54165
Folk dancing- Northeast India	793.319 541
Folk dancing- Orissa	793.319 5413
Folk dancing- Pondicherry	793.319 5486
Folk dancing- Punjab	793.319 54552
Folk dancing- Rajasthan	793.319 544
Folk dancing- Sikkim	793.319 54167
Folk dancing- South Asia	793.319 54
Folk dancing- Southern India	793.319 548
Folk dancing- Tamil Nadu	793.319 5482
Folk dancing- Tripura	793.319 5415
Folk dancing- Uttanchal	793.319 5451
Folk dancing- Uttar Pradesh	793.319 542

Folk dancing- West Bengal	793.319 5414
Folk dancing- Western India	793.319 547
Folk literature	398.2
Folk literature- Andaman and Nicobar Islands	398.209 548 8
Folk literature- Andhra Pradesh	398.209 548 4
Folk literature- Arunachal Pradesh	398.209 541 63
Folk literature- Assam	398.209 541 62
Folk literature- Bengal	398.209 541 4
Folk literature- Bhopal	398.209 543
Folk literature- Bihar	398.209 541 2
Folk literature- Bombay	398.209 547 923
Folk literature- Central Dravidian languages	398.204 948 2
Folk literature- Chhattisgarh	398.209 54137
Folk literature- Dadra and Nagar Haveli	398.209 547 96
Folk literature- Dardic languages	398.204 914 99
Folk literature- Delhi	398.209 545 26
Folk literature- Dravidian languages.	398.204 948
Folk literature- Eastern Himalayan languages.	398.204 954 9
Folk literature- Goa, Daman and Diu	398.209 547 99
Folk literature- Gujarat	398.209 547 5
Folk literature- Haryana	398.209 545 258
Folk literature- Himachal Pradesh	398.209 545 22
Folk literature- India	398.209 54

Folk literature- Indic languages	398.204 911
Folk literature- Indo-Iranian languages	398.204 911
Folk literature- Jammu and Kashmir	398.209 546
Folk literature- Jharkhand	398.209 541 27
Folk literature- Karnataka	398.209 548 7
Folk literature- Kerala	398.209 548 3
Folk literature- Lakshwadweep	398.209 548 1
Folk literature- Madhya Pradesh	398.209 543
Folk literature- Madras	398.209 548 2
Folk literature- Maharashtra	398.209 547 92
Folk literature- Manipur	398.209 541 7
Folk literature- Meghalaya	398.209 541 64
Folk literature- Mizoram	398.209 541 66
Folk literature- Modern Prakrit languages	398.204 914
Folk literature- Munda languages	398.204 959 5
Folk literature- Nagaland	398.209 541 65
Folk literature- North Dravidian languages	398.204 948 3
Folk literature- Northeast India	398.209 541
Folk literature- Orissa	398.209 541 3
Folk literature- People who spoke Vedic (Old Vedic) languages	398.204 912 9
Folk literature- Pondicherry	398.209 548 6
Folk literature- Prakrit languages	398.204 913
Folk literature- Punjab	398.209 545 252
Folk literature- Rajasthan	398.209 544

Folk literature- Sikkim	398.209 541 67
Folk literature- South Asia	398.209 54
Folk literature- South Dravidian languages	398.204 948 1
Folk literature- Southern India	398.209 548
Folk literature- Tamil Nadu	398.209 548 2
Folk literature- Tripura	398.209 541 5
Folk literature- Uttar Pradesh	398.209 542
Folk literature- Uttaranchal	398.209 545 1
Folk literature- West Bengal	398.209 541 4
Folk literature- Western Hindi languages	398.204 914 3
Folk literature- Western India	398.209 547
Folk literature, Assamese	398.204 914 51
Folk literature, Awadhi	398.204 914 9
Folk literature, Bagheli	398.204 914 9
Folk literature, Bengali	398.204 914 4
Folk literature, Bhili	398.204 914 7
Folk literature, Bhojpuri	398.204 914 54
Folk literature, Bihari	398.204 914 54
Folk literature, Brahui	398.204 948 3
Folk literature, Chepang	398:204 954 9
Folk literature, Chhattisgarhi	398.204 914 9
Folk literature, Dardic	398.204 914 99
Folk literature, Eastern Hindi	398.204 914 9
Folk literature, Gadaba	398.204 959 5
Folk literature, Gondi.	398.204 948 2

Folk literature, Gujarati	398.204 914 71
Folk literature, Hindi	398.204 914 31
Folk literature, Ho	398.204 959 5
Folk literature, Indic	398.204 913
Folk literature, Jaipuri	398.204 914 79
Folk literature, Kafiri	398.204 914 9
Folk literature, Kanarese	398.204 948 14
Folk literature, Kandh	398.204 948 2
Folk literature, Kannada	398.204 948 14
Folk literature, Kashmiri	398.204 914 99
Folk literature, Khond	398.204 948 2
Folk literature, Khowar	398.204 914 99
Folk literature, Kiranti	398.204 954 9
Folk literature, Kohistani	398.204 914 99
Folk literature, Konkani	398.204 914 6
Folk literature, Kota	398.204 948 1
Folk literature, Kurukh	398.204 948 3
Folk literature, Lahnda	398.204 914 19
Folk literature, Limbu	398.204 954 9
Folk literature, Magahi.	398.204 914 54
Folk literature, Magari	398.204 954 9
Folk literature, Maithili	398.204 914 54
Folk literature, Malayalam	398.204 948 12
Folk literature, Malto	398.204 948 3
Folk literature, Marathi	398.204 914 6

Folk literature, Marwari	398.204 914 79
Folk literature, Mundari	398.204 959 5
Folk literature, Newari	398.204 954 9
Folk literature, Nuristani	398.204 914 9
Folk literature, Oraon	398.204 948 3
Folk literature, Oriya	398.204 914 56
Folk literature, Pahari.	398.204 914 9
Folk literature, Pali	398.204 913 7
Folk literature, Panjabi	398.204 914 2
Folk literature, Pisacha	398.204 914 99
Folk literature, Rajasthani	398.204 914 79
Folk literature, Romany	398.204 914 97
Folk literature, Santali	398.204 959 5
Folk literature, Shina	398.204 914 99
Folk literature, Sindhi	398.204 914 11
Folk literature, Sunwar	398.204 954 9
Folk literature, Tamil	398.204 948 11
Folk literature, Telugu	398.204 948 27
Folk literature, Toda	398.204 948 1
Folk literature, Urdu	398.204 914 39
Folk music	***See also*** under specific name, e.g. Brahui folk music
Folk songs	782.421 62
Food supply- Andaman and Nicobar Islands	338.195 488

Food supply- Andhra Pradesh	338.195 484
Food supply- Arunachal Pradesh	338.195 416 3
Food supply- Assam	338.195 416 2
Food supply- Bengal	338.195 414
Food supply- Bhopal	338.195 43
Food supply- Bihar	338.195 412
Food supply- Bombay	338.195 479 23
Food supply- Calcutta	338.195 414 7
Food supply- Chandigarh	338.195 45 52
Food supply- Chhattisgarh	338.195 413 7
Food supply- Dadra and Nagar Haveli	338.195 479 6
Food supply- Delhi	338.195 45 6
Food supply- Goa, Daman and Diu	338.195 479 9
Food supply- Gujarat	338.195 475
Food supply- Haryana	338.195 45 58
Food supply- Himachal Pradesh	338.195 452
Food supply- Hyderabad state	338.195 484
Food supply- India	338.195 4
Food supply- Jammu and Kashmir	338.195 46
Food supply- Jharkhand	338.195 412 7
Food supply- Karnataka	338.195 487
Food supply- Kerala	338.195 483
Food supply- Lakshwadweep	338.195 481
Food supply- Madhya Pradesh	338.195 43
Food supply- Madras	338.195 482

Food supply- Maharashtra	338.195 479 2
Food supply- Manipur	338.195 417
Food supply- Meghalaya	338.195 416 4
Food supply- Mizoram	338.195 416 6
Food supply- Nagaland	338.195 416 5
Food supply- Northeast India	338.195 41
Food supply- Orissa	338.195 413
Food supply- Pondicherry	338.195 486
Food supply- Punjab	338.195 45 52
Food supply- Rajasthan	338.195 44
Food supply- Sikkim	338.195 416 7
Food supply- South Asia	338.195 4
Food supply- Southern India	338.195 48
Food supply- Tamil Nadu	338.195 482
Food supply- Tripura	338.195 415
Food supply- Uttar Pradesh	338.195 42
Food supply- Uttaranchal	338.195 451
Food supply- West Bengal	338.195 414
Food supply- Western India	338.195 47
Foreign relations	***See*** International relations
Furniture and furniture makers- India	749.2954

G

Galleries of fine and decorative arts - India	708.954
Ganapataism	294.5515
General classes of religions (Buddhism)	294.334
General classes of religions (Hinduism)	294.514
General classes of religions (Jainism)	294.414
General classes of religions (Sikhism)	294.614
General clubs	367
General clubs- Andaman and Nicobar Islands	367.954 88
General clubs- Andhra Pradesh	367.954 84
General clubs- Arunachal Pradesh	367.954 163
General clubs- Assam	367.954 162
General clubs- Bengal	367.954 14
General clubs- Bhopal	367.954 3
General clubs- Bihar	367.954 12
General clubs- Bombay	367.954 792 3
General clubs- Calcutta	367.954 147
General clubs- Chandigarh	367.954 55 2
General clubs- Chhattisgarh	367.954 137

General clubs- Dadra and Nagar Haveli	367.954 796
General clubs- Delhi	367.954 56
General clubs- Goa, Daman and Diu	367.954 799
General clubs- Gujarat	367.954 75
General clubs- Haryana	367.954 55 8
General clubs- Himachal Pradesh	367.954 522
General clubs- Hyderabad state	367.954 84
General clubs- India	367.954
General clubs- Jammu and Kashmir	367.954 6
General clubs- Jharkhand	367.954 127
General clubs- Karnataka	367.954 87
General clubs- Kerala	367.954 83
General clubs- Lakshwadweep	367.954 81
General clubs- Madhya Pradesh	367.954 3
General clubs- Madras	367.954 82
General clubs- Maharashtra	367.954 792
General clubs- Manipur	367.954 17
General clubs- Meghalaya	367.954 164
General clubs- Mizoram	367.954 166
General clubs- Nagaland	367.954 165
General clubs- Northeast India	367.954 1
General clubs- Orissa	367.954 13
General clubs- Pondicherry	367.954 86
General clubs- Punjab	367.954 55 2
General clubs- Rajasthan	367.954 4

General clubs- Sikkim	367.954 167
General clubs- South Asia	367.954
General clubs- Southern India	367.954 8
General clubs- Tamil Nadu	367.954 82
General clubs- Tripura	367.954 15
General clubs- Uttar Pradesh	367.954 2
General clubs- Uttaranchal	367.954 51
General clubs- West Bengal	367.954 14
General clubs- Western India	367.954 7
General collections	080
General collections in Assamese	089.91451
General collections in Bengali	089.9144
General collections in English	082
General collections in Gujarati	089.9147
General collections in Hindi	089.9143
General collections in Kannada	089.94814
General collections in Malayalam	089.94812
General collections in Marathi	089.9146
General collections in Oriya	089.9145
General collections in Panjabi	089.9142
General collections in Sindhi	089.9141
General collections in Tamil	089.94811
General collections in Telugu	089.94813
General collections in Urdu	089.91439
Geography - Andaman and Nicobar Islands	915.488

Geography - Andhra Pradesh	915.484
Geography - Arunachal Pradesh	915.416 3
Geography - Assam	915.416 2
Geography - Bengal	915.414
Geography - Bhopal	915.43
Geography - Bihar	915.412
Geography - Bombay	915.479 23
Geography - Calcutta	915.414 7
Geography - Chandigarh	915.455 2
Geography - Dadra and Nagar Haveli	915.479 6
Geography - Delhi	915.456
Geography - Goa, Daman and Diu	915.479 9
Geography - Gujarat	915.475
Geography - Haryana	915.455 8
Geography - Himachal Pradesh	915.452
Geography - Hyderabad state	915.484
Geography - India	915.4
Geography - Jammu and Kashmir	915.46
Geography - Karnataka	915.487
Geography - Kerala	915.483
Geography - Lakshwadweep	915.481
Geography - Madhya Pradesh	915.43
Geography - Madras	915.482
Geography - Maharashtra	915.479 2
Geography - Manipur	915.417

Geography - Meghalaya	915.416 4
Geography - Mizoram	915.416 6
Geography - Nagaland	915.416 5
Geography - Northeast India	915.41
Geography - Orissa	915.413
Geography - Pondicherry	915.486
Geography - Punjab	915.455 2
Geography - Rajasthan	915.44
Geography - Sikkim	915.416 7
Geography - South Asia	915.4
Geography - Southern India	915.48
Geography - Tamil Nadu	915.482
Geography - Tripura	915.415
Geography - Uttar Pradesh	915.42
Geography -Uttaranchal	915.451
Geography - West Bengal	915.414
Geography - Western India	915.47
Geography (Buddhism)	294.3091
Geography (Hinduism)	294.5091
Geography (Jainism)	294.4091
Geography (Sikhism)	294.6091
Geology- Andaman and Nicobar Islands	555.488
Geology- Andhra Pradesh	555.484
Geology- Arunachal Pradesh	555.416 3
Geology- Assam	555.416 2

Geology- Bengal	555.414
Geology- Bhopal	555.43
Geology- Bihar	555.412
Geology- Bombay	555.479 23
Geology- Calcutta	555.414 7
Geology- Chandigarh	555.455 2
Geology- Dadra and Nagar Haveli	555.479 6
Geology- Delhi	555.456
Geology- Goa, Daman and Diu	555.479 9
Geology- Gujarat	555.475
Geology- Haryana	555.455 8
Geology- Himachal Pradesh	555.452
Geology- Hyderabad state	555.484
Geology- India	555.4
Geology- Jammu and Kashmir	555.46
Geology- Karnataka	555.487
Geology- Kerala	555.483
Geology- Lakshwadweep	555.481
Geology- Madhya Pradesh	555.43
Geology- Madras	555.482
Geology- Maharashtra	555.479 2
Geology- Manipur	555.417
Geology- Meghalaya	555.416 4
Geology- Mizoram	555.416 6
Geology- Nagaland	555.416 5

Geology- Northeast India	555.41
Geology- Orissa	555.413
Geology- Pondicherry	555.486
Geology- Punjab	555.455 2
Geology- Rajasthan	555.44
Geology- Sikkim	555.416 7
Geology- South Asia	555.4
Geology- Southern India	555.48
Geology- Tamil Nadu	555.482
Geology- Tripura	555.415
Geology- Uttar Pradesh	555.42
Geology- Uttaranchal	555.451
Geology- West Bengal	555.414
Geology- Western India	555.47
Glassmakers	***See*** Glassware and glassmakers
Glassware and glassmakers- India	748.29954
Goa, Daman and Diu- Architecture	720.954 799
Goa, Daman and Diu- Botany	580.954 799
Goa, Daman and Diu- Budget	352.495 479 9
Goa, Daman and Diu- Economic development	338.954 79 9
Goa, Daman and Diu- Economic geography	330.954 799
Goa, Daman and Diu- Education	370.954 799
Goa, Daman and Diu- Fauna	591.954 799

Goa, Daman and Diu- Fine and decorative arts	709.54799
Goa, Daman and Diu- Flora	581.954 799
Goa, Daman and Diu- Folk dancing	793.319 547 99
Goa, Daman and Diu- Geography	915.4799
Goa, Daman and Diu- Geology	555.479 9
Goa, Daman and Diu- History	954.799
Goa, Daman and Diu- Painting and paintings	759.954 799
Goa, Daman and Diu- Public administration	351.547 99
Goa, Daman and Diu- Public finance	336.547 99
Goa, Daman and Diu- Sculpture	730.954 799
God (Buddhism)	294.342 11
God (Hinduism)	294.521 1
God (Jainism)	294.421 1
God (Sikhism)	294.621 1
Goddesses (Buddhism)	294.342 114
Goddesses (Hinduism)	294.521 14
Goddesses (Jainism)	294.421 14
Goddesses (Sikhism)	294.621 14
Gods (Buddhism)	294.342 113
Gods (Hinduism)	294.521 13
Gods (Jainism)	294.421 13
Gods (Sikhism)	294.621 13
Gond (People) - Opinions	303.387 948 2

Gond (People)	305.894 82
Gondi - English dictionary	494.823321
Gondi language	494.823
Gondi language- Applied linguistics	494.8238
Gondi language- Dictionaries	494.8233
Gondi language- Education	494.823071
Gondi language- Grammar	494.8235
Gondi language- History	494.82309
Gondi language- Readers	494.823 86
Gondi language- Research	494.823072
Gondi language- Rhetoric.	808.049 482++
Gondi language- Usage	494.8238
Gondi literature	894.823
Gondi speaking people	305.794 823
Good spirits (Buddhism)	294.342 15
Good spirits (Hinduism)	294.521 5
Good spirits (Jainism)	294.421 5
Good spirits (Sikhism)	294.621 5
Gross national product- India	339.354
Gujar (People).	305.891 47
Gujar folk music.	781 629 147
Gujarat- Architecture	720.954 75
Gujarat- Botany	580.954 75
Gujarat- Budget	352.495 475
Gujarat- Economic development	338.954 75

Gujarat- Economic geography	330.954 75
Gujarat- Education	370.954 75
Gujarat- Fauna	591.954 75
Gujarat- Fine and decorative arts	709.5475
Gujarat- Flora	581.954 75
Gujarat- Folk dancing	793.319 5475
Gujarat- Galleries of fine and decorative arts	708.954 75
Gujarat- Geography	915.475
Gujarat- Geology	555.475
Gujarat- History	954.75
Gujarat- Museums of fine and decorative arts	708.954 75
Gujarat- Painting and paintings	759.954 75
Gujarat- Public administration	351.547 5
Gujarat- Public finance	336.547 5
Gujarat- Sculpture	730.954 75
Gujarati - English dictionary	491.473 21
Gujarati adventure fiction (multiple authors) - Collections	891.47308708**
Gujarati adventure fiction (multiple authors)	891.473087*
Gujarati adventure fiction (multiple authors)- History and criticism	891.47308709**
Gujarati anecdotes, epigrams, graffiti, jokes, quotations (multiple authors)	891.47802
Gujarati anecdotes, epigrams, graffiti, jokes, quotations (single author)	891.478 +CD+02
Gujarati as second language in elementary education	372.659 147 1

Gujarati ballads(multiple authors)	891.471044*
Gujarati ballads(multiple authors)- Collections	891.47104408**
Gujarati ballads(multiple authors)- History and criticism	891.47104409**
Gujarati comedy (multiple authors) - Collections	891.472052308**
Gujarati comedy (multiple authors) - History and criticism	891.472052309**
Gujarati comedy (multiple authors)	891.4720523*
Gujarati conversations (multiple authors)	891.47506*
Gujarati conversations (multiple authors) - Collections	891.4750608**
Gujarati conversations (multiple authors) - History and criticism	891.4750609**
Gujarati debates and public discussions (multiple authors)	891.47503*
Gujarati debates and public discussions (multiple authors)- Collections	891.4750308**
Gujarati debates and public discussions (multiple authors)- History and criticism	891.4750309**
Gujarati detective fiction (multiple authors) - Collections	891.473087208**
Gujarati detective fiction (multiple authors) - History and criticism	891.473087209**
Gujarati detective fiction (multiple authors)	891.4730872*
Gujarati diaries, notebooks, reminiscences (single author)	891.478@
Gujarati diaries, notebooks, reminiscences	

(multiple authors)	891.47803
Gujarati didactic poetry (multiple authors)	891.47105*
Gujarati didactic poetry (multiple authors)- Collections	891.4710508**
Gujarati didactic poetry (multiple authors)- History and criticism	891.4710509**
Gujarati drama	891.472
Gujarati drama (multiple authors) - to 1845 schedule	***See*** Main
Gujarati drama (multiple authors) - 1845-1895	891.4724+
Gujarati drama (multiple authors) - 1895-1919	891.4725+
Gujarati drama (multiple authors) - 1920-1939	891.4726+
Gujarati drama (multiple authors) - 1940-	891.4727+
Gujarati drama (multiple authors) - 1940-1999	891.47271+
Gujarati drama (multiple authors) - 19th century	891.4724+
Gujarati drama (multiple authors) - 2000-	891.47272+
Gujarati drama (multiple authors) - 20th century	891.47271+
Gujarati drama (multiple authors) - Collections	891.472008**
Gujarati drama (multiple authors) - Dictionaries etc	891.472003
Gujarati drama (multiple authors) - History and criticism	891.472009**

Gujarati drama (multiple authors) - Periodicals	891.472005
Gujarati drama (multiple authors) - Philosophy and theory	891.472001
Gujarati drama (multiple authors) - Psychological aspects	891.4720019
Gujarati drama (multiple authors) - Research	891.4720072
Gujarati drama (multiple authors) - Study and teaching	891.472007
Gujarati drama (multiple authors) - Value	891.4720013
Gujarati drama (single author) - to 1845 schedule	***See*** Main
Gujarati drama (single author)- 1845 -1895	891.472 4
Gujarati drama (single author)- 1895 - 1919	891.472 5
Gujarati drama (single author)- 1920- 1939	891.472 6
Gujarati drama (single author)- 1940 -	891.472 7
Gujarati drama (single author)- 1940-1999	891.472 71
Gujarati drama (single author)- 19th century	891.472 4
Gujarati drama (single author)- 2000-	891.472 72
Gujarati drama (single author)- 20th century	891.472 71
Gujarati drama for cinema (multiple authors)	891.47203*
Gujarati drama for cinema (multiple authors) - Collections	891.4720308**
Gujarati drama for cinema (multiple authors) - History and criticism	891.4720309**
Gujarati drama for radio (multiple authors)	891.472022*
Gujarati drama for radio (multiple authors) -	

History and criticism	891.47202209**
Gujarati drama for radio (multiple authors) - Collections	891.47202208**
Gujarati drama for television (multiple authors)	891.472025*
Gujarati drama for television (multiple authors) - Collections	891.47202508**
Gujarati drama for television (multiple authors) - History and criticism	891.47202509**
Gujarati drama(multiple authors)	891.472
Gujarati dramatic poetry (multiple authors)	891.47102*
Gujarati dramatic poetry (multiple authors)- Collections	891.4710208**
Gujarati dramatic poetry (multiple authors)- History and criticism	891.4710209**
Gujarati encyclopaedias	039.9147
Gujarati ephemeral and light verse (multiple authors)	891.47108*
Gujarati ephemeral and light verse (multiple authors) - History and criticism	891.4710809**
Gujarati ephemeral and light verse (multiple authors)- Collections	891.4710808**
Gujarati epic poetry (multiple authors)	891.471032*
Gujarati epic poetry (multiple authors)- Collections	891.47103208**
Gujarati epic poetry (multiple authors)- History and criticism	891.47103209**
Gujarati epigrams	***See*** Gujarati anecdotes ...

Gujarati essays	891.474
Gujarati essays (multiple authors) - to 1845	***See*** Main schedule
Gujarati essays (multiple authors) - 1845-1895	891.4744+
Gujarati essays (multiple authors) - 1895-1919	891.4745+
Gujarati essays (multiple authors) - 1920-1939	891.4746+
Gujarati essays (multiple authors) -1940-	891.4747+
Gujarati essays (multiple authors) - 1940-1999	891.47471+
Gujarati essays (multiple authors) - 19th century	891.4744+
Gujarati essays (multiple authors) -2000-	891.47472+
Gujarati essays (multiple authors) - 20th century	891.47471+
Gujarati essays (multiple authors) - Collections	891.474008**
Gujarati essays (multiple authors) - Dictionaries etc	891.474003
Gujarati essays (multiple authors) - History and criticism	891.474009**
Gujarati essays (multiple authors) - Periodicals	891.474005
Gujarati essays (multiple authors) - Philosophy and theory	891.474001
Gujarati essays (multiple authors) - Psychological aspects Gujarati essays (multiple authors) -	891.4740019

Research	891.4740072
Gujarati essays (multiple authors) - Study and teaching	891.474007
Gujarati essays (multiple authors) -Value	891.4740013
Gujarati essays (single author)- - to 1845	***See*** Main schedule
Gujarati essays (single author)- 1845 -1895	891.474 4
Gujarati essays (single author)- 1895 - 1919	891.474 5
Gujarati essays (single author)- 1920- 1939	891.474 6
Gujarati essays (single author)- 1940 -	891.474 7
Gujarati essays (single author)- 1940-1999	891.474 71
Gujarati essays (single author)- 19th century	891.474 4
Gujarati essays (single author)- 2000-	891.474 72
Gujarati essays (single author)- 20th century	891.474 71
Gujarati experimental and non-formalized works (single author)	891.478+CD+09
Gujarati experimental and non-functional works (multiple authors)	891.47807
Gujarati fantasy fiction (multiple authors)	891.47308766*
Gujarati fantasy fiction (multiple authors)- Collections	891.4730876608**
Gujarati fantasy fiction (multiple authors)- History and criticism	891.4730876609**
Gujarati farce (multiple authors)	891.47205232*
Gujarati farce (multiple authors)- Collections	891.4720523208**
Gujarati farce (multiple authors) - History and criticism	891.4720523209**
Gujarati fiction	891.473

Gujarati fiction (multiple authors) - to 1845	***See*** Main schedule
Gujarati fiction (multiple authors) - 1845-1895	891.4734+
Gujarati fiction (multiple authors) - 1895-1919	891.4735+
Gujarati fiction (multiple authors) - 1920-1939	891.4736+
Gujarati fiction (multiple authors) - 1940-	891.4737+
Gujarati fiction (multiple authors) - 1940-1999	891.47371+
Gujarati fiction (multiple authors) - 19th century	891.4734+
Gujarati fiction (multiple authors) - 2000-	891.47372+
Gujarati fiction (multiple authors) - 20th century	891.47371+
Gujarati fiction (multiple authors) - Collections	891.473008**
Gujarati fiction (multiple authors) - Dictionaries etc	891.473003
Gujarati fiction (multiple authors) - History and criticism	891.473009**
Gujarati fiction (multiple authors) - Periodicals	891.473005
Gujarati fiction (multiple authors) - Philosophy and theory	891.473001
Gujarati fiction (multiple authors) - Psychological aspects	891.4730019
Gujarati fiction (multiple authors) - Research	891.4730072

Gujarati fiction (multiple authors) - Study and teaching	891.473007
Gujarati fiction (multiple authors) - Value	891.4730013
Gujarati fiction (single author)- 1845 -1895	891.473 4
Gujarati fiction (single author)- 1895 - 1919	891.473 5
Gujarati fiction (single author)- 1920- 1939	891.473 6
Gujarati fiction (single author)- 1940 -	891.473 7
Gujarati fiction (single author)- 1940-1999	891.473 71
Gujarati fiction (single author)- 19th century	891.473 4
Gujarati fiction (single author)- 2000-	891.473 72
Gujarati fiction (single author)- 20th century	891.473 71
Gujarati fiction (single author)- to 1845	***See*** Main schedule
Gujarati folk music.	781 629 147
Gujarati ghost fiction (multiple authors)	891.47308733*
Gujarati ghost fiction (multiple authors) - Collections	891.4730873308**
Gujarati ghost fiction (multiple authors)- History and criticism	891.4730873309**
Gujarati graffiti	***See*** Gujarati anecdotes ...
Gujarati historical drama (multiple authors)	891.4720514*
Gujarati historical drama(multiple authors)- Collections	891.472051408**
Gujarati historical drama(multiple authors)- History and criticism	891.472051409**
Gujarati historical fiction (multiple authors) Gujarati historical fiction (multiple authors)-	891.473081*

Collections	891.47308108**
Gujarati historical fiction (multiple authors)-History and criticism	891.47308109**
Gujarati horror fiction (multiple authors)	891.47308738*
Gujarati horror fiction (multiple authors)-Collections	891.4730873808**
Gujarati horror fiction (multiple authors)-History and criticism	891.4730873809**
Gujarati humour and satire	891.477
Gujarati humour and satire (multiple authors) - -to 1845	***See*** Main schedule
Gujarati humour and satire (multiple authors) -1845-1895	891.4774+
Gujarati humour and satire (multiple authors) -1895-1919	891.4775+
Gujarati humour and satire (multiple authors) -1920-1939	891.4776+
Gujarati humour and satire (multiple authors) -1940-	891.4777+
Gujarati humour and satire (multiple authors) -1940-1999	891.47771+
Gujarati humour and satire (multiple authors) -19th century	891.4774+
Gujarati humour and satire (multiple authors) -2000-	891.47772+
Gujarati humour and satire (multiple authors) -20th century	891.47771+
Gujarati humour and satire (multiple authors) -Collections Gujarati humour and satire (multiple	891.477008**

authors) -Dictionaries etc	891.477003
Gujarati humour and satire (multiple authors) -History and criticism	891.477009**
Gujarati humour and satire (multiple authors) -Periodicals	891.477005
Gujarati humour and satire (multiple authors) -Philosophy and theory	891.477001
Gujarati humour and satire (multiple authors) -Psychological aspects	891.4770019
Gujarati humour and satire (multiple authors) -Research	891.4770072
Gujarati humour and satire (multiple authors) -Study and teaching	891.477007
Gujarati humour and satire (multiple authors) -Value	891.4770013
Gujarati humourous and satirical poetry (multiple authors)	891.47107*
Gujarati humourous and satirical poetry (multiple authors)- Collections	891.4710708**
Gujarati humourous and satirical poetry (multiple authors)- History and criticism	891.4710709**
Gujarati jokes	***See*** Gujarati anecdotes ...
Gujarati language	491.47
Gujarati language- Applied linguistics	491.478
Gujarati language- Bilingual dictionaries	491.4732-39
Gujarati language- Bilingualism	491.470 42
Gujarati language- Content analysis	491.470 141
Gujarati language- Dialects	491.477

Gujarati language- Dictionaries	491.473
Gujarati language- Discourse analysis	491.470 141
Gujarati language- Education	491.470 71
Gujarati language- Education, research, etc	491.470 7
Gujarati language- Encyclopaedias and concordances	491.470 3
Gujarati language- Etymology	491.472
Gujarati language- Functionalism	491.470 18
Gujarati language- Grammar	491.475
Gujarati language- History	491.470 9
Gujarati language- Intonation	491.471 6
Gujarati language- Lexicography	491.473 028
Gujarati language- Lexicology	491.470 14
Gujarati language- Miscellany	491.470 2
Gujarati language- Multilingualism	491.470 42
Gujarati language- Organizations	491.470 6
Gujarati language- Orthography	491.471 52
Gujarati language- Pauses	491.471 6
Gujarati language- Periodicals	491.470 5
Gujarati language- Persons (men, women, etc)	491.470 8
Gujarati language- Philosophy and theory	491.470 1
Gujarati language- Phonetics	491.471 58
Gujarati language- Phonology, etc Gujarati language- Pitch	491.471 5 491.471 6

Gujarati language- Pronunciation	491.471 52
Gujarati language- Readers	491.478 6
Gujarati language- Research	491.470 72
Gujarati language- Rhetonic	808.049147
Gujarati language- Schools and theories	491.470 18
Gujarati language- Semantics	491.470 143
Gujarati language- Semiotics	491.470 141
Gujarati language- Slang	491.477
Gujarati language- Special topics	491.470 4
Gujarati language- Specialized dictionaries	491.473 1
Gujarati language- Spelling	491.471 52
Gujarati language- Stress	491.471 6
Gujarati language- Structural linguistics	491.470 18
Gujarati language- Suprasegmental features	491.471 6
Gujarati language- Terminology	491.470 14
Gujarati language- Usage	491.478
Gujarati language- Variations (Dialects etc)	491.477
Gujarati language- Writing systems	491.471 1
Gujarati letters	891.476
Gujarati letters (multiple authors) – to 1845	***See*** Main schedule
Gujarati letters (multiple authors) - 1845-1895	891.4764+
Gujarati letters (multiple authors) - 1895-1919 Gujarati letters (multiple authors) -	891.4765+

1920-1939	891.4766+
Gujarati letters (multiple authors) -1940-	891.4767+
Gujarati letters (multiple authors) - 1940-1999	891.47671+
Gujarati letters (multiple authors) - 19th century	891.4764+
Gujarati letters (multiple authors) -2000-	891.47672+
Gujarati letters (multiple authors) - 20th century	891.47671+
Gujarati letters (multiple authors) - Collections	891.476008**
Gujarati letters (multiple authors) - Dictionaries etc	891.476003
Gujarati letters (multiple authors) - History and criticism	891.476009**
Gujarati letters (multiple authors) - Periodicals	891.476005
Gujarati letters (multiple authors) - Philosophy and theory	891.476001
Gujarati letters (multiple authors) - Psychological aspects	891.4760019
Gujarati letters (multiple authors) -Research	891.4760072
Gujarati letters (multiple authors) - Study and teaching	891.476007
Gujarati letters (multiple authors) -Value	891.4760013
Gujarati letters (single author)- to 1845	***See*** Main schedule
Gujarati letters (single author)- 1845 -1895	891.476 4
Gujarati letters (single author)- 1895 - 1919	891.476 5

Gujarati letters (single author)- 1920- 1939	891.476 6
Gujarati letters (single author)- 1940 -	891.476 7
Gujarati letters (single author)- 1940-1999	891.476 71
Gujarati letters (single author)- 19th century	891.476 4
Gujarati letters (single author)- 2000-	891.476 72
Gujarati letters (single author)- 20th century	891.476 71
Gujarati light verse	***See*** Gujarati ephemeral and light verse
Gujarati limericks (multiple authors)	891.471075*
Gujarati limericks(multiple authors)- Collections	891.47107508**
Gujarati limericks(multiple authors)- History and criticism	891.47107509**
Gujarati literature	891.47
Gujarati literature (collections of multiple forms)	891.4708
Gujarati literature (collections of multiple forms) - 19th century	891.470804
Gujarati literature (collections of multiple forms) - 20th century	891.4708071
Gujarati literature (collections of multiple forms) – 21st century	891.4708072
Gujarati literature (collections of multiple forms) - Allegory	891.4708015
Gujarati literature (collections of multiple forms) - Animals	891.47080362++
Gujarati literature (collections of multiple forms) - Artistic themes	891.47080357

Gujarati literature (collections of multiple forms) - Atmosphere	891.4708032161
Gujarati literature (collections of multiple forms) - Characters	891.4708027
Gujarati literature (collections of multiple forms) - Comedy	891.4708017
Gujarati literature (collections of multiple forms) - Evening	891.4708033
Gujarati literature (collections of multiple forms) - Fantasy	891.4708015
Gujarati literature (collections of multiple forms) - Forests	891.4708032152
Gujarati literature (collections of multiple forms) - Historical themes	891.47080358
Gujarati literature (collections of multiple forms) - Horror	891.47080164
Gujarati literature (collections of multiple forms) - Human characteristics (Biological, moral, psychological)	891.47080353
Gujarati literature (collections of multiple forms) - Legendary objects/themes	891.4708037
Gujarati literature (collections of multiple forms) - Literary themes	891.47080357
Gujarati literature (collections of multiple forms) - Love	891.470803543
Gujarati literature (collections of multiple forms) - Marriage	891.470803543
Gujarati literature (collections of multiple forms) - Morning	891.4708033
Gujarati literature (collections of multiple	

forms) - Mountains	891.4708032143
Gujarati literature (collections of multiple forms) - Myth	891.4708015
Gujarati literature (collections of multiple forms) - Mythological objects/themes	891.4708037
Gujarati literature (collections of multiple forms) - Philosophic themes	891.47080384
Gujarati literature (collections of multiple forms) - Places	891.4708032++
Gujarati literature (collections of multiple forms) - Plants	891.47080364
Gujarati literature (collections of multiple forms) - Political themes	891.47080358
Gujarati literature (collections of multiple forms) - Religious themes	891.47080382++
Gujarati literature (collections of multiple forms) - Rivers	891.47080321693
Gujarati literature (collections of multiple forms) - Romanticism	891.47080145
Gujarati literature (collections of multiple forms) - Scientific themes	891.47080356
Gujarati literature (collections of multiple forms) - Sea	891.4708032162
Gujarati literature (collections of multiple forms) - Seasons	891.4708033
Gujarati literature (collections of multiple forms) - Sex	891.470803538
Gujarati literature (collections of multiple forms) - Social themes	891.47080355
Gujarati literature (collections of multiple	

forms) - Space	891.470803219
Gujarati literature (collections of multiple forms) - Specific kinds of persons, e.g. heroes	891.47080352++
Gujarati literature (collections of multiple forms) - Specific persons (real or imaginary)	891.47080351
Gujarati literature (collections of multiple forms) - Stream of consciousness	891.4708025
Gujarati literature (collections of multiple forms) - Supernatural objects/themes	891.4708037
Gujarati literature (collections of multiple forms) - Symbolism	891.4708015
Gujarati literature (collections of multiple forms) - Technical themes	891.47080356
Gujarati literature (collections of multiple forms) - Times (seasons, parts of day, etc)	891.4708033
Gujarati literature (collections of multiple forms) - Towns	891.47080321732
Gujarati literature (collections of multiple forms) - Tragedy	891.47080162
Gujarati literature (collections of multiple forms) - Villages	891.47080321734
Gujarati literature (collections of multiple forms) - Weather	891.4708036
Gujarati literature (collections of multiple forms) emphasizing subjects	891.470804++
Gujarati literature (collections of multiple forms) for/by children	891.470809282
Gujarati literature (collections of multiple forms) for/by persons of racial, ethnic and	

national groups	891.470808++
Gujarati literature (collections of multiple forms) for/by persons of specific classes	891.4708092++
Gujarati literature (collections of multiple forms) for/by persons resident in specific regions	891.4708091++
Gujarati literature (collections of multiple forms) for/by women	891.470809287
Gujarati literature (multiple forms) - Supernatural objects/themes - History and criticism	891.470937
Gujarati literature (multiple authors) - Concordances	891.4703
Gujarati literature (multiple authors) - Dictionaries	891.4703
Gujarati literature (multiple authors) - Education	891.47071
Gujarati literature (multiple authors) - Encyclopaedias	891.4703
Gujarati literature (multiple authors) - Organizations	891.4706
Gujarati literature (multiple authors) - Periodicals	891.4705
Gujarati literature (multiple authors) - Philosophy and theory	891.4701
Gujarati literature (multiple authors) - Research	891.47072
Gujarati literature (multiple authors) - Research in India	891.47072054
Gujarati literature (multiple authors) -	

Study and teaching	891.4707
Gujarati literature (multiple forms) - 19th century	891.4709004
Gujarati literature (multiple forms) – 2000-	891.47090072
Gujarati literature (multiple forms) - 20th century	891.47090071
Gujarati literature (multiple forms) - Allegory – History and criticism	891.470915
Gujarati literature (multiple forms) - Animals - History and criticism	891.4709362++
Gujarati literature (multiple forms) - Artistic themes - History and criticism	891.4709357
Gujarati literature (multiple forms) - Atmosphere - History and criticism	891.470932161
Gujarati literature (multiple forms) - Characters - History and criticism	891.470927
Gujarati literature (multiple forms) - Comedy - History and criticism	891.470917
Gujarati literature (multiple forms) - Evening - History and criticism	891.470933
Gujarati literature (multiple forms) - Fantasy - History , criticism	891.470915
Gujarati literature (multiple forms) - Forests History and criticism	891.470932152
Gujarati literature (multiple forms) - Historical themes - History and criticism	891.4709358
Gujarati literature (multiple forms) - History and criticism	891.4709
Gujarati literature (multiple forms) - Horror - History and criticism	891.4709164

Gujarati literature (multiple forms) - Human characteristics (Biological, moral and psychological) - History and criticism	891.4709353
Gujarati literature (multiple forms) - Legendary objects/themes - History and criticism	891.470937
Gujarati literature (multiple forms) - Literary themes - History and criticism	891.4709357
Gujarati literature (multiple forms) - Love - History and criticism	891.47093543
Gujarati literature (multiple forms) - Marriage - History and criticism	891.47093543
Gujarati literature (multiple forms) - Morning - History and criticism	891.470933
Gujarati literature (multiple forms) - Mountains - History and criticism	891.470932143
Gujarati literature (multiple forms) - Myth - History and criticism	891.470915
Gujarati literature (multiple forms) - Mythological objects/themes - History and criticism	891.470937
Gujarati literature (multiple forms) - Persons of racial, ethnic and national groups - History and criticism	891.47098++
Gujarati literature (multiple forms) - Persons of specific classes - History and criticism	891.470992++
Gujarati literature (multiple forms) - Persons resident in specific regions - History and criticism	891.470991++

Gujarati literature (multiple forms) - Philosophic themes - History and criticism	891.4709384
Gujarati literature (multiple forms) - Places - History and criticism	891.470932++
Gujarati literature (multiple forms) - Plants - History and criticism	891.4709364
Gujarati literature (multiple forms) - Political themes - History and criticism	891.4709358
Gujarati literature (multiple forms) - Religious themes - History and criticism	891.4709382
Gujarati literature (multiple forms) - Rivers - History and criticism	891.4709321693
Gujarati literature (multiple forms) - Romanticism - History and criticism	891.4709145
Gujarati literature (multiple forms) - Scientific themes - History and criticism	891.4709356
Gujarati literature (multiple forms) - Sea - History and criticism	891.470932162
Gujarati literature (multiple forms) - Seasons - History and criticism	891.470933
Gujarati literature (multiple forms) - Sex - History and criticism	891.47093538
Gujarati literature (multiple forms) - Social themes - History and criticism	891.4709355
Gujarati literature (multiple forms) - Space - History and criticism	891.47093219
Gujarati literature (multiple forms) - Specific kinds of persons, e.g. heroes, - History and criticism	891.4709352++
Gujarati literature (multiple forms) -	

Specific persons - History and criticism	891.4709351
Gujarati literature (multiple forms) - Stream of consciousness - History and criticism	891.470925
Gujarati literature (multiple forms) - Subjects - History and criticism	891.47094++
Gujarati literature (multiple forms) - Symbolism- History ,criticism	891.470915
Gujarati literature (multiple forms) - Technical themes - History and criticism	891.4709356
Gujarati literature (multiple forms) - Times - History and criticism	891.470933
Gujarati literature (multiple forms) - Towns - History and criticism	891.4709321732
Gujarati literature (multiple forms) - Tragedy - History and criticism	891.4709162
Gujarati literature (multiple forms) - Villages - History and criticism	891.4709321734
Gujarati literature (multiple forms) - Weather - History and criticism	891.470936
Gujarati literature (single author)- to 1845 - Biography, collections, criticism	***See*** Main schedule
Gujarati literature (single author)- 1845 – 1895- Biography, collections, criticism	891.478 409
Gujarati literature (single author)- 1895 - 1919 - Biography, collections, criticism	891.478 509
Gujarati literature (single author)- 1920- 1939 - Biography, collections, criticism	891.478 609
Gujarati literature (single author)- 1940 - Biography, collections, criticism	891.478 709

Gujarati literature (single author)- 1940-1999 - Biography, collections, criticism	891.478 7109
Gujarati literature (single author)- 19th century- Biography, collections, criticism	891.478 409
Gujarati literature (single author)- 2000- Biography, collections, criticism	891.478 7209
Gujarati literature (single author)- 20th century - Biography, collections, criticism	891.478 7109
Gujarati literature for/by children - History and criticism	891.47099282
Gujarati literature for/by women - History and criticism	891.47099287
Gujarati love fiction (multiple authors)	891.473085*
Gujarati love fiction (multiple authors)- Collections	891.47308508**
Gujarati love fiction (multiple authors)- History and criticism	891.47308509**
Gujarati melodrama (multiple authors)	891.4720527*
Gujarati melodrama (multiple authors)- Collections	891.472052708**
Gujarati melodrama (multiple authors)- History and criticism	891.472052709**
Gujarati miscellaneous writings (multiple authors)	891.478
Gujarati miscellaneous writings (multiple authors) - to 1845	***See*** Main schedule
Gujarati miscellaneous writings (multiple authors) -1845-1895	891.4784++

Gujarati miscellaneous writings (multiple authors) -1895-1919	891.4785++
Gujarati miscellaneous writings (multiple authors) -1920-1939	891.4786++
Gujarati miscellaneous writings (multiple authors) -1940-	891.4787++
Gujarati miscellaneous writings (multiple authors) -1940-1999	891.47871++
Gujarati miscellaneous writings (multiple authors) -19th century	891.4784++
Gujarati miscellaneous writings (multiple authors) -2000-	891.47872++
Gujarati miscellaneous writings (multiple authors) -20th century	891.47871++
Gujarati miscellaneous writings (multiple authors) -Collections	891.478008**
Gujarati miscellaneous writings (multiple authors) -Dictionaries etc	891.478003
Gujarati miscellaneous writings (multiple authors) -History and criticism	891.478009**
Gujarati miscellaneous writings (multiple authors) -Periodicals	891.478005
Gujarati miscellaneous writings (multiple authors) -Philosophy and theory	891.478001
Gujarati miscellaneous writings (multiple authors) -Psychological aspects	891.4780019
Gujarati miscellaneous writings (multiple authors) -Research	891.4780072
Gujarati miscellaneous writings (multiple authors) -Study and teaching	891.478007

Gujarati miscellaneous writings (multiple authors) -Value	891.4780013
Gujarati miscellaneous writings (single author)	891.478
Gujarati miscellaneous writings (single author)- - to 1845	***See*** Main schedule
Gujarati miscellaneous writings (single author)- 1845 -1895	891.478 4
Gujarati miscellaneous writings (single author)- 1895 - 1919	891.478 5
Gujarati miscellaneous writings (single author)- 1920- 1939	891.478 6
Gujarati miscellaneous writings (single author)- 1940 -	891.478 7
Gujarati miscellaneous writings (single author)- 1940-1999	891.478 71
Gujarati miscellaneous writings (single author)- 19th century	891.478 4
Gujarati miscellaneous writings (single author)- 2000-	891.478 72
Gujarati miscellaneous writings (single author)- 20th century	891.478 71
Gujarati monologues (multiple authors)	891.472045*
Gujarati monologues (multiple authors)-Collections	891.47204508**
Gujarati monologues (multiple authors)-History and criticism	891.47204509**
Gujarati morality plays	***See*** Gujarati religious and morality plays

Gujarati mystery fiction (multiple authors)	891.4730872*
Gujarati mystery fiction (multiple authors)- Collections	891.473087208**
Gujarati mystery fiction (multiple authors)- History and criticism	891.473087209**
Gujarati narrative poetry (multiple authors)	891.47103*
Gujarati narrative poetry (multiple authors)- Collections	891.4710308**
Gujarati narrative poetry (multiple authors)- History and criticism	891.4710309**
Gujarati notebooks	***See*** Gujarati diaries...
Gujarati odes (multiple authors)	891.471043
Gujarati odes (multiple authors)- Collections	891.47104308**
Gujarati odes (multiple authors)- History and criticism	891.47104309**
Gujarati one act plays (multiple authors)	891.472.041*
Gujarati one act plays (multiple authors)- Collections	891.472.041 08**
Gujarati one act plays (multiple authors)- History and criticism	891.472.041 09**
Gujarati oratory (multiple authors)	*See* Gujarati public speeches
Gujarati periodicals	059.9147
Gujarati poetry	891.471
Gujarati poetry (multiple authors) - to 1845	***See*** Main schedule
Gujarati poetry (multiple authors) - 1845-1895	891.4714+

Gujarati poetry (multiple authors) - 1895-1919	891.4715+
Gujarati poetry (multiple authors) - 1920-1939	891.4716+
Gujarati poetry (multiple authors) - 1940-	891.4717+
Gujarati poetry (multiple authors) - 1940-1999	891.47171+
Gujarati poetry (multiple authors) - 19th century	891.4714+
Gujarati poetry (multiple authors) - 2000-	891.47172+
Gujarati poetry (multiple authors) - 20th century	891.47171+
Gujarati poetry (multiple authors)- Collections	891.471008**
Gujarati poetry (multiple authors)- Dictionaries etc	891.471003
Gujarati poetry (multiple authors)- History and criticism	891.471009**
Gujarati poetry (multiple authors)- Periodicals	891.471005
Gujarati poetry (multiple authors)- Philosophy and theory	891.471001
Gujarati poetry (multiple authors)- Psychological aspects	891.4710019
Gujarati poetry (multiple authors)- Research	891.4710072
Gujarati poetry (multiple authors)- Study and teaching	891.471007
Gujarati poetry (multiple authors)- Value	891.4710013

Gujarati poetry (single author)- to 1845	***See*** Main schedule
Gujarati poetry (single author)- 1845 -1895	891.471 4
Gujarati poetry (single author)- 1895 - 1919	891.471 5
Gujarati poetry (single author)- 1920- 1939	891.471 6
Gujarati poetry (single author)- 1940 -	891.471 7
Gujarati poetry (single author)- 1940-1999	891.471 71
Gujarati poetry (single author)- 19th century	891.471 4
Gujarati poetry (single author)- 2000-	891.471 72
Gujarati poetry (single author)- 20th century	891.471 71
Gujarati prose (single author)- to 1845	***See*** Main schedule
Gujarati prose (single author)- 1845 -1895	891.478 408
Gujarati prose (single author)- 1895 - 1919	891.478 508
Gujarati prose (single author)- 1920- 1939	891.478 608
Gujarati prose (single author)- 1940 -	891.478 708
Gujarati prose (single author)- 1940-1999	891.478 7108
Gujarati prose (single author)- 19th century	891.478 408
Gujarati prose (single author)- 2000-	891.478 7208
Gujarati prose (single author)- 20th century	891.478 7108
Gujarati prose literature	891.47808
Gujarati psychological, realistic, sociological fiction (multiple authors)- Collections	891.47308308**
Gujarati psychological, realistic, sociological fiction (multiple authors) - History and criticism	891.47308309**
Gujarati psychological, realistic,	

sociological fiction (multiple authors)	891.473083
Gujarati public discussions	***See*** Gujarati debates and public discussions
Gujarati public speeches (multiple authors)	891.47501
Gujarati public speeches (multiple authors)- Collections	891.4750108
Gujarati public speeches (multiple authors)- History and criticism	891.4750109
Gujarati quotations	***See*** Gujarati anecdotes ...
Gujarati realistic fiction	***See*** Gujarati psychological... fiction
Gujarati recitations (multiple authors)	891.47504+
Gujarati religious and morality plays (multiple authors)	891.4720516+
Gujarati reminiscences	***See*** Gujarati diaries...
Gujarati romantic fiction (multiple authors)	891.473085*
Gujarati romantic fiction (multiple authors)- Collections	891.47308508**
Gujarati romantic fiction (multiple authors)- History and criticism	891.47308509**
Gujarati satire	***See*** Gujarati humour and satire
Gujarati satirical poetry	***See*** Gujarati humourous and satirical poetry
Gujarati science fiction (multiple authors)	891.47308762*

Gujarati science fiction (multiple authors)-Collections	891.4730876208**
Gujarati science fiction (multiple authors)-History and criticism	891.4730876209**
Gujarati serious drama (multiple authors)	891.472051+
Gujarati short stories (multiple authors)	891.47301*
Gujarati short stories (multiple authors)-Collections	891.4730108**
Gujarati short stories (multiple authors)-History and criticism	891.4730109**
Gujarati sociological fiction (multiple authors)	***See*** Gujarati psychological... fiction
Gujarati sonnets (multiple authors)	891.471042*
Gujarati sonnets(multiple authors)-Collections	891.47104208**
Gujarati sonnets(multiple authors)-History and criticism	891.47104209**
Gujarati speaking people	305.791 471
Gujarati speeches (multiple authors)	891.475
Gujarati speeches (multiple authors) - to 1845	***See*** Main schedule
Gujarati speeches (multiple authors) - 1845-1895	891.4754+
Gujarati speeches (multiple authors) - 1895-1919	891.4755+
Gujarati speeches (multiple authors) - 1920-1939	891.4756+
Gujarati speeches (multiple authors) -	

1940-	891.4757+
Gujarati speeches (multiple authors) - 1940-1999	891.47571+
Gujarati speeches (multiple authors) - 19th century	891.4754+
Gujarati speeches (multiple authors) -2000-	891.47572+
Gujarati speeches (multiple authors) - 20th century	891.47571+
Gujarati speeches (multiple authors) – 21st century	891.47572+
Gujarati speeches (multiple authors) - Collections	891.475008**
Gujarati speeches (multiple authors) - Dictionaries etc	891.475003
Gujarati speeches (multiple authors) - History and criticism	891.475009**
Gujarati speeches (multiple authors) - Periodicals	891.475005
Gujarati speeches (multiple authors) - Philosophy and theory	891.475001
Gujarati speeches (multiple authors) - Psychological aspects	891.4750019
Gujarati speeches (multiple authors) - Research	891.4750072
Gujarati speeches (multiple authors) - Study and teaching	891.475007
Gujarati speeches (multiple authors) -Value	891.4750013
Gujarati speeches (single author)	891.475
Gujarati speeches (single author)- to 1845	***See*** Main schedule

Gujarati speeches (single author)- 1845 -1895	891.475 4
Gujarati speeches (single author)- 1895 - 1919	891.475 5
Gujarati speeches (single author)- 1920- 1939	891.475 6
Gujarati speeches (single author)- 1940 -	891.475 7
Gujarati speeches (single author)- 1940-1999	891.475 71
Gujarati speeches (single author)- 19th century	891.475 4
Gujarati speeches (single author)- 2000-	891.475 72
Gujarati speeches (single author)- 20th century	891.475 71
Gujarati suspense fiction (multiple authors)	891.4730872*
Gujarati suspense fiction (multiple authors)- Collections	891.473087208**
Gujarati suspense fiction (multiple authors)- History and criticism	891.473087209**
Gujarati tragedy (multiple authors)	891.4720512*
Gujarati tragedy (multiple authors)- Collections	891.472051208**
Gujarati tragedy (multiple authors)- History and criticism	891.472051209**
Gujarati variety drama (multiple authors)	891.472057*
Gujarati variety drama (multiple authors)- Collections	891.47205708**
Gujarati variety drama (multiple authors)- History and criticism	891.47205709**

Gujaratis - Opinions	303.387 914 7
Guru Nanak	294.663
Gurus (Buddhism)	294.361
Gurus (Hinduism)	294.561
Gurus (Jainism)	294.461
Gurus (Sikhism)	294.661

H

Haryana- Architecture	720.954 558
Haryana- Botany	580.954 558
Haryana- Budget	352.495 45 58
Haryana- Economic development	338.954 55 8
Haryana- Economic geography	330.954 55 8
Haryana- Education	370.954 5 58
Haryana- Fauna	591.954 558
Haryana- Fine and decorative arts	709.545 58
Haryana- Flora	581.954 558
Haryana- Folk dancing	793.319 54558
Haryana- Galleries of fine and decorative arts	708.954 558
Haryana- Geography	915.4558
Haryana -Geology	555.455 8
Haryana- History	954.558
Haryana- Museums of fine and decorative arts	708.954 558
Haryana- Painting and paintings	759.954 558
Haryana- Public administration	351.545 58

Haryana- Public finance	336.545 58
Haryana- Sculpture	730.954 558
Heaven (Buddhism)	294.342 3
Heaven (Hinduism)	294.523
Heaven (Jainism)	294.423
Heaven (Sikhism)	294.623
Hell (Buddhism)	294.342 3
Hell (Hinduism)	294.523
Hell (Jainism)	294.423
Hell (Sikhism)	294.623
Hereditary societies	***See*** Hereditary, military, patriotic societies
Hereditary, military, patriotic societies	369.2
Hereditary, military, patriotic societies- Andaman and Nicobar Islands	369.254 88
Hereditary, military, patriotic societies- Andhra Pradesh	369.254 84
Hereditary, military, patriotic societies- Arunachal Pradesh	369.254 163
Hereditary, military, patriotic societies- Assam	369.254 162
Hereditary, military, patriotic societies- Bengal	369.254 14
Hereditary, military, patriotic societies- Bhopal	369.254 3
Hereditary, military, patriotic societies- Bihar	369.254 12

Hereditary, military, patriotic societies- Bombay	369.254 792 3
Hereditary, military, patriotic societies- Calcutta	369.254 147
Hereditary, military, patriotic societies- Chandigarh	369.254 55 2
Hereditary, military, patriotic societies- Chhattisgarh	369.254 137
Hereditary, military, patriotic societies- Dadra and Nagar Haveli	369.254 796
Hereditary, military, patriotic societies- Delhi	369.254 56
Hereditary, military, patriotic societies- Goa, Daman and Diu	369.254 799
Hereditary, military, patriotic societies- Gujarat	369.254 75
Hereditary, military, patriotic societies- Haryana	369.254 55 8
Hereditary, military, patriotic societies- Himachal Pradesh	369.254 52
Hereditary, military, patriotic societies- Hyderabad state	369.254 84
Hereditary, military, patriotic societies- India	369.254
Hereditary, military, patriotic societies- Jammu and Kashmir	369.254 6
Hereditary, military, patriotic societies- Jharkhand	369.254 127
Hereditary, military, patriotic societies- Karnataka	369.254 87
Hereditary, military, patriotic societies- Kerala	369.254 83

Hereditary, military, patriotic societies-Lakshwadweep	369.254 81
Hereditary, military, patriotic societies-Madhya Pradesh	369.254 3
Hereditary, military, patriotic societies-Madras	369.254 82
Hereditary, military, patriotic societies-Maharashtra	369.254 792
Hereditary, military, patriotic societies-Manipur	369.254 17
Hereditary, military, patriotic societies-Meghalaya	369.254 164
Hereditary, military, patriotic societies-Mizoram	369.254 166
Hereditary, military, patriotic societies-Nagaland	369.254 165
Hereditary, military, patriotic societies-Northeast India	369.254 1
Hereditary, military, patriotic societies-Orissa	369.254 13
Hereditary, military, patriotic societies-Pondicherry	369.254 86
Hereditary, military, patriotic societies-Punjab	369.254 55 2
Hereditary, military, patriotic societies-Punjab region- India	369.254 52
Hereditary, military, patriotic societies-Rajasthan	369.254 4
Hereditary, military, patriotic societies-Sikkim	369.254 167

Hereditary, military, patriotic societies-South Asia	369.254
Hereditary, military, patriotic societies-Southern India	369.254 8
Hereditary, military, patriotic societies-Tamil Nadu	369.254 82
Hereditary, military, patriotic societies-Tripura	369.254 15
Hereditary, military, patriotic societies-Uttar Pradesh	369.254 2
Hereditary, military, patriotic societies-Uttaranchal	369.254 51
Hereditary, military, patriotic societies-West Bengal	369.254 14
Hereditary, military, patriotic societies-Western India	369.254 7
Heroes as objects of worship (Buddhism)	294.342 13
Heroes as objects of worship (Hinduism)	294.5213
Heroes as objects of worship (Jainism)	294.4213
Heroes as objects of worship (Sikhism)	294.6213
Higher education	378
Higher education- Andaman and Nicobar Islands	378.548 8
Higher education- Andhra Pradesh	378.548 4
Higher education- Arunachal Pradesh	378.541 63
Higher education- Assam	378.541 62
Higher education- Bengal	378.541 4
Higher education- Bhopal	378.543

Higher education- Bihar	378.541 2
Higher education- Bombay	378.547 923
Higher education- Calcutta	378.541 47
Higher education- Chandigarh	378.545 52
Higher education- Chhattisgarh	378.541 37
Higher education- Dadra and Nagar Haveli	378.547 96
Higher education- Delhi	378.545 6
Higher education- Goa, Daman and Diu	378.547 99
Higher education- Gujarat	378.547 5
Higher education- Haryana	378.545 58
Higher education- Himachal Pradesh	378.545 2
Higher education- Hyderabad state	378.548 4
Higher education- India	378.54
Higher education- Jammu and Kashmir	378.546
Higher education- Jharkhand	378.541 27
Higher education- Karnataka	378.548 7
Higher education- Kerala	378.548 3
Higher education- Lakshwadweep	378.548 1
Higher education- Madhya Pradesh	378.543
Higher education- Madras	378.548 2
Higher education- Maharashtra	378.547 92
Higher education- Manipur	378.541 7
Higher education- Meghalaya	378.541 64
Higher education- Mizoram	378.541 66
Higher education- Nagaland	378.541 65

Higher education- Northeast India	378.541
Higher education- Orissa	378.541 3
Higher education- Pondicherry	378.548 6
Higher education- Punjab	378.545 52
Higher education- Rajasthan	378.544
Higher education- Sikkim	378.541 67
Higher education- South Asia	378.54
Higher education- Southern India	378.548
Higher education- Tamil Nadu	378.548 2
Higher education- Tripura	378.541 5
Higher education- Uttar Pradesh	378.542
Higher education- Uttaranchal	378.545 1
Higher education- West Bengal	378.541 4
Higher education- Western India	378.547
Himachal Pradesh- Architecture	720.954 52
Himachal Pradesh- Botany	580.954 52
Himachal Pradesh- Budget	352.495 452
Himachal Pradesh- Economic development	338.954 52
Himachal Pradesh- Economic geography	330.954 52
Himachal Pradesh- Education	370.954 52
Himachal Pradesh- Fauna	591.954 52
Himachal Pradesh- Fine and decorative arts	709.5452
Himachal Pradesh- Flora	581.954 52
Himachal Pradesh- Folk dancing	793.319 5452
Himachal Pradesh- Galleries of fine and	

decorative arts	708.954 52
Himachal Pradesh- Geography	915.452
Himachal Pradesh- Geology	555.452
Himachal Pradesh- History	954.52
Himachal Pradesh- Museums of fine and decorative arts	708.954 52
Himachal Pradesh- Painting and paintings	759.954 52
Himachal Pradesh- Public administration	351.545 2
Himachal Pradesh- Public finance	336.545 2
Himachal Pradesh- Sculpture	730.954 52
Hindi - English dictionary	491.43321
Hindi adventure fiction (multiple authors) - Collections	891.43308708**
Hindi adventure fiction (multiple authors)	891.433087*
Hindi adventure fiction (multiple authors)- History and criticism	891.43308709**
Hindi anecdotes, epigrams, graffiti, jokes, quotations (multiple authors)	891.43802
Hindi anecdotes, epigrams, graffiti, jokes, quotations (single author)	891.438 +CD+02
Hindi as second language in elementary education	372.659 143 1
Hindi ballads (multiple authors)	891.431044*
Hindi ballads (multiple authors)- Collections	891.43104408**
Hindi ballads (multiple authors)- History and criticism	891.43104409**
Hindi comedy (multiple authors) - Collections	891.432052308**

Hindi comedy (multiple authors) - History and criticism	891.432052309**
Hindi comedy (multiple authors)	891.4320523*
Hindi conversations (multiple authors)	891.43506*
Hindi conversations (multiple authors) - Collections	891.4350608**
Hindi conversations (multiple authors) - History and criticism	891.4350609**
Hindi debates and public discussions (multiple authors)	891.43503*
Hindi debates and public discussions (multiple authors)- Collections	891.4350308**
Hindi debates and public discussions (multiple authors)- History and criticism	891.4350309**
Hindi detective fiction (multiple authors) - Collections	891.433087208**
Hindi detective fiction (multiple authors) - History and criticism	891.433087209**
Hindi detective fiction (multiple authors)	891.4330872*
Hindi diaries, notebooks, reminiscences (multiple authors)	891.43803
Hindi diaries, notebooks, reminiscences (single author)- - to 1345	891.438 103
Hindi diaries, notebooks, reminiscences (single author)-1345-1645	891.438 203
Hindi diaries, notebooks, reminiscences (single author)-1645-1845	891.438 303
Hindi diaries, notebooks, reminiscences (single author)-1845 -1895	891.438 403

Hindi diaries, notebooks, reminiscences (single author)-1895 - 1919	891.438 503
Hindi diaries, notebooks, reminiscences (single author)-1919- 1939	891.438 603
Hindi diaries, notebooks, reminiscences (single author)-1940 -	891.438 703
Hindi diaries, notebooks, reminiscences (single author)-1940-1999	891.438 7103
Hindi diaries, notebooks, reminiscences (single author)-19th century	891.438 403
Hindi diaries, notebooks, reminiscences (single author)-2000-	891.438 7203
Hindi diaries, notebooks, reminiscences (single author)-20th century	891.438 7103
Hindi didactic poetry (multiple authors)	891.43105*
Hindi didactic poetry (multiple authors)- Collections	891.4310508**
Hindi didactic poetry (multiple authors)- History and criticism	891.4310509**
Hindi drama	891.432
Hindi drama (multiple authors) - to 1845	***See*** Main schedule
Hindi drama (multiple authors) - 1845-1895	891.4324+
Hindi drama (multiple authors) - 1895-1919	891.4325+
Hindi drama (multiple authors) - 1920-1939	891.4326+
Hindi drama (multiple authors) - 1940-	891.4327+
Hindi drama (multiple authors) - 1940-1999	891.43271+
Hindi drama (multiple authors) - 19th century	891.4324+
Hindi drama (multiple authors) - 2000-	891.43272+

Hindi drama (multiple authors) - 20th century	891.43271+
Hindi drama (multiple authors) - Collections	891.432008**
Hindi drama (multiple authors) - Dictionaries etc	891.432003
Hindi drama (multiple authors) - History and criticism	891.432009**
Hindi drama (multiple authors) - Periodicals	891.432005
Hindi drama (multiple authors) - Philosophy and theory	891.432001
Hindi drama (multiple authors) - Psychological aspects	891.4320019
Hindi drama (multiple authors) - Research	891.4320072
Hindi drama (multiple authors) - Study and teaching	891.432007
Hindi drama (multiple authors) - Value	891.4320013
Hindi drama (single author) - to 1845	***See*** Main schedule
Hindi drama (single author)- 1845 -1895	891.432 4
Hindi drama (single author)- 1895 - 1919	891.432 5
Hindi drama (single author)- 1919- 1939	891.432 6
Hindi drama (single author)- 1940 -	891.432 7
Hindi drama (single author)- 1940-1999	891.432 71
Hindi drama (single author)- 19th century	891.432 4
Hindi drama (single author)- 2000-	891.432 72
Hindi drama (single author)- 20th century	891.432 71
Hindi drama for cinema (multiple authors)	891.43203*
Hindi drama for cinema (multiple authors) - Collections	891.4320308**

Hindi drama for cinema (multiple authors) - History and criticism	891.4320309**
Hindi drama for radio (multiple authors)	891.432022*
Hindi drama for radio (multiple authors) - Collections	891.43202208**
Hindi drama for radio (multiple authors) - History and criticism	891.43202209**
Hindi drama for television (multiple authors)	891.432025*
Hindi drama for television (multiple authors) - Collections	891.43202508**
Hindi drama for television (multiple authors) - History and criticism	891.43202509**
Hindi dramatic poetry (multiple authors)	891.43102*
Hindi dramatic poetry (multiple authors)- Collections	891.4310208**
Hindi dramatic poetry (multiple authors)- History and criticism	891.4310209**
Hindi encyclopaedias	039.9143
Hindi ephemeral and light verse (multiple authors)	891.43108*
Hindi ephemeral and light verse (multiple authors)- Collections	891.4310808**
Hindi ephemeral and light verse (multiple authors) - History and criticism	891.4310809**
Hindi epic poetry (multiple authors)	891.431032*
Hindi epic poetry (multiple authors)- Collections	891.43103208**
Hindi epic poetry (multiple authors)- History and criticism	891.43103209**

Hindi epigrams	***See*** Hindi anecdotes …
Hindi essays	891.434
Hindi essays (multiple authors) - to 1845	***See*** Main schedule
Hindi essays (multiple authors) -1845-1895	891.4344+
Hindi essays (multiple authors) -1895-1919	891.4345+
Hindi essays (multiple authors) -1920-1939	891.4346+
Hindi essays (multiple authors) -1940-	891.4347+
Hindi essays (multiple authors) -1940-1999	891.43471+
Hindi essays (multiple authors) -19th century	891.4344+
Hindi essays (multiple authors) -2000-	891.43472+
Hindi essays (multiple authors) -20th century	891.43471+
Hindi essays (multiple authors) -Collections	891.434008**
Hindi essays (multiple authors) -Dictionaries etc	891.434003
Hindi essays (multiple authors) - History and criticism	891.434009**
Hindi essays (multiple authors) -Periodicals	891.434005
Hindi essays (multiple authors) - Philosophy and theory	891.434001
Hindi essays (multiple authors) - Psychological aspects	891.4340019
Hindi essays (multiple authors) -Research	891.4340072
Hindi essays (multiple authors) - Study and teaching	891.434007
Hindi essays (multiple authors) -Value	891.4340013
Hindi essays (single author)- to 1845	***See*** Main schedule

Hindi essays (single author)- 1845 -1895	891.434 4
Hindi essays (single author)- 1895 - 1919	891.434 5
Hindi essays (single author)- 1920- 1939	891.434 6
Hindi essays (single author)- 1940 -	891.434 7
Hindi essays (single author)- 1940-1999	891.434 71
Hindi essays (single author)- 19th century	891.434 4
Hindi essays (single author)- 2000-	891.434 72
Hindi essays (single author)- 20th century	891.434 71
Hindi experimental and non-formalized works (single author)	891.438+CD+07
Hindi experimental and non-formalized works (multiple authors)	891.43807
Hindi fantasy fiction (multiple authors)	891.43308766*
Hindi fantasy fiction (multiple authors)- Collections	891.4330876608**
Hindi fantasy fiction (multiple authors)- History and criticism	891.4330876609**
Hindi farce (multiple authors) - History and criticism	891.4320523209**
Hindi farce (multiple authors)	891.43205232*
Hindi farce (multiple authors)- Collections	891.4320523208**
Hindi farce (multiple authors)- History and Criticism	891.4320523209*
Hindi fiction	891.433
Hindi fiction (multiple authors) - to 1845	***See*** Main schedule
Hindi fiction (multiple authors) - 1845-1895	891.4334+
Hindi fiction (multiple authors) - 1895-1919	891.4335+

Hindi fiction (multiple authors) - 1920-1939	891.4336+
Hindi fiction (multiple authors) - 1940-	891.4337+
Hindi fiction (multiple authors) - 1940-1999	891.43371+
Hindi fiction (multiple authors) - 19th century	891.4334+
Hindi fiction (multiple authors) - 2000-	891.43372+
Hindi fiction (multiple authors) - 20th century	891.43371+
Hindi fiction (multiple authors) - Collections	891.433008**
Hindi fiction (multiple authors) - Dictionaries etc	891.433003
Hindi fiction (multiple authors) - History and criticism	891.433009**
Hindi fiction (multiple authors) - Periodicals	891.433005
Hindi fiction (multiple authors) - Philosophy and theory	891.433001
Hindi fiction (multiple authors) - Psychological aspects	891.4330019
Hindi fiction (multiple authors) - Research	891.4330072
Hindi fiction (multiple authors) - Study and teaching	891.433007
Hindi fiction (multiple authors) - Value	891.4330013
Hindi fiction (single authors) - to 1845	***See*** Main Schedule
Hindi fiction (single author)- 1845 -1895	891.433 4
Hindi fiction (single author)- 1895 - 1919	891.433 5
Hindi fiction (single author)- 1920- 1939	891.433 6
Hindi fiction (single author)- 1940 -	891.433 7
Hindi fiction (single author)- 1940-1999	891.433 71

Hindi fiction (single author)- 19th century	891.433 4
Hindi fiction (single author)- 2000-	891.433 72
Hindi fiction (single author)- 20th century	891.433 71
Hindi fiction (single author)- to 1845	***See*** Main schedule
Hindi folk music	781 629 143
Hindi ghost fiction (multiple authors) - Collections	891.4330873308**
Hindi ghost fiction (multiple authors)	891.43308733*
Hindi ghost fiction (multiple authors)- History and criticism	891.4330873309**
Hindi graffiti	***See*** Hindi anecdotes ...
Hindi historical drama (multiple authors)	891.4320514*
Hindi historical drama (multiple authors)- Collections	891.432051408**
Hindi historical drama (multiple authors)- History and criticism	891.432051409**
Hindi historical fiction (multiple authors)	891.433081*
Hindi historical fiction (multiple authors)- Collections	891.43308108**
Hindi historical fiction (multiple authors)- History and criticism	891.43308109**
Hindi horror fiction (multiple authors)	891.43308738*
Hindi horror fiction (multiple authors)- Collections	891.4330873808**
Hindi horror fiction (multiple authors)- History and criticism	891.4330873809**
Hindi humour and satire	891.437

Hindi humour and satire (multiple authors) - to 1845	***See*** Main schedule
Hindi humour and satire (multiple authors) - 1845-1895	891.4374+
Hindi humour and satire (multiple authors) - 1895-1919	891.4375+
Hindi humour and satire (multiple authors) - 1920-1939	891.4376+
Hindi humour and satire (multiple authors) - 1940-	891.4377+
Hindi humour and satire (multiple authors) - 1940-1999	891.43771+
Hindi humour and satire (multiple authors) - 19th century	891.4374+
Hindi humour and satire (multiple authors) - 2000-	891.43772+
Hindi humour and satire (multiple authors) - 20th century	891.43771+
Hindi humour and satire (multiple authors) - Collections	891.437008**
Hindi humour and satire (multiple authors) - Dictionaries etc	891.437003
Hindi humour and satire (multiple authors) - History and criticism	891.437009**
Hindi humour and satire (multiple authors) - Periodicals	891.437005
Hindi humour and satire (multiple authors) - Philosophy and theory	891.437001
Hindi humour and satire (multiple authors) - Psychological aspects	891.4370019

Hindi humour and satire (multiple authors) - Research	891.4370072
Hindi humour and satire (multiple authors) - Study and teaching	891.437007
Hindi humour and satire (multiple authors) - Value	891.4370013
Hindi humourous and satirical poetry (multiple authors)	891.43107*
Hindi humourous and satirical poetry (multiple authors)- Collections	891.4310708**
Hindi humourous and satirical poetry (multiple authors)- History and criticism	891.4310709**
Hindi jokes	***See*** Hindi anecdotes ...
Hindi language	491.43
Hindi language- Applied linguistics	491.438
Hindi language- Bilingual dictionaries	491.4332-39
Hindi language- Bilingualism	491.430 42
Hindi language- Concordances	491.430 3
Hindi language- Content analysis	491.430 141
Hindi language- Dialects	491.437
Hindi language- Dictionaries	491.433
Hindi language- Discourse analysis	491.430 141
Hindi language- Education	491.430 71
Hindi language- Encyclopaedias	491.430 3
Hindi language- Etymology	491.432
Hindi language- Functionalism	491.430 18

Hindi language- Grammar	491.435
Hindi language- History	491.430 9
Hindi language- Intonation	491.431 6
Hindi language- Lexicography	491.433 028
Hindi language- Lexicology	491.430 14
Hindi language- Miscellany	491.430 2
Hindi language- Multilingualism	491.430 42
Hindi language- Organizations	491.430 6
Hindi language- Orthography	491.431 52
Hindi language- Pauses	491.431 6
Hindi language- Periodicals	491.430 5
Hindi language- Persons (men, women, etc)	491.430 8
Hindi language- Philosophy and theory	491.430 1
Hindi language- Phonetics	491.431 58
Hindi language- Phonology	491.431 5
Hindi language- Pitch	491.431 6
Hindi language- Pronunciation	491.431 52
Hindi language- Readers	491.438 6
Hindi language- Research	491.43072
Hindi language- Rhetoric	808.049 1431+
Hindi language- Schools and theories of linguistics	491.430 18
Hindi language- Semantics	491.430 143
Hindi language- Semiotics	491.430 141
Hindi language- Slang	491.437

Hindi language- Special topics	491.430 4
Hindi language- Specialized dictionaries	491.4331
Hindi language- Spelling	491.431 52
Hindi language- Stress	491.431 6
Hindi language- Structural linguistics	491.430 18
Hindi language- Suprasegmental features	491.431 6
Hindi language- Terminology	491.430 14
Hindi language- Usage	491.438
Hindi language- Variations (Dialects etc)	491.437
Hindi language- Writing systems	491.431 1
Hindi letters	891.436
Hindi letters (multiple authors) – to 1845	***See*** Main schedule
Hindi letters (multiple authors) -1845-1895	891.4364+
Hindi letters (multiple authors) -1895-1919	891.4365+
Hindi letters (multiple authors) -1920-1939	891.4366+
Hindi letters (multiple authors) -1940-	891.4367+
Hindi letters (multiple authors) -1940-1999	891.43671+
Hindi letters (multiple authors) -19th century	891.4364+
Hindi letters (multiple authors) -2000-	891.43672+
Hindi letters (multiple authors) -20th century	891.43671+
Hindi letters (multiple authors) -Collections	891.436008**
Hindi letters (multiple authors) - Dictionaries etc	891.436003
Hindi letters (multiple authors) - History and criticism	891.436009**

Hindi letters (multiple authors) -Periodicals	891.436005
Hindi letters (multiple authors) - Philosophy and theory	891.436001
Hindi letters (multiple authors) - Psychological aspects	891.4360019
Hindi letters (multiple authors) -Research	891.4360072
Hindi letters (multiple authors) - Study and teaching	891.436007
Hindi letters (multiple authors) -Value	891.4360013
Hindi letters (single author)- to 1845	***See*** Main schedule
Hindi letters (single author)- 1845 -1895	891.436 4
Hindi letters (single author)- 1895 - 1919	891.436 5
Hindi letters (single author)- 1919- 1939	891.436 6
Hindi letters (single author)- 1940 -	891.436 7
Hindi letters (single author)- 1940-1999 (20th century)	891.436 71
Hindi letters (single author)- 19th century	891.436 4
Hindi letters (single author)- 2000-	891.436 72
Hindi letters (single author)- 20th century	891.436 71
Hindi light verse	***See*** Hindi ephemeral and light verse
Hindi limericks (multiple authors)	891.431075*
Hindi limericks(multiple authors)- Collections	891.43107508**
Hindi limericks(multiple authors)- History and criticism	891.43107509**
Hindi literature	891.43

Hindi literature (collections of multiple forms)	891.4308
Hindi literature (collections of multiple forms) - 19th century	891.430804
Hindi literature (collections of multiple forms) - 20th century	891.4308071
Hindi literature (collections of multiple forms) – 21st century	891.4308072
Hindi literature (collections of multiple forms) - Allegory	891.4308015
Hindi literature (collections of multiple forms) - Animals	891.43080362++
Hindi literature (collections of multiple forms) - Artistic themes	891.43080357
Hindi literature (collections of multiple forms) - Atmosphere	891.4308032161
Hindi literature (collections of multiple forms) - Characters	891.4308027
Hindi literature (collections of multiple forms) - Comedy	891.4308017
Hindi literature (collections of multiple forms) - Evening	891.4308033
Hindi literature (collections of multiple forms) - Fantasy	891.4308015
Hindi literature (collections of multiple forms) - Forests	891.4308032152
Hindi literature (collections of multiple forms) - Historical themes	891.43080358
Hindi literature (collections of multiple forms) - Horror	891.43080164
Hindi literature (collections of multiple	

forms) - Human characteristics (Biological, moral and psychological)	891.43080353
Hindi literature (collections of multiple forms) - Legendary objects/themes	891.4308037
Hindi literature (collections of multiple forms) - Literary themes	891.43080357
Hindi literature (collections of multiple forms) - Love	891.430803543
Hindi literature (collections of multiple forms) - Marriage	891.430803543
Hindi literature (collections of multiple forms) - Morning	891.4308033
Hindi literature (collections of multiple forms) - Mountains	891.4308032143
Hindi literature (collections of multiple forms) - Myth	891.4308015
Hindi literature (collections of multiple forms) - Mythological objects/themes	891.4308037
Hindi literature (collections of multiple forms) - Philosophic themes	891.43080384
Hindi literature (collections of multiple forms) - Places	891.4308032++
Hindi literature (collections of multiple forms) - Plants	891.43080364
Hindi literature (collections of multiple forms) - Political themes	891.43080358
Hindi literature (collections of multiple forms) - Religious themes	891.43080382++
Hindi literature (collections of multiple forms) - Rivers	891.43080321693

Hindi literature (collections of multiple forms) - Romanticism	891.43080145
Hindi literature (collections of multiple forms) - Scientific themes	891.43080356
Hindi literature (collections of multiple forms) - Sea	891.4308032162
Hindi literature (collections of multiple forms) - Seasons	891.4308033
Hindi literature (collections of multiple forms) - Sex	891.430803538
Hindi literature (collections of multiple forms) - Social themes	891.43080355
Hindi literature (collections of multiple forms) - Space	891.430803219
Hindi literature (collections of multiple forms) - Specific kinds of persons, e.g. heroes	891.43080352+
Hindi literature (collections of multiple forms) - Specific persons (real or imaginary)	891.43080351
Hindi literature (collections of multiple forms) - Stream of consciousness	891.4308025
Hindi literature (collections of multiple forms) - Supernatural objects/themes	891.4308037
Hindi literature (collections of multiple forms) - Symbolism	891.4308015
Hindi literature (collections of multiple forms) - Technical themes	891.43080356
Hindi literature (collections of multiple forms) - Times (seasons, parts of day, etc)	891.4308033
Hindi literature (collections of multiple	

forms) - Towns	891.43080321732
Hindi literature (collections of multiple forms) - Tragedy	891.43080162
Hindi literature (collections of multiple forms) - Villages	891.43080321734
Hindi literature (collections of multiple forms) - Weather	891.4308036
Hindi literature (collections of multiple forms) emphasizing subjects	891.430804++
Hindi literature (collections of multiple forms) for/by children	891.430809282
Hindi literature (collections of multiple forms) for/by persons of racial, ethnic and national groups	891.430808++
Hindi literature (collections of multiple forms) for/by persons of specific classes	891.4308092++
Hindi literature (collections of multiple forms) for/by persons resident in specific regions	891.4308091++
Hindi literature (collections of multiple forms) for/by women	891.430809287
Hindi literature (multiple authors) - Concordances	891.4303
Hindi literature (multiple authors) - Dictionaries	891.4303
Hindi literature (multiple authors) - Education	891.43071
Hindi literature (multiple authors) - Encyclopaedias	891.4303
Hindi literature (multiple authors) -	

Organizations	891.4306
Hindi literature (multiple authors) - Periodicals	891.4305
Hindi literature (multiple authors) - Philosophy and theory	891.4301
Hindi literature (multiple authors) - Research	891.43072
Hindi literature (multiple authors) - Research in India	891.43072054
Hindi literature (multiple authors) - Study and teaching	891.4307
Hindi literature (multiple forms) - 19th century	891.4309004
Hindi literature (multiple forms) - 2000-	891.43090072
Hindi literature (multiple forms) - 20th century	891.43090071
Hindi literature (multiple forms) - Allegory – History and criticism	891.430915
Hindi literature (multiple forms) - Animals - History and criticism	891.4309362++
Hindi literature (multiple forms) - Artistic themes - History and criticism	891.4309357
Hindi literature (multiple forms) - Atmosphere - History and criticism	891.430932161
Hindi literature (multiple forms) - Characters - History and criticism	891.430927
Hindi literature (multiple forms) - Comedy - History and criticism	891.430917
Hindi literature (multiple forms) - Evening - History and criticism	891.430933
Hindi literature (multiple forms) -	

Fantasy – History and criticism	891.430915
Hindi literature (multiple forms) - Forests History and criticism	891.430932152
Hindi literature (multiple forms) - Historical themes - History and criticism	891.4309358
Hindi literature (multiple forms) - History and criticism	891.4309
Hindi literature (multiple forms) - Horror - History and criticism	891.4309164
Hindi literature (multiple forms) - Human characteristics (Biological, moral, psychological) - History and criticism	891.4309353
Hindi literature (multiple forms) - Legendary objects/themes - History and criticism	891.430937
Hindi literature (multiple forms) - Literary themes - History and criticism	891.4309357
Hindi literature (multiple forms) - Love - History and criticism	891.43093543
Hindi literature (multiple forms) - Marriage - History and criticism	891.43093543
Hindi literature (multiple forms) - Morning - History and criticism	891.430933
Hindi literature (multiple forms) - Mountains - History and criticism	891.430932143
Hindi literature (multiple forms) - Myth - History and criticism	891.430915
Hindi literature (multiple forms) - Mythological objects/themes - History and criticism	891.430937

Hindi literature (multiple forms) - Persons of racial, ethnic and national groups - History and criticism	891.43098++
Hindi literature (multiple forms) - Persons of specific classes - History and criticism	891.430992++
Hindi literature (multiple forms) - Persons resident in specific regions -History and criticism	891.430991++
Hindi literature (multiple forms) - Philosophic themes - History and criticism	891.4309384
Hindi literature (multiple forms) - Places - History and criticism	891.430932++
Hindi literature (multiple forms) - Plants - History and criticism	891.4309364
Hindi literature (multiple forms) - Political themes - History and criticism	891.4309358
Hindi literature (multiple forms) - Religious themes - History and criticism	891.4309382++
Hindi literature (multiple forms) - Rivers - History and criticism	891.4309321693
Hindi literature (multiple forms) - Romanticism - History and criticism	891.4309145
Hindi literature (multiple forms) - Scientific themes - History and criticism	891.4309356
Hindi literature (multiple forms) - Sea - History and criticism	891.430932162
Hindi literature (multiple forms) - Seasons - History and criticism	891.430933
Hindi literature (multiple forms) - Sex - History and criticism	891.43093538

Hindi literature (multiple forms) - Social themes - History and criticism	891.4309355
Hindi literature (multiple forms) - Space - History and criticism	891.43093219
Hindi literature (multiple forms) - Specific kinds of persons (e.g. heroes) - History and criticism	891.4309352++
Hindi literature (multiple forms) - Specific persons - History and criticism	891.4309351
Hindi literature (multiple forms) - Stream of consciousness - History and criticism	891.430925
Hindi literature (multiple forms) - Supernatural objects/themes - History and criticism	891.430937
Hindi literature (multiple forms) - Subjects - History and criticism	891.43094++
Hindi literature (multiple forms) - Symbolism- History, criticism	891.430915
Hindi literature (multiple forms) - Technical themes - History and criticism	891.4309356
Hindi literature (multiple forms) - Times - History and criticism	891.430933
Hindi literature (multiple forms) - Towns - History and criticism	891.4309321732
Hindi literature (multiple forms) - Tragedy - History and criticism	891.4309162
Hindi literature (multiple forms) - Villages - History and criticism	891.4309321734
Hindi literature (multiple forms) - Weather - History and criticism	891.430936

Hindi literature (single author)- - to 1845 - Biography, collections, criticism	***See*** Main schedule
Hindi literature (single author)- 1845 - 1895 - Biography, collections, criticism	891.438 409
Hindi literature (single author)- 1895 - 1919 - Biography, collections, criticism	891.438 509
Hindi literature (single author)- 1920- 1939 - Biography, collections, criticism	891.438 609
Hindi literature (single author)- 1940 - Biography, collections, criticism	891.438 709
Hindi literature (single author)- 1940- 1999 - Biography, collections, criticism	891.438 7109
Hindi literature (single author)- 19th century- Biography, collections, criticism	891.438 409
Hindi literature (single author)- 2000- Biography, collections, criticism	891.438 7209
Hindi literature (single author)- 20th century - Biography, collections, criticism	891.438 7109
Hindi literature for/by children - History and criticism	891.43099282
Hindi literature for/by women - History and criticism	891.43099287
Hindi love fiction (multiple authors)	891.433085*
Hindi love fiction (multiple authors)- Collections	891.43308508**
Hindi love fiction (multiple authors)- History and criticism	891.43308509**
Hindi melodrama (multiple authors)	891.4320527*

Hindi melodrama (multiple authors)-Collections	891.432052708**
Hindi melodrama (multiple authors)-History and criticism	891.432052709**
Hindi miscellaneous writings	891.438
Hindi miscellaneous writings (multiple authors) - to 1845	***See*** Main schedule
Hindi miscellaneous writings (multiple authors) -1845-1895	891.4384++
Hindi miscellaneous writings (multiple authors) -1895-1919	891.4385++
Hindi miscellaneous writings (multiple authors) -1920-1939	891.4386++
Hindi miscellaneous writings (multiple authors) -1940-	891.4387++
Hindi miscellaneous writings (multiple authors) -1940-1999	891.43871++
Hindi miscellaneous writings (multiple authors) -19th century	891.4384++
Hindi miscellaneous writings (multiple authors) -2000-	891.43872++
Hindi miscellaneous writings (multiple authors) -20th century	891.43871++
Hindi miscellaneous writings (multiple authors) -Collections	891.438008**
Hindi miscellaneous writings (multiple authors) -Dictionaries etc	891.438003
Hindi miscellaneous writings (multiple authors) -History and criticism	891.438009**
Hindi miscellaneous writings (multiple	

authors) -Periodicals	891.438005
Hindi miscellaneous writings (multiple authors) -Philosophy and theory	891.438001
Hindi miscellaneous writings (multiple authors) -Psychological aspects	891.4380019
Hindi miscellaneous writings (multiple authors) -Research	891.4380072
Hindi miscellaneous writings (multiple authors) -Study and teaching	891.438007
Hindi miscellaneous writings (multiple authors) -Value	891.4380013
Hindi miscellaneous writings (single author)- - to 1845	***See*** Main schedule
Hindi miscellaneous writings (single author)- 1845 -1895 (19th century)	891.438 4
Hindi miscellaneous writings (single author)- 1895 - 1919	891.438 5
Hindi miscellaneous writings (single author)- 1920- 1939	891.438 6
Hindi miscellaneous writings (single author)- 1940 -	891.438 7
Hindi miscellaneous writings (single author)- 1940-1999	891.438 71
Hindi miscellaneous writings (single author)- 2000-	891.438 72
Hindi monologues (multiple authors)	891.432045*
Hindi monologues (multiple authors)-Collections	891.43204508**
Hindi monologues (multiple authors)-	

History and criticism	891.43204509**
Hindi morality plays	***See*** Hindi religious and morality plays
Hindi mystery fiction (multiple authors)	891.4330872*
Hindi mystery fiction (multiple authors)- Collections	891.433087208**
Hindi mystery fiction (multiple authors)- History and criticism	891.433087209**
Hindi narrative poetry (multiple authors)	891.43103*
Hindi narrative poetry (multiple authors)- Collections	891.4310308**
Hindi narrative poetry (multiple authors)- History and criticism	891.4310309**
Hindi notebooks (multiple authors)	891.43803
Hindi odes (multiple authors)	891.431043*
Hindi odes (multiple authors)- Collections	891.43104308**
Hindi odes (multiple authors)- History and criticism	891.43104309**
Hindi one act plays (multiple authors)	891.432.041*
Hindi one act plays (multiple authors)- Collections	891.432.041 08**
Hindi one act plays (multiple authors)- History and criticism	891.432.041 09**
Hindi oratory (multiple authors)	***See*** Hindi public speeches
Hindi periodicals	059.9143
Hindi poetry	891.431
Hindi poetry (multiple authors) - - to 1845	***See*** Main schedule

Hindi poetry (multiple authors) - 1845-1895	891.4314+
Hindi poetry (multiple authors) - 1895-1919	891.4315+
Hindi poetry (multiple authors) - 1920-1939	891.4316+
Hindi poetry (multiple authors) - 1940-	891.4317+
Hindi poetry (multiple authors) - 1940-1999	891.43171+
Hindi poetry (multiple authors) - 19th century	891.4314+
Hindi poetry (multiple authors) - 2000-	891.43172+
Hindi poetry (multiple authors) - 20th century	891.43171+
Hindi poetry (multiple authors)- Collections	891.431008**
Hindi poetry (multiple authors)- Dictionaries etc	891.431003
Hindi poetry (multiple authors)- History and criticism	891.431009**
Hindi poetry (multiple authors)- Periodicals	891.431005
Hindi poetry (multiple authors)- Philosophy and theory	891.431001
Hindi poetry (multiple authors)- Psychological aspects	891.4310019
Hindi poetry (multiple authors)- Research	891.4310072
Hindi poetry (multiple authors)- Study and teaching	891.431007
Hindi poetry (multiple authors)- Value	891.4310013
Hindi poetry (single author)- - to 1845	***See*** Main schedule
Hindi poetry (single author)- 1845 -1895	891.431 4
Hindi poetry (single author)- 1895 - 1919	891.431 5
Hindi poetry (single author)- 1920- 1939	891.431 6

Hindi poetry (single author)- 1940 -	891.431 7
Hindi poetry (single author)- 1940-1999	891.431 71
Hindi poetry (single author)- 19th century	891.431 4
Hindi poetry (single author)- 2000-	891.431 72
Hindi poetry (single author)- 20th century	891.431 71
Hindi prose (single author)- - to 1845	***See*** Main schedule
Hindi prose (single author)- 1845 -1895	891.438 408
Hindi prose (single author)- 1895 - 1919	891.438 508
Hindi prose (single author)- 1920- 1939	891.438 608
Hindi prose (single author)- 1940 -	891.438 708
Hindi prose (single author)- 1940-1999	891.438 7108
Hindi prose (single author)- 19th century	891.438 408
Hindi prose (single author)- 2000-	891.438 7208
Hindi prose (single author)- 20th century	891.438 7108
Hindi prose literature (multiple authors)	891.43808
Hindi psychological, realistic, sociological fiction (multiple authors)	891.433083*
Hindi psychological, realistic, sociological fiction (multiple authors)- Collections	891.43308308**
Hindi psychological, realistic, sociological fiction (multiple authors)- History and criticism	891.43308309**
Hindi public discussions	***See*** Hindi debates and public discussions
Hindi public speeches (multiple authors)	891.43501*
Hindi public speeches (multiple authors)-	

Collections	891.4350108**
Hindi public speeches (multiple authors)-History and criticism	891.4350109**
Hindi quotations	***See*** Hindi anecdotes ...
Hindi realistic fiction	***See*** Hindi psychological... fiction
Hindi recitations (multiple authors)	891.435 04+
Hindi religious and morality plays (multiple authors)	891.432 051 6+
Hindi reminiscences See Hindi diaries...	
Hindi romantic fiction (multiple authors)	891.433 085*
Hindi romantic fiction (multiple authors)-Collections	891.433 085 08**
Hindi romantic fiction (multiple authors)-History and criticism	891.433 085 09**
Hindi satire	***See*** Hindi humour and satire
Hindi satirical poetry	***See*** Hindi humourous and satirical poetry
Hindi science fiction (multiple authors)	891.43308762*
Hindi science fiction (multiple authors)-Collections	891.4330876208**
Hindi science fiction (multiple authors)-History and criticism	891.4330876209**
Hindi serious drama (multiple authors)	891.432051*
Hindi short stories (multiple authors)	891.43301*

Hindi short stories (multiple authors)- Collections	891.4330108**
Hindi short stories (multiple authors)- History and criticism	891.4330109**
Hindi sociological fiction (multiple authors)	***See*** Hindi psychological ... fiction
Hindi sonnets (multiple authors)	891.431042*
Hindi sonnets (multiple authors)- Collections	891.43104208**
Hindi sonnets (multiple authors)- History and criticism	891.43104209**
Hindi speeches	891.435
Hindi speeches (multiple authors) — to 1845	***See*** Main schedule
Hindi speeches (multiple authors) - 1845-1895	891.4354+
Hindi speeches (multiple authors) - 1895-1919	891.4355+
Hindi speeches (multiple authors) - 1920-1939	891.4356+
Hindi speeches (multiple authors) -1940-	891.4357+
Hindi speeches (multiple authors) - 1940-1999	891.43571+
Hindi speeches (multiple authors) - 19th century	891.4354+
Hindi speeches (multiple authors) -2000-	891.43572+
Hindi speeches (multiple authors) - 20th century	891.43571+
Hindi speeches (multiple authors) -	

Collections	891.435008**
Hindi speeches (multiple authors) - Dictionaries etc	891.435003
Hindi speeches (multiple authors) - History and criticism	891.435009**
Hindi speeches (multiple authors) - Periodicals	891.435005
Hindi speeches (multiple authors) - Philosophy and theory	891.435001
Hindi speeches (multiple authors) - Psychological aspects	891.4350019
Hindi speeches (multiple authors) - Research	891.4350072
Hindi speeches (multiple authors) - Study and teaching	891.435007
Hindi speeches (multiple authors) -Value	891.4350013
Hindi speeches (single author)- - to 1845	***See*** Main schedule
Hindi speeches (single author)- 1845 -1895	891.435 4
Hindi speeches (single author)- 1895 - 1919	891.435 5
Hindi speeches (single author)- 1920- 1939	891.435 6
Hindi speeches (single author)- 1940 -	891.435 7
Hindi speeches (single author)- 1940-1999	891.435 71
Hindi speeches (single author)- 19th century	891.435 4
Hindi speeches (single author)- 2000-	891.435 72
Hindi speeches (single author)- 20th century	891.435 71
Hindi suspense fiction (multiple authors)	891.4330872*
Hindi suspense fiction (multiple authors)-	

Collections	891.433087208**
Hindi suspense fiction (multiple authors)- History and criticism	891.433087209**
Hindi tragedy (multiple authors)	891.4320512*
Hindi tragedy (multiple authors)- Collections	891.432051208**
Hindi tragedy (multiple authors)- History and criticism	891.432051209**
Hindi variety drama (multiple authors)	891.432057*
Hindi variety drama (multiple authors)- Collections	891.43205708**
Hindi variety drama (multiple authors)- History and criticism	891.43205709**
Hindis (People)	305.891 43
Hindis - Opinions	303.387 914 3
Hindu philosophy	181.045
Hindu schools	371.0745
Hindu sculpture	730.954
Hindu tantras	294.595
Hindu temples and shrines	294.535; 726.145
Hinduism	294.5
Hinduism- Abuse within a family	294.517 832 7
Hinduism- Adults – victims of abuse as children	294.517 832 73
Hinduism- Alms giving	294.544 6
Hinduism and communication media	294.5175
Hinduism and literature	294.5175

Hinduism and medicine	294.5175
Hinduism and psychology	294.5175
Hinduism and science	294.5175
Hinduism and technology	294.5175
Hinduism- Animism	294.521
Hinduism- Asceticism	294.544 7
Hinduism- Associations	294.565
Hinduism- Atonement	294.522
Hinduism- Attitude towards age groups	294.517 834
Hinduism- Attitude towards ethnic groups	294.517 834
Hinduism- Attitude towards language groups	294.517 834
Hinduism- Attitude towards social classes	294.517 834
Hinduism- Attitude towards the sexes	294.517 834
Hinduism- Attributes of God	294.521 12
Hinduism- Attributes of the gods	294.521 12
Hinduism- Biography	294.5092
Hinduism- Ceremonial and ritual observances	294.544 6
Hinduism- Ceremonies	294.538
Hinduism- Child abuse and neglect	294.517 832 71
Hinduism- Concordances	294.503
Hinduism- Congregations	294.565
Hinduism- Conscience	294.548
Hinduism- Contemplation	294.543
Hinduism- Conversion	294.542

Hinduism- Cosmology	294.524
Hinduism- Creation	294.524
Hinduism- Creation of humankind	294.522
Hinduism- Crime	294.517 833
Hinduism- Death	294.523
Hinduism- Deities	294.5211
Hinduism- Demons	294.521 6
Hinduism- Devotional literature	294.543 2
Hinduism- Dharma	294.548
Hinduism- Dictionaries	294.503
Hinduism- Divination	294.532
Hinduism- Divinities	294.5211
Hinduism- Doctrines	294.52
Hinduism- Ecology	294.517 836
Hinduism- Economic order	294.517 85
Hinduism- Education	294.5071
Hinduism- Emblems	294.537
Hinduism- Encyclopaedias	294.503
Hinduism- End of the world	294.523
Hinduism- Enlightenment	294.542
Hinduism- Eschatology	294.523
Hinduism- Ethics	294.548
Hinduism- Ethics of communication	294.5486 5
Hinduism- Ethics of consumption	294.5486 8
Hinduism- Ethics of leisure	294.5486 5

Hinduism- Ethics of public performances	294.5486 5
Hinduism- Ethics of recreation	294.5486 5
Hinduism- Ethics of reproduction	294.5486 6
Hinduism- Ethics of sex	294.5486 6
Hinduism- Ethics of social relations	294.5486 7
Hinduism- Evil spirits	294.521 6
Hinduism- Exercise of religious authority	294.565
Hinduism- Family ethics	294.5486 3
Hinduism- Family life	294.544 1
Hinduism- Fire	294.521 2
Hinduism- General classes of religions	294.514
Hinduism- Geography	294.5091
Hinduism- God	294.5211
Hinduism- Goddesses	294.521 14
Hinduism- Gods	294.521 13
Hinduism- Good spirits	294.521 5
Hinduism- Gurus	294.561
Hinduism- Heaven	294.523
Hinduism- Hell	294.523
Hinduism- History	294.509
Hinduism- Holy days	294.536
Hinduism- Humankind	294.522
Hinduism- Hunger	294.517 832 6
Hinduism- Images	294.521 8
Hinduism- Immortality	294.523

Hinduism- Individual observances	294.544 6
Hinduism- Institutions	294.565
Hinduism- International affairs	294.517 87
Hinduism- Inter-religious relations and attitudes	294.517
Hinduism- Karma	294.522
Hinduism- Laws and decisions	294.594
Hinduism- Leaders and organization	294.56
Hinduism- Leaders and their work (role, function, duties)	294.561
Hinduism- Mandalas	294.537
Hinduism- Mantras	294.537
Hinduism- Marriage	294.544 1
Hinduism- Meditation	294.543 5
Hinduism- Meditational literature	294.543 2
Hinduism- Miracles	294.521 17
Hinduism- Missions	294.572
Hinduism- Moral theology	294.548
Hinduism- Mysticism	294.542 2
Hinduism- Mythology and mythological foundations	294.513
Hinduism- Nature	294.521 2
Hinduism- Nuclear weapon and nuclear war	294.517 873 2
Hinduism- Objects of warship and veneration	294.521
Hinduism- Observance of restrictions and limitations	294.544 6

Hinduism- Occupational ethics	294.5486 4
Hinduism- Offerings	294.534
Hinduism- Omen	294.532
Hinduism- Oracles	294.532
Hinduism- Oral traditions	294.593
Hinduism- Orders	294.565
Hinduism- Organizations	294.565
Hinduism- Other worlds	294.523
Hinduism- Parties	294.565
Hinduism- Peace	294.517 873
Hinduism- Penances	294.534
Hinduism- Periodicals	294.505
Hinduism- Personified abstraction	294.521 4
Hinduism- Persons (male, female, etc)	294.508
Hinduism- Persons as objects of worship and veneration	294.521 3
Hinduism- Persons experiencing illness, trouble, addiction, bereavement	294.544 2
Hinduism- Philosophy and theory	294.501
Hinduism- Pilgrimages	294.5351
Hinduism- Political ethics	294.548 62
Hinduism- Politics	294.517 7
Hinduism- Population	294.517 836
Hinduism- Prayer	294.543
Hinduism- Prayer books	294.543 3

Hinduism- Priests	294.561
Hinduism- Prophecies	294.532
Hinduism- Prophecy	294.521 17
Hinduism- Providence	294.521 17
Hinduism- Public worship and other practices	294.53
Hinduism- Punishment	294.517 833
Hinduism- Punishment (Eschatology)	294.523
Hinduism- Reform movements, sources of	294.585
Hinduism- Refugees	294.517 832 8
Hinduism- Reincarnation	294.523 7
Hinduism- Relationship with communication media	294.517 5
Hinduism- Relationship with literature	294.517 5
Hinduism- Relationship with medicine	294.517 5
Hinduism- Relationship with other religions and irreligions	294.517 2
Hinduism- Relationship with psychology	294.517 5
Hinduism- Relationship with science	294.517 5
Hinduism- Relationship with secular disciplines	294.517 5
Hinduism- Relationship with technology	294.517 5
Hinduism- Religious calendar	294.536
Hinduism- Religious education	294.575
Hinduism- Religious experience	294.542
Hinduism- Religious festivals	294.536

Hinduism- Religious freedom	294.517 72
Hinduism- Religious healing	294.531
Hinduism- Religious life	294.544
Hinduism- Religious practice	294.544
Hinduism- Repentance	294.522
Hinduism- Revelation	294.521 17
Hinduism- Rewards (Eschatology)	294.523
Hinduism- Rites	294.538
Hinduism- Role in society	294.517 1
Hinduism- Sacred books	294.582
Hinduism- Sacred places	294.535
Hinduism- Sacred times	294.536
Hinduism- Sacrifices	294.534
Hinduism- Salvation	294.522
Hinduism- Scriptures	294.582
Hinduism- Sects and reform movements	294.55
Hinduism- Sex	294.521 2
Hinduism- Sexual abuse	294.517 832 72
Hinduism- Sexual relations, marriage, divorce and family	294.517 835
Hinduism- Sin	294.522
Hinduism- Sin (Moral theology)	294.548
Hinduism- Social problems	294.517 83
Hinduism- Social theology	294.517
Hinduism- Social welfare problems	294.517 832

Hinduism- Social welfare services	294.517 832
Hinduism- Socioeconomic problems	294.517 8
Hinduism- Soul	294.522
Hinduism- Sounds	294.537
Hinduism- Sources	294.59
Hinduism- Sources of sects and reform movement	294.595
Hinduism- Specific moral issues	294.5486
Hinduism- Specific sins	294.5486
Hinduism- Specific vices	294.5486
Hinduism- Specific virtues	294.5486
Hinduism- Spiritism	294.521
Hinduism- Spirituality	294.54
Hinduism- Sun	294.521 2
Hinduism- Symbolic objects	294.537
Hinduism- Symbolism	294.537
Hinduism- Theocracy	294.517 73
Hinduism- Theodicy	294.521 18
Hinduism- Theory	294.501
Hinduism- Trees	294.521 2
Hinduism- Vice	294.548
Hinduism- Victims of political oppression	294.517 832 8
Hinduism- Virtue	294.548
Hinduism- War	294.517 873
Hinduism- Water	294.521 2

Hinduism- Witchcraft	294.533
Hinduism- World (miracles, prophecy, providence, revelation)	294.521 17
Hinduism- Worship	294.543
Hinduism- Yoga	294.543 6
Hinduism as an academic subject	294.5071
Hindus	305.6945
Hindus - Opinions	303.388 294 5
Hindustani music	780.954
History – Ancient India	954.01 or 934
History - Andaman and Nicobar Islands	954.88
History - Andhra Pradesh	954.84
History - Arunachal Pradesh	954.16 3
History - Assam	954.16 2
History - Bengal	954.14
History - Bhopal	954.3
History - Bihar	954.12
History - Bombay	954.79 23
History - Calcutta	954.14 7
History - Chandigarh	954.55 2
History - Chhatisgarh	954.13 7
History - Dadra and Nagar Haveli	954.79 6
History - Delhi	954.56
History - Goa, Daman and Diu	954.79 9
History - Gujarat	954.75

History - Haryana	954.55 8
History - Himachal Pradesh	954.52
History - Hyderabad state	954.84
History – India	954
History – India - - to 647	954.01
History – India – 647-1785	954.02
History – India – 647-997	954.021
History – India – 997-1196	954.022 3
History – India – 997-1206 (Period of Muslim conquests)	954.022
History – India – 1196-1206	954.022 5
History – India – 1206-1290 (Period of Slave kings of Delhi)	954.023 2
History – India – 1206-1414	954.023
History – India – 1290-1320	954.023 4
History – India – 1414-1451	954.024 2
History – India – 1414-1526	954.024
History – India – 1451 – 1526	954.024 5
History – India – 1526 – 1530	954.025 2
History – India – 1526-1707	954.025
History – India – 1530 –1556	954.025 3
History – India – 1556-1605	954.025 4
History – India – 1605-1627	954.025 6
History – India – 1628-1658	954.025 7
History – India – 1658-1707	954.025 8

History – India – 16th century	954.025 4
History – India – 1707 –1744	954.029 2
History – India - 1707 –1785 (Period of European penetration)	954.029
History – India – 1744 – 1757 (Period of Anglo-French conflict)	954.029 4
History – India – 1757-1772	954.029 6
History – India – 1772 –1785	954.029 8
History – India – 1785 –1947	954.03
History – India – 1785-1798	954.031 1
History – India – 1785-1858	954.031
History – India – 1798-1807	954.031 2
History – India – 17th century	954.025 8
History – India – 1807-1828	954.031 3
History – India – 1828-1842	954.031 4
History – India – 1842-1848	954.031 5
History – India – 1848-1856	954.031 6
History – India – 1856-1862	954.031 7
History – India - 1858-1868	954.035 1
History – India – 1858-1947 (Period of control by Crown)	954.035
History – India – 1869-1876	954.035 2
History – India - 1876-1884	954.035 3
History – India – 1884-1894	954.035 4
History – India - 1894-1905	954.035 5
History – India – 18th century	954.029

History – India – 1905-1916	954.035 6
History – India – 1916-1926	954.035 7
History – India – 1926-1936	954.035 8
History – India – 1936-1947	954.035 9
History – India – 1947-1971	954.04
History – India – 1971-	954.05
History – India – 1977-	954.052
History – India – 19th century	954.031
History – India – 20th century	954.035
History – India – Akbar's reign	954.025 4
History – India – Anglo-French conflict	954.029 4
History – India – Atal Vihari Vajpayee's regime	954.052
History – India – Aurangzeb's reign	954.025 8
History – India - Babur's reign	954.025 2
History – India - Baron Hardinge's governorship	954.035 6
History – India - Baron Lawrence's governorship	954.035 1
History – India - Baron Metcalfe's governorship	954.031 4
History – India – Battle of Plassey 1757	954.029 4
History – India – British period	954.03
History – India – Chandra Shekhar's regime	954.052
History – India – Charan Singh's regime	954.052
History – India – Civil Disobedience	

Movement	954.035 7
History – India - Dandi March 1930	954.035 8
History – India - Earl (1st) of Minto's governorship	954.031 3
History – India - Earl (4th) of Minto's governorship	954.035 6
History – India - Earl (8th) of Elgin's governorship	954.035 1
History – India - Earl (9th) of Elgin's governorship	954.035 5
History – India - Earl Amherst's governorship	954.031 3
History – India - Earl Canning's governorship	954.031 7
History – India - Earl Mountbatten's governorship	954.035 9
History – India - Earl of Allenborough's governorship	954.031 5
History – India - Earl of Auckland's governorship	954.031 4
History – India - Earl of Halifax's governorship	954.035 8
History – India - Earl of Lyton's governorship	954.035 3
History – India - Earl of Mayo's governorship	954.035 2
History – India - Earl of Northbrook's governorship	954.035 2
History – India - Earl of Wavell's governorship	954.035 9

History – India – East India Company's rule	954.031
History – India – Freedom struggle	954.035
History – India – Ghazni dynasty	954.022 3
History – India – Ghor dynasty	954.022 5
History – India – Humayun's reign	954.025 3
History – India – Indira Gandhi's regime	954.045
History – India – Indo-Chinese War	954.042
History – India - Jahangir's reign	954.025 6
History – India - Jalianwallabagh massacre	954.035 7
History – India – Jawaharlal Nehru's regime	954.042
History – India - John Shore's governorship	954.031 1
History – India – Khalji dynasty	954.023 4
History – India – Khilafat movement	954.035 7
History – India – Lal Bahadur Shastri's regime	954.043
History – India – Lodi dynasty	954.024 5
History – India - Lord Bentinck's governorship	954.031 4
History – India - Lord Clive's governorship	954.029 6
History – India - Lord Teignmouth's governorship	954.031 1
History – India – Manmohan Singh's regime	954.052
History – India - Marquess Cornwallis's governorship	954.031 2
History – India - Marquess of Hastings's governorship	954.031 3

History – India – Marquess of Lansdowne's governorship	954.035 4
History – India – Marquess of Linlithgow's governorship	954.035 9
History – India - Marquess of Reading's governorship	954.035 7
History – India - Marquess of Ripon's governorship	954.035 3
History – India - Marquess of Willingdon's governorship	954.035 8
History – India - Marquess Wellesley's governorship	954.031 2
History – India - Marquis Cornwallis's governorship	954.031 1
History – India - Marquis of Curzon's governorship	954.035 5
History – India - Marquis of Dalhousie's governorship	954.031 6
History – India – Marquis of Dufferin's governorship	954.035 4
History – India – Mogul period	954.025
History – India – Moplah rebellion in Malabar	954.035 7
History – India – Morarji Desai's regime	954.052
History – India – National movement	954.035
History – India – P V Narasimha Rao's regime	954.052
History – India – Quit India Movement	954.035 9
History – India – Rajiv Gandhi's regime	954.052

History – India - Sayyid dynasty	954.024 2
History – India – Sepoy Mutiny	954.031 7
History – India - Shahjahan's reign	954.025.7
History – India - Sher Shah's reign	954.025 3
History – India – Sir George Barlow's governorship	954.031 2
History – India – Sir John Macpherson's governorship	954.031 1
History – India – V P Singh's regime	954.052
History – India - Viscount Chemsford's governorship	954.035 7
History – India - Viscout Hardinge's governorship	954.031 5
History – India – Warren Hastings's governorship	954.029 8
History – Indo– Chinese War 1965	954.042
History – Indo– Pakistan War 1965	954.043
History – Indo– Pakistan War 1971	954.051
History - Jammu and Kashmir	954.6
History - Jharkhand	954.127
History - Karnataka	954.87
History - Kerala	954.83
History - Lakshwadweep	954.81
History - Madhya Pradesh	954.3
History - Madras	954.82
History - Maharashtra	954.79 2

History - Manipur	954.17
History - Meghalaya	954.16 4
History - Mizoram	954.16 6
History - Nagaland	954.16 5
History - Northeast India	954.1
History - Orissa	954.13
History - Pondicherry	954.86
History - Punjab	954.55 2
History - Rajasthan	954.4
History - Sikkim	954.16 7
History - South Asia	954.
History - Southern India	954.8
History - Tamil Nadu	954.82
History - Tripura	954.15
History - Uttar Pradesh	954.2
History - Uttaranchal	954.51
History - West Bengal	954.14
History - Western India	954.7
History (Buddhism)	294.309
History (Hinduism)	294.509
History (Jainism)	294.409
History (Sikhism)	294.609
Holy days (Buddhism)	294.343 6
Holy days (Hinduism)	294.536
Holy days (Jainism)	294.436

Holy days (Sikhism)	294.636
Humankind (Buddhism)	294.342 2
Humankind (Hinduism)	294.522
Humankind (Jainism)	294.422
Humankind (Sikhism)	294.622
Hunger (Buddhism)	294.337 83 26
Hunger (Hinduism)	294.517 832 6
Hunger (Jainism)	294.417 832 6
Hunger (Sikhism)	294.617 832 6
Hyderabad state- Architecture	720.954 84
Hyderabad state- Botany	580.954 84
Hyderabad state- Fauna	591.954 84
Hyderabad state- Fine and decorative arts	709.5484
Hyderabad state- Flora	581.954 84
Hyderabad state- Folk dancing	793.319 5484
Hyderabad state- Galleries of fine and decorative arts	708.954 84
Hyderabad state- Geography	915.484
Hyderabad state- Geology	555.484
Hyderabad state- History	954.84
Hyderabad state- Museums of fine and decorative arts	708.954 84
Hyderabad state- Painting and paintings	759.954 84
Hyderabad state- Public administration	351.548 4
Hyderabad state- Public finance	336.548 4
Hyderabad state- Sculpture	730.954 84

I

Images (Buddhism)	294.342 18
Images (Hinduism)	294.521 8
Images (Jainism)	294.421 8
Images (Sikhism)	294.621 8
Immortality (Buddhism)	294.342 3
Immortality (Hinduism)	294.523
Immortality (Jainism)	294.423
Immortality (Sikhism)	294.623
India - a reference annual	*030.954*
India- Architecture	720.954
India- Botany	580.954
India- Budget	352.495 4
India- Caricatures collection	741.5954
India- Carpets	746.754
India- Cartoons collection	741.5954
India- Comics collection	741.5954
India- Economic development	338.954
India- Economic geography	330.954

India- Education	370.954
India- Fauna	591.954
India- Fine and decorative arts	709.54
India- Flora	581.954
India- Folk dancing	793.319 54
India- Furniture and furniture makers	749.2954
India- Galleries of fine and decorative arts	708.954
India- Geography	915.4
India- Geology	555.4
India- Glassware and glassmakers	748.29954
India- Gross national product	339.354
India- History	***See*** History- India
India- Museums of fine and decorative arts	708.954
India- National dances	793.319 54
India- Painting and paintings	759.954
India- Printmaking	769.954
India- Public administration	351.54
India- Public finance	336.54
India- Rugs	746.754
India- Sculpture	730.954
India- Stained, painted, leaded, mosaic glass and glass makers	748.59954
Indian architecture, Ancient	722.44
Indian folk music. Anglo-Indian folk music	781 629 1411
Indian National Bibliography. Indian	

Books in Print	015.54
Indian sculpture, Ancient	732.44
Indians	305.891 411
Indians - Opinions	303.387 914 11
Indic languages	491.1
Indic literatures	891.1
Indic people	305.891 4
Indic philosophy (both ancient and modern)	181.4
Individual observances (Buddhism).	294.344 46
Individual observances (Hinduism)	294.544 6
Individual observances (Jainism)	294.444 6
Individual observances (Sikhism)	294.644 6
Indo-Aryans	305.891 4
Indo-Iranian languages	491.1
Indo-Iranian literatures	891.1
Indology	954
Initiative and referendum in India	328.254
Institutions (Buddhism)	294.365
Institutions (Hinduism)	294.565
Institutions (Jainism)	294.465
Institutions (Sikhism)	294.665
Insurance- India	368.954
International affairs (Buddhism)	294.337 87
International affairs (Hinduism)	294.517 87
International affairs (Jainism)	294.417 87

International affairs (Sikhism)	294.617 87
International assistance (aid) by UK	338.9141
International assistance (aid) by UK to India	338.9141054
International commerce of India	382.0954
International law- cases brought by India	341.026 854
International relation between India and Australia	327.54094
International relation between India and Bangladesh	327.5405492
International relation between India and Bhutan	327.5405498
International relation between India and Canada	327.54071
International relation between India and China	327.54051
International relation between India and Developed countries	327.5401722
International relation between India and Developing countries	327.5401724
International relation between India and England	327.54042
International relation between India and European countries	327.5404
International relation between India and Indonesia	327.540598
International relation between India and Japan	327.54052
International relation between India and Malaysia	327.540595

International relation between India and Maldives	327.5405495
International relation between India and Middle East	327.54056
International relation between India and Myanmar	327.540591
International relation between India and Nepal	327.5405496
International relation between India and Pakistan	327.5405491
International relation between India and Russia	327.54047
International relation between India and Singapore	327.5405957
International relation between India and Sri Lanka	327.5405493
International relation between India and Thailand	327.540593
International relation between India and UK	327.54041
International relation between India and USA	327.54073
International society for Krishna consciousness	294.551 2
Inter-religious relations and attitudes (Buddhism)	294.337
Inter-religious relations and attitudes (Hinduism)	294.517
Inter-religious relations and attitudes (Jainism)	294.417
Inter-religious relations and attitudes (Sikhism)	294.617

J

Jails	*See* Prisons
Jain sculpture	730.954
Jain schools	371.0744
Jain temples and shrines	726.144
Jainism	294.4
Jainism - Abuse within a family	294.417 832 7
Jainism - Adults – victims of abuse as children	294.417 832 73
Jainism - Alms giving	294.444 6
Jainism - Ancestors	294.421 3
Jainism - Animism	294.421
Jainism - Asceticism	294.444 7
Jainism - Associations	294.465
Jainism - Atonement	294.422
Jainism - Attitude towards age groups	294.417 834
Jainism - Attitude towards ethnic groups	294.417 834
Jainism - Attitude towards language groups	294.417 834
Jainism - Attitude towards social classes	294.417 834
Jainism - Attitude towards the sexes	294.417 834

Jainism - Attributes of God	294.421 12
Jainism - Attributes of the gods	294.421 12
Jainism - Biography	294.4092
Jainism - Ceremonial and ritual observances	294.444 6
Jainism - Ceremonies	294.438
Jainism - Child abuse and neglect	294.417 832 71
Jainism - Concordances	294.403
Jainism - Congregations	294.465
Jainism - Conscience	294.45
Jainism - Contemplation	294.443
Jainism - Conversion	294.442
Jainism - Cosmology	294.424
Jainism - Creation	294.424
Jainism - Creation of humankind	294.422
Jainism - Crime	294.417 833
Jainism – Dead persons	294.421 3
Jainism - Death	294.423
Jainism - Deities	294.4211
Jainism - Devotional literature	294.443 2
Jainism - Dictionaries	294.403
Jainism - Divination	294.432
Jainism - Divinities	294.4211
Jainism - Doctrines	294.42
Jainism - Ecology	294.417 836
Jainism - Economic order	294.417 85

Jainism - Education	294.4071
Jainism - Emblems	294.437
Jainism - Encyclopaedias	294.403
Jainism - End of the world	294.423
Jainism - Enlightenment	294.442
Jainism - Eschatology	294.423
Jainism - Ethics	294.45
Jainism - Ethics of communication	294.456 5
Jainism - Ethics of consumption	294.456 8
Jainism - Ethics of leisure	294.456 5
Jainism - Ethics of public performances	294.456 5
Jainism - Ethics of recreation	294.456 5
Jainism - Ethics of reproduction	294.456 6
Jainism - Ethics of sex	294.456 6
Jainism - Ethics of social relations	294.456 7
Jainism - Evil spirits	294.421 6
Jainism - Exercise of religious authority	294.465
Jainism - Family ethics	294.456 3
Jainism - Family life	294.444 1
Jainism - Fire	294.421 2
Jainism - Founders	294.463
Jainism - General classes of religions	294.414
Jainism - Geography	294.4091
Jainism - God	294.4211
Jainism - Goddesses	294.421 14

Jainism - Gods	294.421 13
Jainism - Good spirits	294.421 5
Jainism - Gurus	294.461
Jainism - Heaven	294.423
Jainism - Hell	294.423
Jainism - Heroes	294.421 3
Jainism - History	294.409
Jainism - Holy days	294.436
Jainism - Humankind	294.422
Jainism - Hunger	294.417 832 6
Jainism - Images	294.421 8
Jainism - Immortality	294.423
Jainism - Individual observances	294.444 6
Jainism - Institutions	294.465
Jainism - International affairs	294.417 87
Jainism – Inter-religious relations and attitudes	294.417
Jainism - Karma	294.422
Jainism - Laws and decisions	294.484
Jainism - Leaders and organization	294.46
Jainism - Leaders and their work (role, function, duties)	294.461
Jainism - Mantras	294.437
Jainism - Marriage	294.444 1
Jainism - Meditation	294.443 5

Jainism - Meditation literature	294.443 2
Jainism - Miracles	294.421 17
Jainism - Missions	294.472
Jainism - Monarchs	294.421 3
Jainism - Moral theology	294.45
Jainism - Mysticism	294.442 2
Jainism - Mythology and mythological foundations	294.413
Jainism - Nature	294.421 2
Jainism - Nuclear weapon and nuclear war	294.417 873 2
Jainism - Objects of warship and veneration	294.421
Jainism - Observance of restrictions and limitations	294.444 6
Jainism - Occupational ethics	294.456 4
Jainism - Offerings	294.434
Jainism - Omen	294.432
Jainism - Oracles	294.432
Jainism - Oral traditions	294.483
Jainism - Orders	294.465
Jainism - Organizations	294.465
Jainism - Other worlds	294.423
Jainism - Parties	294.465
Jainism - Peace	294.417 873
Jainism - Penances	294.434
Jainism - Periodicals	294.405

Jainism - Relationship with other religions and irreligions	294.417 2
Jainism - Relationship with psychology	294.417 5
Jainism - Relationship with science	294.417 5
Jainism - Relationship with secular disciplines	294.417 5
Jainism - Relationship with technology	294.417 5
Jainism - Religious calendar	294.436
Jainism - Religious education	294.475
Jainism - Religious experience	294.442
Jainism - Religious festivals	294.436
Jainism - Religious freedom	294.417 72
Jainism - Religious healing	294.431
Jainism - Religious life	294.444
Jainism - Religious practice	294.444
Jainism - Repentance	294.422
Jainism - Rewards (Eschatology)	294.423
Jainism - Rites	294.438
Jainism - Role in society	294.417 1
Jainism - Sacred books	294.482
Jainism - Sacred places	294.435
Jainism - Sacred times	294.436
Jainism - Sacrifices	294.434
Jainism - Saints	294.421 3
Jainism - Salvation	294.422

Jainism - Scriptures	294.482
Jainism - Sects and reform movements	294.49
Jainism - Sex	294.421 2
Jainism - Sexual abuse	294.417 832 72
Jainism - Sexual relations, marriage, divorce and family	294.417 835
Jainism - Sin	294.422
Jainism - Sin (Moral theology)	294.45
Jainism - Social problems	294.417 83
Jainism - Social theology	294.417
Jainism - Social welfare problems	294.417 832
Jainism - Social welfare services	294.417 832
Jainism - Socioeconomic problems	294.417 8
Jainism - Soul	294.422
Jainism - Sounds	294.437
Jainism - Sources	294.48
Jainism - Sources of sects	294.485
Jainism - Specific moral issues	294.456
Jainism - Specific sins	294.456
Jainism - Specific vices	294.456
Jainism - Specific virtues	294.456
Jainism - Spiritism	294.421
Jainism - Sun	294.421 2
Jainism - Symbolic objects	294.437
Jainism - Symbolism	294.437

Jainism - Theocracy	294.417 73
Jainism - Theodicy	294.421 18
Jainism - Theory	294.401
Jainism - Trees	294.421 2
Jainism - Vice	294.45
Jainism - Victims of political oppression	294.417 832 8
Jainism - Virtue	294.45
Jainism - War	294.417 873
Jainism - Water	294.421 2
Jainism - World (miracles, prophecy, providence, revelation)	294.421 17
Jainism - Worship	294.443
Jainism - Yoga	294.443 6
Jainism and communication media	294.4175
Jainism and literature	294.4175
Jainism and medicine	294.4175
Jainism and science	294.4175
Jainism and technology	294.4175
Jainist philosophy	181.044
Jains	305.6944
Jains - Opinions	303.388 294 4
Jammu and Kashmir- Architecture	720.954 6
Jammu and Kashmir- Botany	580.954 6
Jammu and Kashmir- Budget	352.495 46
Jammu and Kashmir- Economic	

Jharkhand- Painting and paintings	759.954 127
Jharkhand- Public administration	351.541 27
Jharkhand- Public finance	336.541 27
Jharkhand- Zoogeography	591.954 127
Jnana Yoga	294.543 6
Journalism - Andaman and Nicobar Islands	079.5488
Journalism - Andhra Pradesh	079.5484
Journalism - Arunachal Pradesh	079.54163
Journalism - Assam	079.54162
Journalism - Bihar	079.5412
Journalism - Chhattisgarh	079.54137
Journalism - Delhi	079.5456
Journalism - Goa, Daman and Diu	079.54799
Journalism - Gujarat	079.5475
Journalism - Haryana	079.54558
Journalism - Himachal Pradesh	079.5452
Journalism - India	079.54
Journalism - Jammu and Kashmir	079.546
Journalism - Jharkhand	079.54127
Journalism - Karnataka	079.5487
Journalism - Kerala	079.5483
Journalism - Lakshwadweep	079.5481
Journalism - Madhya Pradesh	079.543
Journalism - Maharashtra	079.54792
Journalism - Manipur	079.5417

Journalism - Meghalaya	079.54164
Journalism - Mizoram	079.54166
Journalism - Nagaland	079.54165
Journalism - Northeast India	079.541
Journalism - Orissa	079.5413
Journalism - Pondicherry	079.5486
Journalism - Punjab	079.54552
Journalism - Rajasthan	079.544
Journalism - Southern India	079.548
Journalism - Tamil Nadu	079.5482
Journalism - Tripura	079.5415
Journalism - Uttar Pradesh	079.542
Journalism - Uttaranchal	079.545 1
Journalism - West Bengal	079.5414
Journalism - Western India	079.547

K

Kafiri languages	491.49
Kafiri literatures	891.49
Kanarese (People)	305.894 814
Kanarese - Opinions	303.387 948 14
Kanarese as second language in elementary education	372.659 481 4
Kanarese folk music	781 629 4814
Kanarese speaking people	305.794 814
Kandh (People)	305.894 82
Kandh language	***See*** Khond language
Kannad speaking people	305.794 814
Kannada - English dictionary	494.814 321
Kannada adventure fiction (multiple authors)	894.8143087*
Kannada adventure fiction (multiple authors) -Collections	894.814308708**
Kannada adventure fiction (multiple authors)- History and criticism	894.814308709**
Kannada anecdotes, epigrams, graffiti, jokes, quotations (multiple authors)	894.814802

Kannada anecdotes, epigrams, graffiti, jokes, quotations (single author)	894.8148 +CD+02
Kannada as second language in elementary education	372.659 481 4
Kannada ballads (multiple authors)	894.8141044*
Kannada ballads (multiple authors)- Collections	894.814104408**
Kannada ballads (multiple authors)- History and criticism	894.814104409**
Kannada comedy (multiple authors)	894.81420523*
Kannada comedy (multiple authors) - Collections	894.8142052308**
Kannada comedy (multiple authors) - History and criticism	894.8142052309**
Kannada conversations (multiple authors)	894.814506*
Kannada conversations (multiple authors) - Collections	894.81450608**
Kannada conversations (multiple authors) - History and criticism	894.81450609**
Kannada debates and public discussions (multiple authors)	894.814503*
Kannada debates and public discussions (multiple authors)- Collections	894.81450308**
Kannada debates and public discussions (multiple authors)- History and criticism	894.81450309**
Kannada detective fiction (multiple authors)	894.81430872*
Kannada detective fiction (multiple authors) - Collections	894.8143087208**
Kannada detective fiction (multiple	

authors) - History and criticism	894.8143087209**
Kannada diaries, notebooks, reminiscences (multiple authors)	894.814 803
Kannada diaries, notebooks, reminiscences (single author)	894.814 8@
Kannada didactic poetry (multiple authors)	894.814105*
Kannada didactic poetry (multiple authors)- Collections	894.81410508**
Kannada didactic poetry (multiple authors)- History and criticism	894.81410509**
Kannada drama	894.8142
Kannada drama (multiple authors) - - to 1845	***See*** Main schedule
Kannada drama (multiple authors) - 1845-1895	894.81424+
Kannada drama (multiple authors) - 1895-1919	894.81425+
Kannada drama (multiple authors) - 1920-1939	894.81426+
Kannada drama (multiple authors) - 1940-	894.81427+
Kannada drama (multiple authors) - 1940-1999	894.814271+
Kannada drama (multiple authors) - 19th century	894.81424+
Kannada drama (multiple authors) - 2000-	894.814272+
Kannada drama (multiple authors) - 20th century	894.814271+
Kannada drama (multiple authors) – 21st century	894.814272+

Kannada drama (multiple authors) - Collections	894.8142008**
Kannada drama (multiple authors) - Dictionaries etc	894.8142003
Kannada drama (multiple authors) - History and criticism	894.8142009**
Kannada drama (multiple authors) - Periodicals	894.8142005
Kannada drama (multiple authors) - Philosophy and theory	894.8142001
Kannada drama (multiple authors) - Psychological aspects	894.81420019
Kannada drama (multiple authors) - Research	894.81420072
Kannada drama (multiple authors) - Study and teaching	894.8142007
Kannada drama (multiple authors) - Value	894.81420013
Kannada drama (single author) - to 1845	***See*** Main schedule
Kannada drama (single author)- 1845 -1895	894.8142 4
Kannada drama (single author)- 1895 - 1919	894.8142 5
Kannada drama (single author)- 1920- 1939	894.8142 6
Kannada drama (single author)- 1940 -	894.8142 7
Kannada drama (single author)- 1940-1999	894.8142 71
Kannada drama (single author)- 19th century	894.8142 4
Kannada drama (single author)- 2000-	894.8142 72
Kannada drama (single author)- 20th century	894.8142 71
Kannada drama for cinema (multiple authors)	894.814203*

Kannada drama for cinema (multiple authors) - Collections	894.81420308**
Kannada drama for cinema (multiple authors) - History and criticism	894.81420309**
Kannada drama for radio (multiple authors)	894.8142022*
Kannada drama for radio (multiple authors) - History and criticism	894.814202209**
Kannada drama for radio (multiple authors) - Collections	894.814202208**
Kannada drama for television (multiple authors)	894.8142025*
Kannada drama for television (multiple authors) - Collections	894.814202508**
Kannada drama for television (multiple authors) - History and criticism	894.814202509**
Kannada dramatic poetry (multiple authors)	894.814102*
Kannada dramatic poetry (multiple authors)- Collections	894.81410208**
Kannada dramatic poetry (multiple authors)- History and criticism	894.81410209**
Kannada encyclopaedias	039.94814
Kannada ephemeral and light verse (multiple authors)	894.814108*
Kannada ephemeral and light verse (multiple authors)- Collections	894.81410808**
Kannada ephemeral and light verse (multiple authors) - History and criticism	894.81410809**
Kannada epic poetry (multiple authors)	894.8141032*
Kannada epic poetry (multiple authors)-	

Collections	894.814103208**
Kannada epic poetry (multiple authors)-History and criticism	894.814103209**
Kannada epigrams	*See* Kannadaanecdotes
Kannada essays	894.8144
Kannada essays (multiple authors) - - to 1845	*See* Main schedule
Kannada essays (multiple authors) - 1845-1895	894.81444+
Kannada essays (multiple authors) - 1895-1919	894.81445+
Kannada essays (multiple authors) - 1920-1939	894.81446+
Kannada essays (multiple authors) -1940-	894.81447+
Kannada essays (multiple authors) - 1940-1999	894.814471+
Kannada essays (multiple authors) - 19th century	894.81444+
Kannada essays (multiple authors) -2000-	894.814472+
Kannada essays (multiple authors) - 20th century	894.814471+
Kannada essays (multiple authors) - Collections	894.8144008**
Kannada essays (multiple authors) - Dictionaries etc	894.8144003
Kannada essays (multiple authors) - History and criticism	894.8144009**
Kannada essays (multiple authors) -	

Periodicals	894.8144005
Kannada essays (multiple authors) - Philosophy and theory	894.8144001
Kannada essays (multiple authors) - Psychological aspects	894.81440019
Kannada essays (multiple authors) - Research	894.81440072
Kannada essays (multiple authors) - Study and teaching	894.8144007
Kannada essays (multiple authors) -Value	894.81440013
Kannada essays (single author)- - to 1845	***See*** Main Schedule
Kannada essays (single author)- 1845 -1895	894.8144 4
Kannada essays (single author)- 1895 - 1919	894.8144 5
Kannada essays (single author)- 1920- 1939	894.8144 6
Kannada essays (single author)- 1940 -	894.8144 7
Kannada essays (single author)- 1940-1999	894.8144 71
Kannada essays (single author)- 19th century	894.8144 4
Kannada essays (single author)- 2000-	894.8144 72
Kannada essays (single author)- 20th century	894.8144 71
Kannada experimental and non-formalized works (multiple authors)	894.814807
Kannada experimental and non-formalized works (single author)	894.8148
Kannada fantasy fiction (multiple authors)	894.814308766*
Kannada fantasy fiction (multiple authors)-	

Collections	894.81430876608**
Kannada fantasy fiction (multiple authors)- History and criticism	894.81430876609**
Kannada farce (multiple authors)	894.814205232*
Kannada farce (multiple authors) - History and criticism	894.81420523209**
Kannada farce (multiple authors)- Collections	894.81420523208**
Kannada fiction	894.8143
Kannada fiction (multiple authors) - to 1845	***See*** Main schedule
Kannada fiction (multiple authors) - 1845-1895	894.81434+
Kannada fiction (multiple authors) - 1895-1919	894.81435+
Kannada fiction (multiple authors) - 1920-1939	894.81436+
Kannada fiction (multiple authors) - 1940-	894.81437+
Kannada fiction (multiple authors) - 1940-1999	894.814371+
Kannada fiction (multiple authors) - 19th century	894.81434+
Kannada fiction (multiple authors) - 2000-	894.814372+
Kannada fiction (multiple authors) - 20th century	894.814371+
Kannada fiction (multiple authors) – 21st century	894.814372+
Kannada fiction (multiple authors) - Collections	894.8143008**

Kannada fiction (multiple authors) - Dictionaries etc	894.8143003
Kannada fiction (multiple authors) - History and criticism	894.8143009**
Kannada fiction (multiple authors) - Periodicals	894.8143005
Kannada fiction (multiple authors) - Philosophy and theory	894.8143001
Kannada fiction (multiple authors) - Psychological aspects	894.81430019
Kannada fiction (multiple authors) - Research	894.81430072
Kannada fiction (multiple authors) - Study and teaching	894.8143007
Kannada fiction (multiple authors) - Value	894.81430013
Kannada fiction (single author)- - to 1845	***See*** Main schedule
Kannada fiction (single author)- 1845 -1895	894.8143 4
Kannada fiction (single author)- 1895 - 1919	894.8143 5
Kannada fiction (single author)- 1920- 1939	894.8143 6
Kannada fiction (single author)- 1940 -	894.8143 7
Kannada fiction (single author)- 1940-1999	894.8143 71
Kannada fiction (single author)- 19th century	894.8143 4
Kannada fiction (single author)- 2000-	894.8143 72
Kannada fiction (single author)- 20th century	894.8143 71
Kannada ghost fiction (multiple authors)	894.814308733*
Kannada ghost fiction (multiple authors)- Collections	894.81430873308**

Kannada ghost fiction (multiple authors)- History and criticism	894.81430873309**
Kannada graffiti	***See*** Kannada anecdotes ...
Kannada historical drama (multiple authors)	894.81420514*
Kannada historical drama (multiple authors)- Collections	894.8142051408**
Kannada historical drama (multiple authors)- History and criticism	894.8142051409**
Kannada historical fiction (multiple authors)	894.8143081*
Kannada historical fiction (multiple authors)- Collections	894.814308108**
Kannada historical fiction (multiple authors)- History and criticism	894.814308109**
Kannada horror fiction (multiple authors)	894.814308738*
Kannada horror fiction (multiple authors)- Collections	894.81430873808**
Kannada horror fiction (multiple authors)- History and criticism	894.81430873809**
Kannada humour and satire	894.8147
Kannada humour and satire (multiple authors) — to 1845	***See*** Main schedule
Kannada humour and satire (multiple authors) -1845-1895	894.81474+
Kannada humour and satire (multiple authors) -1895-1919	894.81475+
Kannada humour and satire (multiple authors) -1920-1939	894.81476+
Kannada humour and satire (multiple	

authors) -1940-	894.81477+
Kannada humour and satire (multiple authors) -1940-1999	894.814771+
Kannada humour and satire (multiple authors) -19th century	894.81474+
Kannada humour and satire (multiple authors) –2000-	894.814772+
Kannada humour and satire (multiple authors) -20th century	894.814771+
Kannada humour and satire (multiple authors) -Collections	894.8147008**
Kannada humour and satire (multiple authors) -Dictionaries etc	894.8147003
Kannada humour and satire (multiple authors) -History and criticism	894.8147009**
Kannada humour and satire (multiple authors) -Periodicals	894.8147005
Kannada humour and satire (multiple authors) -Philosophy and theory	894.8147001
Kannada humour and satire (multiple authors) -Psychological aspects	894.81470019
Kannada humour and satire (multiple authors) -Research	894.81470072
Kannada humour and satire (multiple authors) -Study and teaching	894.8147007
Kannada humour and satire (multiple authors) -Value	894.81470013
Kannada humourous and satirical poetry (multiple authors)	894.814107*
Kannada humourous and satirical poetry	

(multiple authors)- Collections	894.81410708**
Kannada humourous and satirical poetry (multiple authors)- History and criticism	894.81410709**
Kannada jokes	***See*** Kannada anecdotes ...
Kannada language	494.814
Kannada language- Applied linguistics	494.8148
Kannada language- Bilingual dictionaries	494.81432-39
Kannada language- Bilingualism	494.8140 42
Kannada language- Concordances	494.8140 3
Kannada language- Content analysis	494.8140 141
Kannada language- Dialects	494.8147
Kannada language- Dictionaries	494.8143
Kannada language- Discourse analysis	494.8140 141
Kannada language- Education	494.8140 71
Kannada language- Encyclopaedias	494.8140 3
Kannada language- Etymology	494.8142
Kannada language- Functionalism	494.8140 18
Kannada language- Grammar	494.8145
Kannada language- History	494.8140 9
Kannada language- Intonation	494.8141 6
Kannada language- Lexicography	494.8143 028
Kannada language- Lexicology	494.8140 14
Kannada language- Miscellany	494.8140 2
Kannada language- Multilingualism	494.8140 42

Kannada language- Organizations	494.8140 6
Kannada language- Orthography	494.8141 52
Kannada language- Pauses	494.8141 6
Kannada language- Periodicals	494.8140 5
Kannada language- Persons (men, women, etc)	494.8140 8
Kannada language- Philosophy and theory	494.8140 1
Kannada language- Phonetics	494.8141 58
Kannada language- Phonology	494.8141 5
Kannada language- Pitch	494.8141 6
Kannada language- Pronunciation	494.8141 52
Kannada language- Readers	494.814 86
Kannada language- Research	494.814 072
Kannada language- Rhetoric	808.049 4814++
Kannada language- Schools and theories of linguistics	494.8140 18
Kannada language- Semantics	494.8140 143
Kannada language- Semiotics	494.8140 141
Kannada language- Slang	494.8147
Kannada language- Special topics	494.8140 4
Kannada language- Specialized dictionaries	494.81431
Kannada language- Spelling	494.8141 52
Kannada language- Stress	494.8141 6
Kannada language- Structural linguistics	494.8140 18
Kannada language- Suprasegmental features	494.8141 6

Kannada language- Terminology	494.8140 14
Kannada language- Usage	494.8148
Kannada language- Variations (Dialects etc)	494.8147
Kannada language- Writing systems	494.8141 1
Kannada letters	894.8146
Kannada letters (multiple authors) - to 1845	***See*** Main schedule
Kannada letters (multiple authors) - 1845-1895	894.81464+
Kannada letters (multiple authors) - 1895-1919	894.81465+
Kannada letters (multiple authors) - 1920-1939	894.81466+
Kannada letters (multiple authors) -1940-	894.81467+
Kannada letters (multiple authors) - 1940-1999	894.814671+
Kannada letters (multiple authors) - 19th century	894.81464+
Kannada letters (multiple authors) -2000-	894.814672+
Kannada letters (multiple authors) - 20th century	894.814671+
Kannada letters (multiple authors) - Collections	894.8146008**
Kannada letters (multiple authors) - Dictionaries etc	894.8146003
Kannada letters (multiple authors) - History and criticism	894.8146009**
Kannada letters (multiple authors) - Periodicals	894.8146005

Kannada letters (multiple authors) - Philosophy and theory	894.8146001
Kannada letters (multiple authors) - Psychological aspects	894.81460019
Kannada letters (multiple authors) - Research	894.81460072
Kannada letters (multiple authors) - Study and teaching	894.8146007
Kannada letters (multiple authors) -Value	894.81460013
Kannada letters (single author)- - to 1845	***See*** Main schedule
Kannada letters (single author)- 1845 -1895	894.8146 4
Kannada letters (single author)- 1895 - 1919	894.8146 5
Kannada letters (single author)- 1920- 1939	894.8146 6
Kannada letters (single author)- 1940 -	894.8146 7
Kannada letters (single author)- 1940-1999	894.8146 71
Kannada letters (single author)- 19th century	894.8146 4
Kannada letters (single author)- 2000-	894.8146 72
Kannada letters (single author)- 20th century	894.8146 71
Kannada light verse	***See*** Kannada ephemeral and light verse
Kannada limericks (multiple authors)	894.8141075*
Kannada limericks (multiple authors)- Collections	894.814107508**
Kannada limericks (multiple authors)- History and criticism	894.814107509**
Kannada literature	894.814

Kannada literature (collections of multiple forms)	894.81408
Kannada literature (collections of multiple forms) - 19th century	894.8140804
Kannada literature (collections of multiple forms) - 20th century	894.81408071
Kannada literature (collections of multiple forms) – 21st century	894.81408072
Kannada literature (collections of multiple forms) - Allegory	894.81408015
Kannada literature (collections of multiple forms) - Animals	894.814080362++
Kannada literature (collections of multiple forms) - Artistic themes	894.814080357
Kannada literature (collections of multiple forms) - Atmosphere	894.81408032161
Kannada literature (collections of multiple forms) - Characters	894.81408027
Kannada literature (collections of multiple forms) - Comedy	894.81408017
Kannada literature (collections of multiple forms) - Evening	894.81408033
Kannada literature (collections of multiple forms) - Fantasy	894.81408015
Kannada literature (collections of multiple forms) - Forests	894.81408032152
Kannada literature (collections of multiple forms) - Historical themes	894.814080358
Kannada literature (collections of multiple forms) - Horror	894.814080164

Kannada literature (collections of multiple forms) - Human characteristics (Biological, moral, psychological)	894.814080353
Kannada literature (collections of multiple forms) - Legendary objects/themes	894.81408037
Kannada literature (collections of multiple forms) - Literary themes	894.814080357
Kannada literature (collections of multiple forms) - Love	894.8140803543
Kannada literature (collections of multiple forms) - Marriage	894.8140803543
Kannada literature (collections of multiple forms) - Morning	894.81408033
Kannada literature (collections of multiple forms) - Mountains	894.81408032143
Kannada literature (collections of multiple forms) - Myth	894.81408015
Kannada literature (collections of multiple forms) - Mythological objects/themes	894.81408037
Kannada literature (collections of multiple forms) - Philosophic themes	894.814080384
Kannada literature (collections of multiple forms) - Places	894.81408032++
Kannada literature (collections of multiple forms) - Plants	894.814080364
Kannada literature (collections of multiple forms) - Political themes	894.814080358
Kannada literature (collections of multiple forms) - Religious themes	894.814080382++
Kannada literature (collections of multiple	

forms) - Rivers	894.814080321693
Kannada literature (collections of multiple forms) - Romanticism	894.814080145
Kannada literature (collections of multiple forms) - Scientific themes	894.814080356
Kannada literature (collections of multiple forms) - Sea	894.81408032162
Kannada literature (collections of multiple forms) - Seasons	894.81408033
Kannada literature (collections of multiple forms) - Sex	894.8140803538
Kannada literature (collections of multiple forms) - Social themes	894.814080355
Kannada literature (collections of multiple forms) - Space	894.8140803219
Kannada literature (collections of multiple forms) - Specific kinds of persons, e.g. heroes	894.814080352++
Kannada literature (collections of multiple forms) - Specific persons (real or imaginary)	894.814080351
Kannada literature (collections of multiple forms) - Stream of consciousness	894.81408025
Kannada literature (collections of multiple forms) - Supernatural objects/themes	894.81408037
Kannada literature (collections of multiple forms) - Symbolism	894.81408015
Kannada literature (collections of multiple forms) - Technical themes	894.814080356
Kannada literature (collections of multiple forms) - Times (seasons, parts of day, etc)	894.81408033

Kannada literature (collections of multiple forms) - Towns	894.814080321732
Kannada literature (collections of multiple forms) - Tragedy	894.814080162
Kannada literature (collections of multiple forms) - Villages	894.814080321734
Kannada literature (collections of multiple forms) - Weather	894.81408036
Kannada literature (collections of multiple forms) emphasizing subjects	894.8140804++
Kannada literature (collections of multiple forms) for/by children	894.8140809282
Kannada literature (collections of multiple forms) for/by persons of racial, ethnic and national groups	894.8140808++
Kannada literature (collections of multiple forms) for/by persons of specific classes	894.81408092++
Kannada literature (collections of multiple forms) for/by persons resident in specific regions	894.81408091++
Kannada literature (collections of multiple forms) for/by women	894.8140809287
Kannada literature (multiple authors) - Concordances	894.81403
Kannada literature (multiple authors) - Dictionaries	894.81403
Kannada literature (multiple authors) - Education	894.814071
Kannada literature (multiple authors) - Encyclopaedias	894.81403

Kannada literature (multiple authors) - Organizations	894.81406
Kannada literature (multiple authors) - Periodicals	894.81405
Kannada literature (multiple authors) - Philosophy and theory	894.81401
Kannada literature (multiple authors) - Research	894.814072
Kannada literature (multiple authors) - Research in India	894.814072054
Kannada literature (multiple authors) - Study and teaching	894.81407
Kannada literature (multiple forms) - Supernatural objects/themes - History and criticism	894.8140937
Kannada literature (multiple forms) - 19th century	894.81409004
Kannada literature (multiple forms) – 2000-	894.814090072
Kannada literature (multiple forms) - 20th century	894.814090071
Kannada literature (multiple forms) - Allegory – History and criticism	894.8140915
Kannada literature (multiple forms) - Animals - History and criticism	894.81409362++
Kannada literature (multiple forms) - Artistic themes - History and criticism	894.81409357
Kannada literature (multiple forms) - Atmosphere - History and criticism	894.8140932161
Kannada literature (multiple forms) - Characters - History and criticism	894.8140927

Kannada literature (multiple forms) - Comedy - History and criticism	894.8140917
Kannada literature (multiple forms) - Evening - History and criticism	894.8140933
Kannada literature (multiple forms) - Fantasy - History , description, criticism	894.8140915
Kannada literature (multiple forms) - Forests- History and criticism	894.8140932152
Kannada literature (multiple forms) - Historical themes - History and criticism	894.81409358
Kannada literature (multiple forms) - History and criticism	894.81409
Kannada literature (multiple forms) - Horror - History and criticism	894.81409164
Kannada literature (multiple forms) - Human characteristics (Biological, moral, psychological) - History and criticism	894.81409353
Kannada literature (multiple forms) - Legendary objects/themes - History and criticism	894.8140937
Kannada literature (multiple forms) - Literary themes - History and criticism	894.81409357
Kannada literature (multiple forms) - Love - History and criticism	894.814093543
Kannada literature (multiple forms) - Marriage - History and criticism	894.814093543
Kannada literature (multiple forms) - Morning - History and criticism	894.8140933
Kannada literature (multiple forms) - Mountains - History and criticism	894.8140932143

Kannada literature (multiple forms) - Myth - History and criticism	894.8140915
Kannada literature (multiple forms) - Mythological objects/themes - History and criticism	894.8140937
Kannada literature (multiple forms) - Persons of racial, ethnic and national groups - History and criticism	894.814098++
Kannada literature (multiple forms) - Persons of specific classes - History and criticism	894.8140992++
Kannada literature (multiple forms) - Persons resident in specific regions - History and criticism	894.8140991++
Kannada literature (multiple forms) - Philosophic themes - History and criticism	894.81409384
Kannada literature (multiple forms) - Places - History and criticism	894.8140932++
Kannada literature (multiple forms) - Plants - History and criticism	894.81409364
Kannada literature (multiple forms) - Political themes - History and criticism	894.81409358
Kannada literature (multiple forms) - Religious themes - History and criticism	894.81409382++
Kannada literature (multiple forms) - Rivers - History and criticism	894.81409321693
Kannada literature (multiple forms) - Romanticism - History and criticism	894.81409145
Kannada literature (multiple forms) - Scientific themes - History and criticism	894.81409356
Kannada literature (multiple forms) - Sea -	

History and criticism	894.8140932162
Kannada literature (multiple forms) - Seasons - History and criticism	894.8140933
Kannada literature (multiple forms) - Sex - History and criticism	894.814093538
Kannada literature (multiple forms) - Social themes - History and criticism	894.81409355
Kannada literature (multiple forms) - Space - History and criticism	894.814093219
Kannada literature (multiple forms) - Specific kinds of persons, (e.g. heroes) - History and criticism	894.81409352++
Kannada literature (multiple forms) - Specific persons - History and criticism	894.81409351
Kannada literature (multiple forms) - Stream of consciousness - History and criticism	894.8140925
Kannada literature (multiple forms) - Subjects - History and criticism	894.814094++
Kannada literature (multiple forms) - Symbolism- History and criticism	894.8140915
Kannada literature (multiple forms) - Technical themes - History and criticism	894.81409356
Kannada literature (multiple forms) - Times - History and criticism	894.8140933
Kannada literature (multiple forms) - Towns - History and criticism	894.81409321732
Kannada literature (multiple forms) - Tragedy - History and criticism	894.81409162
Kannada literature (multiple forms) -	

Villages - History and criticism	894.81409321734
Kannada literature (multiple forms) - Weather - History and criticism	894.8140936
Kannada literature (single author)- to 1845 - Biography, collections, criticism	***See*** Main schedule
Kannada literature (single author)- 1845 - 1895 - Biography, collections, criticism	894.8148 409
Kannada literature (single author)- 1895 - 1919 - Biography, collections, criticism	894.8148 509
Kannada literature (single author)- 1920-1939 - Biography, collections, criticism	894.8148 609
Kannada literature (single author)- 1940 - Biography, collections, criticism	894.8148 709
Kannada literature (single author)- 1940-1999 - Biography, collections, criticism	894.8148 7109
Kannada literature (single author)- 19th century - Biography, collections, criticism	894.8148 409
Kannada literature (single author)- 2000- Biography, collections, criticism	894.8148 7209
Kannada literature (single author)- 20th century - Biography, collections, criticism	894.8148 7109
Kannada literature for/by children - History and criticism	894.814099282
Kannada literature for/by women - History and criticism	894.814099287
Kannada love fiction (multiple authors)	894.8143085*
Kannada love fiction (multiple authors)- Collections	894.814308508**

Kannada love fiction (multiple authors)-History and criticism	894.814308509**
Kannada melodrama (multiple authors)	894.81420527*
Kannada melodrama (multiple authors)-Collections	894.8142052708**
Kannada melodrama (multiple authors)-History and criticism	894.8142052709**
Kannada miscellaneous writings (multiple authors)	894.8148
Kannada miscellaneous writings (multiple authors) - to 1845	***See*** Main schedule
Kannada miscellaneous writings (multiple authors) -1845-1895	894.81484++
Kannada miscellaneous writings (multiple authors) -1895-1919	894.81485++
Kannada miscellaneous writings (multiple authors) -1920-1939	894.81486++
Kannada miscellaneous writings (multiple authors) -1940-	894.81487++
Kannada miscellaneous writings (multiple authors) -1940-1999	894.814871++
Kannada miscellaneous writings (multiple authors) -19th century	894.81484++
Kannada miscellaneous writings (multiple authors) -2000-	894.814872++
Kannada miscellaneous writings (multiple authors) -20th century	894.814871++
Kannada miscellaneous writings (multiple authors) -Collections	894.8148008**
Kannada miscellaneous writings	

(multiple authors) -Dictionaries etc	894.8148003
Kannada miscellaneous writings (multiple authors) -History and criticism	894.8148009**
Kannada miscellaneous writings (multiple authors) -Periodicals	894.8148005
Kannada miscellaneous writings (multiple authors) -Philosophy and theory	894.8148001
Kannada miscellaneous writings (multiple authors) -Psychological aspects	894.81480019
Kannada miscellaneous writings (multiple authors) -Research	894.81480072
Kannada miscellaneous writings (multiple authors) -Study and teaching	894.8148007
Kannada miscellaneous writings (multiple authors) -Value	894.81480013
Kannada miscellaneous writings (single author)- - to 1845	***See*** Main schedule
Kannada miscellaneous writings (single author)- 1845 -1895	894.8148 4
Kannada miscellaneous writings (single author)- 1895 - 1919	894.8148 5
Kannada miscellaneous writings (single author)- 1920- 1939	894.8148 6
Kannada miscellaneous writings (single author)- 1940 -	894.8148 7
Kannada miscellaneous writings (single author)- 1940-1999	894.8148 71
Kannada miscellaneous writings (single author)- 19th century	894.8148 4
Kannada miscellaneous writings	

(single author)- 2000-	894.8148 72
Kannada miscellaneous writings (single author)- 20th century	894.8148 71
Kannada monologues (multiple authors)	894.8142045*
Kannada monologues (multiple authors)- Collections	894.814204508**
Kannada monologues (multiple authors)- History and criticism	894.814204509**
Kannada morality plays	***See*** Kannada religious and morality plays
Kannada mystery fiction (multiple authors)	894.81430872*
Kannada mystery fiction (multiple authors)- Collections	894.8143087208**
Kannada mystery fiction (multiple authors)- History and criticism	894.8143087209**
Kannada narrative poetry (multiple authors)	894.814103*
Kannada narrative poetry (multiple authors)- Collections	894.81410308**
Kannada narrative poetry (multiple authors)- History and criticism	894.81410309**
Kannada notebooks	***See*** Kannada diaries...
Kannada odes (multiple authors)	894.8141043*
Kannada odes (multiple authors)- Collections	894.814104308**
Kannada odes (multiple authors)- History and criticism	894.814104309**
Kannada one act plays (multiple authors)	894.814 204 1*

Kannada one act plays (multiple authors)-Collections	894.814 204 108**
Kannada one act plays (multiple authors)-History and criticism	894.814 204 109**
Kannada oratory (multiple authors)	***See*** Kannada public speeches
Kannada periodicals	059.94814
Kannada poetry	894.8141
Kannada poetry (multiple authors) - to 1845	***See*** Main schedule
Kannada poetry (multiple authors) - 1845-1895	894.81414+
Kannada poetry (multiple authors) - 1895-1919	894.81415+
Kannada poetry (multiple authors) - 1920-1939	894.81416+
Kannada poetry (multiple authors) - 1940-	894.81417+
Kannada poetry (multiple authors) - 1940-1999	894.814171+
Kannada poetry (multiple authors) - 19th century	894.81414+
Kannada poetry (multiple authors) – 2000-	894.814172+
Kannada poetry (multiple authors) - 20th century	894.814171+
Kannada poetry (multiple authors)-Collections	894.8141008**
Kannada poetry (multiple authors)-Dictionaries etc	894.8141003
Kannada poetry (multiple authors)-	

History and criticism	894.8141009**
Kannada poetry (multiple authors)- Periodicals	894.8141005
Kannada poetry (multiple authors)- Philosophy and theory	894.8141001
Kannada poetry (multiple authors)- Psychological aspects	894.81410019
Kannada poetry (multiple authors)- Research	894.81410072
Kannada poetry (multiple authors)- Study and teaching	894.8141007
Kannada poetry (multiple authors)- Value	894.81410013
Kannada poetry (single author)- - to 1845	***See*** Main schedule
Kannada poetry (single author)- 1845 -1895	894.8141 4
Kannada poetry (single author)- 1895 - 1919	894.8141 5
Kannada poetry (single author)- 1920- 1939	894.8141 6
Kannada poetry (single author)- 1940 -	894.8141 7
Kannada poetry (single author)- 1940-1999	894.8141 71
Kannada poetry (single author)- 19th century	894.8141 4
Kannada poetry (single author)- 2000-	894.8141 72
Kannada poetry (single author)- 20th century	894.8141 71
Kannada prose (single author)- - to 1845	***See*** Main schedule
Kannada prose (single author)- 1845 -1895	894.8148 408
Kannada prose (single author)- 1895 - 1919	894.8148 508
Kannada prose (single author)- 1919- 1939	894.8148 608
Kannada prose (single author)- 1940 -	894.8148 708

Kannada prose (single author)- 1940-1999	894.8148 7108
Kannada prose (single author)- 19th century	894.8148 408
Kannada prose (single author)- 2000-	894.8148 7208
Kannada prose (single author)- 20th century	894.8148 7108
Kannada prose literature (multiple authors)	894.814808
Kannada psychological, realistic, sociological fiction (multiple authors)	894.8143083*
Kannada psychological, realistic, sociological fiction (multiple authors)- Collections	894.814308308**
Kannada psychological, realistic, sociological fiction (multiple authors) - History and criticism	894.814308309**
Kannada public discussions	***See*** Kannada debates and public discussions
Kannada public speeches (multiple authors)	894.814 501
Kannada public speeches (multiple authors)- Collections	894.81450108
Kannada public speeches (multiple authors)- History and criticism	894.81450109
Kannada quotations	***See*** Kannada anecdotes …
Kannada realistic fiction	***See*** Kannada psychological... fiction
Kannada recitations (multiple authors)	894.814504+
Kannada religious and morality plays (multiple authors)	894.81420516+

Kannada reminiscences	***See*** Kannada diaries...
Kannada romantic fiction (multiple authors)	894.8143085*
Kannada romantic fiction (multiple authors)-Collections	894.814308508**
Kannada romantic fiction (multiple authors)-History and criticism	894.814308509**
Kannada satire	***See*** Kannada humour and satire
Kannada satirical poetry	***See*** Kannada humourous and satirical poetry
Kannada science fiction (multiple authors)	894.814308762*
Kannada science fiction (multiple authors)-Collections	894.81430876208**
Kannada science fiction (multiple authors)-History and criticism	894.81430876209**
Kannada serious drama (multiple authors)	894.8142051+
Kannada short stories (multiple authors)	894.814301*
Kannada short stories (multiple authors)-Collections	894.81430108**
Kannada short stories (multiple authors)-History and criticism	894.81430109**
Kannada sociological fiction (multiple authors)	***See*** Kannada psychological... fiction
Kannada sonnets (multiple authors)	894.8141042*
Kannada sonnets (multiple authors)-Collections	894.814104208**

Kannada sonnets (multiple authors)-History and criticism	894.814104209**
Kannada speeches (multiple authors)	894.8145
Kannada speeches (multiple authors) — to 1845	***See*** Main schedule
Kannada speeches (multiple authors) - 1845-1895	894.81454+
Kannada speeches (multiple authors) - 1895-1919	894.81455+
Kannada speeches (multiple authors) - 1920-1939	894.81456+
Kannada speeches (multiple authors) -1940-	894.81457+
Kannada speeches (multiple authors) - 1940-1999	894.814571+
Kannada speeches (multiple authors) - 19th century	894.81454+
Kannada speeches (multiple authors) -2000-	894.814572+
Kannada speeches (multiple authors) - 20th century	894.814571+
Kannada speeches (multiple authors) - Collections	894.8145008**
Kannada speeches (multiple authors) - Dictionaries etc	894.8145003
Kannada speeches (multiple authors) - History and criticism	894.8145009**
Kannada speeches (multiple authors) - Periodicals	894.8145005
Kannada speeches (multiple authors) - Philosophy and theory	894.8145001

Kannada speeches (multiple authors) - Psychological aspects	894.81450019
Kannada speeches (multiple authors) - Research	894.81450072
Kannada speeches (multiple authors) - Study and teaching	894.8145007
Kannada speeches (multiple authors) - Value	894.81450013
Kannada speeches (single author)	894.8145
Kannada speeches (single author)- to 1845	***See*** Main schedule
Kannada speeches (single author)- 1845 -1895	894.8145 4
Kannada speeches (single author)- 1895 - 1919	894.8145 5
Kannada speeches (single author)- 1920- 1939	894.8145 6
Kannada speeches (single author)- 1940 -	894.8145 7
Kannada speeches (single author)- 1940-1999	894.8145 71
Kannada speeches (single author)- 19th century	894.8145 4
Kannada speeches (single author)- 2000-	894.8145 72
Kannada speeches (single author)- 20th century	894.8145 71
Kannada suspense fiction (multiple authors)	894.81430872*
Kannada suspense fiction (multiple authors)- Collections	894.8143087208**
Kannada suspense fiction (multiple	

authors)- History and criticism	894.8143087209**
Kannada tragedy (multiple authors)	894.81420512*
Kannada tragedy (multiple authors)- Collections	894.8142051208**
Kannada tragedy (multiple authors)- History and criticism	894.8142051209**
Kannada variety drama (multiple authors)	894.8142057*
Kannada variety drama (multiple authors)- Collections	894.814205708**
Kannada variety drama (multiple authors)- History and criticism	894.814205709**
Karma (Buddhism)	294.342 2
Karma (Hinduism)	294.522
Karma (Jainism)	294.422
Karma (Sikhism)	294.622
Karma yoga	294.543 6
Karnatak music	780.954 87
Karnataka- Architecture	720.954 87
Karnataka- Botany	580.954 87
Karnataka- Budget	352.495 487
Karnataka- Economic development	338.954 87
Karnataka- Economic geography	330.954 87
Karnataka- Education	370.954 87
Karnataka- Fauna	591.954 87
Karnataka- Fine and decorative arts	709.548 7
Karnataka- Flora	581.954 87

Karnataka- Folk dancing	793.319 548 7
Karnataka- Galleries of fine and decorative arts	708.954 87
Karnataka- Geography	915.487
Karnataka- Geology	555.487
Karnataka- History	954.87
Karnataka- Museums of fine and decorative arts	708.954 87
Karnataka- Painting and paintings	759.954 87
Karnataka- Public administration	351.548 7
Karnataka- Public finance	336.548 7
Karnataka- Sculpture	730.954 87
Kashmiri folk music.	781 629 149 9
Kashmiri language	491.499
Kashmiri literature	891.499
Kashmiris	305.891 499
Kerala- Architecture	720.954 83
Kerala- Botany	580.954 83
Kerala- Budget	352.495 483
Kerala- Economic development	338.954 83
Kerala- Economic geography	330.954 83
Kerala- Education	370.954 83
Kerala- Fauna	591.954 83
Kerala- Fine and decorative arts	709.5483
Kerala- Flora	581.954 83

Kerala- Folk dancing	793.319 5483
Kerala- Galleries of fine and decorative arts	708.954 83
Kerala- Geography	915.483
Kerala- Geology	555.483
Kerala- History	954.83
Kerala- Museums of fine and decorative arts	708.954 83
Kerala- Painting and paintings	759.954 83
Kerala- Public administration	351.548 3
Kerala- Public finance	336.548 3
Kerala- Sculpture	730.954 83
Khond - English dictionary	494.824 321
Khond language	494.824
Khond language- Applied linguistics	494.824 8
Khond language- Dictionaries	494.824 3
Khond language- Education	494.824 071
Khond language- Grammar	494.824 5
Khond language- History	494.824 09
Khond language- Readers	494.824 86
Khond language- Research	494.824 072
Khond language- Rhetoric	808.049 4824++
Khond language- Usage	494.824 8
Khond literature	894.824
Khond speaking people	305.794 824
Khowar language	491.499
Khowar literature	891.499

Khuddakanikaya	294.382 32
Kohistani folk music	781 629 149 9
Kohistani language	491.499
Kohistani literature	891.499
Kohistanis	305.891 499
Kolkata	***See*** Calcutta
Konkani language	491.467
Konkani literature	891.46
Konkani speaking people	305.791 46
Kundalini yoga	294.543 6
Kurukh (People)	305.894 83
Kurukh folk music	781 629 483

L

Labour law- India	344.54
Lahnda drama	891.419 2
Lahnda- English dictionary	491.419 321
Lahnda essays	891.419 4
Lahnda fiction	891.419 3
Lahnda- Hindi dictionary	491.419 391 431
Lahnda language	491.419
Lahnda language- Applied linguistics	491.419 8
Lahnda language- Dictionaries	491.419 3
Lahnda language- Education	491.419 071
Lahnda language- Grammar	491.419 5
Lahnda language- History	491.419 09
Lahnda language- Readers	491.419 86
Lahnda language- Research	491.419 072
Lahnda language- Rhetoric	808.049 1419++
Lahnda language- Usage	491.419 8
Lahnda letters	891.419 6
Lahnda literature	891.419

Lahnda poetry	891.419 1
Lahnda speaking people	305.791 419
Lahnda speeches	891.419 5
Lakshwadweep- Botany	580.954 81
Lakshwadweep- Budget	352.495 481
Lakshwadweep- Economic development	338.954 81
Lakshwadweep- Economic geography	330.954 81
Lakshwadweep- Education	370.954 81
Lakshwadweep- Fauna	591.954 81
Lakshwadweep- Flora	581.954 81
Lakshwadweep- Folk dancing	793.319 5481
Lakshwadweep- Geography	915.481
Lakshwadweep- Geology	555.481
Lakshwadweep- History	954.81
Lakshwadweep- Public administration	351.548 1
Lakshwadweep- Public finance	336.548 1
Lamaism	294.392 3
Lamaism- Doctrines	294.342 0423
Languages of Indus script	490
Laws (Statutes), regulations, cases- India	348.54
Laws and decisions (Buddhism)	294.384
Laws and decisions (Hinduism)	294.584
Laws and decisions (Jainism)	294.484
Laws and decisions (Sikhism)	294.684
Laws- India	349.54

Legislative process- Gujarat	328.547 5
Legislative process- Haryana	328.545 58
Legislative process- Himachal Pradesh	328.545 2
Legislative process- Hyderabad state	328.548 4
Legislative process- India	328.54
Legislative process- Jammu and Kashmir	328.546
Legislative process- Jharkhand	328.541 27
Legislative process- Karnataka	328.548 7
Legislative process- Kerala	328.548 3
Legislative process- Lakshwadweep	328.548 1
Legislative process- Madhya Pradesh	328.543
Legislative process- Maharashtra	328.547 92
Legislative process- Manipur	328.541 7
Legislative process- Meghalaya	328.541 64
Legislative process- Mizoram	328.541 66
Legislative process- Nagaland	328.541 65
Legislative process- Orissa	328.541 3
Legislative process- Pondicherry	328.548 6
Legislative process- Punjab	328.545 52
Legislative process- Rajasthan	328.544
Legislative process- Sikkim	328.541 67
Legislative process- Tamil Nadu	328.548 2
Legislative process- Tripura	328.541 5
Legislative process- Uttar Pradesh	328.542
Legislative process- Uttaranchal	328.545 1

Legislative process- West Bengal	328.541 4
Limbu	495.49
Limbu speaking people	305.795 49
Lingayats	294.551 3
Literature	294.337 5
Liturgical year (Buddhism)	294.343 6
Liturgical year (Hinduism)	294.536
Liturgical year (Jainism)	294.436
Liturgical year (Sikhism)	294.636
Local public debt - Andaman and Nicobar Islands	336.343 154 88
Local public debt - Andhra Pradesh	336.343 154 84
Local public debt - Arunachal Pradesh	336.343 154 163
Local public debt - Assam	336.343 154 162
Local public debt - Bengal	336.343 154 14
Local public debt - Bihar	336.343 154 12
Local public debt - Bombay	336.343 154 792 3
Local public debt - Chandigarh	336.343 154 55 2
Local public debt - Chhattisgarh	336.343 154 137
Local public debt - Dadra and Nagar Haveli	336.343 154 796
Local public debt - Delhi	336.343 154 56
Local public debt - Goa, Daman and Diu	336.343 154 79
Local public debt - Gujarat	336.343 154 75
Local public debt - Haryana	336.343 154 55 8
Local public debt - Himachal Pradesh	336.343 154 52

Local public debt - Hyderabad state	336.343 154 84
Local public debt - India	336.343 154
Local public debt - Jammu and Kashmir	336.343 154 6
Local public debt - Jharkhand	336.343 154 127
Local public debt - Karnataka	336.343 154 87
Local public debt - Kerala	336.343 154 83
Local public debt - Lakshwadweep	336.343 154 81
Local public debt - Madhya Pradesh	336.343 154 3
Local public debt - Madras	336.343 154 82
Local public debt - Maharashtra	336.343 154 792
Local public debt - Manipur	336.343 154 17
Local public debt - Meghalaya	336.343 154 164
Local public debt - Mizoram	336.343 154 166
Local public debt - Nagaland	336.343 154 165
Local public debt - Orissa	336.343 154 13
Local public debt - Pondicherry	336.343 154 86
Local public debt - Punjab	336.343 154 55 2
Local public debt - Rajasthan	336.343 154 4
Local public debt - Sikkim	336.343 154 167
Local public debt - Tamil Nadu	336.343 154 82
Local public debt - Tripura	336.343 154 15
Local public debt - Uttar Pradesh	336.343 154 2
Local public debt - Uttaranchal	336.343 154 51
Local public debt- West Bengal	336.343 154 14
Local taxes- Andaman and Nicobar Islands	336.201 454 88

Local taxes- Andhra Pradesh	336.201 454 84
Local taxes- Arunachal Pradesh	336.201 454 163
Local taxes- Assam	336.201 454 162
Local taxes- Bengal	336.201 454 14
Local taxes- Bhopal	336.201 454 3
Local taxes- Bihar	336.201 454 12
Local taxes- Bombay	336.201 454 792 3
Local taxes- Calcutta	336.201 454 147
Local taxes- Chandigarh	336.201 454 55 2
Local taxes- Chhattisgarh	336.201 454 137
Local taxes- Dadra and Nagar Haveli	336.201 454 796
Local taxes- Delhi	336.201 454 56
Local taxes- Goa, Daman and Diu	336.201 454 79
Local taxes- Gujarat	336.201 454 75
Local taxes- Haryana	336.201 454 55 8
Local taxes- Himachal Pradesh	336.201 454 52
Local taxes- Hyderabad state	336.201 454 84
Local taxes- India	336.201 454
Local taxes- Jammu and Kashmir	336.201 454 6
Local taxes- Jharkhand	336.201 454 127
Local taxes- Karnataka	336.201 454 87
Local taxes- Kerala	336.201 454 83
Local taxes- Lakshwadweep	336.201 454 81
Local taxes- Madhya Pradesh	336.201 454 3
Local taxes- Madras	336.201 454 82

Local taxes- Maharashtra	336.201 454 792
Local taxes- Manipur	336.201 454 17
Local taxes- Meghalaya	336.201 454 164
Local taxes- Mizoram	336.201 454 166
Local taxes- Nagaland	336.201 454 165
Local taxes- Orissa	336.201 454 13
Local taxes- Pondicherry	336.201 454 86
Local taxes- Punjab	336.201 454 55 2
Local taxes- Rajasthan	336.201 454 4
Local taxes- Sikkim	336.201 454 167
Local taxes- Tamil Nadu	336.201 454 82
Local taxes- Tripura	336.201 454 15
Local taxes- Uttar Pradesh	336.201 454 2
Local taxes- Uttaranchal	336.201 454 51
Local taxes- West Bengal	336.201 454 14

M

Maharashtra- Geology	555.479 2
Maharashtra- History	954.792
Maharashtra- Museums of fine and decorative arts	708.954 792
Maharashtra- Painting and paintings	759.954 792
Maharashtra- Public administration	351.547 92
Maharashtra- Public finance	336.547 92
Maharashtra- Sculpture	730.954 792
Mahasanghika school (Buddhism)	294.391
Mahavira	294.463
Mahayana (Northern) Buddhism- Doctrines	294.342 042
Mahayana (Northern) Buddhism. Madhyamika, Yogacara (Vijnana) schools	294.392
Mahayanist sacred texts	294.382
Mahayanist sacred works	294.385
Maithili language	491.454 7
Maithili literature	891.454
Maithili speaking people	305.791 454
Malayalam - English dictionary	494.812 321
Malayalam adventure fiction (multiple authors)	894.812 3087*
Malayalam adventure fiction (multiple authors) -Collections	894.812 308 708**
Malayalam adventure fiction (multiple authors)- History and criticism	894.812 308 709**
Malayalam anecdotes, epigrams, graffiti, jokes, quotations (multiple authors)	894.812802

Malayalam anecdotes, epigrams, graffiti, jokes, quotations (single author)	894.8128 +CD+02
Malayalam as second language in elementary education	372.659 481 2
Malayalam ballads (multiple authors)	894.8121044*
Malayalam ballads (multiple authors)- Collections	894.812104408**
Malayalam ballads (multiple authors)- History and criticism	894.812104409**
Malayalam comedy (multiple authors)	894.81220523*
Malayalam comedy (multiple authors) - Collections	894.8122052308**
Malayalam comedy (multiple authors) - History and criticism	894.8122052309**
Malayalam conversations (multiple authors)	894.812506*
Malayalam conversations (multiple authors) - Collections	894.81250608**
Malayalam conversations (multiple authors) - History and criticism	894.81250609**
Malayalam debates and public discussions (multiple authors)	894.812503*
Malayalam debates and public discussions (multiple authors)- Collections	894.81250308**
Malayalam debates and public discussions (multiple authors)- History and criticism	894.81250309**
Malayalam detective fiction (multiple authors)	894.81230872*
Malayalam detective fiction (multiple authors) - Collections	894.8123087208**

Malayalam detective fiction (multiple authors) - History and criticism	894.8123087209**
Malayalam diaries, notebooks, reminiscences (multiple authors)	894.812803
Malayalam diaries, notebooks, reminiscences (single author)	894.8128@
Malayalam didactic poetry (multiple authors)	894.812105*
Malayalam didactic poetry (multiple authors)- Collections	894.81210508**
Malayalam didactic poetry (multiple authors)- History and criticism	894.81210509**
Malayalam drama	894.8122
Malayalam drama (multiple authors) - to 1845	***See*** Main schedule
Malayalam drama (multiple authors) - 1845-1895	894.81224+
Malayalam drama (multiple authors) - 1895-1919	894.81225+
Malayalam drama (multiple authors) - 1920-1939	894.81226+
Malayalam drama (multiple authors) - 1940-	894.81227+
Malayalam drama (multiple authors) - 1940-1999	894.812271+
Malayalam drama (multiple authors) - 19th century	894.81224+
Malayalam drama (multiple authors) - 2000-	894.812272+
Malayalam drama (multiple authors) - 20th century	894.812271+

Malayalam drama (multiple authors) - Collections	894.8122008**
Malayalam drama (multiple authors) - Dictionaries etc	894.8122003
Malayalam drama (multiple authors) - History and criticism	894.8122009**
Malayalam drama (multiple authors) - Periodicals	894.8122005
Malayalam drama (multiple authors) - Philosophy and theory	894.8122001
Malayalam drama (multiple authors) - Psychological aspects	894.81220019
Malayalam drama (multiple authors) - Research	894.81220072
Malayalam drama (multiple authors) - Study and teaching	894.8122007
Malayalam drama (multiple authors) - Value	894.81220013
Malayalam drama (single author) - to 1845	***See*** Main schedule
Malayalam drama (single author)- 1845 -1895	894.8122 4
Malayalam drama (single author)- 1895 - 1919	894.8122 5
Malayalam drama (single author)- 1920- 1939	894.8122 6
Malayalam drama (single author)- 1940 -	894.8122 7
Malayalam drama (single author)- 1940-1999	894.8122 71
Malayalam drama (single author)- 19th century	894.8122 4

Malayalam drama (single author)- 2000-	894.8122 72
Malayalam drama (single author)- 20th century	894.8122 71
Malayalam drama for cinema (multiple authors)	894.812203*
Malayalam drama for cinema (multiple authors) - Collections	894.81220308**
Malayalam drama for cinema (multiple authors) - History and criticism	894.81220309**
Malayalam drama for radio (multiple authors)	894.8122022*
Malayalam drama for television (multiple authors)	894.8122025*
Malayalam drama for radio (multiple authors) - History and criticism	894.812202209**
Malayalam drama for radio (multiple authors) - Collections	894.812202208**
Malayalam drama for television (multiple authors) - Collections	894.812202508**
Malayalam drama for television (multiple authors) - History and criticism	894.812202509**
Malayalam dramatic poetry (multiple authors)	894.812102*
Malayalam dramatic poetry (multiple authors)- Collections	894.81210208**
Malayalam dramatic poetry (multiple authors)- History and criticism	894.81210209**
Malayalam encyclopaedias	039.94812
Malayalam ephemeral and light verse (multiple authors)	894.812108*

Malayalam ephemeral and light verse (multiple authors)- Collections	894.81210808**
Malayalam ephemeral and light verse (multiple authors) - History and criticism	894.81210809**
Malayalam epic poetry (multiple authors)	894.8121032*
Malayalam epic poetry (multiple authors)- Collections	894.812103208**
Malayalam epic poetry (multiple authors)- History and criticism	894.812103209**
Malayalam epigrams	***See*** Malayalam anecdotes ...
Malayalam essays	894.8124
Malayalam essays (multiple authors) - to 1845	***See*** Main schedule
Malayalam essays (multiple authors) - 1845-1895	894.81244+
Malayalam essays (multiple authors) - 1895-1919	894.81245+
Malayalam essays (multiple authors) - 1920-1939	894.81246+
Malayalam essays (multiple authors) -1940-	894.81247+
Malayalam essays (multiple authors) - 1940-1999	894.812471+
Malayalam essays (multiple authors) - 19th century	894.81244+
Malayalam essays (multiple authors) - 2000-	894.812472+
Malayalam essays (multiple authors) - 20th century	894.812471+

Malayalam essays (multiple authors) - Collections	894.8124008**
Malayalam essays (multiple authors) - Dictionaries etc	894.8124003
Malayalam essays (multiple authors) - History and criticism	894.8124009**
Malayalam essays (multiple authors) - Periodicals	894.8124005
Malayalam essays (multiple authors) - Philosophy and theory	894.8124001
Malayalam essays (multiple authors) - Psychological aspects	894.81240019
Malayalam essays (multiple authors) - Research	894.81240072
Malayalam essays (multiple authors) - Study and teaching	894.8124007
Malayalam essays (multiple authors) - Value	894.81240013
Malayalam essays (single author)- to 1845	***See*** Main schedule
Malayalam essays (single author)- 1845 -1895	894.8124 4
Malayalam essays (single author)- 1895 - 1919	894.8124 5
Malayalam essays (single author)- 1920- 1939	894.8124 6
Malayalam essays (single author)- 1940 -	894.8124 7
Malayalam essays (single author)- 1940-1999	894.8124 71
Malayalam essays (single author)-	

19th century	894.8124 4
Malayalam essays (single author)- 2000-	894.8124 72
Malayalam essays (single author)- 20th century	894.8124 71
Malayalam experimental and non-formalized works (single author)	894.8128+CD+07
Malayalam experimental and non-formalized works (multiple authors)	894.812807
Malayalam fantasy fiction (multiple authors)	894.812308766*
Malayalam fantasy fiction (multiple authors)- Collections	894.81230876608**
Malayalam fantasy fiction (multiple authors)- History and criticism	894.81230876609**
Malayalam farce (multiple authors)	894.812205232*
Malayalam farce (multiple authors) - History and criticism	894.81220523209**
Malayalam farce (multiple authors)- Collections	894.81220523208**
Malayalam fiction	894.8123
Malayalam fiction (multiple authors) - to 1845	***See*** Main schedule
Malayalam fiction (multiple authors) - 1845-1895	894.81234+
Malayalam fiction (multiple authors) - 1895-1919	894.81235+
Malayalam fiction (multiple authors) - 1920-1939	894.81236+
Malayalam fiction (multiple authors) - 1940-	894.81237+

Malayalam fiction (multiple authors) - 1940-1999	894.812371+
Malayalam fiction (multiple authors) - 19th century	894.81234+
Malayalam fiction (multiple authors) - 2000-	894.812372+
Malayalam fiction (multiple authors) - 20th century	894.812371+
Malayalam fiction (multiple authors) - Collections	894.8123008**
Malayalam fiction (multiple authors) - Dictionaries etc	894.8123003
Malayalam fiction (multiple authors) - History and criticism	894.8123009**
Malayalam fiction (multiple authors) - Periodicals	894.8123005
Malayalam fiction (multiple authors) - Philosophy and theory	894.8123001
Malayalam fiction (multiple authors) - Psychological aspects	894.81230019
Malayalam fiction (multiple authors) - Research	894.81230072
Malayalam fiction (multiple authors) - Study and teaching	894.8123007
Malayalam fiction (multiple authors) - Value	894.81230013
Malayalam fiction (single author)- - to 1845	***See*** Main schedule
Malayalam fiction (single author)- 1845 -1895	894.8123 4
Malayalam fiction (single author)- 1895 - 1919	894.8123 5

Malayalam fiction (single author)- 1920- 1939	894.8123 6
Malayalam fiction (single author)- 1940 -	894.8123 7
Malayalam fiction (single author)- 1940-1999	894.8123 71
Malayalam fiction (single author)- 19th century	894.8123 4
Malayalam fiction (single author)- 2000-	894.8123 72
Malayalam fiction (single author)- 20th century	894.8123 71
Malayalam ghost fiction (multiple authors)	894.812308733*
Malayalam ghost fiction (multiple authors) - Collections	894.81230873308**
Malayalam ghost fiction (multiple authors)- History and criticism	894.81230873309**
Malayalam graffiti	***See*** Malayalam anecdotes ...
Malayalam historical drama (multiple authors)	894.81220514*
Malayalam historical drama (multiple authors)- Collections	894.8122051408**
Malayalam historical drama (multiple authors)- History and criticism	894.8122051409**
Malayalam historical fiction (multiple authors)	894.8123081*
Malayalam historical fiction (multiple authors)- Collections	894.812308108**
Malayalam historical fiction (multiple authors)- History and criticism	894.812308109**

Malayalam horror fiction (multiple authors)	894.812308738*
Malayalam horror fiction (multiple authors)- Collections	894.81230873808**
Malayalam horror fiction (multiple authors)- History and criticism	894.81230873809**
Malayalam humour and satire	894.8127
Malayalam humour and satire (multiple authors) — to 1845	***See*** Main schedule
Malayalam humour and satire (multiple authors) -1845-1895	894.81274+
Malayalam humour and satire (multiple authors) -1895-1919	894.81275+
Malayalam humour and satire (multiple authors) -1920-1939	894.81276+
Malayalam humour and satire (multiple authors) -1940-	894.81277+
Malayalam humour and satire (multiple authors) -1940-1999	894.812771+
Malayalam humour and satire (multiple authors) -19th century	894.81274+
Malayalam humour and satire (multiple authors) -2000-	894.812772+
Malayalam humour and satire (multiple authors) -20th century	894.812771+
Malayalam humour and satire (multiple authors) -Collections	894.8127008**
Malayalam humour and satire (multiple authors) -Dictionaries etc	894.8127003
Malayalam humour and satire (multiple authors) -History and criticism	894.8127009**

Malayalam humour and satire (multiple authors) -Periodicals	894.8127005
Malayalam humour and satire (multiple authors) -Philosophy and theory	894.8127001
Malayalam humour and satire (multiple authors) -Psychological aspects	894.81270019
Malayalam humour and satire (multiple authors) -Research	894.81270072
Malayalam humour and satire (multiple authors) -Study and teaching	894.8127007
Malayalam humour and satire (multiple authors) -Value	894.81270013
Malayalam humourous and satirical poetry (multiple authors)	894.812107*
Malayalam humourous and satirical poetry (multiple authors)- Collections	894.81210708**
Malayalam humourous and satirical poetry (multiple authors)- History and criticism	894.81210709**
Malayalam jokes ***See*** Malayalam anecdotes	894.812802
Malayalam language	494.812
Malayalam language- Applied linguistics	494.8128
Malayalam language- Bilingual dictionaries	494.81232-39
Malayalam language- Bilingualism	494.812 042
Malayalam language- Concordances	494.812 03
Malayalam language- Content analysis	494.812 0141
Malayalam language- Dialects	494.812 7
Malayalam language- Dictionaries	494.812 3
Malayalam language- Discourse analysis	494.812 0141

Malayalam language- Education	494.812 071
Malayalam language- Encyclopaedias	494.812 03
Malayalam language- Etymology	494.812 2
Malayalam language- Functionalism	494.812 018
Malayalam language- Grammar	494.812 5
Malayalam language- History	494.812 09
Malayalam language- Intonation	494.812 16
Malayalam language- Lexicography	494.812 302 8
Malayalam language- Lexicology	494.812 014
Malayalam language- Miscellany	494.812 02
Malayalam language- Multilingualism	494.812 042
Malayalam language- Organizations	494.812 06
Malayalam language- Orthography	494.812 152
Malayalam language- Pauses	494.812 16
Malayalam language- Periodicals	494.812 05
Malayalam language- Persons (men, women, etc)	494.812 08
Malayalam language- Philosophy and theory	494.812 01
Malayalam language- Phonetics	494.812 158
Malayalam language- Phonology, etc	494.812 15
Malayalam language- Pitch	494.812 16
Malayalam language- Pronunciation	494.812 152
Malayalam language- Readers	494.812 86
Malayalam language- Research	494.812 072
Malayalam language -Rhetoric	808.049 4812++

Malayalam language- Schools and theories of linguistics	494.812 018
Malayalam language- Semantics	494.812 014 3
Malayalam language- Semiotics	494.812 014 1
Malayalam language- Slang	494.812 7
Malayalam language- Special topics	494.812 04
Malayalam language- Specialized dictionaries	494.812 31
Malayalam language- Spelling	494.812 152
Malayalam language- Stress	494.812 16
Malayalam language- Structural linguistics	494.812 018
Malayalam language- Suprasegmental features	494.812 16
Malayalam language- Terminology	494.812 014
Malayalam language- Theory	494.812 01
Malayalam language- Usage	494.812 8
Malayalam language- Variations	494.812 7
Malayalam language- Writing systems	494.812 11
Malayalam letters	894.8126
Malayalam letters (multiple authors) - to 1845	***See*** Main schedule
Malayalam letters (multiple authors) - 1845-1895	894.81264+
Malayalam letters (multiple authors) - 1895-1919	894.81265+
Malayalam letters (multiple authors) - 1920-1939	894.81266+

Malayalam letters (multiple authors) -1940-	894.81267+
Malayalam letters (multiple authors) - 1940-1999	894.812671+
Malayalam letters (multiple authors) - 19th century	894.81264+
Malayalam letters (multiple authors) -2000-	894.812672+
Malayalam letters (multiple authors) - 20th century	894.812671+
Malayalam letters (multiple authors) - Collections	894.8126008**
Malayalam letters (multiple authors) - Dictionaries etc	894.8126003
Malayalam letters (multiple authors) - History and criticism	894.8126009**
Malayalam letters (multiple authors) - Periodicals	894.8126005
Malayalam letters (multiple authors) - Philosophy and theory	894.8126001
Malayalam letters (multiple authors) - Psychological aspects	894.81260019
Malayalam letters (multiple authors) - Research	894.81260072
Malayalam letters (multiple authors) - Study and teaching	894.8126007
Malayalam letters (multiple authors) -Value	894.81260013
Malayalam letters (single author)- - to 1845	***See*** Main schedule
Malayalam letters (single author)- 1845 -1895	894.8126 4
Malayalam letters (single author)- 1895 - 1919	894.8126 5

Malayalam letters (single author)- 1920- 1939	894.8126 6
Malayalam letters (single author)- 1940 -	894.8126 7
Malayalam letters (single author)- 1940-1999	894.8126 71
Malayalam letters (single author)- 19th century	894.8126 4
Malayalam letters (single author)- 2000-	894.8126 72
Malayalam letters (single author)- 20th century	894.8126 71
Malayalam light verse	***See*** Malayalam ephemeral and light verse
Malayalam limericks (multiple authors)	894.8121075*
Malayalam limericks (multiple authors)- Collections	894.812107508**
Malayalam limericks (multiple authors)- History and criticism	894.812107509**
Malayalam literature	894.812
Malayalam literature (collections of multiple forms)	894.81208
Malayalam literature (collections of multiple forms) - 19th century	894.8120804
Malayalam literature (collections of multiple forms) - 20th century	894.81208071
Malayalam literature (collections of multiple forms) – 21st century	894.81208072
Malayalam literature (collections of multiple forms) - Allegory	894.81208015

Malayalam literature (collections of multiple forms) - Animals	894.812080362++
Malayalam literature (collections of multiple forms) - Artistic themes	894.812080357
Malayalam literature (collections of multiple forms) - Atmosphere	894.81208032161
Malayalam literature (collections of multiple forms) - Characters	894.81208027
Malayalam literature (collections of multiple forms) - Comedy	894.81208017
Malayalam literature (collections of multiple forms) - Evening	894.81208033
Malayalam literature (collections of multiple forms) - Fantasy	894.81208015
Malayalam literature (collections of multiple forms) - Forests	894.81208032152
Malayalam literature (collections of multiple forms) - Historical themes	894.812080358
Malayalam literature (collections of multiple forms) - Horror	894.812080164
Malayalam literature (collections of multiple forms) - Human characteristics (Biological, moral, psychological)	894.812080353
Malayalam literature (collections of multiple forms) - Legendary objects/themes	894.81208037
Malayalam literature (collections of multiple forms) - Literary themes	894.812080357
Malayalam literature (collections of multiple forms) - Love	894.8120803543
Malayalam literature (collections of multiple forms) - Marriage	894.8120803543

Malayalam literature (collections of multiple forms) - Morning	894.81208033
Malayalam literature (collections of multiple forms) - Mountains	894.81208032143
Malayalam literature (collections of multiple forms) - Myth	894.81208015
Malayalam literature (collections of multiple forms) - Mythological objects/ themes	894.81208037
Malayalam literature (collections of multiple forms) - Philosophic themes	894.812080384
Malayalam literature (collections of multiple forms) - Places	894.81208032++
Malayalam literature (collections of multiple forms) - Plants	894.812080364
Malayalam literature (collections of multiple forms) - Political themes	894.812080358
Malayalam literature (collections of multiple forms) - Religious themes	894.812080382++
Malayalam literature (collections of multiple forms) - Rivers	894.812080321693
Malayalam literature (collections of multiple forms) - Romanticism	894.812080145
Malayalam literature (collections of multiple forms) - Scientific themes	894.812080356
Malayalam literature (collections of multiple forms) - Sea	894.81208032162
Malayalam literature (collections of multiple forms) - Seasons	894.81208033
Malayalam literature (collections of multiple forms) - Sex	894.8120803538

Malayalam literature (collections of multiple forms) - Social themes	894.812080355
Malayalam literature (collections of multiple forms) - Space	894.8120803219
Malayalam literature (collections of multiple forms) - Specific kinds of persons, e.g. heroes	894.812080352++
Malayalam literature (collections of multiple forms) - Specific persons (real or imaginary)	894.812080351
Malayalam literature (collections of multiple forms) - Stream of consciousness	894.81208025
Malayalam literature (collections of multiple forms) - Supernatural objects/themes	894.81208037
Malayalam literature (collections of multiple forms) - Symbolism	894.81208015
Malayalam literature (collections of multiple forms) - Technical themes	894.812080356
Malayalam literature (collections of multiple forms) - Times (seasons, parts of day, etc)	894.81208033
Malayalam literature (collections of multiple forms) - Towns	894.812080321732
Malayalam literature (collections of multiple forms) - Tragedy	894.812080162
Malayalam literature (collections of multiple forms) - Villages	894.812080321734
Malayalam literature (collections of multiple forms) - Weather	894.81208036
Malayalam literature (collections of multiple forms) emphasizing subjects	894.8120804++
Malayalam literature (collections of multiple forms) for/by children	894.8120809282

Malayalam literature (collections of multiple forms) for/by persons of racial, ethnic and national groups	894.8120808++
Malayalam literature (collections of multiple forms) for/by persons of specific classes	894.81208092++
Malayalam literature (collections of multiple forms) for/by persons resident in specific regions	894.81208091++
Malayalam literature (collections of multiple forms) for/by women	894.8120809287
Malayalam literature (multiple authors) - Concordances	894.81203
Malayalam literature (multiple authors) - Dictionaries	894.81203
Malayalam literature (multiple authors) - Education	894.812071
Malayalam literature (multiple authors) - Encyclopaedias	894.81203
Malayalam literature (multiple authors) - Organizations	894.81206
Malayalam literature (multiple authors) - Periodicals	894.81205
Malayalam literature (multiple authors) - Philosophy and theory	894.81201
Malayalam literature (multiple authors) - Research	894.812072
Malayalam literature (multiple authors) - Research in India	894.812072054
Malayalam literature (multiple authors) - Study and teaching	894.81207

Malayalam literature (multiple forms) - Supernatural objects/themes - History and criticism	894.8120937
Malayalam literature (multiple forms) - 19th century	894.81209004
Malayalam literature (multiple forms) – 2000-	894.812090072
Malayalam literature (multiple forms) - 20th century	894.812090071
Malayalam literature (multiple forms) - Allegory – History and criticism	894.8120915
Malayalam literature (multiple forms) - Animals - History and criticism	894.81209362++
Malayalam literature (multiple forms) - Artistic themes - History and criticism	894.81209357
Malayalam literature (multiple forms) - Atmosphere - History and criticism	894.8120932161
Malayalam literature (multiple forms) - Characters - History and criticism	894.8120927
Malayalam literature (multiple forms) - Comedy - History and criticism	894.8120917
Malayalam literature (multiple forms) - Evening - History and criticism	894.8120933
Malayalam literature (multiple forms) - Fantasy - History , description, criticism	894.8120915
Malayalam literature (multiple forms) - Forests- History and criticism	894.8120932152
Malayalam literature (multiple forms) - Historical themes - History and criticism	894.81209358
Malayalam literature (multiple forms) - History and criticism	894.81209

Malayalam literature (multiple forms) - Horror - History and criticism	894.81209164
Malayalam literature (multiple forms) - Human characteristics (Biological, moral, psychological) - History and criticism	894.81209353
Malayalam literature (multiple forms) - Legendary objects/themes - History and criticism	894.8120937
Malayalam literature (multiple forms) - Literary themes - History and criticism	894.81209357
Malayalam literature (multiple forms) - Love - History and criticism	894.812093543
Malayalam literature (multiple forms) - Marriage - History and criticism	894.812093543
Malayalam literature (multiple forms) - Morning - History and criticism	894.8120933
Malayalam literature (multiple forms) - Mountains - History and criticism	894.8120932143
Malayalam literature (multiple forms) - Myth - History and criticism	894.8120915
Malayalam literature (multiple forms) - Mythological objects/themes - History and criticism	894.8120937
Malayalam literature (multiple forms) - Persons of racial, ethnic and national groups - History and criticism	894.812098++
Malayalam literature (multiple forms) - Persons of specific classes - History and criticism	894.8120992++
Malayalam literature (multiple forms) - Persons resident in specific regions - History and criticism	894.8120991++

Malayalam literature (multiple forms) - Philosophic themes - History and criticism	894.81209384
Malayalam literature (multiple forms) - Places - History and criticism	894.8120932++
Malayalam literature (multiple forms) - Plants - History and criticism	894.81209364
Malayalam literature (multiple forms) - Political themes - History and criticism	894.81209358
Malayalam literature (multiple forms) - Religious themes - History and criticism	894.81209382++
Malayalam literature (multiple forms) - Rivers - History and criticism	894.81209321693
Malayalam literature (multiple forms) - Romanticism - History and criticism	894.81209145
Malayalam literature (multiple forms) - Scientific themes - History and criticism	894.81209356
Malayalam literature (multiple forms) - Sea - History and criticism	894.8120932162
Malayalam literature (multiple forms) - Seasons - History and criticism	894.8120933
Malayalam literature (multiple forms) - Sex - History and criticism	894.812093538
Malayalam literature (multiple forms) - Social themes - History and criticism	894.81209355
Malayalam literature (multiple forms) - Space - History and criticism	894.812093219
Malayalam literature (multiple forms) - Specific kinds of persons, e.g. heroes, - History and criticism	894.81209352++
Malayalam literature (multiple forms) - Specific persons - History and criticism	894.81209351

Malayalam literature (multiple forms) - Stream of consciousness - History and criticism	894.8120925
Malayalam literature (multiple forms) - Subjects - History and criticism	894.812094++
Malayalam literature (multiple forms) - Symbolism- History , description, criticism	894.8120915
Malayalam literature (multiple forms) - Technical themes - History and criticism	894.81209356
Malayalam literature (multiple forms) - Times - History and criticism	894.8120933
Malayalam literature (multiple forms) - Towns - History and criticism	894.81209321732
Malayalam literature (multiple forms) - Tragedy - History and criticism	894.81209162
Malayalam literature (multiple forms) - Villages - History and criticism	894.81209321734
Malayalam literature (multiple forms) - Weather - History and criticism	894.8120936
Malayalam literature (single author)- to 1845 - Biography, collections, criticism	***See*** Main schedule
Malayalam literature (single author)- 1845 - 1895 - Biography, collections, criticism	894.8128 409
Malayalam literature (single author)- 1895 - 1919 - Biography, collections, criticism	894.8128 509
Malayalam literature (single author)- 1920-1939 - Biography, collections, criticism	894.8128 609
Malayalam literature (single author)- 1940 - Biography, collections, criticism	894.8128 709
Malayalam literature (single author)- 1940-1999 - Biography, collections, criticism	894.8128 7109

Malayalam literature (single author)- 19th century- Biography, collections, criticism	894.8128 409
Malayalam literature (single author)- 2000- Biography, collections, criticism	894.8128 7209
Malayalam literature (single author)- 20th century - Biography, collections, criticism	894.8128 7109
Malayalam literature for/by children - History and criticism	894.812099282
Malayalam literature for/by women - History and criticism	894.812099287
Malayalam love fiction (multiple authors)	894.8123085*
Malayalam love fiction (multiple authors)- Collections	894.812308508**
Malayalam love fiction (multiple authors)- History and criticism	894.812308509**
Malayalam melodrama (multiple authors)	894.81220527*
Malayalam melodrama (multiple authors)- Collections	894.8122052708**
Malayalam melodrama (multiple authors)- History and criticism	894.8122052709**
Malayalam miscellaneous writings	894.8128
Malayalam miscellaneous writings (multiple authors) - to 1845	***See*** Main schedule
Malayalam miscellaneous writings (multiple authors) -1845-1895	894.81284++
Malayalam miscellaneous writings (multiple authors) -1895-1919	894.81285++

Malayalam miscellaneous writings (multiple authors) -1920-1939	894.81286++
Malayalam miscellaneous writings (multiple authors) -1940-	894.81287++
Malayalam miscellaneous writings (multiple authors) -1940-1999	894.812871++
Malayalam miscellaneous writings (multiple authors) -19th century	894.81284++
Malayalam miscellaneous writings (multiple authors) –2000-	894.812872++
Malayalam miscellaneous writings (multiple authors) -20th century	894.812871++
Malayalam miscellaneous writings (multiple authors) -Collections	894.8128008**
Malayalam miscellaneous writings (multiple authors) -Dictionaries etc	894.8128003
Malayalam miscellaneous writings (multiple authors) -History and criticism	894.8128009**
Malayalam miscellaneous writings (multiple authors) -Periodicals	894.8128005
Malayalam miscellaneous writings (multiple authors) -Philosophy and theory	894.8128001
Malayalam miscellaneous writings (multiple authors) -Psychological aspects	894.81280019
Malayalam miscellaneous writings (multiple authors) -Research	894.81280072
Malayalam miscellaneous writings (multiple authors) -Study and teaching	894.8128007
Malayalam miscellaneous writings (multiple authors) -Value	894.81280013

Malayalam miscellaneous writings (single author)	894.8128
Malayalam miscellaneous writings (single author)- - to 1845	***See*** Main schedule
Malayalam miscellaneous writings (single author)- 1845 -1895	894.8128 4
Malayalam miscellaneous writings (single author)- 1895 - 1919	894.8128 5
Malayalam miscellaneous writings (single author)- 1920- 1939	894.8128 6
Malayalam miscellaneous writings (single author)- 1940 -	894.8128 7
Malayalam miscellaneous writings (single author)- 1940-1999	894.8128 71
Malayalam miscellaneous writings (single author)- 19th century	894.8128 4
Malayalam miscellaneous writings (single author)- 2000-	894.8128 72
Malayalam miscellaneous writings (single author)- 20th century	894.8128 71
Malayalam monologues (multiple authors)	894.8122045*
Malayalam monologues (multiple authors)- Collections	894.812204508**
Malayalam monologues (multiple authors)- History and criticism	894.812204509**
Malayalam morality plays	***See*** Malayalam religious and morality plays
Malayalam mystery fiction (multiple authors)	894.81230872*

Malayalam mystery fiction (multiple authors)- Collections	894.8123087208**
Malayalam mystery fiction (multiple authors)- History and criticism	894.8123087209**
Malayalam narrative poetry (multiple authors)	894.812103*
Malayalam narrative poetry (multiple authors)- Collections	894.81210308**
Malayalam narrative poetry (multiple authors)- History and criticism	894.81210309**
Malayalam notebooks ***See*** Malayalam diaries ...	894.812803
Malayalam odes (multiple authors)	894.8121043*
Malayalam odes (multiple authors)- Collections	894.812104308**
Malayalam odes (multiple authors)- History and criticism	894.812104309**
Malayalam one act plays (multiple authors)	894.812 204 1*
Malayalam one act plays (multiple authors)- Collections	894.812 204 108**
Malayalam one act plays (multiple authors)- History and criticism	894.812 204 109**
Malayalam oratory (multiple authors)	***See*** Malayalam public speeches
Malayalam periodicals	059.94812
Malayalam poetry	894.8121
Malayalam poetry (multiple authors) - to 1845	***See*** Main schedule
Malayalam poetry (multiple authors) - 1845-1895	894.81214+

Malayalam poetry (multiple authors) - 1895-1919	894.81215+
Malayalam poetry (multiple authors) - 1920-1939	894.81216+
Malayalam poetry (multiple authors) - 1940-	894.81217+
Malayalam poetry (multiple authors) - 1940-1999	894.812171+
Malayalam poetry (multiple authors) - 19th century	894.81214+
Malayalam poetry (multiple authors) – 2000-	894.812172+
Malayalam poetry (multiple authors) - 20th century	894.812171+
Malayalam poetry (multiple authors)- Collections	894.8121008**
Malayalam poetry (multiple authors)- Dictionaries etc	894.8121003
Malayalam poetry (multiple authors)- History and criticism	894.8121009**
Malayalam poetry (multiple authors)- Periodicals	894.8121005
Malayalam poetry (multiple authors)- Philosophy and theory	894.8121001
Malayalam poetry (multiple authors)- Psychological aspects	894.81210019
Malayalam poetry (multiple authors)- Research	894.81210072
Malayalam poetry (multiple authors)- Study and teaching	894.8121007
Malayalam poetry (multiple authors)- Value	894.81210013

Malayalam poetry (single author)- - to 1845	***See*** Main schedule
Malayalam poetry (single author)- 1845 -1895	894.8121 4
Malayalam poetry (single author)- 1895 - 1919	894.8121 5
Malayalam poetry (single author)- 1920- 1939	894.8121 6
Malayalam poetry (single author)- 1940 -	894.8121 7
Malayalam poetry (single author)- 1940-1999	894.8121 71
Malayalam poetry (single author)- 19th century	894.8121 4
Malayalam poetry (single author)- 2000-	894.8121 72
Malayalam poetry (single author)- 20th century	894.8121 71
Malayalam prose (single author)- to 1845	***See*** Main schedule
Malayalam prose (single author)- 1845 -1895	894.8128 408
Malayalam prose (single author)- 1895 - 1919	894.8128 508
Malayalam prose (single author)- 1920- 1939	894.8128 608
Malayalam prose (single author)- 1940 -	894.8128 708
Malayalam prose (single author)- 1940-1999	894.8128 7108
Malayalam prose (single author)- 19th century	894.8128 408
Malayalam prose (single author)- 2000-	894.8128 7208
Malayalam prose (single author)- 20th century	894.8128 7108

Malayalam prose literature (multiple authors)	894.812808
Malayalam psychological, realistic, sociological fiction (multiple authors) - History and criticism	894.812308309**
Malayalam psychological, realistic, sociological fiction (multiple authors)- Collections	894.812308308**
Malayalam psychological, realistic, sociological fiction (multiple authors)	894.8123083*
Malayalam public discussions	***See*** Malayalam debates and public discussions
Malayalam public speeches (multiple authors)	894.812501
Malayalam public speeches (multiple authors)- Collections	894.81250108
Malayalam public speeches (multiple authors)- History and criticism	894.81250109
Malayalam quotations	***See*** Malayalam anecdotes ...
Malayalam realistic fiction	***See*** Malayalam psychological... fiction
Malayalam recitations (multiple authors)	894.812504+
Malayalam religious and morality plays (multiple authors)	894.81220516+
Malayalam reminiscences	***See*** Malayalam diaries ...
Malayalam romantic fiction (multiple authors)	894.8123085*

Malayalam romantic fiction (multiple authors)- Collections	894.812308508**
Malayalam romantic fiction (multiple authors)- History and criticism	894.812308509**
Malayalam satire	***See*** Malayalam humour and satire
Malayalam satirical poetry	***See*** Malayalam humourous and satirical poetry
Malayalam science fiction (multiple authors)	894.812308762*
Malayalam science fiction (multiple authors)- Collections	894.81230876208**
Malayalam science fiction (multiple authors)- History and criticism	894.81230876209**
Malayalam serious drama (multiple authors)	894.8122051+
Malayalam short stories (multiple authors)	894.812301*
Malayalam short stories (multiple authors)- Collections	894.81230108**
Malayalam short stories (multiple authors)- History and criticism	894.81230109**
Malayalam sociological fiction (multiple authors)	***See*** Malayalam psychological... fiction
Malayalam sonnets (multiple authors)	894.8121042*
Malayalam sonnets (multiple authors)- Collections	894.812104208**
Malayalam sonnets (multiple authors)- History and criticism	894.812104209**
Malayalam speaking people	305.794 812

Malayalam speeches (multiple authors)	894.8125
Malayalam speeches (multiple authors) — to 1845	***See*** Main schedule
Malayalam speeches (multiple authors) - 1845-1895	894.81254+
Malayalam speeches (multiple authors) - 1895-1919	894.81255+
Malayalam speeches (multiple authors) - 1920-1939	894.81256+
Malayalam speeches (multiple authors) - 1940-	894.81257+
Malayalam speeches (multiple authors) - 1940-1999	894.812571+
Malayalam speeches (multiple authors) - 19th century	894.81254+
Malayalam speeches (multiple authors) - 20th century	894.812571+
Malayalam speeches (multiple authors) - Collections	894.8125008**
Malayalam speeches (multiple authors) - Dictionaries etc	894.8125003
Malayalam speeches (multiple authors) - History and criticism	894.8125009**
Malayalam speeches (multiple authors) - Periodicals	894.8125005
Malayalam speeches (multiple authors) - Philosophy and theory	894.8125001
Malayalam speeches (multiple authors) - Psychological aspects	894.81250019
Malayalam speeches (multiple authors) - Research	894.81250072

Malayalam speeches (multiple authors) - Study and teaching	894.8125007
Malayalam speeches (multiple authors) - Value	894.81250013
Malayalam speeches (single author)- to 1845	***See*** Main schedule
Malayalam speeches (single author)- 1845 -1895	894.8125 4
Malayalam speeches (single author)- 1895 - 1919	894.8125 5
Malayalam speeches (single author)- 1920- 1939	894.8125 6
Malayalam speeches (single author)- 1940 -	894.8125 7
Malayalam speeches (single author)- 1940-1999	894.8125 71
Malayalam speeches (single author)- 19th century	894.8125 4
Malayalam speeches (single author)- 2000-	894.8125 72
Malayalam speeches (single author)- 20th century	894.8125 71
Malayalam suspense fiction (multiple authors)	894.81230872*
Malayalam suspense fiction (multiple authors)- Collections	894.8123087208**
Malayalam suspense fiction (multiple authors)- History and criticism	894.8123087209**
Malayalam tragedy (multiple authors)	894.81220512*
Malayalam tragedy (multiple authors)- Collections	894.8122051208**

Malayalam tragedy (multiple authors)- History and criticism	894.8122051209**
Malayalam variety drama (multiple authors)	894.8122057*
Malayalam variety drama (multiple authors)- Collections	894.812205708**
Malayalam variety drama (multiple authors)- History and criticism	894.812205709**
Malayali folk music	781 629 4812
Malayalis	305.894 812
Malayalis - Opinions	303.387 948 12
Maldivian language	491.487
Maldivian literature	891.48
Mandalas (Hinduism)	294.537
Manipur- Architecture	720.954 17
Manipur- Budget	352.495 417
Manipur- Economic development	338.954 17
Manipur- Economic geography	330.954 17
Manipur- Education	370.954 17
Manipur- Fauna	591.954 17
Manipur- Flora	581.954 17
Manipur- Folk dancing	793.319 5417
Manipur- Geography	915.417
Manipur- Geology	555.417
Manipur- History	954.17
Manipur- Painting and paintings	759.954 17
Manipur- Public administration	351.541 7

Manipur- Public finance	336.541 7
Manipur- Sculpture	730.954 17
Mantras (Buddhism)	294.343 7
Mantras (Hinduism)	294.537
Mantras (Jainism)	294.437
Mantras (Sikhism)	294.637
Mamis Code	294.592 6
Maratha folk music	781 629 48
Marathas	305.894 8
Marathas - Opinions	303.387 948
Marathi - English dictionary	491.463 21
Marathi adventure fiction (multiple authors)	891.463087*
Marathi adventure fiction (multiple authors) -Collections	891.46308708**
Marathi adventure fiction (multiple authors)- History and criticism	891.46308709**
Marathi anecdotes, epigrams, graffiti, jokes, quotations (multiple authors)	891.46802
Marathi anecdotes, epigrams, graffiti, jokes, quotations (single author)	891.468 +CD+02
Marathi as second language in elementary education	372.659 146
Marathi ballads (multiple authors)	891.461044*
Marathi ballads (multiple authors)- Collections	891.46104408**
Marathi ballads (multiple authors)- History and criticism	891.46104409**

Marathi comedy (multiple authors)	891.4620523*
Marathi comedy (multiple authors) - Collections	891.462052308**
Marathi comedy (multiple authors) - History and criticism	891.462052309**
Marathi conversations (multiple authors)	891.46506*
Marathi conversations (multiple authors) - Collections	891.4650608**
Marathi conversations (multiple authors) - History and criticism	891.4650609**
Marathi debates and public discussions (multiple authors)	891.46503*
Marathi debates and public discussions (multiple authors)- Collections	891.4650308**
Marathi debates and public discussions (multiple authors)- History and criticism	891.4650309**
Marathi detective fiction (multiple authors)	891.4630872*
Marathi detective fiction (multiple authors) - Collections	891.463087208**
Marathi detective fiction (multiple authors) - History and criticism	891.463087209**
Marathi diaries, notebooks, reminiscences (multiple authors)	891.46803
Marathi diaries, notebooks, reminiscences (single author)	891.468@
Marathi didactic poetry (multiple authors)	891.46105*
Marathi didactic poetry (multiple authors)- Collections	891.4610508**
Marathi didactic poetry (multiple authors)- History and criticism	891.4610509**

Marathi drama	891.462
Marathi drama (multiple authors) - -to 1845	***See*** Main schedule
Marathi drama (multiple authors) - 1845-1895	891.4624+
Marathi drama (multiple authors) - 1895-1919	891.4625+
Marathi drama (multiple authors) - 1920-1939	891.4626+
Marathi drama (multiple authors) - 1940-	891.4627+
Marathi drama (multiple authors) - 1940-1999	891.46271+
Marathi drama (multiple authors) - 19th century	891.4624+
Marathi drama (multiple authors) - 2000 -	891.46272+
Marathi drama (multiple authors) - 20th century	891.46271+
Marathi drama (multiple authors) - Collections	891.462008**
Marathi drama (multiple authors) - Dictionaries etc	891.462003
Marathi drama (multiple authors) - History and criticism	891.462009**
Marathi drama (multiple authors) - Periodicals	891.462005
Marathi drama (multiple authors) - Philosophy and theory	891.462001
Marathi drama (multiple authors) - Psychological aspects	891.4620019
Marathi drama (multiple authors) - Research	891.4620072

Marathi drama (multiple authors) - Study and teaching	891.462007
Marathi drama (multiple authors) - Value	891.4620013
Marathi drama (single author) - to 1845	***See*** Main schedule
Marathi drama (single author)- 1845 -1895	891.462 4
Marathi drama (single author)- 1895 - 1919	891.462 5
Marathi drama (single author)- 1920- 1939	891.462 6
Marathi drama (single author)- 1940 -	891.462 7
Marathi drama (single author)- 1940-1999	891.462 71
Marathi drama (single author)- 19th century	891.462 4
Marathi drama (single author)- 2000 -	891.462 72
Marathi drama (single author)- 20th century	891.462 71
Marathi drama for cinema (multiple authors)	891.46203*
Marathi drama for cinema (multiple authors) - Collections	891.4620308**
Marathi drama for cinema (multiple authors) - History and criticism	891.4620309**
Marathi drama for radio (multiple authors)	891.462022*
Marathi drama for radio (multiple authors) - Collections	891.46202208**
Marathi drama for radio (multiple authors) - History and criticism	891.46202209**
Marathi drama for television (multiple authors)	891.462025*
Marathi drama for television (multiple authors) - Collections	891.46202508**
Marathi drama for television (multiple authors) - History and criticism	891.46202509**

Marathi dramatic poetry (multiple authors)	891.46102*
Marathi dramatic poetry (multiple authors)- Collections	891.4610208**
Marathi dramatic poetry (multiple authors)- History and criticism	891.4610209**
Marathi encyclopaedias	039.9146
Marathi ephemeral and light verse (multiple authors)	891.46108*
Marathi ephemeral and light verse (multiple authors)- Collections	891.4610808**
Marathi ephemeral and light verse (multiple authors) - History and criticism	891.4610809**
Marathi epic poetry (multiple authors)	891.461032*
Marathi epic poetry (multiple authors)- Collections	891.46103208**
Marathi epic poetry (multiple authors)- History and criticism	891.46103209**
Marathi epigrams	***See*** Marathi anecdotes ...
Marathi essays	891.464
Marathi essays (multiple authors) - - to 1845	***See*** Main schedule
Marathi essays (multiple authors) - 1845-1895	891.4644+
Marathi essays (multiple authors) - 1895-1919	891.4645+
Marathi essays (multiple authors) - 1920-1939	891.4646+
Marathi essays (multiple authors) -1940-	891.4647+

Marathi essays (multiple authors) - 1940-1999	891.46471+
Marathi essays (multiple authors) - 19th century	891.4644+
Marathi essays (multiple authors) –2000-	891.46472+
Marathi essays (multiple authors) - 20th century	891.46471+
Marathi essays (multiple authors) - Collections	891.464008**
Marathi essays (multiple authors) - Dictionaries etc	891.464003
Marathi essays (multiple authors) - History and criticism	891.464009**
Marathi essays (multiple authors) - Periodicals	891.464005
Marathi essays (multiple authors) - Philosophy and theory	891.464001
Marathi essays (multiple authors) - Psychological aspects	891.4640019
Marathi essays (multiple authors) -Research	891.4640072
Marathi essays (multiple authors) - Study and teaching	891.464007
Marathi essays (multiple authors) -Value	891.4640013
Marathi essays (single author)- - to 1845	***See*** Main schedule
Marathi essays (single author)- 1845 -1895	891.464 4
Marathi essays (single author)- 1895 - 1919	891.464 5
Marathi essays (single author)- 1920- 1939	891.464 6
Marathi essays (single author)- 1940 -	891.464 7

Marathi essays (single author)- 1940-1999	891.464 71
Marathi essays (single author)- 19th century	891.464 4
Marathi essays (single author)- 2000-	891.464 72
Marathi essays (single author)- 20th century	891.464 71
Marathi experimental and non-formalized works (single author)	891.468+CD+07
Marathi experimental and non-formalised works (multiple authors)	891.46807
Marathi fantasy fiction (multiple authors)	891.46308766*
Marathi fantasy fiction (multiple authors)- Collections	891.4630876608**
Marathi fantasy fiction (multiple authors)- History and criticism	891.4630876609**
Marathi farce (multiple authors)	891.46205232*
Marathi farce (multiple authors)- Collections	891.4620523208**
Marathi farce (multiple authors)- History and criticism	891.4620523209**
Marathi fiction	891.463
Marathi fiction (multiple authors) - - to 1845	***See*** Main schedule
Marathi fiction (multiple authors) - 1845-1895	891.4634+
Marathi fiction (multiple authors) - 1895-1919	891.4635+
Marathi fiction (multiple authors) - 1920-1939	891.4636+
Marathi fiction (multiple authors) - 1940-	891.4637+
Marathi fiction (multiple authors) - 1940-1999	891.46371+

Marathi fiction (multiple authors) - 19th century	891.4634+
Marathi fiction (multiple authors) - 2000-	891.46372+
Marathi fiction (multiple authors) - 20th century	891.46371+
Marathi fiction (multiple authors) - Collections	891.463008**
Marathi fiction (multiple authors) - Dictionaries etc	891.463003
Marathi fiction (multiple authors) - History and criticism	891.463009**
Marathi fiction (multiple authors) - Periodicals	891.463005
Marathi fiction (multiple authors) - Philosophy and theory	891.463001
Marathi fiction (multiple authors) - Psychological aspects	891.4630019
Marathi fiction (multiple authors) - Research	891.4630072
Marathi fiction (multiple authors) - Study and teaching	891.463007
Marathi fiction (multiple authors) - Value	891.4630013
Marathi fiction (single author)- - to 1845	***See*** Main schedule
Marathi fiction (single author)- 1845 -1895	891.463 4
Marathi fiction (single author)- 1895 - 1919	891.463 5
Marathi fiction (single author)- 1920 - 1939	891.463 6
Marathi fiction (single author)- 1940 -	891.463 7
Marathi fiction (single author)- 1940-1999	891.463 71
Marathi fiction (single author)- 19th century	891.463 4

Marathi fiction (single author)- 2000-	891.463 72
Marathi fiction (single author)- 20th century	891.463 71
Marathi ghost fiction (multiple authors)	891.46308733*
Marathi ghost fiction (multiple authors) - Collections	891.4630873308**
Marathi ghost fiction (multiple authors)- History and criticism	891.4630873309**
Marathi graffiti	***See*** Marathi anecdotes ...
Marathi historical drama (multiple authors)	891.4620514*
Marathi historical drama (multiple authors)- Collections	891.462051408**
Marathi historical drama (multiple authors)- History and criticism	891.462051409**
Marathi historical fiction (multiple authors)	891.463081*
Marathi historical fiction (multiple authors)- Collections	891.46308108**
Marathi historical fiction (multiple authors)- History and criticism	891.46308109**
Marathi horror fiction (multiple authors)	891.46308738*
Marathi horror fiction (multiple authors)- Collections	891.4630873808**
Marathi horror fiction (multiple authors)- History and criticism	891.4630873809**
Marathi humour and satire	891.467
Marathi humour and satire (multiple authors) — to 1845	***See*** Main schedule
Marathi humour and satire (multiple authors) -1845-1895	891.4674+

Marathi humour and satire (multiple authors) -1895-1919	891.4675+
Marathi humour and satire (multiple authors) -1920-1939	891.4676+
Marathi humour and satire (multiple authors) -1940-	891.4677+
Marathi humour and satire (multiple authors) -1940-1999	891.46771+
Marathi humour and satire (multiple authors) -19th century	891.4674+
Marathi humour and satire (multiple authors) –2000-	891.46772+
Marathi humour and satire (multiple authors) -20th century	891.46771+
Marathi humour and satire (multiple authors) -Collections	891.467008**
Marathi humour and satire (multiple authors) -Dictionaries etc	891.467003
Marathi humour and satire (multiple authors) -History and criticism	891.467009**
Marathi humour and satire (multiple authors) -Periodicals	891.467005
Marathi humour and satire (multiple authors) -Philosophy and theory	891.467001
Marathi humour and satire (multiple authors) -Psychological aspects	891.4670019
Marathi humour and satire (multiple authors) -Research	891.4670072
Marathi humour and satire (multiple authors) -Study and teaching	891.467007

Marathi humour and satire (multiple authors) -Value	891.4670013
Marathi humourous and satirical poetry (multiple authors)	891.46107*
Marathi humourous and satirical poetry (multiple authors)- Collections	891.4610708**
Marathi humourous and satirical poetry (multiple authors)- History and criticism	891.4610709**
Marathi jokes	***See*** Marathi anecdotes,...
Marathi jokes (multiple authors)	891.46802
Marathi language	491.46
Marathi language- Applied linguistics	491.468
Marathi language- Bilingual dictionaries	491.463 2-39
Marathi language- Bilingualism	491.460 42
Marathi language- Concordances	491.460 3
Marathi language- Content analysis	491.460 141
Marathi language- Dialects	491.467
Marathi language- Dictionaries	491.463
Marathi language- Discourse analysis	491.460 141
Marathi language- Education	491.460 71
Marathi language- Encyclopaedias	491.460 3
Marathi language- Etymology	491.462
Marathi language- Functionalism	491.460 18
Marathi language- Grammar	491.465
Marathi language- History	491.460 9

Marathi language- Intonation	491.461 6
Marathi language- Lexicography	491.463 028
Marathi language- Lexicology	491.460 14
Marathi language- Miscellany	491.460 2
Marathi language- Multilingualism	491.460 42
Marathi language- Organizations	491.460 6
Marathi language- Orthography	491.461 52
Marathi language- Pauses	491.461 6
Marathi language- Periodicals	491.460 5
Marathi language- Persons (men, women, etc)	491.460 8
Marathi language- Philosophy and theory	491.460 1
Marathi language- Phonetics	491.461 58
Marathi language- Phonology, etc	491.461 5
Marathi language- Pitch	491.461 6
Marathi language- Pronunciation	491.461 52
Marathi language- Readers	491.468 6
Marathi language- Research	491.460 72
Marathi language -Rhetoric	808.049 146++
Marathi language- Schools and theories of linguistics	491.460 18
Marathi language- Semantics	491.460 143
Marathi language- Semiotics	491.460 141
Marathi language- Slang	491.467
Marathi language- Special topics	491.460 4

Marathi language- Specialized dictionaries	491.463 1
Marathi language- Spelling	491.461 52
Marathi language- Stress	491.461 6
Marathi language- Structural linguistics	491.460 18
Marathi language- Suprasegmental features	491.461 6
Marathi language- Terminology	491.460 14
Marathi language- Theory	491.460 1
Marathi language- Usage	491.468
Marathi language- Variations (Dialects etc).	491.467
Marathi language- Writing systems	491.461 1
Marathi letters	891.466
Marathi letters (multiple authors) - - to 1845	***See*** Main schedule
Marathi letters (multiple authors) - 1845-1895	891.4664+
Marathi letters (multiple authors) - 1895-1919	891.4665+
Marathi letters (multiple authors) - 1920-1939	891.4666+
Marathi letters (multiple authors) -1940-	891.4667+
Marathi letters (multiple authors) - 1940-1999	891.46671+
Marathi letters (multiple authors) -19th century	891.4664+
Marathi letters (multiple authors) –2000-	891.46672+
Marathi letters (multiple authors) - 20th century	891.46671+
Marathi letters (multiple authors) - Collections	891.466008**

Marathi letters (multiple authors) - Dictionaries etc	891.466003
Marathi letters (multiple authors) - History and criticism	891.466009**
Marathi letters (multiple authors) - Periodicals	891.466005
Marathi letters (multiple authors) - Philosophy and theory	891.466001
Marathi letters (multiple authors) - Psychological aspects	891.4660019
Marathi letters (multiple authors) -Research	891.4660072
Marathi letters (multiple authors) - Study and teaching	891.466007
Marathi letters (multiple authors) -Value	891.4660013
Marathi letters (single author)- - to 1845	***See*** Main schedule
Marathi letters (single author)- 1845 -1895	891.466 4
Marathi letters (single author)- 1895 - 1919	891.466 5
Marathi letters (single author)- 1920 - 1939	891.466 6
Marathi letters (single author)- 1940 -	891.466 7
Marathi letters (single author)- 1940-1999	891.466 71
Marathi letters (single author)- 19th century	891.466 4
Marathi letters (single author)- 2000-	891.466 72
Marathi letters (single author)- 20th century	891.466 71
Marathi light verse	***See*** Marathi ephemeral and light verse
Marathi limericks (multiple authors)	891.461075*

Marathi limericks (multiple authors)-Collections	891.46107508**
Marathi limericks (multiple authors)-History and criticism	891.46107509**
Marathi literature	891.46
Marathi literature (collections of multiple forms)	891.4608
Marathi literature (collections of multiple forms) - 19th century	891.460804
Marathi literature (collections of multiple forms) - 20th century	891.4608071
Marathi literature (collections of multiple forms) – 21st century	891.4608072
Marathi literature (collections of multiple forms) - Allegory	891.4608015
Marathi literature (collections of multiple forms) - Animals	891.46080362++
Marathi literature (collections of multiple forms) - Artistic themes	891.46080357
Marathi literature (collections of multiple forms) - Atmosphere	891.4608032161
Marathi literature (collections of multiple forms) - Characters	891.4608027
Marathi literature (collections of multiple forms) - Comedy	891.4608017
Marathi literature (collections of multiple forms) - Evening	891.4608033
Marathi literature (collections of multiple forms) - Fantasy	891.4608015

Marathi literature (collections of multiple forms) - Forests	891.4608032152
Marathi literature (collections of multiple forms) - Historical themes	891.46080358
Marathi literature (collections of multiple forms) - Horror	891.46080164
Marathi literature (collections of multiple forms) - Human characteristics (Biological, moral and psychological)	891.46080353
Marathi literature (collections of multiple forms) - Legendary objects/themes	891.4608037
Marathi literature (collections of multiple forms) - Literary themes	891.46080357
Marathi literature (collections of multiple forms) - Love	891.460803543
Marathi literature (collections of multiple forms) - Marriage	891.460803543
Marathi literature (collections of multiple forms) - Morning	891.4608033
Marathi literature (collections of multiple forms) - Mountains	891.4608032143
Marathi literature (collections of multiple forms) - Myth	891.4608015
Marathi literature (collections of multiple forms) - Mythological objects/themes	891.4608037
Marathi literature (collections of multiple forms) - Philosophic themes	891.46080384
Marathi literature (collections of multiple forms) - Places	891.4608032++
Marathi literature (collections of multiple forms) - Plants	891.46080364

Marathi literature (collections of multiple forms) - Political themes	891.46080358
Marathi literature (collections of multiple forms) - Religious themes	891.46080382++
Marathi literature (collections of multiple forms) - Rivers	891.46080321693
Marathi literature (collections of multiple forms) - Romanticism	891.46080145
Marathi literature (collections of multiple forms) - Scientific themes	891.46080356
Marathi literature (collections of multiple forms) - Sea	891.4608032162
Marathi literature (collections of multiple forms) - Seasons	891.4608033
Marathi literature (collections of multiple forms) - Sex	891.460803538
Marathi literature (collections of multiple forms) - Social themes	891.46080355
Marathi literature (collections of multiple forms) - Space	891.460803219
Marathi literature (collections of multiple forms) - Specific kinds of persons, e.g. heroes	891.46080352++
Marathi literature (collections of multiple forms) - Specific persons (real or imaginary)	891.46080351
Marathi literature (collections of multiple forms) - Stream of consciousness	891.4608025
Marathi literature (collections of multiple forms) - Supernatural objects/themes	891.4608037
Marathi literature (collections of multiple forms) - Symbolism	891.4608015

Marathi literature (collections of multiple forms) - Technical themes	891.46080356
Marathi literature (collections of multiple forms) - Times (seasons, parts of day, etc)	891.4608033
Marathi literature (collections of multiple forms) - Towns	891.46080321732
Marathi literature (collections of multiple forms) - Tragedy	891.46080162
Marathi literature (collections of multiple forms) - Villages	891.46080321734
Marathi literature (collections of multiple forms) - Weather	891.4608036
Marathi literature (collections of multiple forms) emphasizing subjects	891.460804++
Marathi literature (collections of multiple forms) for/by children	891.460809282
Marathi literature (collections of multiple forms) for/by persons of racial, ethnic and national groups	891.460808++
Marathi literature (collections of multiple forms) for/by persons of specific classes	891.4608092++
Marathi literature (collections of multiple forms) for/by persons resident in specific regions	891.4608091++
Marathi literature (collections of multiple forms) for/by women	891.460809287
Marathi literature (multiple authors) - Concordances	891.4603
Marathi literature (multiple authors) - Dictionaries	891.4603

Marathi literature (multiple authors) - Education	891.46071
Marathi literature (multiple authors) - Encyclopaedias	891.4603
Marathi literature (multiple authors) - Organizations	891.4606
Marathi literature (multiple authors) - Periodicals	891.4605
Marathi literature (multiple authors) - Philosophy and theory	891.4601
Marathi literature (multiple authors) - Research	891.46072
Marathi literature (multiple authors) - Research in India	891.46072054
Marathi literature (multiple authors) - Study and teaching	891.4607
Marathi literature (multiple forms) - Supernatural objects/themes - History and criticism	891.460937
Marathi literature (multiple forms) - 19th century	891.4609004
Marathi literature (multiple forms) – 2000-	891.46090072
Marathi literature (multiple forms) - 20th century	891.46090071
Marathi literature (multiple forms) - Allegory – History and criticism	891.460915
Marathi literature (multiple forms) - Animals - History and criticism	891.4609362++
Marathi literature (multiple forms) - Artistic themes - History and criticism	891.4609357

Marathi literature (multiple forms) - Atmosphere - History and criticism	891.460932161
Marathi literature (multiple forms) - Characters - History and criticism	891.460927
Marathi literature (multiple forms) - Comedy - History and criticism	891.460917
Marathi literature (multiple forms) - Evening - History and criticism	891.460933
Marathi literature (multiple forms) - Fantasy - History , description, criticism	891.460915
Marathi literature (multiple forms) - Forests - History and criticism	891.460932152
Marathi literature (multiple forms) - Historical themes - History and criticism	891.4609358
Marathi literature (multiple forms) - History and criticism	891.4609
Marathi literature (multiple forms) - Horror - History and criticism	891.4609164
Marathi literature (multiple forms) - Human characteristics (Biological, moral, psychological) - History and criticism	891.4609353
Marathi literature (multiple forms) - Legendary objects/themes - History and criticism	891.460937
Marathi literature (multiple forms) - Literary themes - History and criticism	891.4609357
Marathi literature (multiple forms) - Love - History and criticism	891.46093543
Marathi literature (multiple forms) - Marriage - History and criticism	891.46093543

Marathi literature (multiple forms) - Morning - History and criticism	891.460933
Marathi literature (multiple forms) - Mountains - History and criticism	891.460932143
Marathi literature (multiple forms) - Myth - History and criticism	891.460915
Marathi literature (multiple forms) - Mythological objects/themes - History and criticism	891.460937
Marathi literature (multiple forms) - Persons of racial, ethnic and national groups - History and criticism	891.46098++
Marathi literature (multiple forms) - Persons of specific classes - History and criticism	891.460992++
Marathi literature (multiple forms) - Persons resident in specific regions - History and criticism	891.460991++
Marathi literature (multiple forms) - Philosophic themes - History and criticism	891.4609384
Marathi literature (multiple forms) - Places - History and criticism	891.460932++
Marathi literature (multiple forms) - Plants - History and criticism	891.4609364
Marathi literature (multiple forms) - Political themes - History and criticism	891.4609358
Marathi literature (multiple forms) - Religious themes - History and criticism	891.4609382++
Marathi literature (multiple forms) - Rivers - History and criticism	891.4609321693
Marathi literature (multiple forms) - Romanticism - History and criticism	891.4609145

Marathi literature (multiple forms) - Scientific themes - History and criticism	891.4609356
Marathi literature (multiple forms) - Sea - History and criticism	891.460932162
Marathi literature (multiple forms) - Seasons - History and criticism	891.460933
Marathi literature (multiple forms) - Sex - History and criticism	891.46093538
Marathi literature (multiple forms) - Social themes - History and criticism	891.4609355
Marathi literature (multiple forms) - Space - History and criticism	891.46093219
Marathi literature (multiple forms) - Specific kinds of persons, e.g. heroes, - History and criticism	891.4609352++
Marathi literature (multiple forms) - Specific persons - History and criticism	891.4609351
Marathi literature (multiple forms) - Stream of consciousness - History and criticism	891.460925
Marathi literature (multiple forms) - Subjects - History and criticism	891.46094++
Marathi literature (multiple forms) - Symbolism- History, description, criticism	891.460915
Marathi literature (multiple forms) - Technical themes - History and criticism	891.4609356
Marathi literature (multiple forms) - Times - History and criticism	891.460933
Marathi literature (multiple forms) - Towns - History and criticism	891.4609321732

Marathi literature (multiple forms) - Tragedy - History and criticism	891.4609162
Marathi literature (multiple forms) - Villages - History and criticism	891.4609321734
Marathi literature (multiple forms) - Weather - History and criticism	891.460936
Marathi literature (single author)- - to 1845 - Biography, collections, criticism	***See*** Main schedule
Marathi literature (single author)- 1845 - 1895 - Biography, collections, criticism	891.468 409
Marathi literature (single author)- 1895 - 1919 - Biography, collections, criticism	891.468 509
Marathi literature (single author)- 1920 1939 - Biography, collections, criticism	891.468 609
Marathi literature (single author)- 1940 - Biography, collections, criticism	891.468 709
Marathi literature (single author)- 1940-1999 - Biography, collections, criticism	891.468 7109
Marathi literature (single author)- 19th century - Biography, collections, criticism	891.468 409
Marathi literature (single author)- 20th century - Biography, collections, criticism	891.468 7109
Marathi literature (single author)- 2000- Biography, collections, criticism	891.468 7209
Marathi literature for/by children - History and criticism	891.46099282
Marathi literature for/by women - History and criticism	891.46099287
Marathi love fiction (multiple authors)	891.463085*

Marathi love fiction (multiple authors)-Collections	891.46308508**
Marathi love fiction (multiple authors)-History and criticism	891.46308509**
Marathi melodrama (multiple authors)	891.4620527*
Marathi melodrama (multiple authors)-Collections	891.462052708**
Marathi melodrama (multiple authors)-History and criticism	891.462052709**
Marathi miscellaneous writings (multiple authors)	891.468
Marathi miscellaneous writings (multiple authors) - to 1845	*See* Main schedule
Marathi miscellaneous writings (multiple authors) -1845-1895	891.4684++
Marathi miscellaneous writings (multiple authors) -1895-1919	891.4685++
Marathi miscellaneous writings (multiple authors) -1920-1939	891.4686++
Marathi miscellaneous writings (multiple authors) -1940-	891.4687++
Marathi miscellaneous writings (multiple authors) -1940-1999	891.46871++
Marathi miscellaneous writings (multiple authors) -19th century	891.4684++
Marathi miscellaneous writings (multiple authors) –2000-	891.46872++
Marathi miscellaneous writings (multiple authors) -20th century	891.46871++
Marathi miscellaneous writings (multiple authors) -Collections	891.468008**

Marathi miscellaneous writings (multiple authors) -Dictionaries etc	891.468003
Marathi miscellaneous writings (multiple authors) -History and criticism	891.468009**
Marathi miscellaneous writings (multiple authors) -Periodicals	891.468005
Marathi miscellaneous writings (multiple authors) -Philosophy and theory	891.468001
Marathi miscellaneous writings (multiple authors) -Psychological aspects	891.4680019
Marathi miscellaneous writings (multiple authors) -Research	891.4680072
Marathi miscellaneous writings (multiple authors) -Study and teaching	891.468007
Marathi miscellaneous writings (multiple authors) -Value	891.4680013
Marathi miscellaneous writings (single author)- - to 1845	***See*** Main schedule
Marathi miscellaneous writings (single author)- 1845 -1895	891.468 4
Marathi miscellaneous writings (single author)- 1895 - 1919	891.468 5
Marathi miscellaneous writings (single author)- 1920 - 1939	891.468 6
Marathi miscellaneous writings (single author)- 1940 -	891.468 7
Marathi miscellaneous writings (single author)- 1940-1999	891.468 71
Marathi miscellaneous writings (single author)- 19th century	891.468 4
Marathi miscellaneous writings (single author)- 2000-	891.468 72

Marathi miscellaneous writings (single author)- 20th century	891.468 71
Marathi monologues (multiple authors)	891.462045*
Marathi monologues (multiple authors)- Collections	891.46204508**
Marathi monologues (multiple authors)- History and criticism	891.46204509**
Marathi morality plays	***See*** Marathi religious... plays
Marathi mystery fiction (multiple authors)	891.4630872*
Marathi mystery fiction (multiple authors)- Collections	891.463087208**
Marathi mystery fiction (multiple authors)- History and criticism	891.463087209**
Marathi narrative poetry (multiple authors)	891.46103*
Marathi narrative poetry (multiple authors)- Collections	891.4610308**
Marathi narrative poetry (multiple authors)- History and criticism	891.4610309**
Marathi notebooks	***See*** Marathi diaries...
Marathi odes (multiple authors)	891.461043*
Marathi odes (multiple authors)- Collections	891.46104308**
Marathi odes (multiple authors)- History and criticism	891.46104309**
Marathi one act plays (multiple authors)	891.462 041*
Marathi one act plays (multiple authors)- Collections	891.462 041 08**
Marathi one act plays (multiple authors)- History and criticism	891.462 041 09**

Marathi oratory (multiple authors)	*See* Marathi public speeches
Marathi periodicals	059.9146
Marathi poetry	891.461
Marathi poetry (multiple authors) - - to 1845	*See* Main schedule
Marathi poetry (multiple authors)-1845-1895	891.4614+
Marathi poetry (multiple authors)-1895-1919	891.4615+
Marathi poetry (multiple authors)-1920-1939	891.4616+
Marathi poetry (multiple authors)-1940-	891.4617+
Marathi poetry (multiple authors)-1940-1999	891.46171+
Marathi poetry (multiple authors) - 19th century	891.4614+
Marathi poetry (multiple authors) – 2000-	891.46172+
Marathi poetry (multiple authors) - 20th century	891.46171+
Marathi poetry (multiple authors)- Collections	891.461008**
Marathi poetry (multiple authors)- Dictionaries etc	891.461003
Marathi poetry (multiple authors)- History and criticism	891.461009**
Marathi poetry (multiple authors)- Periodicals	891.461005
Marathi poetry (multiple authors)- Philosophy and theory	891.461001
Marathi poetry (multiple authors)- Psychological aspects	891.4610019
Marathi poetry (multiple authors)- Research	891.4610072

Marathi poetry (multiple authors)- Study and teaching	891.461007
Marathi poetry (multiple authors)- Value	891.4610013
Marathi poetry (single author)- - to 1845	***See*** Main schedule
Marathi poetry (single author)- 1845 -1895	891.461 4
Marathi poetry (single author)- 1895 - 1919	891.461 5
Marathi poetry (single author)- 1920 - 1939	891.461 6
Marathi poetry (single author)- 1940 -	891.461 7
Marathi poetry (single author)- 1940-1999	891.461 71
Marathi poetry (single author)- 19th century	891.461 4
Marathi poetry (single author)- 2000-	891.461 72
Marathi poetry (single author)- 20th century	891.461 71
Marathi prose (single author)- - to 1845	***See*** Main schedule
Marathi prose (single author)- 1845 -1895	891.468 408
Marathi prose (single author)- 1895 - 1919	891.468 508
Marathi prose (single author)- 1920 - 1939	891.468 608
Marathi prose (single author)- 1940 -	891.468 708
Marathi prose (single author)- 1940-1999	891.468 7108
Marathi prose (single author)- 19th century	891.468 408
Marathi prose (single author)- 2000-	891.468 7208
Marathi prose (single author)- 20th century	891.468 7108
Marathi prose literature (multiple authors)	891.46808
Marathi psychological, realistic, sociological fiction (multiple authors)	891.463083*
Marathi psychological, realistic, sociological fiction (multiple authors) - History and criticism	891.46308309**

Marathi psychological, realistic, sociological fiction (multiple authors) - Collections	891.46308308**
Marathi public discussions	***See*** Marathi debates ... discussions
Marathi public speeches (multiple authors)	891.46501*
Marathi public speeches (multiple authors)- Collections	891.4650108**
Marathi public speeches (multiple authors)- History and criticism	891.4650109**
Marathi quotations	***See*** Marathi anecdotes ..
Marathi quotations (multiple authors)	891.46802
Marathi realistic fiction	***See*** Marathi psychological... fiction
Marathi recitations (multiple authors)	891.46504+
Marathi religious and morality plays (multiple authors)	891.4620516+
Marathi reminiscences	***See*** Marathi diaries ...
Marathi romantic fiction (multiple authors)	891.463085*
Marathi romantic fiction (multiple authors)- Collections	891.46308508**
Marathi romantic fiction (multiple authors)- History and criticism	891.46308509**
Marathi satire	***See*** Marathi humour and satire
Marathi satirical poetry	***See*** Marathi

	humourous ... poetry
Marathi science fiction (multiple authors)	891.46308762*
Marathi science fiction (multiple authors)- Collections	891.4630876208**
Marathi science fiction (multiple authors)- History and criticism	891.4630876209**
Marathi serious drama (multiple authors)	891.462051+
Marathi short stories (multiple authors)	891.46301*
Marathi short stories (multiple authors)- Collections	891.4630108**
Marathi short stories (multiple authors)- History and criticism	891.4630109**
Marathi sociological fiction (multiple authors)	***See*** Marathi psychological ... fiction
Marathi sonnets (multiple authors)	891.461042*
Marathi sonnets (multiple authors)- Collections	891.46104208**
Marathi sonnets (multiple authors)- History and criticism	891.46104209**
Marathi speaking people	305.791 46
Marathi speeches	891.465
Marathi speeches (multiple authors) — to 1845	***See*** Main schedule
Marathi speeches (multiple authors) - 1845-1895	891.4654+
Marathi speeches (multiple authors) - 1895-1919	891.4655+

Marathi speeches (multiple authors) - 1920-1939	891.4656+
Marathi speeches (multiple authors) -1940-	891.4657+
Marathi speeches (multiple authors) - 1940-1999	891.46571+
Marathi speeches (multiple authors) - 19th century	891.4654+
Marathi speeches (multiple authors) - 20th century	891.46571+
Marathi speeches (multiple authors) - Collections	891.465008**
Marathi speeches (multiple authors) - Dictionaries etc	891.465003
Marathi speeches (multiple authors) - History and criticism	891.465009**
Marathi speeches (multiple authors) - Periodicals	891.465005
Marathi speeches (multiple authors) - Philosophy and theory	891.465001
Marathi speeches (multiple authors) - Psychological aspects	891.4650019
Marathi speeches (multiple authors) - Research	891.4650072
Marathi speeches (multiple authors) - Study and teaching	891.465007
Marathi speeches (multiple authors) -Value	891.4650013
Marathi speeches (single author)- - to 1845	***See*** Main schedule
Marathi speeches (single author)- 1845 - 1895	891.465 4

Marathi speeches (single author)- 1895 - 1919	891.465 5
Marathi speeches (single author)- 1920 - 1939	891.465 6
Marathi speeches (single author)- 1940 -	891.465 7
Marathi speeches (single author)- 1940-1999	891.465 71
Marathi speeches (single author)- 19th century	891.465 4
Marathi speeches (single author)- 2000-	891.465 72
Marathi speeches (single author)- 20th century	891.465 71
Marathi suspense fiction (multiple authors)	891.4630872*
Marathi suspense fiction (multiple authors)- Collections	891.463087208**
Marathi suspense fiction (multiple authors)- History and criticism	891.463087209**
Marathi tragedy (multiple authors)	891.4620512*
Marathi tragedy (multiple authors)- Collections	891.462051208**
Marathi tragedy (multiple authors)- History and criticism	891.462051209**
Marathi variety drama (multiple authors)	891.462057*
Marathi variety drama (multiple authors)- Collections	891.46205708**
Marathi variety drama (multiple authors)- History and criticism	891.46205709**
Marriage (Buddhism)	294.337 835
Marriage (Hinduism)	294.517835

Marriage (Jainism)	294.417835
Marriage (Sikhism)	294.617835
Marwari speaking people	305.791 479
Medicine (Buddhism)	294.337 5
Medicine (Hinduism)	294.5175
Medicine (Jainism)	294.4175
Medicine (Sikhism)	294.6175
Meditation (Buddhism)	294.344 35
Meditation (Hinduism)	294.543 5
Meditation (Jainism)	294.443 5
Meditation (Sikhism)	294.643 5
Meditation literature (Buddhism)	294.343 2
Meditation literature (Hinduism)	294.543 2
Meditation literature (Jainism)	294.443 2
Meditation literature (Sikhism)	294.643 2
Meghalaya- Architecture	720.954 164
Meghalaya- Budget	352.495 416 4
Meghalaya- Economic development	338.954 16 4
Meghalaya- Economic geography	330.954 164
Meghalaya- Education	370.954 16 4
Meghalaya- Fauna	591.954 164
Meghalaya- Flora	581.954 16 4
Meghalaya- Folk dancing	793.319 54164
Meghalaya- Geography	915.4164
Meghalaya- Geology	555.416 4

Meghalaya- History	954.164
Meghalaya- Painting and paintings	759.954 164
Meghalaya- Public administration	351.541 64
Meghalaya- Public finance	336.541 64
Meghalaya- Sculpture	730.954 164
Middle Indic languages	491.3
Middle Indic literatures	891.3
Migration from India to U. K.	304.841054
Military assistance to India	355.032 54
Military capability- India	355.033 254
Military policy- India	355.033 554
Military relations- India	355.031 095 4
Military relations- India - Russia	355.031 095 409 47
Military situation	355.033
Military situation- India	355.033 054
Military societies	***See*** Hereditary ... societies
Mimamsa philosophy	181.42
Miracles (Buddhism)	294.342 117
Miracles (Hinduism)	294.521 17
Miracles (Jainism)	294.421 17
Miracles (Sikhism)	294.621 17
Miscellaneous writings in Assamese	891.451 8
Miscellaneous writings in Bengali	891.448
Miscellaneous writings in Bihari	891.454 8

Miscellaneous writings in English	828
Miscellaneous writings in Hindi	891.438
Miscellaneous writings in Kannada	891.8148
Miscellaneous writings in Lahnda	891.419 8
Miscellaneous writings in Malayalam	891.8128
Miscellaneous writings in Marathi	891.468
Miscellaneous writings in Oriya	891.456 8
Miscellaneous writings in Pali	891.378
Miscellaneous writings in Panjabi	891.428
Miscellaneous writings in Sanskrit	891.28
Miscellaneous writings in Sindhi	891.418
Miscellaneous writings in Tamil	891.8118
Miscellaneous writings in Telugu	891.8278
Miscellaneous writings in Urdu	891.439 8
Missions (Buddhism)	294.372
Missions (Hinduism)	294.572
Missions (Jainism)	294.472
Missions (Sikhism)	294.672
Mizoram- Architecture	720.954 166
Mizoram- Budget	352.495 416 6
Mizoram- Economic development	338.954 16 6
Mizoram- Economic geography	330.954 166
Mizoram- Education	370.954 16 6
Mizoram- Fauna	591.954 166
Mizoram- Flora	581.954 16 6

Mizoram- Folk dancing	793.319 54166
Mizoram- Geography	915.4166
Mizoram- Geology	555.416 6
Mizoram- History	954.166
Mizoram- Painting and paintings	759.954 166
Mizoram- Public administration	351.541 66
Mizoram- Public finance	336.541 66
Mizoram- Sculpture	730.954 166
Modern Indian literatures	891.4
Modern Indic language speaking people	305.791 4
Modern Indic languages	491.4
Modern Indic literatures	891.4
Monarchs (Buddhism)	294.342 13
Monarchs (Hinduism)	294.5213
Monarchs (Jainism)	294.4213
Monarchs (Sikhism)	294.6213
Moral theology (Buddhism).	294.35
Moral theology (Hinduism)	294.548
Moral theology (Jainism)	294.45
Moral theology (Sikhism)	294.65
Mosaic glass and glass makers	***See*** Stained ... glass makers
Movement of people	304.8
Mumbai	***See*** Bombay
Munda folk music	781.629 595

Munda languages	495.95
Munda literature	895.95
Mundari speaking people	305.795 95
Mundas (People)	305.895 95
Museums of fine and decorative arts- Andaman and Nicobar Islands	708.954 88
Museums of fine and decorative arts- Andhra Pradesh	708.954 84
Museums of fine and decorative arts- Arunachal Pradesh	708.954 163
Museums of fine and decorative arts- Assam	708.954 162
Museums of fine and decorative arts- Bengal	708.954 14
Museums of fine and decorative arts- Bhopal	708.954 3
Museums of fine and decorative arts- Bihar	708.954 12
Museums of fine and decorative arts- Bombay	708.954 7923
Museums of fine and decorative arts- Calcutta	708.954 147
Museums of fine and decorative arts- Chandigarh	708.954 552
Museums of fine and decorative arts- Dadra and Nagar Haveli	708.954 796
Museums of fine and decorative arts- Delhi	708.954 56
Museums of fine and decorative arts- Goa, Daman and Diu	708.954 799

Museums of fine and decorative arts- Gujarat	708.954 75
Museums of fine and decorative arts- Haryana	708.954 558
Museums of fine and decorative arts- Himachal Pradesh	708.954 52
Museums of fine and decorative arts- Hyderabad state	708.954 84
Museums of fine and decorative arts- India	708.954
Museums of fine and decorative arts- Jammu and Kashmir	708.954 6
Museums of fine and decorative arts- Karnataka	708.954 87
Museums of fine and decorative arts- Kerala	708.954 83
Museums of fine and decorative arts- Lakshwadweep	708.954 81
Museums of fine and decorative arts- Madhya Pradesh	708.954 3
Museums of fine and decorative arts- Madras	708.954 82
Museums of fine and decorative arts- Maharashtra	708.954 792
Museums of fine and decorative arts- Manipur	708.954 17
Museums of fine and decorative arts- Meghalaya	708.954 164
Museums of fine and decorative arts- Mizoram	708.954 166
Museums of fine and decorative arts- Nagaland	708.954 165

Museums of fine and decorative arts-Northeast India	708.954 1
Museums of fine and decorative arts-Orissa	708.954 13
Museums of fine and decorative arts-Pondicherry	708.954 86
Museums of fine and decorative arts - Punjab	708.954 552
Museums of fine and decorative arts-Rajasthan	708.954 4
Museums of fine and decorative arts - Sikkim	708.954 167
Museums of fine and decorative arts-South Asia	708.954
Museums of fine and decorative arts-Southern India	708.954 8
Museums of fine and decorative arts-Tamil Nadu	708.954 82
Museums of fine and decorative arts - Tripura	708.954 15
Museums of fine and decorative arts-Uttar Pradesh	708.954 2
Museums of fine and decorative arts-Uttaranchal	708.954 51
Museums of fine and decorative arts-West Bengal	708.954 14
Museums of fine and decorative arts-Western India	708.954 7
Mysticism (Buddhism)	294.344 22
Mysticism (Hinduism)	294.542 2

Mysticism (Jainism)	294.442 2
Mysticism (Sikhism)	294.642 2
Mythology (Buddhism)	294.333
Mythology (Hinduism)	294.513
Mythology (Jainism)	294.413
Mythology (Sikhism)	294.613

N

Nagaland- Architecture	720.954 165
Nagaland- Budget	352.495 416 5
Nagaland- Economic development	338.954 16 5
Nagaland- Economic geography	330.954 165
Nagaland- Education	370.954 16 5
Nagaland- Fauna	591.954 165
Nagaland- Flora	581.954 16 5
Nagaland- Folk dancing	793.319 54165
Nagaland- Geography	915.4165
Nagaland- Geology	555.416 5
Nagaland- History	954.165
Nagaland- Painting and paintings	759.954 165
Nagaland- Public administration	351.541 65
Nagaland- Public finance	336.541 65
Nagaland- Sculpture	730.954 165
National dancing- India	793.319 54
National Library of India	027.554
National public debt- India	336.343 354

National taxes- India	336.201 254
Nationality clubs- India	369.254
Nature (Buddhism)	294.342 12
Nature (Hinduism)	294.521 2
Nature (Jainism)	294.421 2
Nature (Sikhism)	294.621 2
NEFA	***See*** Arunachal Pradesh
Nepali - English dictionary	491.495 321
Nepali adventure fiction (multiple authors)	891.4953087*
Nepali adventure fiction (multiple authors) - Collections	891.495308708**
Nepali adventure fiction (multiple authors)- History and criticism	891.495308709**
Nepali anecdotes, epigrams, graffiti, jokes, quotations (multiple authors)	891.495802
Nepali anecdotes, epigrams, graffiti, jokes, quotations (single author) -	891.4958 +CD+02
Nepali ballads (multiple authors)	891.4951044*
Nepali ballads (multiple authors)- Collections	891.495104408**
Nepali ballads (multiple authors)- History and criticism	891.495104409**
Nepali comedy (multiple authors)	891.49520523*
Nepali comedy (multiple authors) - Collections	891.4952052308**
Nepali comedy (multiple authors) - History and criticism	891.4952052309**

Nepali conversations (multiple authors)	891.495506*
Nepali conversations (multiple authors) - Collections	891.49550608**
Nepali conversations (multiple authors) - History and criticism	891.49550609**
Nepali debates and public discussions (multiple authors)	891.495503*
Nepali debates and public discussions (multiple authors)- Collections	891.49550308**
Nepali debates and public discussions (multiple authors)- History and criticism	891.49550309**
Nepali detective fiction (multiple authors)	891.49530872*
Nepali detective fiction (multiple authors) - Collections	891.4953087208**
Nepali detective fiction (multiple authors) - History and criticism	891.4953087209**
Nepali diaries, notebooks, reminiscences (multiple authors)	891.495803
Nepali diaries, notebooks, reminiscences (single author)	891.4958@
Nepali didactic poetry (multiple authors)	891.495105*
Nepali didactic poetry (multiple authors)- Collections	891.49510508**
Nepali didactic poetry (multiple authors)- History and criticism	891.49510509**
Nepali drama	891.4952
Nepali drama (multiple authors) - - to 1845	***See*** Main schedule
Nepali drama (multiple authors) - 1845-1895	891.49524+
Nepali drama (multiple authors) - 1895-1919	891.49525+

Nepali drama (multiple authors) - 1920-1939	891.49526+
Nepali drama (multiple authors) - 1940-	891.49527+
Nepali drama (multiple authors) - 1940-1999	891.495271+
Nepali drama (multiple authors) - 19th century	891.49524+
Nepali drama (multiple authors) – 2000-	891.495272+
Nepali drama (multiple authors) - 20th century	891.495271+
Nepali drama (multiple authors) - Collections	891.4952008**
Nepali drama (multiple authors) - Dictionaries etc	891.4952003
Nepali drama (multiple authors) - History and criticism	891.4952009**
Nepali drama (multiple authors) - Periodicals	891.4952005
Nepali drama (multiple authors) - Philosophy and theory	891.4952001
Nepali drama (multiple authors) - Psychological aspects	891.49520019
Nepali drama (multiple authors) - Research	891.49520072
Nepali drama (multiple authors) - Study and teaching	891.4952007
Nepali drama (multiple authors) - Value	891.49520013
Nepali drama (single author) - - to 1845	***See*** Main schedule
Nepali drama (single author)- 1845 -1895	891.4952 4
Nepali drama (single author)- 1895 - 1919	891.4952 5
Nepali drama (single author)- 1920 1939	891.4952 6

Nepali drama (single author)- 1940 -	891.4952 7
Nepali drama (single author)- 1940-1999	891.4952 71
Nepali drama (single author)- 19th century	891.4952 4
Nepali drama (single author)- 2000-	891.4952 72
Nepali drama (single author)- 20th century	891.4952 71
Nepali drama for cinema (multiple authors)	891.495203*
Nepali drama for cinema (multiple authors) - Collections	891.49520308**
Nepali drama for cinema (multiple authors) - History and criticism	891.49520309**
Nepali drama for radio (multiple authors)	891.4952022*
Nepali drama for radio (multiple authors) - History and criticism	891.495202209**
Nepali drama for radio (multiple authors) - Collections	891.495202208**
Nepali drama for television (multiple authors)	891.4952025*
Nepali drama for television (multiple authors) - Collections	891.495202508**
Nepali drama for television (multiple authors) - History and criticism	891.495202509**
Nepali dramatic poetry (multiple authors)	891.495102*
Nepali dramatic poetry (multiple authors)- Collections	891.49510208**
Nepali dramatic poetry (multiple authors)- History and criticism	891.49510209**
Nepali ephemeral and light verse (multiple authors)	891.495108*
Nepali ephemeral and light verse (multiple authors)- Collections	891.49510808**

Nepali ephemeral and light verse (multiple authors) - History and criticism	891.49510809**
Nepali epic poetry (multiple authors)	891.4951032*
Nepali epic poetry (multiple authors)- Collections	891.495103208**
Nepali epic poetry (multiple authors)- History and criticism	891.495103209**
Nepali epigrams	***See*** Nepali anecdotes...
Nepali essays (multiple authors)	891.4954
Nepali essays (multiple authors) - - to 1845	***See*** Main schedule
Nepali essays (multiple authors) -1845-1895	891.49544+
Nepali essays (multiple authors) -1895-1919	891.49545+
Nepali essays (multiple authors) -1920-1939	891.49546+
Nepali essays (multiple authors) -1940-	891.49547+
Nepali essays (multiple authors) -1940-1999	891.495471+
Nepali essays (multiple authors) - 19th century	891.49544+
Nepali essays (multiple authors) -2000-	891.495472+
Nepali essays (multiple authors) - 20th century	891.495471+
Nepali essays (multiple authors) - Collections	891.4954008**
Nepali essays (multiple authors) - Dictionaries etc	891.4954003
Nepali essays (multiple authors) - History and criticism	891.4954009**
Nepali essays (multiple authors) - Periodicals	891.4954005

Nepali essays (multiple authors) - Philosophy and theory	891.4954001
Nepali essays (multiple authors) - Psychological aspects	891.49540019
Nepali essays (multiple authors) -Research	891.49540072
Nepali essays (multiple authors) - Study and teaching	891.4954007
Nepali essays (multiple authors) -Value	891.49540013
Nepali essays (single author)- - to 1845	***See*** Main schedule
Nepali essays (single author)- 1845 -1895	891.4954 4
Nepali essays (single author)- 1895 - 1919	891.4954 5
Nepali essays (single author)- 1920 - 1939	891.4954 6
Nepali essays (single author)- 1940 -	891.4954 7
Nepali essays (single author)- 1940-1999	891.4954 71
Nepali essays (single author)- 19th century	891.4954 4
Nepali essays (single author)- 2000-	891.4954 72
Nepali essays (single author)- 20th century	891.4954 71
Nepali experimental and non-formalized works (single author)	891.4958+CD+08
Nepali experimental and non-formalized works (multiple authors)	891.495807
Nepali fantasy fiction (multiple authors)	891.495308766*
Nepali fantasy fiction (multiple authors)- Collections	891.49530876608**
Nepali fantasy fiction (multiple authors)- History and criticism	891.49530876609**
Nepali farce (multiple authors)	891.495205232*

Nepali fiction (multiple authors)	891.4953
Nepali farce (multiple authors) - History and criticism	891.49520523209**
Nepali farce (multiple authors)- Collections	891.49520523208**
Nepali fiction (multiple authors) - - to 1845	***See*** Main schedule
Nepali fiction (multiple authors) - 1845-1895	891.49534+
Nepali fiction (multiple authors) - 1895-1919	891.49535+
Nepali fiction (multiple authors) - 1920-1939	891.49536+
Nepali fiction (multiple authors) - 1940-	891.49537+
Nepali fiction (multiple authors) - 1940-1999	891.495371+
Nepali fiction (multiple authors) - 19th century	891.49534+
Nepali fiction (multiple authors) – 2000-	891.495372+
Nepali fiction (multiple authors) - 20th century	891.495371+
Nepali fiction (multiple authors) - Collections	891.4953008**
Nepali fiction (multiple authors) - Dictionaries etc	891.4953003
Nepali fiction (multiple authors) - History and criticism	891.4953009**
Nepali fiction (multiple authors) - Periodicals	891.4953005
Nepali fiction (multiple authors) - Philosophy and theory	891.4953001
Nepali fiction (multiple authors) - Psychological aspects	891.49530019
Nepali fiction (multiple authors) - Research	891.49530072
Nepali fiction (multiple authors) - Study and teaching	891.4953007
Nepali fiction (multiple authors) - Value	891.49530013

Nepali fiction (single author)- - to 1845	***See*** Main schedule
Nepali fiction (single author)- 1845 -1895	891.4953 4
Nepali fiction (single author)- 1895 - 1919	891.4953 5
Nepali fiction (single author)- 1920 - 1939	891.4953 6
Nepali fiction (single author)- 1940 -	891.4953 7
Nepali fiction (single author)- 1940-1999	891.4953 71
Nepali fiction (single author)- 19th century	891.4953 4
Nepali fiction (single author)- 2000-	891.4953 72
Nepali fiction (single author)- 20th century	891.4953 71
Nepali ghost fiction (multiple authors)	891.495308733*
Nepali ghost fiction (multiple authors) - Collections	891.49530873308**
Nepali ghost fiction (multiple authors)- History and criticism	891.49530873309**
Nepali graffiti (multiple authors)	891.495802
Nepali graffiti	***See*** Nepali anecdotes,...
Nepali historical drama (multiple authors)	891.49520514*
Nepali historical drama (multiple authors)- Collections	891.4952051408**
Nepali historical drama (multiple authors)- History and criticism	891.4952051409**
Nepali historical fiction (multiple authors)	891.4953081*
Nepali historical fiction (multiple authors)- Collections	891.495308108**
Nepali historical fiction (multiple authors)- History and criticism	891.495308109**

Nepali horror fiction (multiple authors)	891.495308738*
Nepali horror fiction (multiple authors)-Collections	891.49530873808**
Nepali horror fiction (multiple authors)-History and criticism	891.49530873809**
Nepali humour and satire	891.4957
Nepali humour and satire (multiple authors) – to 1845	***See*** Main schedule
Nepali humour and satire (multiple authors) -1845-1895	891.49574+
Nepali humour and satire (multiple authors) -1895-1919	891.49575+
Nepali humour and satire (multiple authors) -1920-1939	891.49576+
Nepali humour and satire (multiple authors) -1940-	891.49577+
Nepali humour and satire (multiple authors) -1940-1999	891.495771+
Nepali humour and satire (multiple authors) -19th century	891.49574+
Nepali humour and satire (multiple authors) –2000-	891.495772+
Nepali humour and satire (multiple authors) -20th century	891.495771+
Nepali humour and satire (multiple authors) -Collections	891.4957008**
Nepali humour and satire (multiple authors) -Dictionaries etc	891.4957003
Nepali humour and satire (multiple authors) -History and criticism	891.4957009**

Nepali humour and satire (multiple authors) -Periodicals	891.4957005
Nepali humour and satire (multiple authors) -Philosophy and theory	891.4957001
Nepali humour and satire (multiple authors) -Psychological aspects	891.49570019
Nepali humour and satire (multiple authors) -Research	891.49570072
Nepali humour and satire (multiple authors) -Study and teaching	891.4957007
Nepali humour and satire (multiple authors) -Value	891.49570013
Nepali humourous and satirical poetry (multiple authors)	891.495107*
Nepali humourous and satirical poetry (multiple authors)- Collections	891.49510708**
Nepali humourous and satirical poetry (multiple authors)- History and criticism	891.49510709**
Nepali jokes	***See*** Nepali anecdotes,...
Nepali jokes (multiple authors)	891.495802
Nepali language	491.495
Nepali language- Applied linguistics	491.495 7
Nepali language- Bilingual dictionaries	491.495 32-39
Nepali language- Bilingualism	491.495 042
Nepali language- Concordances	491.495 03
Nepali language- Content analysis	491.495 014 1
Nepali language- Dictionaries	491.495 3

Nepali language- Discourse analysis	491.495 014 1
Nepali language- Education	491.495 071
Nepali language- Encyclopaedias	491.495 03
Nepali language- Etymology	491.495 2
Nepali language- Functionalism	491.495 018
Nepali language- Grammar	491.495 5
Nepali language- History	491.495 09
Nepali language- Intonation	491.495 16
Nepali language- Lexicography	491.495 302 8
Nepali language- Lexicology	491.495 014
Nepali language- Miscellany	491.495 02
Nepali language- Multilingualism	491.495 042
Nepali language- Organizations	491.495 06
Nepali language- Orthography	491.495 152
Nepali language- Pauses	491.495 16
Nepali language- Periodicals	491.495 05
Nepali language- Persons (men, women, etc)	491.495 08
Nepali language- Philosophy and theory	491.495 01
Nepali language- Phonetics	491.495 158
Nepali language- Phonology	491.495 15
Nepali language- Pitch	491.495 16
Nepali language- Pronunciation	491.495 152
Nepali language- Readers	491.495 86
Nepali language- Research	491.495 07

Nepali language- Schools and theories of linguistics	491.495 018
Nepali language- Semantics	491.495 014 3
Nepali language- Semiotics	491.495 014 1
Nepali language- Slang	491.495 7
Nepali language- Special topics	491.495 04
Nepali language- Specialized dictionaries	491.495 31
Nepali language- Spelling	491.495 152
Nepali language- Stress	491.495 16
Nepali language- Structural linguistics	491.495 018
Nepali language- Suprasegmental features	491.495 16
Nepali language- Terminology	491.495 014
Nepali language- Usage	491.495 8
Nepali language- Variations	491.495 7
Nepali language- Writing systems	491.495 11
Nepali letters	891.4956
Nepali letters (multiple authors) - - to 1845	***See*** Main schedule
Nepali letters (multiple authors) -1845-1895	891.49564+
Nepali letters (multiple authors) -1895-1919	891.49565+
Nepali letters (multiple authors) -1920-1939	891.49566+
Nepali letters (multiple authors) -1940-	891.49567+
Nepali letters (multiple authors) -1940-1999	891.495671+
Nepali letters (multiple authors) -19th century	891.49564+
Nepali letters (multiple authors) –2000-	891.495672+
Nepali letters (multiple authors) -20th century	891.495671+

Nepali letters (multiple authors) -Collections	891.4956008**
Nepali letters (multiple authors) - Dictionaries etc	891.4956003
Nepali letters (multiple authors) - History and criticism	891.4956009**
Nepali letters (multiple authors) - Periodicals	891.4956005
Nepali letters (multiple authors) - Philosophy and theory	891.4956001
Nepali letters (multiple authors) - Psychological aspects	891.49560019
Nepali letters (multiple authors) -Research	891.49560072
Nepali letters (multiple authors) - Study and teaching	891.4956007
Nepali letters (multiple authors) -Value	891.49560013
Nepali letters (single author)- - to 1845	***See*** Main schedule
Nepali letters (single author)- 1845 -1895	891.4956 4
Nepali letters (single author)- 1895 - 1919	891.4956 5
Nepali letters (single author)- 1920 1939	891.4956 6
Nepali letters (single author)- 1940 -	891.4956 7
Nepali letters (single author)- 1940-1999	891.4956 71
Nepali letters (single author)- 19th century	891.4956 4
Nepali letters (single author)- 2000-	891.4956 72
Nepali letters (single author)- 20th century	891.4956 71
Nepali light verse	***See*** Nepali ephemeral and light verse
Nepali limericks (multiple authors)	891.4951075*

Nepali limericks (multiple authors)-Collections	891.495107508**
Nepali limericks (multiple authors)-History and criticism	891.495107509**
Nepali literature	891.495
Nepali literature (collections of multiple forms)	891.49508
Nepali literature (collections of multiple forms) - 19th century	891.4950804
Nepali literature (collections of multiple forms) - 20th century	891.49508071
Nepali literature (collections of multiple forms) – 21st century	891.49508072
Nepali literature (collections of multiple forms) - Allegory	891.49508015
Nepali literature (collections of multiple forms) - Animals	891.495080362++
Nepali literature (collections of multiple forms) - Artistic themes	891.495080357
Nepali literature (collections of multiple forms) - Atmosphere	891.49508032161
Nepali literature (collections of multiple forms) - Characters	891.49508027
Nepali literature (collections of multiple forms) - Comedy	891.49508017
Nepali literature (collections of multiple forms) - Evening	891.49508033
Nepali literature (collections of multiple forms) - Fantasy	891.49508015
Nepali literature (collections of multiple forms) - Forests	891.49508032152

Nepali literature (collections of multiple forms) - Historical themes	891.495080358
Nepali literature (collections of multiple forms) - Horror	891.495080164
Nepali literature (collections of multiple forms) - Human characteristics (Biological, moral and psychological)	891.495080353
Nepali literature (collections of multiple forms) - Legendary objects/themes	891.49508037
Nepali literature (collections of multiple forms) - Literary themes	891.495080357
Nepali literature (collections of multiple forms) - Love	891.4950803543
Nepali literature (collections of multiple forms) - Marriage	891.4950803543
Nepali literature (collections of multiple forms) - Morning	891.49508033
Nepali literature (collections of multiple forms) - Mountains	891.49508032143
Nepali literature (collections of multiple forms) - Myth	891.49508015
Nepali literature (collections of multiple forms) - Mythological objects/themes	891.49508037
Nepali literature (collections of multiple forms) - Philosophic themes	891.495080384
Nepali literature (collections of multiple forms) - Places	891.49508032++
Nepali literature (collections of multiple forms) - Plants	891.495080364
Nepali literature (collections of multiple forms) - Political themes	891.495080358

Nepali literature (collections of multiple forms) - Religious themes	891.495080382++
Nepali literature (collections of multiple forms) - Rivers	891.495080321693
Nepali literature (collections of multiple forms) - Romanticism	891.495080145
Nepali literature (collections of multiple forms) - Scientific themes	891.495080356
Nepali literature (collections of multiple forms) - Sea	891.49508032162
Nepali literature (collections of multiple forms) - Seasons	891.49508033
Nepali literature (collections of multiple forms) - Sex	891.4950803538
Nepali literature (collections of multiple forms) - Social themes	891.495080355
Nepali literature (collections of multiple forms) - Space	891.4950803219
Nepali literature (collections of multiple forms) - Specific kinds of persons, e.g. heroes	891.495080352++
Nepali literature (collections of multiple forms) - Specific persons (real or imaginary)	891.495080351
Nepali literature (collections of multiple forms) - Stream of consciousness	891.49508025
Nepali literature (collections of multiple forms) - Supernatural objects/themes	891.49508037
Nepali literature (collections of multiple forms) - Symbolism	891.49508015
Nepali literature (collections of multiple forms) - Technical themes	891.495080356

Nepali literature (collections of multiple forms) - Times (seasons, parts of day, etc)	891.49508033
Nepali literature (collections of multiple forms) - Towns	891.495080321732
Nepali literature (collections of multiple forms) - Tragedy	891.495080162
Nepali literature (collections of multiple forms) - Villages	891.495080321734
Nepali literature (collections of multiple forms) - Weather	891.49508036
Nepali literature (collections of multiple forms) emphasizing subjects	891.4950804++
Nepali literature (collections of multiple forms) for/by children	891.4950809282
Nepali literature (collections of multiple forms) for/by persons of racial, ethnic and national groups	891.4950808++
Nepali literature (collections of multiple forms) for/by persons of specific classes	891.49508092++
Nepali literature (collections of multiple forms) for/by persons resident in specific regions	891.49508091++
Nepali literature (collections of multiple forms) for/by women	891.4950809287
Nepali literature (multiple authors) - Concordances	891.49503
Nepali literature (multiple authors) - Dictionaries	891.49503
Nepali literature (multiple authors) - Education	891.495071

Nepali literature (multiple authors) - Encyclopaedias	891.49503
Nepali literature (multiple authors) - Organizations	891.49506
Nepali literature (multiple authors) - Periodicals	891.49505
Nepali literature (multiple authors) - Philosophy and theory	891.49501
Nepali literature (multiple authors) - Research	891.495072
Nepali literature (multiple authors) - Research in India	891.495072054
Nepali literature (multiple authors) - Study and teaching	891.49507
Nepali literature (multiple forms) - Supernatural objects/themes - History and criticism	891.4950937
Nepali literature (multiple forms) - 19th century	891.49509004
Nepali literature (multiple forms) - 20th century	891.495090071
Nepali literature (multiple forms) - Allegory – History and criticism	891.4950915
Nepali literature (multiple forms) - Animals - History and criticism	891.49509362++
Nepali literature (multiple forms) - Artistic themes - History and criticism	891.49509357
Nepali literature (multiple forms) - Atmosphere - History and criticism	891.4950932161
Nepali literature (multiple forms) - Characters - History and criticism	891.4950927

Nepali literature (multiple forms) - Comedy - History and criticism	891.4950917
Nepali literature (multiple forms) - Evening - History and criticism	891.4950933
Nepali literature (multiple forms) - Fantasy - History, criticism	891.4950915
Nepali literature (multiple forms) - Forests- History and criticism	891.4950932152
Nepali literature (multiple forms) - Historical themes - History and criticism	891.49509358
Nepali literature (multiple forms) - History and criticism	891.49509
Nepali literature (multiple forms) - Horror - History and criticism	891.49509164
Nepali literature (multiple forms) - Human characteristics (Biological, moral and psychological) - History and criticism	891.49509353
Nepali literature (multiple forms) - Legendary objects/themes - History and criticism	891.4950937
Nepali literature (multiple forms) - Literary themes - History and criticism	891.49509357
Nepali literature (multiple forms) - Love - History and criticism	891.495093543
Nepali literature (multiple forms) - Marriage - History and criticism	891.495093543
Nepali literature (multiple forms) - Morning - History and criticism	891.4950933
Nepali literature (multiple forms) - Mountains - History and criticism	891.4950932143

Nepali literature (multiple forms) - Myth - History and criticism	891.4950915
Nepali literature (multiple forms) - Mythological objects/themes - History and criticism	891.4950937
Nepali literature (multiple forms) - Persons of racial, ethnic and national groups - History and criticism	891.495098++
Nepali literature (multiple forms) - Persons of specific classes - History and criticism	891.4950992++
Nepali literature (multiple forms) - Persons resident in specific regions - History and criticism	891.4950991++
Nepali literature (multiple forms) - Philosophic themes - History and criticism	891.49509384
Nepali literature (multiple forms) - Places - History and criticism	891.4950932++
Nepali literature (multiple forms) - Plants - History and criticism	891.49509364
Nepali literature (multiple forms) - Political themes - History and criticism	891.49509358
Nepali literature (multiple forms) - Religious themes - History and criticism	891.49509382++
Nepali literature (multiple forms) - Rivers - History and criticism	891.49509321693
Nepali literature (multiple forms) - Romanticism - History and criticism	891.49509145
Nepali literature (multiple forms) - Scientific themes - History and criticism	891.49509356
Nepali literature (multiple forms) - Sea - History and criticism	891.4950932162

Nepali literature (multiple forms) - Seasons - History and criticism	891.4950933
Nepali literature (multiple forms) - Sex - History and criticism	891.495093538
Nepali literature (multiple forms) - Social themes - History and criticism	891.49509355
Nepali literature (multiple forms) - Space - History and criticism	891.495093219
Nepali literature (multiple forms) - Specific kinds of persons, e.g. heroes, - History and criticism	891.49509352++
Nepali literature (multiple forms) - Specific persons - History and criticism	891.49509351
Nepali literature (multiple forms) - Stream of consciousness - History and criticism	891.4950925
Nepali literature (multiple forms) - Subjects - History and criticism	891.495094++
Nepali literature (multiple forms) - Symbolism- History, criticism	891.4950915
Nepali literature (multiple forms) - Technical themes - History and criticism	891.49509356
Nepali literature (multiple forms) - Times - History and criticism	891.4950933
Nepali literature (multiple forms) - Towns - History and criticism	891.49509321732
Nepali literature (multiple forms) - Tragedy - History and criticism	891.49509162
Nepali literature (multiple forms) - Villages - History and criticism	891.49509321734
Nepali literature (multiple forms) - Weather - History and criticism	891.4950936

Nepali literature (single author)- - to 1845 - Biography, collections, criticism	*See* Main schedule
Nepali literature (single author)- 1845 - 1895 - Biography, collections, criticism	891.4958 409
Nepali literature (single author)- 1895 - 1919 - Biography, collections, criticism	891.4958 509
Nepali literature (single author)- 1920 1939 - Biography, collections, criticism	891.4958 609
Nepali literature (single author)- 1940 - Biography, collections, criticism	891.4958 709
Nepali literature (single author)- 1940-1999 - Biography, collections, criticism	891.4958 7109
Nepali literature (single author)- 19th century- Biography, collections, criticism	891.4958 409
Nepali literature (single author)- 2000- Biography, collections, criticism	891.4958 7209
Nepali literature (single author)- 20th century - Biography, collections, criticism	891.4958 7109
Nepali literature for/by children - History and criticism	891.495099282
Nepali literature for/by women - History and criticism	891.495099287
Nepali love fiction (multiple authors)	891.4953085*
Nepali love fiction (multiple authors)- Collections	891.495308508**
Nepali love fiction (multiple authors)- History and criticism	891.495308509**
Nepali melodrama (multiple authors)	891.49520527*
Nepali melodrama (multiple authors)- Collections	891.4952052708**

Nepali melodrama (multiple authors)-History and criticism	891.4952052709**
Nepali miscellaneous writings (multiple authors)	891.4958
Nepali miscellaneous writings (multiple authors) - to 1845	***See*** Main schedule
Nepali miscellaneous writings (multiple authors) -1845-1895	891.49584++
Nepali miscellaneous writings (multiple authors) -1895-1919	891.49585++
Nepali miscellaneous writings (multiple authors) -1920-1939	891.49586++
Nepali miscellaneous writings (multiple authors) -1940-	891.49587++
Nepali miscellaneous writings (multiple authors) -1940-1999	891.495871++
Nepali miscellaneous writings (multiple authors) -19th century	891.49584++
Nepali miscellaneous writings (multiple authors) –2000-	891.495872++
Nepali miscellaneous writings (multiple authors) -20th century	891.495871++
Nepali miscellaneous writings (multiple authors) -Collections	891.4958008**
Nepali miscellaneous writings (multiple authors) -Dictionaries etc	891.4958003
Nepali miscellaneous writings (multiple authors) -History and criticism	891.4958009**
Nepali miscellaneous writings (multiple authors) -Periodicals	891.4958005

Nepali miscellaneous writings (multiple authors) -Philosophy and theory	891.4958001
Nepali miscellaneous writings (multiple authors) -Psychological aspects	891.49580019
Nepali miscellaneous writings (multiple authors) -Research	891.49580072
Nepali miscellaneous writings (multiple authors) -Study and teaching	891.4958007
Nepali miscellaneous writings (multiple authors) -Value	891.49580013
Nepali miscellaneous writings (single author)- - to 1845	***See*** Main schedule
Nepali miscellaneous writings (single author)- 1845 -1895	891.4958 4
Nepali miscellaneous writings (single author)- 1895 - 1919	891.4958 5
Nepali miscellaneous writings (single author)- 1920 - 1939	891.4958 6
Nepali miscellaneous writings (single author)- 1940 -	891.4958 7
Nepali miscellaneous writings (single author)- 1940-1999	891.4958 71
Nepali miscellaneous writings (single author)- 19th century	891.4958 4
Nepali miscellaneous writings (single author)- 2000-	891.4958 72
Nepali miscellaneous writings (single author)- 20th century	891.4958 71
Nepali monologues (multiple authors)	891.4952045*
Nepali monologues (multiple authors)- Collections	891.495204508**

Nepali monologues (multiple authors)- History and criticism	891.495204509**
Nepali morality plays	***See*** Nepali religious ... plays
Nepali mystery fiction (multiple authors)	891.49530872*
Nepali mystery fiction (multiple authors)- Collections	891.4953087208**
Nepali mystery fiction (multiple authors)- History and criticism	891.4953087209**
Nepali narrative poetry (multiple authors)	891.495103*
Nepali narrative poetry (multiple authors)- Collections	891.49510308**
Nepali narrative poetry (multiple authors)- History and criticism	891.49510309**
Nepali notebooks	***See*** Nepali diaries...
Nepali odes (multiple authors)	891.4951043*
Nepali odes (multiple authors)- Collections	891.495104308**
Nepali odes (multiple authors)- History and criticism	891.495104309**
Nepali one act plays (multiple authors)	891.495 204 1*
Nepali one act plays (multiple authors)- Collections	891.495 204 108**
Nepali one act plays (multiple authors)- History and criticism	891.495 204 109**
Nepali oratory (multiple authors)	***See*** Nepali public speeches
Nepali poetry	891.4951
Nepali poetry (multiple authors) - - to 1845	***See*** Main schedule

Nepali poetry (multiple authors) – 1845-1895	891.49514+
Nepali poetry (multiple authors) – 1895-1919	891.49515+
Nepali poetry (multiple authors) – 1920-1939	891.49516+
Nepali poetry (multiple authors) – 1940-	891.49517+
Nepali poetry (multiple authors) – 1940-1999	891.495171+
Nepali poetry (multiple authors) – 19th century	891.49514+
Nepali poetry (multiple authors) – 2000-	891.495172+
Nepali poetry (multiple authors) – 20th century	891.495171+
Nepali poetry (multiple authors)- Collections	891.4951008**
Nepali poetry (multiple authors)- Dictionaries etc	891.4951003
Nepali poetry (multiple authors)- History and criticism	891.4951009**
Nepali poetry (multiple authors)- Periodicals	891.4951005
Nepali poetry (multiple authors)- Philosophy and theory	891.4951001
Nepali poetry (multiple authors)- Psychological aspects	891.49510019
Nepali poetry (multiple authors)- Research	891.49510072
Nepali poetry (multiple authors)- Study and teaching	891.4951007
Nepali poetry (multiple authors)- Value	891.49510013
Nepali poetry (single author)- - to 1845	***See*** Main schedule

Nepali poetry (single author)- 1845 –1895	891.4951 4
Nepali poetry (single author)- 1895 – 1919	891.4951 5
Nepali poetry (single author)- 1920 – 1939	891.4951 6
Nepali poetry (single author)- 1940 -	891.4951 7
Nepali poetry (single author)- 1940-1999	891.4951 71
Nepali poetry (single author)- 19th century	891.4951 4
Nepali poetry (single author)- 2000-	891.4951 72
Nepali poetry (single author)- 20th century	891.4951 71
Nepali prose (single author)- - to 1845	***See*** Main schedule
Nepali prose (single author)- 1845 –1895	891.4958 408
Nepali prose (single author)- 1895 – 1919	891.4958 508
Nepali prose (single author)- 1920 1939	891.4958 608
Nepali prose (single author)- 1940 -	891.4958 708
Nepali prose (single author)- 1940-1999	891.4958 7108
Nepali prose (single author)- 19th century	891.4958 408
Nepali prose (single author)- 2000-	891.4958 7208
Nepali prose (single author)- 20th century	891.4958 7108
Nepali prose literature (multiple authors)	891.495808
Nepali psychological, realistic, sociological fiction (multiple authors)	891.4953083*
Nepali psychological, realistic, sociological fiction (multiple authors)- Collections	891.495308308**
Nepali psychological, realistic, sociological fiction (multiple authors) – History and criticism	891.495308309**

Nepali public discussions debates ... discussions	***See*** Nepali
Nepali public speeches (multiple authors)	891.495501
Nepali public speeches (multiple authors)- Collections	891.49550108
Nepali public speeches (multiple authors)- History and criticism	891.49550109
Nepali quotations	***See*** Nepali anecdotes,...
Nepali realistic fiction	***See*** Nepali psychological... fiction
Nepali recitations (multiple authors)	891.495504+
Nepali religious and morality plays (multiple authors)	891.49520516+
Nepali reminiscences	***See*** Nepali diaries
Nepali romantic fiction (multiple authors)	891.4953085*
Nepali romantic fiction (multiple authors)- Collections	891.495308508**
Nepali romantic fiction (multiple authors)- History and criticism	891.495308509**
Nepali satire	***See*** Nepali humour and satire
Nepali satirical poetry	***See*** Nepali humourous ... poetry
Nepali science fiction (multiple authors)	891.495308762*
Nepali science fiction (multiple authors)- Collections	891.49530876208**

Nepali science fiction (multiple authors)-History and criticism	891.49530876209**
Nepali serious drama (multiple authors)	891.4952051+
Nepali short stories (multiple authors)	891.495301*
Nepali short stories (multiple authors)-Collections	891.49530108**
Nepali short stories (multiple authors)-History and criticism	891.49530109**
Nepali sociological fiction (multiple authors)	***See*** Nepali psychological... fiction
Nepali sonnets (multiple authors)	891.4951042*
Nepali sonnets (multiple authors)-Collections	891.495104208**
Nepali sonnets (multiple authors)-History and criticism	891.495104209**
Nepali speeches (multiple authors)	891.4955
Nepali speeches (multiple authors) — to 1845	***See*** Main schedule
Nepali speeches (multiple authors) - 1845-1895	891.49554+
Nepali speeches (multiple authors) - 1895-1919	891.49555+
Nepali speeches (multiple authors) - 1920-1939	891.49556+
Nepali speeches (multiple authors) -1940-	891.49557+
Nepali speeches (multiple authors) - 1940-1999	891.495571+
Nepali speeches (multiple authors) - 19th century	891.49554+

Nepali speeches (multiple authors) - 20th century	891.495571+
Nepali speeches (multiple authors) - Collections	891.4955008**
Nepali speeches (multiple authors) - Dictionaries etc	891.4955003
Nepali speeches (multiple authors) - History and criticism	891.4955009**
Nepali speeches (multiple authors) - Periodicals	891.4955005
Nepali speeches (multiple authors) - Philosophy and theory	891.4955001
Nepali speeches (multiple authors) - Psychological aspects	891.49550019
Nepali speeches (multiple authors) - Research	891.49550072
Nepali speeches (multiple authors) - Study and teaching	891.4955007
Nepali speeches (multiple authors) -Value	891.49550013
Nepali speeches (single author)- - to 1845	***See*** Main schedule
Nepali speeches (single author)- 1845 - 1895	891.4955 4
Nepali speeches (single author)- 1895 - 1919	891.4955 5
Nepali speeches (single author)- 1920 - 1939	891.4955 6
Nepali speeches (single author)- 1940 -	891.4955 7
Nepali speeches (single author)- 1940-1999	891.4955 71
Nepali speeches (single author)- 19th century	891.4955 4

Nepali speeches (single author)- 2000-	891.4955 72
Nepali speeches (single author)- 20th century	891.4955 71
Nepali suspense fiction (multiple authors)	891.49530872*
Nepali suspense fiction (multiple authors)- Collections	891.4953087208**
Nepali suspense fiction (multiple authors)- History and criticism	891.4953087209**
Nepali tragedy (multiple authors)	891.49520512*
Nepali tragedy (multiple authors)-Collections	891.4952051208**
Nepali tragedy (multiple authors)- History and criticism	891.4952051209**
Nepali variety drama (multiple authors)	891.4952057*
Nepali variety drama (multiple authors)- Collections	891.495205708**
Nepali variety drama (multiple authors)- History and criticism	891.495205709**
Newari language	495.49
Newari literature	895.49
Newari speaking people	305.795 49
Newspapers- Andaman and Nicobar Islands	079.5488
Newspapers- Andhra Pradesh	079.5484
Newspapers- Arunachal Pradesh	079.54163
Newspapers- Assam	079.54162
Newspapers- Bihar	079.5412
Newspapers- Chhattisgarh	079.541 37
Newspapers- Delhi	079.5456

Newspapers- Goa, Daman and Diu	079.54799
Newspapers- Gujarat	079.5475
Newspapers- Haryana	079.54558
Newspapers- Himachal Pradesh	079.5452
Newspapers- India	079.54
Newspapers- Jammu and Kashmir	079.546
Newspapers- Jharkhand	079.541 27
Newspapers- Karnataka	079.5487
Newspapers- Kerala	079.5483
Newspapers- Lakshwadweep	079.5481
Newspapers- Madhya Pradesh	079.543
Newspapers- Maharashtra	079.54792
Newspapers- Manipur	079.5417
Newspapers- Meghalaya	079.54164
Newspapers- Mizoram	079.54166
Newspapers- Nagaland	079.54165
Newspapers- Northeast India	079.541
Newspapers- Orissa	079.5413
Newspapers- Pondicherry	079.5486
Newspapers- Punjab	079.54552
Newspapers- Rajasthan	079.544
Newspapers- Southern India	079.548
Newspapers- Tamil Nadu	079.5482
Newspapers- Tripura	079.5415
Newspapers- Uttar Pradesh	079.542
Newspapers- Uttaranchal	079.545 1
Newspapers- West Bengal	079.5414

Newspapers- Western India	079.547
Nichiren Shoshu	294.392 8
Nimbarka philosophy	181.4843
North Dravidian folk music	781 629 483
North Dravidians	305.894 83
North East Frontier Agency	***See*** Arunachal Pradesh
Northeast India- Architecture	720.954 1
Northeast India- Economic geography	330.954 1
Northeast India- Fauna	591.954 1
Northeast India- Flora	581.954 1
Northeast India- Folk dancing	793.319 541
Northeast India- Geography	915.41
Northeast India- Geology	555.41
Northeast India- History	954.1
Northeast India- Painting and paintings	759.954 1
Northeast India- Sculpture	730.954 1
Nuclear weapon and nuclear war (Buddhism)	294.33787 32
Nuclear weapon and nuclear war (Hinduism)	294.517 873 2
Nuclear weapon and nuclear war (Jainism)	294.417 873 2
Nuclear weapon and nuclear war (Sikhism)	294.617 873 2
Nuri (People)	305.891 49
Nuri folk music	781 629 149
Nuristani language	491.49
Nuristani literature	891.49

O

Objects of worship and veneration (Buddhism)	294.342 1
Objects of worship and veneration (Hinduism)	294.521
Objects of worship and veneration (Jainism)	294.421
Objects of worship and veneration (Sikhism)	294.621
Observance of restrictions and limitations (Buddhism)	294.344 46
Observance of restrictions and limitations (Hinduism)	294.544 6
Observance of restrictions and limitations (Jainism)	294.444 6
Observance of restrictions and limitations (Sikhism)	294.644 6
Occupational ethics (Buddhism)	294.356 4
Occupational ethics (Hinduism)	294.5486 4
Occupational ethics (Jainism)	294.456 4
Occupational ethics (Sikhism)	294.656 4
Offerings (Buddhism)	294.343 4
Offerings (Hinduism)	294.534

Offerings (Jainism)	294.434
Offerings (Sikhism)	294.634
Old English (Anglo-Saxon)	429
Old Indic languages	491.29
Old Indic literatures	891.29
Omen (Buddhism)	294.343 2
Omen (Hinduism)	294.532
Omen (Jainism)	294.432
Omen (Sikhism)	294.632
Opinions	303.387
Opinions of Assamese	303.387 914 5
Opinions of Bengalis	303.387 914 4
Opinions of Brahmins	303.388 294 5
Opinions of Buddhists	303.388 294 3
Opinions of Dravidians	303.387 948
Opinions of Gujaratis	303.387 914 7
Opinions of Hindis	303.387 914 3
Opinions of Hindus	303.388 294 5
Opinions of Indians	303.387 914 11
Opinions of Indic people	303.387 914
Opinions of Jains	303.388 294 4
Opinions of Kanarese	303.387 948 14
Opinions of Malayalis	303.387 948 12
Opinions of Marathas	303.387 948
Opinions of Oriyas	303.387 914 5

Opinions of Panjabis	303.387 914 2
Opinions of persons of Indic religion	303.388 294
Opinions of Rajasthanis	303.387 914 7
Opinions of South Asians	303.387 914
Opinions of Tamilians	303.387 948 11
Opinions of Telugu people	303.387 948.27
Oracles (Buddhism)	294.343 2
Oracles (Hinduism)	294.532
Oracles (Jainism)	294.432
Oracles (Sikhism)	294.632
Oral traditions (Buddhism)	294.383
Oral traditions (Hinduism)	294.583
Oral traditions (Jainism)	294.483
Oral traditions (Sikhism)	294.683
Oraon speaking people	305.794 83
Orders (Buddhism)	294.365
Orders (Hinduism)	294.565
Orders (Jainism)	294.465
Orders (Sikhism)	294.665
Organizations (Buddhism)	294.365
Organizations (Hinduism)	294.565
Organizations (Jainism)	294.465
Organizations (Sikhism)	294.665
Organizations- Andaman & Nicobar Islands	069.954 88
Organizations- Andhra Pradesh	069.954 84

Organizations- Arunachal Pradesh	069.954 163
Organizations- Assam	069.954 162
Organizations- Bihar	069.954 12
Organizations- Chhattisgarh	069.954 137
Organizations- Delhi	069.954 56
Organizations- Goa, Daman and Diu	069.954 799
Organizations- Gujarat	069.954 75
Organizations- Haryana	069.954 558
Organizations- Himachal Pradesh	069.954 52
Organizations- India	069.954
Organizations- Jammu and Kashmir	069.954 6
Organizations- Jharkhand	069.954 127
Organizations- Karnataka	069.954 87
Organizations- Kerala	069.954 83
Organizations- Lakshwadweep	069.954 81
Organizations- Madhya Pradesh	069.954 3
Organizations- Maharashtra	069.954 792
Organizations- Manipur	069.954 17
Organizations- Meghalaya	069.954 164
Organizations- Mizoram	069.954 166
Organizations- Nagaland	069.954 165
Organizations- Northeast India	069.954 1
Organizations- Orissa	069.954 13
Organizations- Pondicherry	069.954 86
Organizations- Punjab	069.954 552

Organizations- Rajasthan	069.954 4
Organizations- Southern India	069.954 8
Organizations- Tamil Nadu	069.954 82
Organizations- Tripura	069.954 15
Organizations- Uttar Pradesh	069.954 2
Organizations- Uttaranchal	069.954 51
Organizations- West Bengal	069.954 14
Organizations- Western India	069.954 7
Oriental psychology	181
Orissa- Architecture	720.954 13
Orissa- Budget	352.495 413
Orissa- Economic development	338.954 13
Orissa- Economic geography	330.954 13
Orissa- Education	370.954 13
Orissa- Fauna	591.954 13
Orissa- Flora	581.954 13
Orissa- Folk dancing	793.319 5413
Orissa- Geography	915.413
Orissa- Geology	555.413
Orissa- History	954.13
Orissa- Painting and paintings	759.954 13
Orissa- Public administration	351.541 3
Orissa- Public finance	336.541 3
Orissa- Sculpture	730.954 13
Oriya - English dictionary	491.456 321

Oriya adventure fiction (multiple authors)	891.4563087*
Oriya adventure fiction (multiple authors) -Collections	891.456308708**
Oriya adventure fiction (multiple authors)- History and criticism	891.456308709**
Oriya anecdotes, epigrams, graffiti, jokes, quotations (multiple authors)	891.456802
Oriya anecdotes, epigrams, graffiti, jokes, quotations (single author)	891.4568 +CD+02
Oriya as second language in elementary education	372.659 145 6
Oriya ballads (multiple authors)	891.4561044*
Oriya ballads (multiple authors)- Collections	891.456104408**
Oriya ballads (multiple authors)- History and criticism	891.456104409**
Oriya comedy (multiple authors)	891.45620523*
Oriya comedy (multiple authors) - Collections	891.4562052308**
Oriya comedy (multiple authors) - History and criticism	891.4562052309**
Oriya conversations (multiple authors)	891.456506*
Oriya conversations (multiple authors) - Collections	891.45650608**
Oriya conversations (multiple authors) - History and criticism	891.45650609**
Oriya debates and public discussions (multiple authors)	891.456503*
Oriya debates and public discussions (multiple authors)- Collections	891.45650308**

Oriya debates and public discussions (multiple authors)- History and criticism	891.45650309**
Oriya detective fiction (multiple authors)	891.45630872*
Oriya detective fiction (multiple authors) - Collections	891.4563087208**
Oriya detective fiction (multiple authors) - History and criticism	891.4563087209**
Oriya diaries, notebooks, reminiscences (multiple authors)	891.456 803
Oriya diaries, notebooks, reminiscences (single author)	891.456 8@
Oriya didactic poetry (multiple authors)	891.456105*
Oriya didactic poetry (multiple authors)- Collections	891.45610508**
Oriya didactic poetry (multiple authors)- History and criticism	891.45610509**
Oriya drama	891.456 2
Oriya drama (multiple authors) - - to 1845	***See*** Main schedule
Oriya drama (multiple authors) - 1845-1895	891.45624+
Oriya drama (multiple authors) - 1895-1919	891.45625+
Oriya drama (multiple authors) - 1920-1939	891.45626+
Oriya drama (multiple authors) - 1940-	891.45627+
Oriya drama (multiple authors) - 1940-1999	891.456271+
Oriya drama (multiple authors) - 19th century	891.45624+
Oriya drama (multiple authors) – 2000-	891.456272+
Oriya drama (multiple authors) - 20th century	891.456271+
Oriya drama (multiple authors) - Collections	891.4562008**

Oriya drama (multiple authors) - Dictionaries etc	891.4562003
Oriya drama (multiple authors) - History and criticism	891.4562009**
Oriya drama (multiple authors) - Periodicals	891.4562005
Oriya drama (multiple authors) - Philosophy and theory	891.4562001
Oriya drama (multiple authors) - Psychological aspects	891.45620019
Oriya drama (multiple authors) - Research	891.45620072
Oriya drama (multiple authors) - Study and teaching	891.4562007
Oriya drama (multiple authors) - Value	891.45620013
Oriya drama (single author) - to 1845	***See*** Main schedule
Oriya drama (single author)- 1845 -1895	891.4562 4
Oriya drama (single author)- 1895 - 1919	891.4562 5
Oriya drama (single author)- 1920 - 1939	891.4562 6
Oriya drama (single author)- 1940 -	891.4562 7
Oriya drama (single author)- 1940-1999	891.4562 71
Oriya drama (single author)- 19th century	891.4562 4
Oriya drama (single author)- 2000-	891.4562 72
Oriya drama (single author)- 20th century	891.4562 71
Oriya drama for cinema (multiple authors)	891.456203*
Oriya drama for cinema (multiple authors) - Collections	891.45620308**
Oriya drama for cinema (multiple authors) - History and criticism	891.45620309**

Oriya drama for radio (multiple authors)	891.4562022*
Oriya drama for radio (multiple authors) - Collections	891.456202208**
Oriya drama for radio (multiple authors) - History and criticism	891.456202209**
Oriya drama for television (multiple authors)	891.4562025*
Oriya drama for television (multiple authors) - Collections	891.456202508**
Oriya drama for television (multiple authors) - History and criticism	891.456202509**
Oriya dramatic poetry (multiple authors)	891.456102*
Oriya dramatic poetry (multiple authors)- Collections	891.45610208**
Oriya dramatic poetry (multiple authors)- History and criticism	891.45610209**
Oriya encyclopaedias	039.91456
Oriya ephemeral and light verse (multiple authors)	891.456108*
Oriya ephemeral and light verse (multiple authors)- Collections	891.45610808**
Oriya ephemeral and light verse (multiple authors) - History and criticism	891.45610809**
Oriya epic poetry (multiple authors)	891.4561032*
Oriya epic poetry (multiple authors)- Collections	891.456103208**
Oriya epic poetry (multiple authors)- History and criticism	891.456103209**
Oriya epigrams	***See*** Oriya anecdotes ...

Oriya essays	891.456 4
Oriya essays (multiple authors)	891.4564
Oriya essays (multiple authors) - to 1845	***See*** Main schedule
Oriya essays (multiple authors) -1845-1895	891.45644+
Oriya essays (multiple authors) -1895-1919	891.45645+
Oriya essays (multiple authors) -1920-1939	891.45646+
Oriya essays (multiple authors) -1940-	891.45647+
Oriya essays (multiple authors) -1940-1999	891.456471+
Oriya essays (multiple authors) -19th century	891.45644+
Oriya essays (multiple authors) –2000-	891.456472+
Oriya essays (multiple authors) -20th century	891.456471+
Oriya essays (multiple authors) -Collections	891.4564008**
Oriya essays (multiple authors) - Dictionaries etc	891.4564003
Oriya essays (multiple authors) - History and criticism	891.4564009**
Oriya essays (multiple authors) -Periodicals	891.4564005
Oriya essays (multiple authors) -Philosophy and theory	891.4564001
Oriya essays (multiple authors) - Psychological aspects	891.45640019
Oriya essays (multiple authors) -Research	891.45640072
Oriya essays (multiple authors) - Study and teaching	891.4564007
Oriya essays (multiple authors) -Value	891.45640013
Oriya essays (single author)- - to 1845	***See*** Main schedule

Oriya essays (single author)- 1845 -1895	891.4564 4
Oriya essays (single author)- 1895 - 1919	891.4564 5
Oriya essays (single author)- 1920 1939	891.4564 6
Oriya essays (single author)- 1940 -	891.4564 7
Oriya essays (single author)- 1940-1999	891.4564 71
Oriya essays (single author)- 19th century	891.4564 4
Oriya essays (single author)- 2000-	891.4564 72
Oriya essays (single author)- 20th century	891.4564 71
Oriya experimental and non-formalized works (multiple authors)	891.456807
Oriya experimental and non-formalized works (single author)	891.4568+CD+07
Oriya fantasy fiction (multiple authors)	891.456308766*
Oriya fantasy fiction (multiple authors)- Collections	891.45630876608**
Oriya fantasy fiction (multiple authors)- History and criticism	891.45630876609**
Oriya farce (multiple authors)	891.456205232*
Oriya farce (multiple authors)- Collections	891.45620523208**
Oriya farce (multiple authors)- History and criticism	891.45620523209**
Oriya fiction	891.4563
Oriya fiction (multiple authors) - - to 1845	***See*** Main schedule
Oriya fiction (multiple authors) - 1845-1895	891.45634+
Oriya fiction (multiple authors) - 1895-1919	891.45635+
Oriya fiction (multiple authors) - 1920-1939	891.45636+

Oriya fiction (multiple authors) - 1940-	891.45637+
Oriya fiction (multiple authors) - 1940-1999	891.456371+
Oriya fiction (multiple authors) - 19th century	891.45634+
Oriya fiction (multiple authors) – 2000-	891.456372+
Oriya fiction (multiple authors) - 20th century	891.456371+
Oriya fiction (multiple authors) - Collections	891.4563008**
Oriya fiction (multiple authors) - Dictionaries etc	891.4563003
Oriya fiction (multiple authors) - History and criticism	891.4563009**
Oriya fiction (multiple authors) - Periodicals	891.4563005
Oriya fiction (multiple authors) - Philosophy and theory	891.4563001
Oriya fiction (multiple authors) - Psychological aspects	891.45630019
Oriya fiction (multiple authors) - Research	891.45630072
Oriya fiction (multiple authors) - Study and teaching	891.4563007
Oriya fiction (multiple authors) - Value	891.45630013
Oriya fiction (single author)- - to 1845	***See*** Main schedule
Oriya fiction (single author)- 1845 -1895	891.4563 4
Oriya fiction (single author)- 1895 - 1919	891.4563 5
Oriya fiction (single author)- 1920 - 1939	891.4563 6
Oriya fiction (single author)- 1940 -	891.4563 7
Oriya fiction (single author)- 1940-1999	891.4563 71
Oriya fiction (single author)- 19th century	891.4563 4

Oriya fiction (single author)- 2000-	891.4563 72
Oriya fiction (single author)- 20th century	891.4563 71
Oriya folk music	781 629 145
Oriya ghost fiction (multiple authors)	891.456308733*
Oriya ghost fiction (multiple authors) - Collections	891.45630873308**
Oriya ghost fiction (multiple authors)- History and criticism	891.45630873309**
Oriya graffiti	***See*** Oriya anecdotes ...
Oriya historical drama (multiple authors)	891.45620514*
Oriya historical drama (multiple authors)- Collections	891.4562051408**
Oriya historical drama (multiple authors)- History and criticism	891.4562051409**
Oriya historical fiction (multiple authors)	891.4563081*
Oriya historical fiction (multiple authors)- Collections	891.456308108**
Oriya historical fiction (multiple authors)- History and criticism	891.456308109**
Oriya horror fiction (multiple authors)	891.456308738*
Oriya horror fiction (multiple authors)- Collections	891.45630873808**
Oriya horror fiction (multiple authors)- History and criticism	891.45630873809**
Oriya humour and satire	891.4567
Oriya humour and satire (multiple authors) — to 1845	***See*** Main schedule

Oriya humour and satire (multiple authors) -1845-1895	891.45674+
Oriya humour and satire (multiple authors) -1895-1919	891.45675+
Oriya humour and satire (multiple authors) -1920-1939	891.45676+
Oriya humour and satire (multiple authors) -1940-	891.45677+
Oriya humour and satire (multiple authors) -1940-1999	891.456771+
Oriya humour and satire (multiple authors) -19th century	891.45674+
Oriya humour and satire (multiple authors) –2000-	891.456772+
Oriya humour and satire (multiple authors) -20th century	891.456771+
Oriya humour and satire (multiple authors) -Collections	891.4567008**
Oriya humour and satire (multiple authors) -Dictionaries etc	891.4567003
Oriya humour and satire (multiple authors) -History and criticism	891.4567009**
Oriya humour and satire (multiple authors) -Periodicals	891.4567005
Oriya humour and satire (multiple authors) -Philosophy and theory	891.4567001
Oriya humour and satire (multiple authors) -Psychological aspects	891.45670019
Oriya humour and satire (multiple authors) -Research	891.45670072

Oriya humour and satire (multiple authors) -Study and teaching	891.4567007
Oriya humour and satire (multiple authors) -Value	891.45670013
Oriya humourous and satirical poetry (multiple authors)	891.456107*
Oriya humourous and satirical poetry (multiple authors)- Collections	891.45610708**
Oriya humourous and satirical poetry (multiple authors)- History and criticism	891.45610709**
Oriya jokes	***See*** Oriya anecdotes ...
Oriya language	491.456
Oriya language- Applied linguistics	491.456 8
Oriya language- Bilingual dictionaries	491.456 32-39
Oriya language- Bilingualism, multilingualism	491.456 042
Oriya language- Concordances	491.456 03
Oriya language- Content analysis	491.456 014 1
Oriya language- Dictionaries	491.456 3
Oriya language- Discourse analysis	491.456 014 1
Oriya language- Education	491.456 071
Oriya language- Encyclopaedias	491.456 03
Oriya language- Etymology	491.456 2
Oriya language- Functionalism	491.456 018
Oriya language- Grammar	491.456 5
Oriya language- History	491.456 09

Oriya language- Intonation	491.456 16
Oriya language- Lexicography	491.456 302 8
Oriya language- Lexicology	491.456 014
Oriya language- Miscellany	491.456 02
Oriya language- Organizations	491.456 06
Oriya language- Orthography	491.456 152
Oriya language- Pauses	491.456 16
Oriya language- Periodicals	491.456 05
Oriya language- Persons (men, women, etc)	491.456 08
Oriya language- Philosophy and theory	491.456 01
Oriya language- Phonetics	491.456 158
Oriya language- Phonology	491.456 15
Oriya language- Pitch	491.456 16
Oriya language- Pronunciation	491.456 152
Oriya language- Readers	491.456 86
Oriya language- Research	491.456 072
Oriya language- Rhetoric	808.049 1456++
Oriya language- Schools and theories of linguistics	491.456 018
Oriya language- Semantics	491.456 014 3
Oriya language- Semiotics	491.456 014 1
Oriya language- Slang	491.456 7
Oriya language- Special topics	491.456 04
Oriya language- Specialized dictionaries	491.456 31
Oriya language- Spelling	491.456 152

Oriya language- Stress	491.456 16
Oriya language- Structural linguistics	491.456 018
Oriya language- Suprasegmental features	491.456 16
Oriya language- Terminology	491.456 014
Oriya language- Usage	491.456 8
Oriya language- Variations (Dialects etc)	491.456 7
Oriya language- Writing systems	491.456 11
Oriya letters (multiple authors) - - to 1845	***See*** Main schedule
Oriya letters (multiple authors) -1845-1895	891.45664+
Oriya letters (multiple authors) -1895-1919	891.45665+
Oriya letters (multiple authors) -1920-1939	891.45666+
Oriya letters (multiple authors) -1940-	891.45667+
Oriya letters (multiple authors) -1940-1999	891.456671+
Oriya letters (multiple authors) -19th century	891.45664+
Oriya letters (multiple authors) –2000-	891.456672+
Oriya letters (multiple authors) -20th century	891.456671+
Oriya letters (multiple authors) -Collections	891.4566008**
Oriya letters (multiple authors) - Dictionaries etc	891.4566003
Oriya letters (multiple authors) -History and criticism	891.4566009**
Oriya letters (multiple authors) -Periodicals	891.4566005
Oriya letters (multiple authors) -Philosophy and theory	891.4566001
Oriya letters (multiple authors) - Psychological aspects	891.45660019

Oriya letters (multiple authors) -Research	891.45660072
Oriya letters (multiple authors) -Study and teaching	891.4566007
Oriya letters (multiple authors) -Value	891.45660013
Oriya letters (single author)- - to 1845	***See*** Main schedule
Oriya letters (single author)- 1845 -1895	891.4566 4
Oriya letters (single author)- 1895 - 1919	891.4566 5
Oriya letters (single author)- 1920 1939	891.4566 6
Oriya letters (single author)- 1940 -	891.4566 7
Oriya letters (single author)- 1940-1999	891.4566 71
Oriya letters (single author)- 19th century	891.4566 4
Oriya letters (single author)- 2000-	891.4566 72
Oriya letters (single author)- 20th century	891.4566 71
Oriya light verse	***See*** Oriya ephemeral …verse
Oriya limericks (multiple authors)	891.4561075*
Oriya limericks (multiple authors)- Collections	891.456107508**
Oriya limericks (multiple authors)- History and criticism	891.456107509**
Oriya literature	891.456
Oriya literature (collections of multiple forms)	891.45608
Oriya literature (collections of multiple forms) - Allegory	891.45608015
Oriya literature (collections of multiple forms) - Animals	891.456080362++

Oriya literature (collections of multiple forms) - Artistic themes	891.456080357
Oriya literature (collections of multiple forms) - Atmosphere	891.45608032161
Oriya literature (collections of multiple forms) - Characters	891.45608027
Oriya literature (collections of multiple forms) - Comedy	891.45608017
Oriya literature (collections of multiple forms) - Evening	891.45608033
Oriya literature (collections of multiple forms) - Fantasy	891.45608015
Oriya literature (collections of multiple forms) - Forests	891.45608032152
Oriya literature (collections of multiple forms) - Historical themes	891.456080358
Oriya literature (collections of multiple forms) - Horror	891.456080164
Oriya literature (collections of multiple forms) - Human characteristics (Biological, moral, psychological)	891.456080353
Oriya literature (collections of multiple forms) - Legendary objects/themes	891.45608037
Oriya literature (collections of multiple forms) - Literary themes	891.456080357
Oriya literature (collections of multiple forms) - Love	891.4560803543
Oriya literature (collections of multiple forms) - Marriage	891.4560803543
Oriya literature (collections of multiple forms) - Morning	891.45608033

Oriya literature (collections of multiple forms) - Mountains	891.45608032143
Oriya literature (collections of multiple forms) - Myth	891.45608015
Oriya literature (collections of multiple forms) - Mythological objects/themes	891.45608037
Oriya literature (collections of multiple forms) - Philosophic themes	891.456080384
Oriya literature (collections of multiple forms) - Places	891.45608032++
Oriya literature (collections of multiple forms) - Plants	891.456080364
Oriya literature (collections of multiple forms) - Political themes	891.456080358
Oriya literature (collections of multiple forms) - Religious themes	891.456080382++
Oriya literature (collections of multiple forms) - Rivers	891.456080321693
Oriya literature (collections of multiple forms) - Romanticism	891.456080145
Oriya literature (collections of multiple forms) - Scientific themes	891.456080356
Oriya literature (collections of multiple forms) - Sea	891.45608032162
Oriya literature (collections of multiple forms) - Seasons	891.45608033
Oriya literature (collections of multiple forms) - Sex	891.4560803538
Oriya literature (collections of multiple forms) - Social themes	891.456080355

Oriya literature (collections of multiple forms) - Space	891.4560803219
Oriya literature (collections of multiple forms) - Specific kinds of persons, e.g. heroes	891.456080352++
Oriya literature (collections of multiple forms) - Specific persons (real or imaginary)	891.456080351
Oriya literature (collections of multiple forms) - Stream of consciousness	891.45608025
Oriya literature (collections of multiple forms) - Supernatural objects/themes	891.45608037
Oriya literature (collections of multiple forms) - Symbolism	891.45608015
Oriya literature (collections of multiple forms) - Technical themes	891.456080356
Oriya literature (collections of multiple forms) - Times (seasons, parts of day, etc)	891.45608033
Oriya literature (collections of multiple forms) - Towns	891.456080321732
Oriya literature (collections of multiple forms) - Tragedy	891.456080162
Oriya literature (collections of multiple forms) - Villages	891.456080321734
Oriya literature (collections of multiple forms) - Weather	891.45608036
Oriya literature (collections of multiple forms) -19th century	891.4560804
Oriya literature (collections of multiple forms) -20th century	891.45608071
Oriya literature (collections of multiple forms) –21st century	891.45608072

Oriya literature (collections of multiple forms) emphasizing subjects	891.4560804++
Oriya literature (collections of multiple forms) for/by children	891.4560809282
Oriya literature (collections of multiple forms) for/by persons of racial, ethnic and national groups	891.4560808++
Oriya literature (collections of multiple forms) for/by persons of specific classes	891.45608092++
Oriya literature (collections of multiple forms) for/by persons resident in specific regions	891.45608091++
Oriya literature (collections of multiple forms) for/by women	891.4560809287
Oriya literature (multiple authors) - Concordances	891.45603
Oriya literature (multiple authors) - Dictionaries	891.45603
Oriya literature (multiple authors) - Education	891.456071
Oriya literature (multiple authors) - Encyclopaedias	891.45603
Oriya literature (multiple authors) - Organizations	891.45606
Oriya literature (multiple authors) - Periodicals	891.45605
Oriya literature (multiple authors) - Philosophy and theory	891.45601
Oriya literature (multiple authors) - Research	891.456072

Oriya literature (multiple authors) - Research in India	891.456072054
Oriya literature (multiple authors) - Study and teaching	891.45607++
Oriya literature (multiple forms) - 19th century	891.45609004
Oriya literature (multiple forms) – 2000-	891.456090072
Oriya literature (multiple forms) - 20th century	891.456090071
Oriya literature (multiple forms) - Allegory – History and criticism	891.4560915
Oriya literature (multiple forms) - Animals - History and criticism	891.45609362++
Oriya literature (multiple forms) - Artistic themes - History and criticism	891.45609357
Oriya literature (multiple forms) - Atmosphere - History and criticism	891.4560932161
Oriya literature (multiple forms) - Characters - History and criticism	891.4560927
Oriya literature (multiple forms) - Comedy - History and criticism	891.4560917
Oriya literature (multiple forms) - Evening - History and criticism	891.4560933
Oriya literature (multiple forms) - Fantasy - History and criticism	891.4560915
Oriya literature (multiple forms) - Forests- History and criticism	891.4560932152
Oriya literature (multiple forms) - Historical themes - History and criticism	891.45609358
Oriya literature (multiple forms) - History and criticism	891.45609

Oriya literature (multiple forms) - Horror - History and criticism	891.45609164
Oriya literature (multiple forms) - Human characteristics (Biological, moral, psychological) - History and criticism	891.45609353
Oriya literature (multiple forms) - Legendary objects/themes - History and criticism	891.4560937
Oriya literature (multiple forms) - Literary themes - History and criticism	891.45609357
Oriya literature (multiple forms) - Love - History and criticism	891.456093543
Oriya literature (multiple forms) - Marriage - History and criticism	891.456093543
Oriya literature (multiple forms) - Morning - History and criticism	891.4560933
Oriya literature (multiple forms) - Mountains - History and criticism	891.4560932143
Oriya literature (multiple forms) - Myth - History and criticism	891.4560915
Oriya literature (multiple forms) - Mythological objects/themes - History and criticism	891.4560937
Oriya literature (multiple forms) - Persons of racial, ethnic and national groups - History and criticism	891.456098++
Oriya literature (multiple forms) - Persons of specific classes - History and criticism	891.4560992++
Oriya literature (multiple forms) - Persons resident in specific regions - History and criticism	891.4560991++
Oriya literature (multiple forms) - Philosophic themes - History and criticism	891.45609384

Oriya literature (multiple forms) - Places - History and criticism	891.4560932++
Oriya literature (multiple forms) - Plants - History and criticism	891.45609364
Oriya literature (multiple forms) - Political themes - History and criticism	891.45609358
Oriya literature (multiple forms) - Religious themes - History and criticism	891.45609382++
Oriya literature (multiple forms) - Rivers - History and criticism	891.45609321693
Oriya literature (multiple forms) - Romanticism - History and criticism	891.45609145
Oriya literature (multiple forms) - Scientific themes - History and criticism	891.45609356
Oriya literature (multiple forms) - Sea - History and criticism	891.4560932162
Oriya literature (multiple forms) - Seasons - History and criticism	891.4560933
Oriya literature (multiple forms) - Sex - History and criticism	891.456093538
Oriya literature (multiple forms) - Social themes - History and criticism	891.45609355
Oriya literature (multiple forms) - Space - History and criticism	891.456093219
Oriya literature (multiple forms) - Specific kinds of persons, e.g. heroes, - History and criticism	891.45609352++
Oriya literature (multiple forms) - Specific persons - History and criticism	891.45609351
Oriya literature (multiple forms) - Stream of consciousness - History and criticism	891.4560925

Oriya literature (multiple forms) - Subjects - History and criticism	891.456094++
Oriya literature (multiple forms) - Supernatural objects/themes - History and criticism	891.4560937
Oriya literature (multiple forms) - Symbolism- History , description, criticism	891.4560915
Oriya literature (multiple forms) - Technical themes - History and criticism	891.45609356
Oriya literature (multiple forms) - Times - History and criticism	891.4560933
Oriya literature (multiple forms) - Towns - History and criticism	891.45609321732
Oriya literature (multiple forms) - Tragedy - History and criticism	891.45609162
Oriya literature (multiple forms) - Villages - History and criticism	891.45609321734
Oriya literature (multiple forms) - Weather - History and criticism	891.4560936
Oriya literature (single author)- - to 1845 - Biography, collections, criticism	***See*** Main schedule
Oriya literature (single author)- 1845 - 1895 - Biography, collections, criticism	891.4568 409
Oriya literature (single author)- 1895 - 1919 - Biography, collections, criticism	891.4568 509
Oriya literature (single author)- 1920 1939 - Biography, collections, criticism	891.4568 609
Oriya literature (single author)- 1940 - Biography, collections, criticism	891.4568 709
Oriya literature (single author)- 1940- 1999 - Biography, collections, criticism	891.4568 7109

Oriya literature (single author)- 19th century- Biography, collections, criticism	891.4568 409
Oriya literature (single author)- 2000- Biography, collections, criticism	891.4568 7209
Oriya literature (single author)- 20th century - Biography, collections, criticism	891.4568 7109
Oriya literature for/by children - History and criticism	891.456099282
Oriya literature for/by women - History and criticism	891.456099287
Oriya love fiction (multiple authors)	891.4563085*
Oriya love fiction (multiple authors)- Collections	891.456308508**
Oriya love fiction (multiple authors)- History and criticism	891.456308509**
Oriya melodrama (multiple authors)	891.45620527*
Oriya melodrama (multiple authors)- Collections	891.4562052708**
Oriya melodrama (multiple authors)- History and criticism	891.4562052709**
Oriya miscellaneous writings	891.4568
Oriya miscellaneous writings (multiple authors) - to 1845	***See*** Main schedule
Oriya miscellaneous writings (multiple authors) -1845-1895	891.45684++
Oriya miscellaneous writings (multiple authors) -1895-1919	891.45685++
Oriya miscellaneous writings (multiple authors) -1920-1939	891.45686++

Oriya miscellaneous writings (multiple authors) -1940-	891.45687++
Oriya miscellaneous writings (multiple authors) -1940-1999	891.456871++
Oriya miscellaneous writings (multiple authors) -19th century	891.45684++
Oriya miscellaneous writings (multiple authors) –2000-	891.456872++
Oriya miscellaneous writings (multiple authors) -20th century	891.456871++
Oriya miscellaneous writings (multiple authors) -Collections	891.4568008**
Oriya miscellaneous writings (multiple authors) -Dictionaries etc	891.4568003
Oriya miscellaneous writings (multiple authors) -History and criticism	891.4568009**
Oriya miscellaneous writings (multiple authors) -Periodicals	891.4568005
Oriya miscellaneous writings (multiple authors) -Philosophy and theory	891.4568001
Oriya miscellaneous writings (multiple authors) -Psychological aspects	891.45680019
Oriya miscellaneous writings (multiple authors) -Research	891.45680072
Oriya miscellaneous writings (multiple authors) -Study and teaching	891.4568007
Oriya miscellaneous writings (multiple authors) -Value	891.45680013
Oriya miscellaneous writings (single author)- - to 1845	***See*** Main schedule

Oriya miscellaneous writings (single author)- 1845 -1895	891.4568 4
Oriya miscellaneous writings (single author)- 1895 - 1919	891.4568 5
Oriya miscellaneous writings (single author)- 1920 - 1939	891.4568 6
Oriya miscellaneous writings (single author)- 1940 -	891.4568 7
Oriya miscellaneous writings (single author)- 1940-1999	891.4568 71
Oriya miscellaneous writings (single author)- 19th century	891.4568 4
Oriya miscellaneous writings (single author)- 2000-	891.4568 72
Oriya miscellaneous writings (single author)- 20th century	891.4568 71
Oriya monologues (multiple authors)	891.4562045*
Oriya monologues (multiple authors)- Collections	891.456204508**
Oriya monologues (multiple authors)- History and criticism	891.456204509**
Oriya morality plays	***See*** Oriya religious ... plays
Oriya mystery fiction (multiple authors)	891.45630872*
Oriya mystery fiction (multiple authors)- Collections	891.4563087208**
Oriya mystery fiction (multiple authors)- History and criticism	891.4563087209**
Oriya narrative poetry (multiple authors)	891.456103*

Oriya narrative poetry (multiple authors)- Collections	891.45610308**
Oriya narrative poetry (multiple authors)- History and criticism	891.45610309**
Oriya notebooks	***See*** Oriya diaries ...
Oriya odes (multiple authors)	891.4561043*
Oriya odes (multiple authors)- Collections	891.456104308**
Oriya odes (multiple authors)- History and criticism	891.456104309**
Oriya one act plays (multiple authors)	891.456 204 1*
Oriya one act plays (multiple authors)- Collections	891.456 204 108**
Oriya one act plays (multiple authors)- History and criticism	891.456 204 109**
Oriya oratory (multiple authors)	***See*** Oriya public speeches
Oriya people	305.891 45
Oriya periodicals	059.91456
Oriya poetry	891.4561
Oriya poetry (multiple authors) - - to 1845	***See*** Main schedule
Oriya poetry (multiple authors) - 1845-1895	891.45614+
Oriya poetry (multiple authors) - 1895-1919	891.45615+
Oriya poetry (multiple authors) - 1920-1939	891.45616+
Oriya poetry (multiple authors) - 1940-	891.45617+
Oriya poetry (multiple authors) - 1940-1999	891.456171+
Oriya poetry (multiple authors) - 19th century	891.45614+

Oriya poetry (multiple authors) - 2000-	891.456172+
Oriya poetry (multiple authors) - 20th century	891.456171+
Oriya poetry (multiple authors)- Collections	891.4561008**
Oriya poetry (multiple authors)- Dictionaries etc	891.4561003
Oriya poetry (multiple authors)- History and criticism	891.4561009**
Oriya poetry (multiple authors)- Periodicals	891.4561005
Oriya poetry (multiple authors)- Philosophy and theory	891.4561001
Oriya poetry (multiple authors)- Psychological aspects	891.45610019
Oriya poetry (multiple authors)- Research	891.45610072
Oriya poetry (multiple authors)- Study and teaching	891.4561007
Oriya poetry (multiple authors)- Value	891.45610013
Oriya poetry (single author)- - to 1845	***See*** Main schedule
Oriya poetry (single author)- 1845 -1895	891.4561 4
Oriya poetry (single author)- 1895 - 1919	891.4561 5
Oriya poetry (single author)- 1920 - 1939	891.4561 6
Oriya poetry (single author)- 1940 -	891.4561 7
Oriya poetry (single author)- 1940-1999	891.4561 71
Oriya poetry (single author)- 19th century	891.4561 4
Oriya poetry (single author)- 2000-	891.4561 72
Oriya poetry (single author)- 20th century	891.4561 71
Oriya prose (single author)- - to 1845	***See*** Main schedule

Oriya prose (single author)- 1845 -1895	891.4568 408
Oriya prose (single author)- 1895 - 1919	891.4568 508
Oriya prose (single author)- 1920 - 1939	891.4568 608
Oriya prose (single author)- 1940 -	891.4568 708
Oriya prose (single author)- 1940-1999	891.4568 7108
Oriya prose (single author)- 19th century	891.4568 408
Oriya prose (single author)- 2000-	891.4568 7208
Oriya prose (single author)- 20th century	891.4568 7108
Oriya prose literature (multiple authors)	891.456808
Oriya psychological, realistic, sociological fiction (multiple authors) - History and criticism	891.4563083
Oriya public discussions	***See*** Oriya debates ...
Oriya public speeches (multiple authors)- Collections	891.45650108**
Oriya public speeches (multiple authors)- History and criticism	891.45650109**
Oriya quotations	***See*** Oriya anecdotes ...
Oriya recitations (multiple authors)	891.456504+
Oriya religious and morality plays (multiple authors)	891.45620516+
Oriya reminiscences	***See*** Oriya diaries ...
Oriya romantic fiction (multiple authors)	891.4563085*
Oriya romantic fiction (multiple authors)- Collections	891.456308508**

Oriya romantic fiction (multiple authors)- History and criticism	891.456308509**
Oriya satire	*See* Oriya humour ...
Oriya satirical poetry	*See* Oriya humourous ... poetry
Oriya science fiction (multiple authors)	891.456308762*
Oriya science fiction (multiple authors)- Collections	891.45630876208**
Oriya science fiction (multiple authors)- History and criticism	891.45630876209**
Oriya serious drama (multiple authors)	891.4562051+
Oriya short stories (multiple authors)	891.456301*
Oriya short stories (multiple authors)- Collections	891.45630108**
Oriya short stories (multiple authors)- History and criticism	891.45630109**
Oriya sociological fiction (multiple authors)	891.4563083+
Oriya sonnets (multiple authors)	891.4561042*
Oriya sonnets (multiple authors)- Collections	891.456104208**
Oriya sonnets (multiple authors)- History and criticism	891.456104209**
Oriya speaking people	305.791 456
Oriya speeches	891.4565
Oriya speeches (multiple authors) — to 1845	*See* Main schedule
Oriya speeches (multiple authors) - 1845-1895	891.45654+

Oriya speeches (multiple authors) - 1895-1919	891.45655+
Oriya speeches (multiple authors) - 1920-1939	891.45656+
Oriya speeches (multiple authors) -1940-	891.45657+
Oriya speeches (multiple authors) - 1940-1999	891.456571+
Oriya speeches (multiple authors) - 19th century	891.45654+
Oriya speeches (multiple authors) –2000-	891.456572+
Oriya speeches (multiple authors) - 20th century	891.456571+
Oriya speeches (multiple authors) - Collections	891.4565008**
Oriya speeches (multiple authors) - Dictionaries etc	891.4565003
Oriya speeches (multiple authors) - History and criticism	891.4565009**
Oriya speeches (multiple authors) - Periodicals	891.4565005
Oriya speeches (multiple authors) - Philosophy and theory	891.4565001
Oriya speeches (multiple authors) - Psychological aspects	891.45650019
Oriya speeches (multiple authors) - Research	891.45650072
Oriya speeches (multiple authors) - Study and teaching	891.4565007
Oriya speeches (multiple authors) -Value	891.45650013
Oriya speeches (single author)- - to 1845	***See*** Main schedule

Oriya speeches (single author)- 1845 -1895	891.4565 4
Oriya speeches (single author)- 1895 - 1919	891.4565 5
Oriya speeches (single author)- 1920 - 1939	891.4565 6
Oriya speeches (single author)- 1940 -	891.4565 7
Oriya speeches (single author)- 1940-1999	891.4565 71
Oriya speeches (single author)- 19th century	891.4565 4
Oriya speeches (single author)- 2000-	891.4565 72
Oriya speeches (single author)- 20th century	891.4565 71
Oriya suspense fiction (multiple authors)	891.45630872*
Oriya suspense fiction (multiple authors)- Collections	891.4563087208**
Oriya suspense fiction (multiple authors)- History and criticism	891.4563087209**
Oriya tragedy (multiple authors)	891.45620512*
Oriya tragedy (multiple authors)- Collections	891.4562051208**
Oriya tragedy (multiple authors)- History and criticism	891.4562051209**
Oriya variety drama (multiple authors)	891.4562057*
Oriya variety drama (multiple authors)- Collections	891.456205708**
Oriya variety drama (multiple authors)- History and criticism	891.456205709**
Oriyas - Opinions	303.387 914 5
Other worlds (Buddhism)	294.342 3
Other worlds (Hinduism)	294.523
Other worlds (Jainism)	294.423
Other worlds (Sikhism)	294.623

P

Pagodas	294.3435
Pahari (People)	305.891 496
Pahari folk music	781 629 1496
Pahari languages	491.49
Pahari literatures	891.49
Painted glass and glass makers	***See*** Stained... glass makers
Painting and paintings- Andaman and Nicobar Islands	759.954 88
Painting and paintings- Andhra Pradesh	759.954 84
Painting and paintings- Arunachal Pradesh	759.954 163
Painting and paintings- Assam	759.954 162
Painting and paintings- Bengal	759.954 14
Painting and paintings- Bhopal	759.954 3
Painting and paintings- Bihar	759.954 12
Painting and paintings- Bombay	759.954 7923
Painting and paintings- Calcutta	759.954 147
Painting and paintings- Chandigarh	759.954 552
Painting and paintings- Chhattisgarh	759.954 137

Painting and paintings- Dadra and Nagar Haveli	759.954 796
Painting and paintings- Delhi	759.954 56
Painting and paintings- Goa, Daman and Diu	759.954 799
Painting and paintings- Gujarat	759.954 75
Painting and paintings- Haryana	759.954 558
Painting and paintings- Himachal Pradesh	759.954 52
Painting and paintings- Hyderabad state	759.954 84
Painting and paintings- India	759.954
Painting and paintings- Jammu and Kashmir	759.954 6
Painting and paintings- Jharkhand	759.9127
Painting and paintings- Karnataka	759.954 87
Painting and paintings- Kerala	759.954 83
Painting and paintings- Lakshwadweep	759.954 81
Painting and paintings- Madhya Pradesh	759.954 3
Painting and paintings- Madras	759.954 82
Painting and paintings- Maharashtra	759.954 792
Painting and paintings- Manipur	759.954 17
Painting and paintings- Meghalaya	759.954 164
Painting and paintings- Mizoram	759.954 166
Painting and paintings- Nagaland	759.954 165
Painting and paintings- Northeast India	759.954 1
Painting and paintings- Orissa	759.954 13
Painting and paintings- Pondicherry	759.954 86

Painting and paintings- Punjab	759.954 552
Painting and paintings- Rajasthan	759.954 4
Painting and paintings- Sikkim	759.954 167
Painting and paintings- South Asia	759.954
Painting and paintings- Southern India	759.954 8
Painting and paintings- Tamil Nadu	759.954 82
Painting and paintings- Tripura	759.954 15
Painting and paintings- Uttar Pradesh	759.954 2
Painting and paintings- Uttaranchal	759.51
Painting and paintings- West Bengal	759.954 14
Painting and paintings- Western India	759.954 7
Pali drama	891.372
Pali essays	891.374
Pali fiction	891.373
Pali language	491.37
Pali language- Applied linguistics	491.378
Pali language- Bilingual dictionaries	491.373 2-39
Pali language- Concordances	491.370 3
Pali language- Dictionaries	491.373
Pali language- Education	491.370 71
Pali language- Encyclopaedias	491.370 3
Pali language- Grammar	491.375
Pali language- History	491.370 9
Pali language- Lexicography	491.373 028
Pali language- Lexicology	491.370 14

Pali language- Periodicals	491.370 5
Pali language- Philosophy and theory	491.370 1
Pali language- Readers	491.378 6
Pali language- Research	491.370 72
Pali language- Rhetoric	808.049 137++
Pali language- Specialized dictionaries	491.373 1
Pali language- Terminology	491.370 14
Pali language- Usage	491.378
Pali language- Variations (Dialects etc)	491.377
Pali language- Writing systems	491.37 11
Pali letters	891.376
Pali literature	891.37
Pali poetry	891.371
Pali speeches	891.375
Pali–English dictionary	491.417 321
Pali-Hindi dictionary	491.3739 143 1
Panjabi - English dictionary	491.423 21
Panjabi - Hindi dictionary	491.423 91431
Panjabi adventure fiction (multiple authors)	891.423087*
Panjabi adventure fiction (multiple authors) - Collections	891.42308708**
Panjabi adventure fiction (multiple authors)- History and criticism	891.42308709**
Panjabi anecdotes, epigrams, graffiti, jokes, quotations (multiple authors)	891.42802
Panjabi anecdotes, epigrams, graffiti, jokes, quotations (single author)	891.428 +CD+02

Panjabi as second language in elementary education	372.659 142
Panjabi ballads (multiple authors)	891.421044*
Panjabi ballads (multiple authors)- Collections	891.42104408**
Panjabi ballads (multiple authors)- History and criticism	891.42104409**
Panjabi comedy (multiple authors)	891.4220523*
Panjabi comedy (multiple authors) - Collections	891.422052308**
Panjabi comedy (multiple authors) - History and criticism	891.422052309**
Panjabi conversations (multiple authors)	891.42506*
Panjabi conversations (multiple authors) - Collections	891.4250608**
Panjabi conversations (multiple authors) - History and criticism	891.4250609**
Panjabi debates and public discussions (multiple authors)	891.42503*
Panjabi debates and public discussions (multiple authors)- Collections	891.4250308**
Panjabi debates and public discussions (multiple authors)- History and criticism	891.4250309**
Panjabi detective fiction (multiple authors)	891.4230872*
Panjabi detective fiction (multiple authors) - Collections	891.423087208**
Panjabi detective fiction (multiple authors) - History and criticism	891.423087209**
Panjabi diaries, notebooks, reminiscences (multiple authors)	891.42803

Panjabi diaries, notebooks, reminiscences (single author)	891.428@
Panjabi didactic poetry (multiple authors)	891.42105*
Panjabi didactic poetry (multiple authors)-Collections	891.4210508**
Panjabi didactic poetry (multiple authors)-History and criticism	891.4210509**
Panjabi drama	891.422
Panjabi drama (multiple authors) - -to 1845 schedule	See Main
Panjabi drama (multiple authors) - 1845-1895	891.4224+
Panjabi drama (multiple authors) - 1895-1919	891.4225+
Panjabi drama (multiple authors) - 1920-1939	891.4226+
Panjabi drama (multiple authors) - 1940-	891.4227+
Panjabi drama (multiple authors) - 1940-1999	891.42271+
Panjabi drama (multiple authors) - 19th century	891.4224+
Panjabi drama (multiple authors) - 2000-	891.42272+
Panjabi drama (multiple authors) - 20th century	891.42271+
Panjabi drama (multiple authors) - Collections	891.422008**
Panjabi drama (multiple authors) - Dictionaries etc	891.422003
Panjabi drama (multiple authors) - History and criticism	891.422009**

Panjabi drama (multiple authors) - Periodicals	891.422005
Panjabi drama (multiple authors) - Philosophy and theory	891.422001
Panjabi drama (multiple authors) - Psychological aspects	891.4220019
Panjabi drama (multiple authors) - Research	891.4220072
Panjabi drama (multiple authors) - Study and teaching	891.422007
Panjabi drama (multiple authors) - Value	891.4220013
Panjabi drama (single author) - to 1845	***See*** Main schedule
Panjabi drama (single author)- 1845 -1895	891.422 4
Panjabi drama (single author)- 1895 - 1919	891.422 5
Panjabi drama (single author)- 1920 - 1939	891.422 6
Panjabi drama (single author)- 1940 -	891.422 7
Panjabi drama (single author)- 1940-1999	891.422 71
Panjabi drama (single author)- 19th century	891.422 4
Panjabi drama (single author)- 2000-	891.422 72
Panjabi drama (single author)- 20th century	891.422 71
Panjabi drama for cinema (multiple authors)	891.42203*
Panjabi drama for cinema (multiple authors) - Collections	891.4220308**
Panjabi drama for cinema (multiple authors) - History and criticism	891.4220309**
Panjabi drama for radio (multiple authors)	891.422022*
Panjabi drama for radio (multiple authors) - Collections	891.42202208**

Panjabi drama for radio (multiple authors) - History and criticism	891.42202209**
Panjabi drama for television (multiple authors)	891.422025*
Panjabi drama for television (multiple authors) - Collections	891.42202508**
Panjabi drama for television (multiple authors) - History and criticism	891.42202509**
Panjabi dramatic poetry (multiple authors)	891.42102*
Panjabi dramatic poetry (multiple authors)- Collections	891.4210208**
Panjabi dramatic poetry (multiple authors)- History and criticism	891.4210209**
Panjabi encyclopaedias	039.9142
Panjabi ephemeral and light verse (multiple authors)	891.42108*
Panjabi ephemeral and light verse (multiple authors)- Collections	891.4210808**
Panjabi ephemeral and light verse (multiple authors) - History and criticism	891.4210809**
Panjabi epic poetry (multiple authors)	891.421032*
Panjabi epic poetry (multiple authors)- Collections	891.42103208**
Panjabi epic poetry (multiple authors)- History and criticism	891.42103209**
Panjabi epigrams	***See*** Panjabi anecdotes ...
Panjabi essays	891.424
Panjabi essays (multiple authors) - - to 1845	***See*** Main schedule

Panjabi essays (multiple authors) - 1845-1895	891.4244+
Panjabi essays (multiple authors) - 1895-1919	891.4245+
Panjabi essays (multiple authors) - 1920-1939	891.4246+
Panjabi essays (multiple authors) -1940-	891.4247+
Panjabi essays (multiple authors) - 1940-1999	891.42471+
Panjabi essays (multiple authors) - 19th century	891.4244+
Panjabi essays (multiple authors) -2000-	891.42472+
Panjabi essays (multiple authors) - 20th century	891.42471+
Panjabi essays (multiple authors) - Collections	891.424008**
Panjabi essays (multiple authors) - Dictionaries etc	891.424003
Panjabi essays (multiple authors) - History and criticism	891.424009**
Panjabi essays (multiple authors) - Periodicals	891.424005
Panjabi essays (multiple authors) - Philosophy and theory	891.424001
Panjabi essays (multiple authors) - Psychological aspects	891.4240019
Panjabi essays (multiple authors) -Research	891.4240072
Panjabi essays (multiple authors) - Study and teaching	891.424007

Panjabi essays (multiple authors) -Value	891.4240013
Panjabi essays (single author)- - to 1845	See Main schedule
Panjabi essays (single author)- 1845 -1895	891.424 4
Panjabi essays (single author)- 1895 - 1919	891.424 5
Panjabi essays (single author)- 1920 - 1939	891.424 6
Panjabi essays (single author)- 1940 -	891.424 7
Panjabi essays (single author)- 1940-1999	891.424 71
Panjabi essays (single author)- 19th century	891.424 4
Panjabi essays (single author)- 2000-	891.424 72
Panjabi essays (single author)- 20th century	891.424 71
Panjabi experimental and non-formalized works (single author)	891.428+CD+07
Panjabi experimental and non-formalized works (multiple authors)	891.42807
Panjabi fantasy fiction (multiple authors)	891.42308766*
Panjabi fantasy fiction (multiple authors)- Collections	891.4230876608**
Panjabi fantasy fiction (multiple authors)- History and criticism	891.4230876609**
Panjabi farce (multiple authors)	891.42205232*
Panjabi farce (multiple authors)- Collections	891.4220523208**
Panjabi farce (multiple authors)- History and criticism	891.4220523209**
Panjabi fiction	891.423
Panjabi fiction (multiple authors) - -to 1845	***See*** Main schedule
Panjabi fiction (multiple authors) - 1845-1895 Panjabi fiction (multiple authors) -	891.4234+

1895-1919	891.4235+
Panjabi fiction (multiple authors) - 1920-1939	891.4236+
Panjabi fiction (multiple authors) - 1940-	891.4237+
Panjabi fiction (multiple authors) - 1940-1999	891.42371+
Panjabi fiction (multiple authors) - 19th century	891.4234+
Panjabi fiction (multiple authors) - 2000-	891.42372+
Panjabi fiction (multiple authors) - 20th century	891.42371+
Panjabi fiction (multiple authors) - Collections	891.423008**
Panjabi fiction (multiple authors) - Dictionaries etc	891.423003
Panjabi fiction (multiple authors) - History and criticism	891.423009**
Panjabi fiction (multiple authors) - Periodicals	891.423005
Panjabi fiction (multiple authors) - Philosophy and theory	891.423001
Panjabi fiction (multiple authors) - Psychological aspects	891.4230019
Panjabi fiction (multiple authors) - Research	891.4230072
Panjabi fiction (multiple authors) - Study and teaching	891.423007
Panjabi fiction (multiple authors) - Value	891.4230013
Panjabi fiction (single author)- - to 1845	***See*** Main schedule

Panjabi fiction (single author)- 1845 -1895	891.423 4
Panjabi fiction (single author)- 1895 - 1919	891.423 5
Panjabi fiction (single author)- 1920 - 1939	891.423 6
Panjabi fiction (single author)- 1940 -	891.423 7
Panjabi fiction (single author)- 1940-1999	891.423 71
Panjabi fiction (single author)- 19th century	891.423 4
Panjabi fiction (single author)- 2000-	891.423 72
Panjabi fiction (single author)- 20th century	891.423 71
Panjabi folk music	781 629 142
Panjabi ghost fiction (multiple authors)	891.42308733*
Panjabi ghost fiction (multiple authors) - Collections	891.4230873308**
Panjabi ghost fiction (multiple authors)- History and criticism	891.4230873309**
Panjabi graffiti	***See*** Panjabi anecdotes ...
Panjabi historical drama (multiple authors)	891.4220514*
Panjabi historical drama (multiple authors)- Collections	891.422051408**
Panjabi historical drama (multiple authors)- History and criticism	891.422051409**
Panjabi historical fiction (multiple authors)	891.423081*
Panjabi historical fiction (multiple authors)- Collections	891.42308108**
Panjabi historical fiction (multiple authors)- History and criticism	891.42308109**
Panjabi horror fiction (multiple authors)	891.42308738*

tPanjabi horror fiction (multiple authors)-Collections	891.4230873808**
Panjabi horror fiction (multiple authors)-History and criticism	891.4230873809**
Panjabi humour and satire	891.427
Panjabi humour and satire (multiple authors) — to 1845	***See*** Main schedule
Panjabi humour and satire (multiple authors) -1845-1895	891.4274+
Panjabi humour and satire (multiple authors) -1895-1919	891.4275+
Panjabi humour and satire (multiple authors) -1920-1939	891.4276+
Panjabi humour and satire (multiple authors) -1940-	891.4277+
Panjabi humour and satire (multiple authors) -1940-1999	891.42771+
Panjabi humour and satire (multiple authors) -19th century	891.4274+
Panjabi humour and satire (multiple authors) -2000-	891.42772+
Panjabi humour and satire (multiple authors) -20th century	891.42771+
Panjabi humour and satire (multiple authors) -Collections	891.427008**
Panjabi humour and satire (multiple authors) -Dictionaries etc	891.427003
Panjabi humour and satire (multiple authors) -History and criticism	891.427009**
Panjabi humour and satire (multiple authors) -Periodicals	891.427005

Panjabi humour and satire (multiple authors) -Philosophy and theory	891.427001
Panjabi humour and satire (multiple authors) -Psychological aspects	891.4270019
Panjabi humour and satire (multiple authors) -Research	891.4270072
Panjabi humour and satire (multiple authors) -Study and teaching	891.427007
Panjabi humour and satire (multiple authors) -Value	891.4270013
Panjabi humourous and satirical poetry (multiple authors)	891.42107*
Panjabi humourous and satirical poetry (multiple authors)- Collections	891.4210708**
Panjabi humourous and satirical poetry (multiple authors)- History and criticism	891.4210709**
Panjabi jokes	***See*** Panjabi anecdotes ...
Panjabi language	491.42
Panjabi language- Applied linguistics	491.42 8
Panjabi language- Bilingual dictionaries	491.42 32-39
Panjabi language- Bilingualism	491.42 042
Panjabi language- Concordances	491.42 03
Panjabi language- Content analysis	491.42 014 1
Panjabi language- Dictionaries	491.42 3
Panjabi language- Discourse analysis	491.42 014 1
Panjabi language- Education	491.42 071
Panjabi language- Encyclopaedias	491.42 03

Panjabi language- Etymology	491.42 2
Panjabi language- Functionalism	491.42 018
Panjabi language- Grammar	491.42 5
Panjabi language- History	491.42 09
Panjabi language- Intonation	491.42 16
Panjabi language- Lexicography	491.42 302 8
Panjabi language- Lexicology	491.42 014
Panjabi language- Miscellany	491.42 02
Panjabi language- Multilingualism	491.42 042
Panjabi language- Organizations	491.42 06
Panjabi language- Orthography	491.42 152
Panjabi language- Pauses	491.42 16
Panjabi language- Periodicals	491.42 05
Panjabi language- Persons (men, women, etc)	491.42 08
Panjabi language- Philosophy and theory	491.42 01
Panjabi language- Phonetics	491.42 158
Panjabi language- Phonology	491.42 15
Panjabi language- Pitch	491.42 16
Panjabi language- Pronunciation	491.42 152
Panjabi language- Readers	491.428 6
Panjabi language- Research	491.42 072
Panjabi language- Rhetoric	808.049 142++
Panjabi language- Schools and theories of linguistics	491.42 018

Panjabi language- Semantics	491.42 014 3
Panjabi language- Semiotics	491.42 014 1
Panjabi language- Slang	491.42 7
Panjabi language- Special topics	491.42 04
Panjabi language- Specialized dictionaries	491.42 31
Panjabi language- Spelling	491.42 152
Panjabi language- Stress	491.42 16
Panjabi language- Structural linguistics	491.42 018
Panjabi language- Suprasegmental features	491.42 16
Panjabi language- Terminology	491.42 014
Panjabi language- Usage	491.42 8
Panjabi language- Variations (Dialects etc)	491.42 7
Panjabi language- Writing systems	491.42 11
Panjabi letters	891.426
Panjabi letters (multiple authors) - - to 1845	***See*** Main schedule
Panjabi letters (multiple authors) - 1845-1895	891.4264+
Panjabi letters (multiple authors) - 1895-1919	891.4265+
Panjabi letters (multiple authors) - 1920-1939	891.4266+
Panjabi letters (multiple authors) -1940-	891.4267+
Panjabi letters (multiple authors) - 1940-1999	891.42671+
Panjabi letters (multiple authors) - 19th century	891.4264+

Panjabi letters (multiple authors) -2000-	891.42672+
Panjabi letters (multiple authors) - 20th century	891.42671+
Panjabi letters (multiple authors) - Collections	891.426008**
Panjabi letters (multiple authors) - Dictionaries etc	891.426003
Panjabi letters (multiple authors) - History and criticism	891.426009**
Panjabi letters (multiple authors) - Periodicals	891.426005
Panjabi letters (multiple authors) - Philosophy and theory	891.426001
Panjabi letters (multiple authors) - Psychological aspects	891.4260019
Panjabi letters (multiple authors) -Research	891.4260072
Panjabi letters (multiple authors) - Study and teaching	891.426007
Panjabi letters (multiple authors) -Value	891.4260013
Panjabi letters (single author)- - to 1845	***See*** Main schedule
Panjabi letters (single author)- 1845 -1895	891.426 4
Panjabi letters (single author)- 1895 - 1919	891.426 5
Panjabi letters (single author)- 1920 1939	891.426 6
Panjabi letters (single author)- 1940 -	891.426 7
Panjabi letters (single author)- 1940-1999	891.426 71
Panjabi letters (single author)- 19th century	891.426 4
Panjabi letters (single author)- 2000-	891.426 72
Panjabi letters (single author)- 20th century	891.426 71

Panjabi light verse	***See*** Panjabi ephemeral ... verse
Panjabi limericks (multiple authors)	891.421075*
Panjabi limericks (multiple authors)-Collections	891.42107508**
Panjabi limericks (multiple authors)-History and criticism	891.42107509**
Panjabi literature	891.42
Panjabi literature (collections of multiple forms)	891.4208
Panjabi literature (collections of multiple forms) - 19th century	891.420804
Panjabi literature (collections of multiple forms) - 20th century	891.4208071
Panjabi literature (collections of multiple forms) – 21st century	891.4208072
Panjabi literature (collections of multiple forms) - Allegory	891.4208015
Panjabi literature (collections of multiple forms) - Animals	891.42080362++
Panjabi literature (collections of multiple forms) - Artistic themes	891.42080357
Panjabi literature (collections of multiple forms) - Atmosphere	891.4208032161
Panjabi literature (collections of multiple forms) - Characters	891.4208027
Panjabi literature (collections of multiple forms) - Comedy	891.4208017
Panjabi literature (collections of multiple forms) - Evening	891.4208033

Panjabi literature (collections of multiple forms) - Fantasy	891.4208015
Panjabi literature (collections of multiple forms) - Forests	891.4208032152
Panjabi literature (collections of multiple forms) - Historical themes	891.42080358
Panjabi literature (collections of multiple forms) - Horror	891.42080164
Panjabi literature (collections of multiple forms) - Human characteristics (Biological, moral, psychological)	891.42080353
Panjabi literature (collections of multiple forms) - Legendary objects/themes	891.4208037
Panjabi literature (collections of multiple forms) - Literary themes	891.42080357
Panjabi literature (collections of multiple forms) - Love	891.420803543
Panjabi literature (collections of multiple forms) - Marriage	891.420803543
Panjabi literature (collections of multiple forms) - Morning	891.4208033
Panjabi literature (collections of multiple forms) - Mountains	891.4208032143
Panjabi literature (collections of multiple forms) - Myth	891.4208015
Panjabi literature (collections of multiple forms) - Mythological objects/themes	891.4208037
Panjabi literature (collections of multiple forms) - Philosophic themes	891.42080384
Panjabi literature (collections of multiple forms) - Places	891.4208032++

Panjabi literature (collections of multiple forms) - Plants	891.42080364
Panjabi literature (collections of multiple forms) - Political themes	891.42080358
Panjabi literature (collections of multiple forms) - Religious themes	891.42080382++
Panjabi literature (collections of multiple forms) - Rivers	891.42080321693
Panjabi literature (collections of multiple forms) - Romanticism	891.42080145
Panjabi literature (collections of multiple forms) - Scientific themes	891.42080356
Panjabi literature (collections of multiple forms) - Sea	891.4208032162
Panjabi literature (collections of multiple forms) - Seasons	891.4208033
Panjabi literature (collections of multiple forms) - Sex	891.420803538
Panjabi literature (collections of multiple forms) - Social themes	891.42080355
Panjabi literature (collections of multiple forms) - Space	891.420803219
Panjabi literature (collections of multiple forms) - Specific kinds of persons, e.g. heroes	891.42080352++
Panjabi literature (collections of multiple forms) - Specific persons (real or imaginary)	891.42080351
Panjabi literature (collections of multiple forms) - Stream of consciousness	891.4208025
Panjabi literature (collections of multiple forms) - Supernatural objects/themes	891.4208037

Panjabi literature (collections of multiple forms) - Symbolism	891.4208015
Panjabi literature (collections of multiple forms) - Technical themes	891.42080356
Panjabi literature (collections of multiple forms) - Times (seasons, parts of day, etc)	891.4208033
Panjabi literature (collections of multiple forms) - Towns	891.42080321732
Panjabi literature (collections of multiple forms) - Tragedy	891.42080162
Panjabi literature (collections of multiple forms) - Villages	891.42080321734
Panjabi literature (collections of multiple forms) - Weather	891.4208036
Panjabi literature (collections of multiple forms) emphasizing subjects	891.420804++
Panjabi literature (collections of multiple forms) for/by children	891.420809282
Panjabi literature (collections of multiple forms) for/by persons of racial, ethnic and national groups	891.420808++
Panjabi literature (collections of multiple forms) for/by persons of specific classes	891.4208092++
Panjabi literature (collections of multiple forms) for/by persons resident in specific regions	891.4208091++
Panjabi literature (collections of multiple forms) for/by women	891.420809287
Panjabi literature (multiple authors) - Concordances	891.4203
Panjabi literature (multiple authors) - Dictionaries	891.4203

Panjabi literature (multiple authors) - Education	891.42071
Panjabi literature (multiple authors) - Encyclopaedias	891.4203
Panjabi literature (multiple authors) - Organizations	891.4206
Panjabi literature (multiple authors) - Periodicals	891.4205
Panjabi literature (multiple authors) - Philosophy and theory	891.4201
Panjabi literature (multiple authors) - Research	891.42072
Panjabi literature (multiple authors) - Research in India	891.42072054
Panjabi literature (multiple authors) - Study and teaching	891.4207
Panjabi literature (multiple forms) - 19th century	891.4209004
Panjabi literature (multiple forms) – 2000-	891.42090072
Panjabi literature (multiple forms) - 20th century	891.42090071
Panjabi literature (multiple forms) - Allegory – History and criticism	891.420915
Panjabi literature (multiple forms) - Animals - History and criticism	891.4209362++
Panjabi literature (multiple forms) - Artistic themes - History and criticism	891.4209357
Panjabi literature (multiple forms) - Atmosphere - History and criticism	891.420932161
Panjabi literature (multiple forms) - Characters - History and criticism	891.420927

Panjabi literature (multiple forms) - Comedy - History and criticism	891.420917
Panjabi literature (multiple forms) - Evening - History and criticism	891.420933
Panjabi literature (multiple forms) - Fantasy - History , description, criticism	891.420915
Panjabi literature (multiple forms) - Forests - History and criticism	891.420932152
Panjabi literature (multiple forms) - Historical themes - History and criticism	891.4209358
Panjabi literature (multiple forms) - History and criticism	891.4209
Panjabi literature (multiple forms) - Horror - History and criticism	891.4209164
Panjabi literature (multiple forms) - Human characteristics (Biological, moral, psychological) - History and criticism	891.4209353
Panjabi literature (multiple forms) - Legendary objects/themes - History and criticism	891.420937
Panjabi literature (multiple forms) - Literary themes - History and criticism	891.4209357
Panjabi literature (multiple forms) - Love - History and criticism	891.42093543
Panjabi literature (multiple forms) - Marriage - History and criticism	891.42093543
Panjabi literature (multiple forms) - Morning - History and criticism	891.420933
Panjabi literature (multiple forms) - Mountains - History and criticism	891.420932143

Panjabi literature (multiple forms) - Myth - History and criticism	891.420915
Panjabi literature (multiple forms) - Mythological objects/themes - History and criticism	891.420937
Panjabi literature (multiple forms) - Persons of racial, ethnic and national groups - History and criticism	891.42098++
Panjabi literature (multiple forms) - Persons of specific classes - History and criticism	891.420992++
Panjabi literature (multiple forms) - Persons resident in specific regions - History and criticism	891.420991++
Panjabi literature (multiple forms) - Philosophic themes - History and criticism	891.4209384
Panjabi literature (multiple forms) - Places - History and criticism	891.420932++
Panjabi literature (multiple forms) - Plants - History and criticism	891.4209364
Panjabi literature (multiple forms) - Political themes - History and criticism	891.4209358
Panjabi literature (multiple forms) - Religious themes - History and criticism	891.4209382++
Panjabi literature (multiple forms) - Rivers - History and criticism	891.4209321693
Panjabi literature (multiple forms) - Romanticism - History and criticism	891.4209145
Panjabi literature (multiple forms) - Scientific themes - History and criticism	891.4209356
Panjabi literature (multiple forms) - Sea - History and criticism	891.420932162

Panjabi literature (multiple forms) - Seasons - History and criticism	891.420933
Panjabi literature (multiple forms) - Sex - History and criticism	891.42093538
Panjabi literature (multiple forms) - Social themes - History and criticism	891.4209355
Panjabi literature (multiple forms) - Space - History and criticism	891.42093219
Panjabi literature (multiple forms) - Specific kinds of persons, e.g. heroes - History and criticism	891.4209352++
Panjabi literature (multiple forms) - Specific persons - History and criticism	891.4209351
Panjabi literature (multiple forms) - Stream of consciousness - History and criticism	891.420925
Panjabi literature (multiple forms) - Subjects - History and criticism	891.42094++
Panjabi literature (multiple forms) - Supernatural objects/themes - History and criticism	891.420937
Panjabi literature (multiple forms) - Symbolism- History and criticism	891.420915
Panjabi literature (multiple forms) - Technical themes - History and criticism	891.4209356
Panjabi literature (multiple forms) - Times - History and criticism	891.420933
Panjabi literature (multiple forms) - Towns - History and criticism	891.4209321732
Panjabi literature (multiple forms) - Tragedy - History and criticism	891.4209162

Panjabi literature (multiple forms) - Villages - History and criticism	891.4209321734
Panjabi literature (multiple forms) - Weather - History and criticism	891.420936
Panjabi literature (single author) - to 1845 - Biography, collections, criticism	***See*** Main schedule
Panjabi literature (single author)-1845-1895 - Biography, collections, criticism	891.428 409
Panjabi literature (single author)- 1895-1919 - Biography, collections, criticism	891.428 509
Panjabi literature (single author)- 1920-1939 - Biography, collections, criticism	891.428 609
Panjabi literature (single author)- 1940-1999 - Biography, collections, criticism	891.428 7109
Panjabi literature (single author)- 1940- Biography, collections, criticism	891.428 709
Panjabi literature (single author)- 19th century - Biography, collections, criticism	891.428 409
Panjabi literature (single author)- 2000- Biography, collections, criticism	891.428 7209
Panjabi literature (single author)- 20th century - Biography, collections, criticism	891.428 7109
Panjabi literature for/by children - History and criticism	891.42099282
Panjabi literature for/by women - History and criticism	891.42099287
Panjabi love fiction (multiple authors)	891.423085*
Panjabi love fiction (multiple authors)- Collections	891.42308508**

Panjabi love fiction (multiple authors)-History and criticism	891.42308509**
Panjabi melodrama (multiple authors)	891.4220527*
Panjabi melodrama (multiple authors)-Collections	891.422052708**
Panjabi melodrama (multiple authors)-History and criticism	891.422052709**
Panjabi miscellaneous writings (multiple authors)	891.428
Panjabi miscellaneous writings (multiple authors) - to 1845	***See*** Main schedule
Panjabi miscellaneous writings (multiple authors) -1845-1895	891.4284++
Panjabi miscellaneous writings (multiple authors) -1895-1919	891.4285++
Panjabi miscellaneous writings (multiple authors) -1920-1939	891.4286++
Panjabi miscellaneous writings (multiple authors) -1940-	891.4287++
Panjabi miscellaneous writings (multiple authors) -1940-1999	891.42871++
Panjabi miscellaneous writings (multiple authors) -19th century	891.4284++
Panjabi miscellaneous writings (multiple authors) -2000-	891.42872++
Panjabi miscellaneous writings (multiple authors) -20th century	891.42871++
Panjabi miscellaneous writings (multiple authors) -Collections	891.428008**

Panjabi miscellaneous writings (multiple authors) -Dictionaries etc	891.428003
Panjabi miscellaneous writings (multiple authors) -History and criticism	891.428009**
Panjabi miscellaneous writings (multiple authors) -Periodicals	891.428005
Panjabi miscellaneous writings (multiple authors) -Philosophy and theory	891.428001
Panjabi miscellaneous writings (multiple authors) -Psychological aspects	891.4280019
Panjabi miscellaneous writings (multiple authors) -Research	891.4280072
Panjabi miscellaneous writings (multiple authors) -Study and teaching	891.428007
Panjabi miscellaneous writings (multiple authors) -Value	891.4280013
Panjabi miscellaneous writings (single author)- - to 1845	***See*** Main schedule
Panjabi miscellaneous writings (single author)- 1845 -1895	891.428 4
Panjabi miscellaneous writings (single author)- 1895 - 1919	891.428 5
Panjabi miscellaneous writings (single author)- 1920 - 1939	891.428 6
Panjabi miscellaneous writings (single author)- 1940 -	891.428 7
Panjabi miscellaneous writings (single author)- 1940-1999	891.428 71
Panjabi miscellaneous writings (single author)- 19th century	891.428 4

Panjabi miscellaneous writings (single author)- 2000-	891.428 72
Panjabi miscellaneous writings (single author)- 20th century	891.428 71
Panjabi monologues (multiple authors)	891.422045*
Panjabi monologues (multiple authors)- Collections	891.42204508**
Panjabi monologues (multiple authors)- History and criticism	891.42204509**
Panjabi morality plays	***See*** Panjabi religious ... plays
Panjabi mystery fiction (multiple authors)	891.4230872*
Panjabi mystery fiction (multiple authors)- Collections	891.423087208**
Panjabi mystery fiction (multiple authors)- History and criticism	891.423087209**
Panjabi narrative poetry (multiple authors)	891.42103*
Panjabi narrative poetry (multiple authors)- Collections	891.4210308**
Panjabi narrative poetry (multiple authors)- History and criticism	891.4210309**
Panjabi notebooks	***See*** Panjabi diaries...
Panjabi odes (multiple authors)	891.421043*
Panjabi odes (multiple authors)- Collections	891.42104308**
Panjabi odes (multiple authors)- History and criticism	891.42104309**
Panjabi one act plays (multiple authors)	891.422041*
Panjabi one act plays (multiple authors)- Collections	891.422041 08**

Panjabi one act plays (multiple authors)-History and criticism	891.422041 09**
Panjabi oratory (multiple authors)	***See*** Panjabi public speeches
Panjabi periodicals	059.9142
Panjabi poetry	891.421
Panjabi poetry (multiple authors) - - to 1845	***See*** Main schedule
Panjabi poetry (multiple authors) - 1845-1895	891.4214+
Panjabi poetry (multiple authors) - 1895-1919	891.4215+
Panjabi poetry (multiple authors) - 1920-1939	891.4216+
Panjabi poetry (multiple authors) - 1940-	891.4217+
Panjabi poetry (multiple authors) - 1940-1999	891.42171+
Panjabi poetry (multiple authors) - 19th century	891.4214+
Panjabi poetry (multiple authors) – 2000-	891.42172+
Panjabi poetry (multiple authors) - 20th century	891.42171+
Panjabi poetry (multiple authors)-Collections	891.421008**
Panjabi poetry (multiple authors)-Dictionaries etc	891.421003
Panjabi poetry (multiple authors)-History and criticism	891.421009**
Panjabi poetry (multiple authors)-Periodicals	891.421005

Panjabi poetry (multiple authors)- Philosophy and theory	891.421001
Panjabi poetry (multiple authors)- Psychological aspects	891.4210019
Panjabi poetry (multiple authors)- Research	891.4210072
Panjabi poetry (multiple authors)- Study and teaching	891.421007
Panjabi poetry (multiple authors)- Value	891.4210013
Panjabi poetry (single author)- - to 1845	***See*** Main schedule
Panjabi poetry (single author)- 1845 -1895	891.421 4
Panjabi poetry (single author)- 1895 - 1919	891.421 5
Panjabi poetry (single author)- 1920 - 1939	891.421 6
Panjabi poetry (single author)- 1940 -	891.421 7
Panjabi poetry (single author)- 1940-1999	891.421 71
Panjabi poetry (single author)- 19th century	891.421 4
Panjabi poetry (single author)- 2000-	891.421 72
Panjabi poetry (single author)- 20th century	891.421 71
Panjabi prose (single author)- - to 1845	***See*** Main schedule
Panjabi prose (single author)- 1845 -1895	891.428 408
Panjabi prose (single author)- 1895 - 1919	891.428 508
Panjabi prose (single author)- 1920 - 1939	891.428 608
Panjabi prose (single author)- 1940 -	891.428 708
Panjabi prose (single author)- 1940-1999	891.428 7108
Panjabi prose (single author)- 19th century	891.428 408
Panjabi prose (single author)- 2000-	891.428 7208

Panjabi prose (single author)- 20th century	891.428 7108
Panjabi prose literature (multiple authors)	891.42808
Panjabi psychological, realistic, sociological fiction (multiple authors)	891.423083*
Panjabi psychological, realistic, sociological fiction (multiple authors)- Collections	891.42308308**
Panjabi psychological, realistic, sociological fiction (multiple authors)- History and criticism	891.42308309**
Panjabi public discussions	***See*** Panjabi debates ...
Panjabi public speeches (multiple authors)	891.42501*
Panjabi public speeches (multiple authors)- Collections	891.4250108**
Panjabi public speeches (multiple authors)- History and criticism	891.4250109**
Panjabi quotations	***See*** Panjabi anecdotes ...
Panjabi realistic fiction	***See*** Panjabi psychological... fiction
Panjabi recitations (multiple authors)	891.42504+
Panjabi religious and morality plays (multiple authors)	891.4220516+
Panjabi reminiscences	***See*** Panjabi diaries...
Punjabi romantic fiction (multiple authors)	891.423 085
Panjabi romantic fiction (multiple authors)- Collections	891.423 085 08**

Panjabi romantic fiction (multiple authors)- History and criticism	891.423 085 09**
Panjabi satire	***See*** Panjabi humour …
Panjabi satirical poetry	***See*** Panjabi humourous … poetry
Panjabi science fiction (multiple authors)	891.42308762*
Panjabi science fiction (multiple authors) - Collections	891.4230876208**
Panjabi science fiction (multiple authors) - History and criticism	891.4230876209**
Panjabi serious drama (multiple authors)	891.422051+
Panjabi short stories (multiple authors)	891.42301*
Panjabi short stories (multiple authors)- Collections	891.4230108**
Panjabi short stories (multiple authors)- History and criticism	891.4230109**
Panjabi sociological fiction (multiple authors)	***See*** Panjabi psychological... fiction
Panjabi sonnets (multiple authors)	891.421042*
Panjabi sonnets (multiple authors)- Collections	891.42104208**
Panjabi sonnets (multiple authors)- History and criticism	891.42104209**
Panjabi speaking people	305.791 42
Panjabi speeches	891.425
Panjabi speeches (multiple authors) — to 1845	***See*** Main schedule

Panjabi speeches (multiple authors) - 1845-1895	891.4254+
Panjabi speeches (multiple authors) - 1895-1919	891.4255+
Panjabi speeches (multiple authors) - 1920-1939	891.4256+
Panjabi speeches (multiple authors) -1940-	891.4257+
Panjabi speeches (multiple authors) - 1940-1999	891.42571+
Panjabi speeches (multiple authors) - 19th century	891.4254+
Panjabi speeches (multiple authors) -2000-	891.42572+
Panjabi speeches (multiple authors) - 20th century	891.42571+
Panjabi speeches (multiple authors) - Collections	891.425008**
Panjabi speeches (multiple authors) - Dictionaries etc	891.425003
Panjabi speeches (multiple authors) - History and criticism	891.425009**
Panjabi speeches (multiple authors) - Periodicals	891.425005
Panjabi speeches (multiple authors) - Philosophy and theory	891.425001
Panjabi speeches (multiple authors) - Psychological aspects	891.4250019
Panjabi speeches (multiple authors) - Research	891.4250072
Panjabi speeches (multiple authors) - Study and teaching	891.425007

Panjabi speeches (multiple authors) -Value	891.4250013
Panjabi speeches (single author)- - to 1845	***See*** Main schedule
Panjabi speeches (single author)- 1845 -1895	891.425 4
Panjabi speeches (single author)- 1895 - 1919	891.425 5
Panjabi speeches (single author)- 1920 - 1939	891.425 6
Panjabi speeches (single author)- 1940 -	891.425 7
Panjabi speeches (single author)- 1940-1999	891.425 71
Panjabi speeches (single author)- 19th century	891.425 4
Panjabi speeches (single author)- 2000-	891.425 72
Panjabi speeches (single author)- 20th century	891.425 71
Panjabi suspense fiction (multiple authors)	891.4230872*
Panjabi suspense fiction (multiple authors)- Collections	891.423087208**
Panjabi suspense fiction (multiple authors)- History and criticism	891.423087209**
Panjabi tragedy (multiple authors)	891.4220512*
Panjabi tragedy (multiple authors)- Collections	891.422051208**
Panjabi tragedy (multiple authors)- History and criticism	891.422051209**
Panjabi variety drama (multiple authors)	891.422057*
Panjabi variety drama (multiple authors)- Collections	891.42205708**

Panjabi variety drama (multiple authors)-History and criticism	891.42205709**
Panjabis	305.891 42
Panjabis - Opinions	303.387 914 2
Parties (Buddhism)	294.365
Parties (Hinduism)	294.565
Parties (Jainism)	294.465
Parties (Sikhism)	294.665
Patanjali's philosophy	181.452
Patriotic societies	***See*** Hereditary... societies
Peace (Buddhism)	294.33787 3
Peace (Hinduism)	294.517 873
Peace (Jainism)	294.417 873
Peace (Sikhism)	294.617 873
Penal institutions	***See*** Prisons
Penances (Buddhism)	294.343 4
Penances (Hinduism)	294.534
Penances (Jainism)	294.434
Penances (Sikhism)	294.634
People speaking Assamese	305.791 451
People speaking Bengali	305.791 44
People speaking Bhojpuri	305.791 454
People speaking Dardic languages	305.791 499
People speaking Dravidian languages.	305.794 8

People speaking Gujarati	305.791 471
People speaking Hindi	305.791 431
People speaking Kanarese	305.794 814
People speaking Kannad	305.794 814
People speaking Kashmiri	305.791 499
People speaking Konkani	305.791 46
People speaking Maithili	305.791 454
People speaking Malayalam	305.794 812
People speaking Marathi	305.791 46
People speaking Modern Indic languages.	305.791 4
People speaking Munda languages	305.795 95
People speaking Oriya	305.791 456
People speaking Panjabi	305.791 42
People speaking Santali	305.795 95
People speaking Sindhi	305.791 411
People speaking Standard Hindi	305.791 431
People speaking Tamil	305.794 811
People speaking Telugu	305.794 8.27
People speaking Urdu	305.791 439
Periodicals	050
Periodicals-Buddhism	294.305
Periodicals-Hinduism	294.505
Periodicals-Jainism	294.405
Periodicals-Sikhism	294.605
Personified abstraction (Buddhism)	294.342 14

Political situation- Delhi	320.954 56
Political situation- Goa, Daman and Diu	320.954 799
Political situation- Gujarat	320.954 75
Political situation- Haryana	320.954 55 8
Political situation- Himachal Pradesh	320.954 52
Political situation- Hyderabad state	320.954 84
Political situation- India	320.954
Political situation- Jammu and Kashmir	320.954 6
Political situation- Jharkhand	320.954 127
Political situation- Karnataka	320.954 87
Political situation- Kerala	320.954 83
Political situation- Lakshwadweep	320.954 81
Political situation- Madhya Pradesh	320.954 3
Political situation- Madras	320.954 82
Political situation- Maharashtra	320.954 792
Political situation- Manipur	320.954 17
Political situation- Meghalaya	320.954 164
Political situation- Mizoram	320.954 166
Political situation- Nagaland	320.954 165
Political situation- Northeast India	320.954 1
Political situation- Orissa	320.954 13
Political situation- Pondicherry	320.954 86
Political situation- Punjab	320.954 55 2
Political situation- Rajasthan	320.954 4
Political situation- Sikkim	320.954 167

Political situation- South Asia	320.954
Political situation- Southern India	320.954 8
Political situation- Tamil Nadu	320.954 82
Political situation- Tripura	320.954 15
Political situation- Uttar Pradesh	320.954 2
Political situation- Uttaranchal	320.954 51
Political situation- West Bengal	320.954 14
Political situation- Western India	320.954 7
Politics (Buddhism)	294.331 77
Politics (Hinduism)	294.517 7
Politics (Jainism)	294.417 7
Politics (Sikhism)	294.617 7
Pondicherry- Architecture	720.954 86
Pondicherry- Budget	352.495 486
Pondicherry- Economic development	338.954 86
Pondicherry- Economic geography	330.954 86
Pondicherry- Education	370.954 86
Pondicherry- Fauna	591.954 86
Pondicherry- Flora	581.954 86
Pondicherry- Folk dancing	793.319 5486
Pondicherry- Geography	915.486
Pondicherry- Geology	555.486
Pondicherry- History	954.86
Pondicherry- Painting and paintings	759.954 86
Pondicherry- Public administration	351.548 6

Pondicherry- Public finance	336.548 6
Pondicherry- Sculpture	730.954 86
Population (Buddhism)	294.33783 6*
Population (Hinduism)	294.517 836
Population (Jainism)	294.417 836
Population (Sikhism)	294.617 836
Postal organization	383.4
Postal organization- Andaman and Nicobar Islands	383.495488
Postal organization- Andhra Pradesh	383.495 484
Postal organization- Arunachal Pradesh	383.495 41 63
Postal organization- Assam	383.495 41 62
Postal organization- Bengal	383.495 41 4
Postal organization- Bihar	383.495 412
Postal organization- Chandigarh	383.495 455 2
Postal organization- Chhattisgarh	383.495 413 7
Postal organization- Dadra and Nagar Haveli	383.495 479 6
Postal organization- Delhi	383.495 456
Postal organization- Goa, Daman and Diu	383.495 479 9
Postal organization- Gujarat	383.495 475
Postal organization- Haryana	383.495 4558
Postal organization- Himachal Pradesh	383.495 452
Postal organization- Hyderabad state	383.495 484
Postal organization- India	383.495 4

Postal organization- Jammu and Kashmir	383.495 46
Postal organization- Jharkhand	383.495 4127
Postal organization- Karnataka	383.495 487
Postal organization- Kerala	383.495 483
Postal organization- Lakshwadweep	383.495 481
Postal organization- Madhya Pradesh	383.495 43
Postal organization- Maharashtra	383.495 479 2
Postal organization- Manipur	383.495 417
Postal organization- Meghalaya	383.495 4164
Postal organization- Mizoram	383.495 4166
Postal organization- Nagaland	383.495 4165
Postal organization- Northeast India	383.495 41
Postal organization- Orissa	383.495 413
Postal organization- Pondicherry	383.495 486
Postal organization- Punjab	383.495 455 2
Postal organization- Rajasthan	383.495 44
Postal organization- Sikkim	383.495 416 7
Postal organization- South Asia	383.495 4
Postal organization- Southern India	383.495 48
Postal organization- Tamil Nadu	383.495 482
Postal organization- Tripura	383.495 415
Postal organization- Uttar Pradesh	383.495 42
Postal organization- Uttaranchal	383.495 451
Postal organization- West Bengal	383.495 414
Postal organization- Western India	383.495 47

Public administration- Tamil Nadu	351.548 2
Public administration- Tripura	351.541 5
Public administration- Uttar Pradesh	351.542
Public administration- Uttaranchal	351.5451
Public administration- West Bengal	351.541 4
Public debt- Andaman and Nicobar Islands	336.343 254 88
Public debt- Andhra Pradesh	336.343 254 84
Public debt- Arunachal Pradesh	336.343 254 163
Public debt- Assam	336.343 254 162
Public debt- Bihar	336.3432541 2
Public debt- Chandigarh	336.343 254 552
Public debt- Chhattisgarh	336.343 254 137
Public debt- Dadra and Nagar Haveli	336.343 254 796
Public debt- Delhi	336.343 254 56
Public debt- Goa, Daman and Diu	336.343 254 79
Public debt- Gujarat	336.343 254 75
Public debt- Haryana	336.343 254 55 8
Public debt- Himachal Pradesh	336.343 254 52
Public debt- Hyderabad state	336.343 254 84
Public debt- Jammu and Kashmir	336.343 254 6
Public debt- Jharkhand	336.343 254 127
Public debt- Karnataka	336.343 254 87
Public debt- Kerala	336.343 254 83
Public debt- Lakshwadweep	336.343 254 81
Public debt- Madhya Pradesh	336.343 254 3

Public debt- Madras	336.343 254 82
Public debt- Maharashtra	336.343 254 792
Public debt- Manipur	336.343 254 17
Public debt- Meghalaya	336.343 254 164
Public debt- Mizoram	336.343 254 166
Public debt- Nagaland	336.343 254 165
Public debt- Orissa	336.343 254 13
Public debt- Pondicherry	336.343 254 86
Public debt- Punjab	336.343 254 55 2
Public debt- Rajasthan	336.343 254 4
Public debt- Sikkim	336.343 254 167
Public debt- Tamil Nadu	336.343 254 82
Public debt- Tripura	336.343 254 15
Public debt- Uttar Pradesh	336.343 254 2
Public debt- Uttaranchal	336.343 254 51
Public debt- West Bengal	336.343 254 14
Public finance at national level	336.012
Public finance in states - India	336.013 54
Public finance in states - Northeast India	336.013 541
Public finance in states - South Asia	336.013 54
Public finance in states - Southern India	336.013 548
Public finance in states - Western India	336.013 547
Public finance- Andaman and Nicobar Islands	336.548 8
Public finance- Andhra Pradesh	336.548 4

Public finance- Arunachal Pradesh	336.541 63
Public finance- Assam	336.541 62
Public finance- Bengal	336.541 4
Public finance- Bihar	336. 541 2
Public finance- Chandigarh	336.545 52
Public finance- Chhattisgarh	336.541 37
Public finance- Dadra and Nagar Haveli	336.547 96
Public finance- Delhi	336.545 6
Public finance- Goa, Daman and Diu	336.547 9
Public finance- Gujarat	336.547 5
Public finance- Haryana	336.545 58
Public finance- Himachal Pradesh	336.545 2
Public finance- Hyderabad state	336.548 4
Public finance- Jammu and Kashmir	336.546
Public finance- Jharkhand	336. 541 27
Public finance- Karnataka	336.548 7
Public finance- Kerala	336.548 3
Public finance- Lakshwadweep	336.548 1
Public finance- Madhya Pradesh	336.543
Public finance- Madras	336.548 2
Public finance- Maharashtra	336.547 92
Public finance- Manipur	336.541 7
Public finance- Meghalaya	336.541 64
Public finance- Mizoram	336.541 66
Public finance- Nagaland	336.541 65

Public finance- Northeast India	336.541
Public finance- Orissa	336.541 3
Public finance- Pondicherry	336.548 6
Public finance- Punjab	336.545 52
Public finance- Rajasthan	336.544
Public finance- Sikkim	336.541 67
Public finance- Tamil Nadu	336.548 2
Public finance- Tripura	336.541 5
Public finance- Uttar Pradesh	336.542
Public finance- Uttaranchal	336.545 1
Public finance- West Bengal	336.541 4
Public libraries in India	027.454
Public policy on education	379
Public policy on education- Andaman and Nicobar Islands	379.548 8
Public policy on education- Andhra Pradesh	379.548 4
Public policy on education- Arunachal Pradesh	379.541 63
Public policy on education- Assam	379.541 62
Public policy on education- Bengal	379.541 4
Public policy on education- Bihar	379.541 2
Public policy on education- Chandigarh	379.545 52
Public policy on education- Chhattisgarh	379.541 37
Public policy on education- Dadra and Nagar Haveli	379.547 96
Public policy on education- Delhi	379.545 6

Public policy on education- Goa, Daman and Diu	379.547 99
Public policy on education- Gujarat	379.547 5
Public policy on education- Haryana	379.545 58
Public policy on education- Himachal Pradesh	379.545 2
Public policy on education- Hyderabad state	379.548 4
Public policy on education- India	379.54
Public policy on education- Jammu and Kashmir	379.546
Public policy on education- Jharkhand	379.541 27
Public policy on education- Karnataka	379.548 7
Public policy on education- Kerala	379.548 3
Public policy on education- Lakshwadweep	379.548 1
Public policy on education- Madhya Pradesh	379.543
Public policy on education- Maharashtra	379.547 92
Public policy on education- Manipur	379.541 7
Public policy on education- Meghalaya	379.541 64
Public policy on education- Mizoram	379.541 66
Public policy on education- Nagaland	379.541 65
Public policy on education- Orissa	379.541 3
Public policy on education- Pondicherry	379.548 6
Public policy on education- Punjab	379.545 52
Public policy on education- Rajasthan	379.544
Public policy on education- Sikkim	379.541 67

Public policy on education- Tamil Nadu	379.548 2
Public policy on education- Tripura	379.541 5
Public policy on education- Uttar Pradesh	379.542
Public policy on education- Uttaranchal	379.545 1
Public policy on education- West Bengal	379.541 4
Public worship and other practices (Buddhism)	294.343
Public worship and other practices (Hinduism)	294.53
Public worship and other practices (Jainism)	294.43
Public worship and other practices (Sikhism)	294.63
Punishment (Eschatology) (Buddhism)	294.342 3
Punishment (Eschatology) (Hinduism)	294.523
Punishment (Eschatology) (Jainism)	294.423
Punishment (Eschatology) (Sikhism)	294.623
Punishment for crime (Buddhism)	294.33783 3*
Punishment for crime (Hinduism)	294.517 833
Punishment for crime (Jainism)	294.417 833
Punishment for crime (Sikhism)	294.617 833
Punjab- Architecture	720.954 552
Punjab- Budget	352.495 4552
Punjab- Economic development	338.954 552
Punjab- Economic geography	330.954 55 2
Punjab- Education	370.954 552
Punjab- Fauna	591.954 552

Punjab- Flora	581.954 552
Punjab- Folk dancing	793.319 54552
Punjab- Geography	915.4552
Punjab- Geology	555.455 2
Punjab- History	954.552
Punjab- Painting and paintings	759.954 552
Punjab- Public administration	351.545 52
Punjab- Public finance	336.545 52
Punjab- Sculpture	730.954 552
Puranas	294.592 5
Pure land sects- Doctrines	294.342 0426

R

Radha Soami Satsang	294
Raja Yoga	294.543 6
Rajasthan- Architecture	720.954 4
Rajasthan- Botany	580.954 4
Rajasthan- Budget	352.495 44
Rajasthan- Economic development	338.954 4
Rajasthan- Economic geography	330.954 4
Rajasthan- Education	370.954 4
Rajasthan- Fauna	591.954 4
Rajasthan- Fine and decorative arts	709.544
Rajasthan- Flora	581.954 4
Rajasthan- Folk dancing	793.319 544
Rajasthan- Galleries of fine and decorative arts	708.954 4
Rajasthan- Geography	915.44
Rajasthan- Geology	555.44
Rajasthan- History	954.4
Rajasthan- Museums of fine and decorative arts	708.954 4

Relationship with medicine (Sikhism)	294.617 5
Relationship with other religions and irreligions (Buddhism)	294.337 2
Relationship with other religions and irreligions (Hinduism)	294.517 2
Relationship with other religions and irreligions (Jainism)	294.417 2
Relationship with other religions and irreligions (Sikhism)	294.617 2
Relationship with psychology (Buddhism)	294.37 5
Relationship with psychology (Hinduism)	294.517 5
Relationship with psychology (Jainism)	294.417 5
Relationship with psychology (Sikhism)	294.617 5
Relationship with science (Buddhism)	294.37 5
Relationship with science (Hinduism)	294.517 5
Relationship with science (Jainism)	294.417 5
Relationship with science (Sikhism)	294.617 5
Relationship with secular disciplines (Buddhism)	294.337 5
Relationship with secular disciplines (Hinduism)	294.517 5
Relationship with secular disciplines (Jainism)	294.417 5
Relationship with secular disciplines (Sikhism)	294.617 5
Relationship with technology (Buddhism)	294.37 5
Relationship with technology (Hinduism)	294.517 5
Relationship with technology (Jainism)	294.417 5

Revenue- Andaman and Nicobar Islands	336.025 488
Revenue- Andhra Pradesh	336.025 484
Revenue- Arunachal Pradesh	336.025 416 3
Revenue- Assam	336.025 416 2
Revenue- Bengal	336.025 414
Revenue- Bihar	336.025 412
Revenue- Chandigarh	336.025 4552
Revenue- Chhattisgarh	336.025 413 7
Revenue- Dadra and Nagar Haveli	336.025 479 6
Revenue- Delhi	336.025 456
Revenue- Goa, Daman and Diu	336.025 479
Revenue- Gujarat	336.025 475
Revenue- Haryana	336.025 4558
Revenue- Himachal Pradesh	336.025 452
Revenue- Hyderabad state	336.025 484
Revenue- India	336.025 4
Revenue- Jammu and Kashmir	336.025 46
Revenue- Jharkhand	336.025 412 7
Revenue- Karnataka	336.025 487
Revenue- Kerala	336.025 483
Revenue- Lakshwadweep	336.025 481
Revenue- Madhya Pradesh	336.025 43
Revenue- Maharashtra	336.025 479 2
Revenue- Manipur	336.025 417
Revenue- Meghalaya	336.025 416 4

Revenue- Mizoram	336.025 416 6
Revenue- Nagaland	336.025 416 5
Revenue- Orissa	336.025 413
Revenue- Pondicherry	336.025 486
Revenue- Punjab	336.025 4552
Revenue- Rajasthan	336.025 44
Revenue- Sikkim	336.025 416 7
Revenue- Tamil Nadu	336.025 482
Revenue- Tripura	336.025 415
Revenue- Uttar Pradesh	336.025 42
Revenue- Uttaranchal	336.025 451
Revenue- West Bengal	336.025 414
Rewards (Eschatology) (Buddhism)	294.342 3
Rewards (Eschatology) (Hinduism)	294.523
Rewards (Eschatology) (Jainism)	294.423
Rewards (Eschatology) (Sikhism)	294.623
Rigveda	294.592 12++
Rinzai	294.392 7
Rinzai doctrines	294.342 042 7
Rinzai Buddhism- Doctrines	294.342 042 7
Rites (Buddhism)	294.3438
Rites (Hinduism)	294.538
Rites (Jainism)	294.438
Rites (Sikhism)	294.638
Role in society (Buddhism)	294.337 1

S

Sacred books (Buddhism)	294.382
Sacred books (Hinduism)	294.582
Sacred books (Jainism)	294.482
Sacred books (Sikhism)	294.682
Sacred music (Buddhism)	781.743
Sacred music (Hinduism)	781.745
Sacred music (Indic religion)	781.74
Sacred music (Jainism)	781.744
Sacred music (Sikhism)	781.746
Sacred places (Buddhism)	294.343 5
Sacred places (Hinduism)	294.535
Sacred places (Jainism)	294.435
Sacred places (Sikhism)	294.635
Sacred times (Buddhism)	294.343 6
Sacred times (Hinduism)	294.536
Sacred times (Jainism)	294.436
Sacred times (Sikhism)	294.636
Sacrifices (Buddhism)	294.343 4

Sanskrit comedy (multiple authors) - Collections	891.22052308**
Sanskrit comedy (multiple authors) - History and criticism	891.22052309**
Sanskrit conversations (multiple authors)	891.2506*
Sanskrit conversations (multiple authors) - Collections	891.250608**
Sanskrit conversations (multiple authors) - History and criticism	891.250609**
Sanskrit debates and public discussions (multiple authors)- Collections	891.250308**
Sanskrit debates and public discussions (multiple authors)	891.2503*
Sanskrit debates and public discussions (multiple authors)- History and criticism	891.250309**
Sanskrit didactic poetry (multiple authors)	891.2105*
Sanskrit didactic poetry (multiple authors)- Collections	891.210508**
Sanskrit didactic poetry (multiple authors)- History and criticism	891.210509**
Sanskrit drama	891.22
Sanskrit drama (multiple authors) - Collections	891.22008**
Sanskrit drama (multiple authors) - Dictionaries etc	891.22003
Sanskrit drama (multiple authors) - History and criticism	891.22009**
Sanskrit drama (multiple authors) - Periodicals	891.22005

Sanskrit drama (multiple authors) - Philosophy and theory	891.22001
Sanskrit drama (multiple authors) - Psychological aspects	891.220019
Sanskrit drama (multiple authors) - Research	891.220072
Sanskrit drama (multiple authors) - Study and teaching	891.22007
Sanskrit drama (multiple authors) - Value	891.220013
Sanskrit dramatic poetry (multiple authors)	891.2102*
Sanskrit dramatic poetry (multiple authors)- Collections	891.210208**
Sanskrit dramatic poetry (multiple authors)- History and criticism	891.210209**
Sanskrit –English dictionary	491.2321
Sanskrit ephemeral and light verse (multiple authors)	891.2108*
Sanskrit ephemeral and light verse (multiple authors)- Collections	891.210808**
Sanskrit ephemeral and light verse (multiple authors) - History and criticism	891.210809**
Sanskrit epic poetry (multiple authors)	891.21032*
Sanskrit epic poetry (multiple authors)- Collections	891.2103208**
Sanskrit epic poetry (multiple authors)- History and criticism	891.2103209**
Sanskrit epigrams (multiple authors)	891.2802
Sanskrit essays	891.24
Sanskrit essays (multiple authors) - Collections	891.24008**

Sanskrit essays (multiple authors) - Dictionaries etc	891.24003
Sanskrit essays (multiple authors) - History and criticism	891.24009**
Sanskrit essays (multiple authors) - Periodicals	891.24005
Sanskrit essays (multiple authors) - Philosophy and theory	891.24001
Sanskrit essays (multiple authors) - Psychological aspects	891.240019
Sanskrit essays (multiple authors) - Research	891.240072
Sanskrit essays (multiple authors) - Study and teaching	891.24007
Sanskrit essays (multiple authors) -Value	891.240013
Sanskrit farce (multiple authors)	891.2205232*
Sanskrit farce (multiple authors)- Collections	891.220523208**
Sanskrit farce (multiple authors)- History and criticism	891.220523209**
Sanskrit fiction	891.23
Sanskrit fiction (multiple authors) - Collections	891.23008**
Sanskrit fiction (multiple authors) - Periodicals	891.23005
Sanskrit fiction (multiple authors) - Philosophy and theory	891.23001
Sanskrit fiction (multiple authors) - Psychological aspects	891.230019
Sanskrit fiction (multiple authors) - Research	891.230072

Sanskrit fiction (multiple authors) - Study and teaching	891.23007
Sanskrit fiction (multiple authors) - Value	891.230013
Sanskrit graffiti (multiple authors)	891.2802
Sanskrit historical drama (multiple authors)	891.220514*
Sanskrit historical drama (multiple authors)- Collections	891.22051408**
Sanskrit historical drama (multiple authors)- History and criticism	891.22051409**
Sanskrit historical fiction (multiple authors)	891.23081*
Sanskrit historical fiction (multiple authors)- Collections	891.2308108**
Sanskrit historical fiction (multiple authors)- History and criticism	891.2308109**
Sanskrit horror fiction (multiple authors)	891.2308738*
Sanskrit horror fiction (multiple authors)- Collections	891.230873808**
Sanskrit horror fiction (multiple authors)- History and criticism	891.230873809**
Sanskrit humour and satire	891.27
Sanskrit humour and satire (multiple authors) -Collections	891.27008**
Sanskrit humour and satire (multiple authors) -Dictionaries etc	891.27003
Sanskrit humour and satire (multiple authors) -History and criticism	891.27009**
Sanskrit humour and satire (multiple authors) -Periodicals	891.27005
Sanskrit humour and satire (multiple authors) -Philosophy and theory	891.27001

Sanskrit humour and satire (multiple authors) -Psychological aspects	891.270019
Sanskrit humour and satire (multiple authors) -Research	891.270072
Sanskrit humour and satire (multiple authors) -Study and teaching	891.27007
Sanskrit humour and satire (multiple authors) -Value	891.270013
Sanskrit humourous and satirical poetry (multiple authors)	891.2107*
Sanskrit humourous and satirical poetry (multiple authors)- Collections	891.210708**
Sanskrit humourous and satirical poetry (multiple authors)- History and criticism	891.210709**
Sanskrit jokes (multiple authors)	891.2802
Sanskrit language	491.2
Sanskrit language- Applied linguistics	491.2 8
Sanskrit language- Bilingual dictionaries	491.2 32-39
Sanskrit language- Bilingualism	491.2 042
Sanskrit language- Concordances	491.2 03
Sanskrit language- Content analysis	491.2 014 1
Sanskrit language- Dictionaries	491.2 3
Sanskrit language- Discourse analysis	491.2 014 1
Sanskrit language- Education	491.2 071
Sanskrit language- Encyclopaedias	491.2 03
Sanskrit language- Etymology	491.2 2
Sanskrit language- Functionalism	491.2 018

Sanskrit language- Grammar	491.2 5
Sanskrit language- History	491.2 09
Sanskrit language- Intonation	491.2 16
Sanskrit language- Lexicography	491.2 302 8
Sanskrit language- Lexicology	491.2 014
Sanskrit language- Miscellany	491.2 02
Sanskrit language- Multilingualism	491.2 042
Sanskrit language- Organizations	491.2 06
Sanskrit language- Orthography	491.2 152
Sanskrit language- Pauses	491.2 16
Sanskrit language- Periodicals	491.2 05
Sanskrit language- Persons (men, women, etc)	491.2 08
Sanskrit language- Philosophy and theory	491.2 01
Sanskrit language- Phonetics	491.2 158
Sanskrit language- Phonology	491.2 15
Sanskrit language- Pitch	491.2 16
Sanskrit language- Pronunciation	491.2 152
Sanskrit language- Readers	491.286
Sanskrit language- Research	491.2 072
Sanskrit language- Rhetoric	808.049 12++
Sanskrit language- Schools and theories of linguistics	491.2 018
Sanskrit language- Semantics	491.2 014 3
Sanskrit language- Semiotics	491.2 014 1

Sanskrit language- Slang	491.2 7
Sanskrit language- Special topics	491.2 04
Sanskrit language- Specialized dictionaries	491.2 31
Sanskrit language- Spelling	491.2 152
Sanskrit language- Stress	491.2 16
Sanskrit language- Structural linguistics	491.2 018
Sanskrit language- Suprasegmental features	491.2 16
Sanskrit language- Terminology	491.2 014
Sanskrit language- Usage	491.2 8
Sanskrit language- Variations	491.2 7
Sanskrit language- Writing systems	491.2 11
Sanskrit letters	891.26
Sanskrit letters (multiple authors) - Collections	891.26008**
Sanskrit letters (multiple authors) - Dictionaries etc	891.26003
Sanskrit letters (multiple authors) - History and criticism	891.26009**
Sanskrit letters (multiple authors) - Philosophy and theory	891.26001
Sanskrit letters (multiple authors) - Psychological aspects	891.260019
Sanskrit letters (multiple authors) -Research	891.260072
Sanskrit letters (multiple authors) - Study and teaching	891.26007
Sanskrit letters (multiple authors) -Value	891.260013
Sanskrit light verse	***See*** Sanskrit ephemeral ...verse

Sanskrit limericks (multiple authors)	891.21075*
Sanskrit limericks (multiple authors)-Collections	891.2107508**
Sanskrit limericks (multiple authors)-History and criticism	891.2107509**
Sanskrit literature	891.2
Sanskrit literature (collections of multiple forms)	891.208
Sanskrit literature (collections of multiple forms) – Allegory	891.208015
Sanskrit literature (collections of multiple forms) - Animals	891.2080362++
Sanskrit literature (collections of multiple forms) - Artistic themes	891.2080357
Sanskrit literature (collections of multiple forms) - Atmosphere	891.208032161
Sanskrit literature (collections of multiple forms) - Characters	891.208027
Sanskrit literature (collections of multiple forms) - Comedy	891.208017
Sanskrit literature (collections of multiple forms) - Evening	891.208033
Sanskrit literature (collections of multiple forms) - Fantasy	891.208015
Sanskrit literature (collections of multiple forms) - Forests	891.208032152
Sanskrit literature (collections of multiple forms) - Historical themes	891.2080358
Sanskrit literature (collections of multiple forms) - Horror	891.2080164

Sanskrit literature (collections of multiple forms) - Human characteristics (Biological, moral, psychological)	891.2080353
Sanskrit literature (collections of multiple forms) - Legendary objects/themes	891.208037
Sanskrit literature (collections of multiple forms) - Literary themes	891.2080357
Sanskrit literature (collections of multiple forms) - Love	891.20803543
Sanskrit literature (collections of multiple forms) - Marriage	891.20803543
Sanskrit literature (collections of multiple forms) - Morning	891.208033
Sanskrit literature (collections of multiple forms) - Mountains	891.208032143
Sanskrit literature (collections of multiple forms) - Myth	891.208015
Sanskrit literature (collections of multiple forms) - Mythological objects/themes	891.208037
Sanskrit literature (collections of multiple forms) - Philosophic themes	891.2080384
Sanskrit literature (collections of multiple forms) - Places	891.208032++
Sanskrit literature (collections of multiple forms) - Plants	891.2080364
Sanskrit literature (collections of multiple forms) - Political themes	891.2080358
Sanskrit literature (collections of multiple forms) - Religious themes	891.2080382++
Sanskrit literature (collections of multiple forms) - Rivers	891.2080321693

Sanskrit literature (collections of multiple forms) - Romanticism	891.2080145
Sanskrit literature (collections of multiple forms) - Scientific themes	891.2080356
Sanskrit literature (collections of multiple forms) - Sea	891.208032162
Sanskrit literature (collections of multiple forms) - Seasons	891.208033
Sanskrit literature (collections of multiple forms) - Sex	891.20803538
Sanskrit literature (collections of multiple forms) - Social themes	891.2080355
Sanskrit literature (collections of multiple forms) - Space	891.20803219
Sanskrit literature (collections of multiple forms) - Specific kinds of persons, e.g. heroes	891.2080352++
Sanskrit literature (collections of multiple forms) - Specific persons (real or imaginary)	891.2080351
Sanskrit literature (collections of multiple forms) - Supernatural objects/themes	891.208037
Sanskrit literature (collections of multiple forms) - Symbolism	891.208015
Sanskrit literature (collections of multiple forms) - Technical themes	891.2080356
Sanskrit literature (collections of multiple forms) - Times (seasons, parts of day, etc)	891.208033
Sanskrit literature (collections of multiple forms) - Towns	891.2080321732
Sanskrit literature (collections of multiple forms) - Tragedy	891.2080162

Sanskrit literature (collections of multiple forms) - Villages	891.2080321734
Sanskrit literature (collections of multiple forms) - Weather	891.208036
Sanskrit literature (collections of multiple forms) emphasizing subjects	891.20804++
Sanskrit literature (collections of multiple forms) for/by children	891.20809282
Sanskrit literature (collections of multiple forms) for/by persons of racial, ethnic and national groups	891.20808++
Sanskrit literature (collections of multiple forms) for/by persons of specific classes	891.208092++
Sanskrit literature (collections of multiple forms) for/by persons resident in specific regions	891.208091++
Sanskrit literature (collections of multiple forms) for/by women	891.20809287
Sanskrit literature (multiple authors)	891.2
Sanskrit literature (multiple authors) - Concordances	891.203
Sanskrit literature (multiple authors) - Dictionaries	891.203
Sanskrit literature (multiple authors) - Education	891.2071
Sanskrit literature (multiple authors) - Encyclopaedias	891.203
Sanskrit literature (multiple authors) - Organizations	891.206
Sanskrit literature (multiple authors) - Periodicals	891.205

Sanskrit literature (multiple authors) - Philosophy and theory	891.201
Sanskrit literature (multiple authors) - Research	891.2072
Sanskrit literature (multiple authors) - Research in India	891.2072054
Sanskrit literature (multiple authors) - Study and teaching	891.207
Sanskrit literature (multiple forms) - Allegory – History and criticism	891.20915
Sanskrit literature (multiple forms) - Animals - History and criticism	891.209362++
Sanskrit literature (multiple forms) - Artistic themes - History and criticism	891.209357
Sanskrit literature (multiple forms) - Atmosphere - History and criticism	891.20932161
Sanskrit literature (multiple forms) - Characters - History and criticism	891.20927
Sanskrit literature (multiple forms) - Comedy - History and criticism	891.20917
Sanskrit literature (multiple forms) - Evening - History and criticism	891.20933
Sanskrit literature (multiple forms) - Fantasy - History , description, criticism	891.20915
Sanskrit literature (multiple forms) - Forests - History and criticism	891.20932152
Sanskrit literature (multiple forms) - Historical themes - History and criticism	891.209358
Sanskrit literature (multiple forms) - History and criticism	891.209

Sanskrit literature (multiple forms) - Horror - History and criticism	891.209164
Sanskrit literature (multiple forms) - Human characteristics (Biological, moral, psychological) - History and criticism	891.209353
Sanskrit literature (multiple forms) - Legendary objects/themes - History and criticism	891.20937
Sanskrit literature (multiple forms) - Literary themes - History and criticism	891.209357
Sanskrit literature (multiple forms) - Love - History and criticism	891.2093543
Sanskrit literature (multiple forms) - Marriage - History and criticism	891.2093543
Sanskrit literature (multiple forms) - Morning - History and criticism	891.20933
Sanskrit literature (multiple forms) - Mountains - History and criticism	891.20932143
Sanskrit literature (multiple forms) - Myth - History and criticism	891.20915
Sanskrit literature (multiple forms) - Mythological objects/themes - History and criticism	891.20937
Sanskrit literature (multiple forms) - Persons of racial, ethnic and national groups - History and criticism	891.2098++
Sanskrit literature (multiple forms) - Persons of specific classes - History and criticism	891.20992++
Sanskrit literature (multiple forms) - Persons resident in specific regions - History and criticism	891.20991++

Sanskrit literature (multiple forms) - Philosophic themes - History and criticism	891.209384
Sanskrit literature (multiple forms) - Places - History and criticism	891.20932++
Sanskrit literature (multiple forms) - Plants - History and criticism	891.209364
Sanskrit literature (multiple forms) - Political themes - History and criticism	891.209358
Sanskrit literature (multiple forms) - Religious themes - History and criticism	891.209382++
Sanskrit literature (multiple forms) - Rivers - History and criticism	891.209321693
Sanskrit literature (multiple forms) - Romanticism - History and criticism	891.209145
Sanskrit literature (multiple forms) - Scientific themes - History and criticism	891.209356
Sanskrit literature (multiple forms) - Sea - History and criticism	891.20932162
Sanskrit literature (multiple forms) - Seasons - History and criticism	891.20933
Sanskrit literature (multiple forms) - Sex - History and criticism	891.2093538
Sanskrit literature (multiple forms) - Social themes - History and criticism	891.209355
Sanskrit literature (multiple forms) - Space - History and criticism	891.2093219
Sanskrit literature (multiple forms) - Specific kinds of persons, e.g. heroes, - History and criticism	891.209352++
Sanskrit literature (multiple forms) - Specific persons - History and criticism	891.209351

Sanskrit literature (multiple forms) - Subjects - History and criticism	891.2094++
Sanskrit literature (multiple forms) - Supernatural objects/themes - History and criticism	891.20937
Sanskrit literature (multiple forms) - Symbolism- History and criticism	891.20915
Sanskrit literature (multiple forms) - Technical themes - History and criticism	891.209356
Sanskrit literature (multiple forms) - Times - History and criticism	891.20933
Sanskrit literature (multiple forms) - Towns - History and criticism	891.209321732
Sanskrit literature (multiple forms) - Tragedy - History and criticism	891.209162
Sanskrit literature (multiple forms) - Villages - History and criticism	891.209321734
Sanskrit literature (multiple forms) - Weather - History and criticism	891.20936
Sanskrit literature for/by children - History and criticism	891.2099282
Sanskrit literature for/by women - History and criticism	891.2099287
Sanskrit love fiction (multiple authors)	891.23085*
Sanskrit love fiction (multiple authors)- Collections	891.2308508**
Sanskrit love fiction (multiple authors)- History and criticism	891.2308509**
Sanskrit melodrama (multiple authors)	891.220527*
Sanskrit melodrama (multiple authors)- Collections	891.22052708**

Sanskrit melodrama (multiple authors)-History and criticism	891.22052709**
Sanskrit miscellaneous writings (multiple authors)	891.28
Sanskrit miscellaneous writings (multiple authors) -Collections	891.28008**
Sanskrit miscellaneous writings (multiple authors) -Dictionaries etc	891.28003
Sanskrit miscellaneous writings (multiple authors) -History and criticism	891.28009**
Sanskrit miscellaneous writings (multiple authors) -Periodicals	891.28005
Sanskrit miscellaneous writings (multiple authors) -Philosophy and theory	891.28001
Sanskrit miscellaneous writings (multiple authors) -Psychological aspects	891.280019
Sanskrit miscellaneous writings (multiple authors) -Research	891.280072
Sanskrit miscellaneous writings (multiple authors) -Study and teaching	891.28007
Sanskrit miscellaneous writings (multiple authors) -Value	891.280013
Sanskrit miscellaneous writings (single author)	891.28
Sanskrit monologues (multiple authors)	891.22045*
Sanskrit monologues (multiple authors)-Collections	891.2204508**
Sanskrit monologues (multiple authors)-History and criticism	891.2204509**
Sanskrit morality plays	***See*** Sanskrit religious ... plays

Sanskrit narrative poetry (multiple authors)	891.2103*
Sanskrit narrative poetry (multiple authors)- Collections	891.210308**
Sanskrit narrative poetry (multiple authors)- History and criticism	891.210309**
Sanskrit odes (multiple authors)	891.21043*
Sanskrit odes (multiple authors)- Collections	891.2104308**
Sanskrit odes (multiple authors)- History and criticism	891.2104309**
Sanskrit one act plays (multiple authors)	891.220.41*
Sanskrit one act plays (multiple authors)- Collections	891.220.410 8**
Sanskrit one act plays (multiple authors)- History and criticism	891.220.410 9**
Sanskrit oratory (multiple authors)	***See*** Sanskrit public speeches
Sanskrit poetry	891.21
Sanskrit poetry (multiple authors)- Collections	891.21008**
Sanskrit poetry (multiple authors)- Dictionaries etc	891.21003
Sanskrit poetry (multiple authors)- History and criticism	891.21009**
Sanskrit poetry (multiple authors)- Periodicals	891.21005
Sanskrit poetry (multiple authors)- Philosophy and theory	891.21001
Sanskrit poetry (multiple authors)- Psychological aspects	891.210019

Sanskrit poetry (multiple authors)- Research	891.210072
Sanskrit poetry (multiple authors)- Study and teaching	891.21007
Sanskrit poetry (multiple authors)- Value	891.210013
Sanskrit prose	891.28
Sanskrit prose literature (multiple authors)	891.2808
Sanskrit psychological fiction (multiple authors	891.23083+
Sanskrit public discussions	***See*** Sanskrit debates ...
Sanskrit public speeches (multiple authors)	891.2501
Sanskrit public speeches (multiple authors)- Collections	891.250108
Sanskrit public speeches (multiple authors)- History and criticism	891.250109
Sanskrit quotations (multiple authors)	891.2802
Sanskrit realistic fiction	891.23083+
Sanskrit recitations (multiple authors)	891.2504+
Sanskrit religious and morality plays (multiple authors)	891.220516+
Sanskrit romantic fiction (multiple authors)	891.23085*
Sanskrit romantic fiction (multiple authors)	891.2308508**
Sanskrit romantic fiction (multiple authors)	891.2308509**
Sanskrit satire	***See*** Sanskrit humour ...
Sanskrit satirical poetry	***See*** Sanskrit humourous ... poetry

Sanskrit serious drama (multiple authors)	891.22051+
Sanskrit short stories (multiple authors)	891.2301+
Sanskrit sociological fiction (multiple authors)	891.23083+
Sanskrit sonnets (multiple authors)	891.21042*
Sanskrit sonnets (multiple authors)- Collections	891.2104208**
Sanskrit sonnets (multiple authors)- History and criticism	891.2104209**
Sanskrit speeches	891.25*
Sanskrit speeches (multiple authors) - Collections	891.25008**
Sanskrit speeches (multiple authors) - Dictionaries etc	891.25003
Sanskrit speeches (multiple authors) - History and criticism	891.25009**
Sanskrit speeches (multiple authors) - Philosophy and theory	891.25001
Sanskrit speeches (multiple authors) - Psychological aspects	891.250019
Sanskrit speeches (multiple authors) - Research	891.250072
Sanskrit speeches (multiple authors) - Study and teaching	891.25007
Sanskrit speeches (multiple authors) -Value	891.250013
Sanskrit tragedy (multiple authors)	891.220512*
Sanskrit tragedy (multiple authors)- Collections	891.22051208**
Sanskrit tragedy (multiple authors)- History and criticism	891.22051209**

Sanskrit variety drama (multiple authors)	891.22057*
Sanskrit variety drama (multiple authors)- Collections	891.2205708**
Sanskrit variety drama (multiple authors)- History and criticism	891.2205709**
Santali speaking people	305.795 95
Saravastivada school (Buddhism)	294.391
Sauraism	294.5517
Sautrantika schools (Buddhism)	294.391
School enrollment- India	371 .219 54
School libraries- India	027.8254
Science and Buddhism	294.337 5
Science and Hinduism	294.517 5
Science and Jainism	294.417 5
Science and Sikhism	294.617 5
Scriptures (Buddhism)	294.382
Scriptures (Hinduism)	294.582
Scriptures (Jainism)	294.482
Scriptures (Sikhism)	294.682
Sculpture- India	730.954
Scytho-Dravidians	305.894 8
Secondary education	373
Secondary education- Andaman and Nicobar Islands	373.548 8
Secondary education- Andhra Pradesh	373.548 4
Secondary education- Arunachal Pradesh	373.541 63

Secondary education- Assam	373.541 62
Secondary education- Bengal	373.541 4
Secondary education- Bihar	373.541 2
Secondary education- Chandigarh	373.545 52
Secondary education- Chhattisgarh	373.541 37
Secondary education- Dadra and Nagar Haveli	373.547 96
Secondary education- Delhi	373.545 6
Secondary education- Goa, Daman and Diu	373.547 99
Secondary education- Gujarat	373.547 5
Secondary education- Haryana	373.545 58
Secondary education- Himachal Pradesh	373.545 2
Secondary education- Hyderabad state	373.548 4
Secondary education- India	373.54
Secondary education- Jammu and Kashmir	373.546
Secondary education- Jharkhand	373.541 27
Secondary education- Karnataka	373.548 7
Secondary education- Kerala	373.548 3
Secondary education- Lakshwadweep	373.548 1
Secondary education- Madhya Pradesh	373.543
Secondary education- Madras	373.548 2
Secondary education- Maharashtra	373.547 92
Secondary education- Manipur	373.541 7
Secondary education- Meghalaya	373.541 64
Secondary education- Mizoram	373.541 66

Secondary education- Nagaland	373.541 65
Secondary education- Northeast India	373.541
Secondary education- Orissa	373.541 3
Secondary education- Pondicherry	373.548 6
Secondary education- Punjab	373.545 52
Secondary education- Rajasthan	373.544
Secondary education- Sikkim	373.541 67
Secondary education- South Asia	373.54
Secondary education- Southern India	373.548
Secondary education- Tamil Nadu	373.548 2
Secondary education- Tripura	373.541 5
Secondary education- Uttar Pradesh	373.542
Secondary education- Uttaranchal	373.545 1
Secondary education- West Bengal	373.541 4
Secondary education- Western India	373.547
Sects (Buddhism)	294.39
Sects (Hinduism)	294.59
Sects (Jainism)	294.49
Sects (Sikhism)	294.69
Serial publications	050
Services (Liturgy and ritual)- Hinduism	782.345
Services (Liturgy and ritual)- Indic religions	782.34
Services (Liturgy and ritual)- Jainism	782.344
Services (Liturgy and ritual)- Sikhism	782.346
Services (Liturgy and ritual)- Buddhism	782.343

Sikhism - Alms giving	294.644 6
Sikhism - Animism	294.621
Sikhism - Asceticism	294.644 7
Sikhism - Associations	294.665
Sikhism - Atonement	294.622
Sikhism - Attitude towards age groups	294.617 834
Sikhism - Attitude towards ethnic groups	294.617 834
Sikhism - Attitude towards language groups	294.617 834
Sikhism - Attitude towards social classes	294.617 834
Sikhism - Attitude towards the sexes	294.617 834
Sikhism - Attributes of God	294.621 12
Sikhism - Attributes of the gods	294.621 12
Sikhism - Biography	294.6092
Sikhism - Ceremonial and ritual observances	294.644 6
Sikhism - Ceremonies	294.638
Sikhism - Child abuse and neglect	294.617 832 71
Sikhism - Concordances	294.603
Sikhism - Congregations	294.665
Sikhism - Conscience	294.65
Sikhism - Contemplation	294.643
Sikhism - Conversion	294.642
Sikhism - Cosmology	294.624
Sikhism - Creation	294.624
Sikhism - Creation of humankind	294.622
Sikhism - Crime	294.617 833

Sikhism - Death	294.623
Sikhism - Deities	294.6211
Sikhism - Demons	294.621 6
Sikhism - Devotional literature	294.643 2
Sikhism - Dictionaries	294.603
Sikhism - Divination (omen, oracles, prophecies)	294.632
Sikhism - Divinities	294.6211
Sikhism - Doctrines	294.62
Sikhism - Ecology	294.617 836
Sikhism - Economic order	294.617 85
Sikhism - Education	294.6071
Sikhism - Emblems	294.637
Sikhism - Encyclopaedias	294.603
Sikhism - End of the world	294.623
Sikhism - Enlightenment	294.642
Sikhism - Eschatology	294.623
Sikhism - Ethics	294.65
Sikhism - Ethics of communication	294.656 5
Sikhism - Ethics of consumption	294.656 8
Sikhism - Ethics of leisure	294.656 5
Sikhism - Ethics of public performances	294.656 5
Sikhism - Ethics of recreation	294.656 5
Sikhism - Ethics of reproduction	294.656 6
Sikhism - Ethics of sex	294.656 6

Sikhism - Karma	294.622
Sikhism - Laws and decisions	294.684
Sikhism - Leaders and organization	294.66
Sikhism - Leaders and their work (role, function, duties)	294.661
Sikhism - Mantras	294.637
Sikhism - Marriage	294.644 1
Sikhism - Meditation	294.643 5
Sikhism - Meditation literature	294.643 2
Sikhism - Miracles	294.621 17
Sikhism - Missions	294.672
Sikhism - Moral theology	294.65
Sikhism - Mysticism	294.642 2
Sikhism - Mythology and mythological foundations	294.613
Sikhism - Nature	294.621 2
Sikhism - Nuclear weapon and nuclear war	294.617 873 2
Sikhism - Objects of warship and veneration	294.621
Sikhism - Observance of restrictions and limitations	294.644 6
Sikhism - Occupational ethics	294.656 4
Sikhism - Offerings	294.634
Sikhism - Omen	294.632
Sikhism - Oracles	294.632
Sikhism - Oral traditions	294.683
Sikhism - Orders	294.665

Sikhism - Organizations	294.665
Sikhism - Other worlds	294.623
Sikhism - Parties	294.665
Sikhism - Peace	294.617 873
Sikhism - Penances	294.634
Sikhism - Periodicals	294.605
Sikhism - Personified abstraction	294.621 4
Sikhism - Persons (male, female, etc)	294.608
Sikhism - Persons as objects of worship and veneration	294.621 3
Sikhism - Persons experiencing illness, trouble, addiction, bereavement	294.644 2
Sikhism - Philosophy and theory	294.601
Sikhism - Pilgrimages	294.6351
Sikhism - Political ethics	294.656 2
Sikhism - Politics	294.617 7
Sikhism - Population	294.617 836
Sikhism - Prayer	294.643
Sikhism - Prayer books	294.643 3
Sikhism - Priests	294.661
Sikhism - Prophecies (Divination)	294.632
Sikhism - Prophecy	294.621 17
Sikhism - Providence	294.621 17
Sikhism - Public worship and other practices	294.63
Sikhism - Punishment	294.617 833

Sikhism - Punishment (Eschatology)	294.623
Sikhism - Reform movements, sources of	294.685
Sikhism - Refugees	294.617 832 8
Sikhism - Reincarnation	294.623 7
Sikhism - Relationship with communication media	294.617 5
Sikhism - Relationship with literature	294.617 5
Sikhism - Relationship with medicine	294.617 5
Sikhism - Relationship with other religions and irreligions	294.617 2
Sikhism - Relationship with psychology	294.617 5
Sikhism - Relationship with science	294.617 5
Sikhism - Relationship with secular disciplines	294.617 5
Sikhism - Relationship with technology	294.617 5
Sikhism - Religious calendar	294.636
Sikhism - Religious education	294.675
Sikhism - Religious experience	294.642
Sikhism - Religious festivals	294.636
Sikhism - Religious freedom	294.617 72
Sikhism - Religious healing	294.631
Sikhism - Religious life	294.644
Sikhism - Religious practice	294.644
Sikhism - Repentance	294.622
Sikhism - Rewards (Eschatology)	294.623
Sikhism - Rites	294.638

Sikhism - Specific vices	294.656
Sikhism - Specific virtues	294.656
Sikhism - Spiritism	294.621
Sikhism - Spirituality	294.64
Sikhism - Sun	294.621 2
Sikhism - Symbolic objects	294.637
Sikhism - Symbolism	294.637
Sikhism - Theocracy	294.617 73
Sikhism - Theodicy	294.621 18
Sikhism - Theory	294.601
Sikhism - Trees	294.621 2
Sikhism - Vice	294.65
Sikhism - Victims of political oppression	294.617 832 8
Sikhism - Virtue	294.65
Sikhism - War	294.617 873
Sikhism - Water	294.621 2
Sikhism - World (miracles, prophecy, providence, revelation)	294.621 17
Sikhism - Worship	294.643
Sikhism - Yoga	294.643 6
Sikhism and communication media	294.617 5
Sikhism and literature	294.617 5
Sikhism and medicine	294.617 5
Sikhism and psychology	294.617 5
Sikhism and science	294.617 5

Sindhi - Hindi dictionary	491.413 914 31
Sindhi adventure fiction (multiple authors)	891.413087*
Sindhi adventure fiction (multiple authors) - Collections	891.41308708**
Sindhi adventure fiction (multiple authors)- History and criticism	891.41308709**
Sindhi anecdotes, epigrams, graffiti, jokes, quotations (multiple authors)	891.41802
Sindhi anecdotes, epigrams, graffiti, jokes, quotations (single author)	891.418+CD+02
Sindhi as second language in elementary education	372.659 141 1
Sindhi ballads (multiple authors)	891.411044*
Sindhi ballads (multiple authors)- Collections	891.41104408**
Sindhi ballads (multiple authors)- History and criticism	891.41104409**
Sindhi comedy (multiple authors)	891.4120523*
Sindhi comedy (multiple authors) - Collections	891.412052308**
Sindhi comedy (multiple authors) - History and criticism	891.412052309**
Sindhi conversations (multiple authors)	891.41506*
Sindhi conversations (multiple authors) - Collections	891.4150608**
Sindhi conversations (multiple authors) - History and criticism	891.4150609**
Sindhi debates and public discussions (multiple authors)	891.41503*

Sindhi debates and public discussions (multiple authors)- Collections	891.4150308**
Sindhi debates and public discussions (multiple authors)- History and criticism	891.4150309**
Sindhi detective fiction (multiple authors)	891.4130872*
Sindhi detective fiction (multiple authors) - Collections	891.413087208**
Sindhi detective fiction (multiple authors) - History and criticism	891.413087209**
Sindhi diaries (multiple authors)	891.41803
Sindhi diaries (single author)	891.418@
Sindhi didactic poetry (multiple authors)	891.41105*
Sindhi didactic poetry (multiple authors)- Collections	891.4110508**
Sindhi didactic poetry (multiple authors)- History and criticism	891.4110509**
Sindhi drama	891.412
Sindhi drama (multiple authors) - - to 1845	***See*** Main schedule
Sindhi drama (multiple authors) - 1845-1895	891.4124+
Sindhi drama (multiple authors) - 1895-1919	891.4125+
Sindhi drama (multiple authors) - 1920-1939	891.4126+
Sindhi drama (multiple authors) - 1940-	891.4127+
Sindhi drama (multiple authors) - 1940-1999	891.41271+
Sindhi drama (multiple authors) - 19th century	891.4124+
Sindhi drama (multiple authors) – 2000-	891.41272+
Sindhi drama (multiple authors) - 20th century	891.41271+

Sindhi drama (multiple authors) - Collections	891.412008**
Sindhi drama (multiple authors) - Dictionaries etc	891.412003
Sindhi drama (multiple authors) - History and criticism	891.412009**
Sindhi drama (multiple authors) - Periodicals	891.412005
Sindhi drama (multiple authors) - Philosophy and theory	891.412001
Sindhi drama (multiple authors) - Psychological aspects	891.4120019
Sindhi drama (multiple authors) - Research	891.4120072
Sindhi drama (multiple authors) - Study and teaching	891.412007
Sindhi drama (multiple authors) - Value	891.4120013
Sindhi drama (single author) - to 1845 schedule	***See*** Main
Sindhi drama (single author)- 1845 -1895	891.412 4
Sindhi drama (single author)- 1895 - 1919	891.412 5
Sindhi drama (single author)- 1920 - 1939	891.412 6
Sindhi drama (single author)- 1940 -	891.412 7
Sindhi drama (single author)- 1940-1999	891.412 71
Sindhi drama (single author)- 19th century	891.412 4
Sindhi drama (single author)- 2000-	891.412 72
Sindhi drama (single author)- 20th century	891.412 71
Sindhi drama for cinema (multiple authors)	891.41203*

Sindhi drama for cinema (multiple authors) - Collections	891.4120308**
Sindhi drama for cinema (multiple authors) - History and criticism	891.4120309**
Sindhi drama for radio (multiple authors)	891.412022*
Sindhi drama for radio (multiple authors) - History and criticism	891.41202209**
Sindhi drama for radio (multiple authors) - Collections	891.41202208**
Sindhi drama for television (multiple authors)	891.412025*
Sindhi drama for television (multiple authors) - Collections	891.41202508**
Sindhi drama for television (multiple authors) - History and criticism	891.41202509**
Sindhi dramatic poetry (multiple authors)	891.41102*
Sindhi dramatic poetry (multiple authors)- Collections	891.4110208**
Sindhi dramatic poetry (multiple authors)- History and criticism	891.4110209**
Sindhi encyclopaedias	039.9141
Sindhi –English dictionary	491.413 21
Sindhi ephemeral and light verse (multiple authors)	891.41108*
Sindhi ephemeral and light verse (multiple authors)- Collections	891.4110808**
Sindhi ephemeral and light verse (multiple authors) - History and criticism	891.4110809**
Sindhi epic poetry (multiple authors)	891.411032*
Sindhi epic poetry (multiple authors)- Collections	891.41103208**

Sindhi epic poetry (multiple authors)- History and criticism	891.41103209**
Sindhi epigrams	***See*** Sindhi anecdotes ...
Sindhi essays	891.414
Sindhi essays (multiple authors) - - to 1845	***See*** Main schedule
Sindhi essays (multiple authors) -1845-1895	891.4144+
Sindhi essays (multiple authors) -1895-1919	891.4145+
Sindhi essays (multiple authors) -1920-1939	891.4146+
Sindhi essays (multiple authors) -1940-	891.4147+
Sindhi essays (multiple authors) -1940-1999	891.41471+
Sindhi essays (multiple authors) - 19th century	891.4144+
Sindhi essays (multiple authors) –2000-	891.41472+
Sindhi essays (multiple authors) - 20th century	891.41471+
Sindhi essays (multiple authors) - Collections	891.414008**
Sindhi essays (multiple authors) - Dictionaries etc	891.414003
Sindhi essays (multiple authors) - History and criticism	891.414009**
Sindhi essays (multiple authors) - Periodicals	891.414005
Sindhi essays (multiple authors) - Philosophy and theory	891.414001
Sindhi essays (multiple authors) - Psychological aspects	891.4140019

Sindhi essays (multiple authors) -Research	891.4140072
Sindhi essays (multiple authors) - Study and teaching	891.414007
Sindhi essays (multiple authors) -Value	891.4140013
Sindhi essays (single author)- - to 1845	***See*** Main schedule
Sindhi essays (single author)- 1845 -1895	891.414 4
Sindhi essays (single author)- 1895 - 1919	891.414 5
Sindhi essays (single author)- 1920 - 1939	891.414 6
Sindhi essays (single author)- 1940 -	891.414 7
Sindhi essays (single author)- 1940-1999	891.414 71
Sindhi essays (single author)- 19th century	891.414 4
Sindhi essays (single author)- 2000-	891.414 72
Sindhi essays (single author)- 20th century	891.414 71
Sindhi fantasy fiction (multiple authors)	891.41308766*
Sindhi fantasy fiction (multiple authors)- Collections	891.4130876608**
Sindhi fantasy fiction (multiple authors)- History and criticism	891.4130876609**
Sindhi farce (multiple authors)	891.41205232*
Sindhi farce (multiple authors)- Collections	891.4120523208**
Sindhi farce (multiple authors)- History and criticism	891.4120523209**
Sindhi fiction	891.413
Sindhi fiction (multiple authors) - - to 1845	***See*** Main schedule
Sindhi fiction (multiple authors) - 1845-1895	891.4134+
Sindhi fiction (multiple authors) - 1895-1919	891.4135+

Sindhi fiction (multiple authors) - 1920-1939	891.4136+
Sindhi fiction (multiple authors) - 1940-	891.4137+
Sindhi fiction (multiple authors) - 1940-1999	891.41371+
Sindhi fiction (multiple authors) - 19th century	891.4134+
Sindhi fiction (multiple authors) – 2000-	891.41372+
Sindhi fiction (multiple authors) - 20th century	891.41371+
Sindhi fiction (multiple authors) - Collections	891.413008**
Sindhi fiction (multiple authors) - Dictionaries etc	891.413003
Sindhi fiction (multiple authors) - History and criticism	891.413009**
Sindhi fiction (multiple authors) - Periodicals	891.413005
Sindhi fiction (multiple authors) - Philosophy and theory	891.413001
Sindhi fiction (multiple authors) - Psychological aspects	891.4130019
Sindhi fiction (multiple authors) - Research	891.4130072
Sindhi fiction (multiple authors) - Study and teaching	891.413007
Sindhi fiction (multiple authors) - Value	891.4130013
Sindhi fiction (single author)- - to 1845	***See*** Main schedule
Sindhi fiction (single author)- 1845 -1895	891.413 4
Sindhi fiction (single author)- 1895 - 1919	891.413 5
Sindhi fiction (single author)- 1920 - 1939	891.413 6
Sindhi fiction (single author)- 1940 -	891.413 7
Sindhi fiction (single author)- 1940-1999	891.413 71

Sindhi fiction (single author)- 19th century	891.413 4
Sindhi fiction (single author)- 2000-	891.413 72
Sindhi fiction (single author)- 20th century	891.413 71
Sindhi folk music.	781 629 48
Sindhi ghost fiction (multiple authors)	891.41308733*
Sindhi ghost fiction (multiple authors) - Collections	891.4130873308**
Sindhi ghost fiction (multiple authors)- History and criticism	891.4130873309**
Sindhi graffiti (multiple authors)	891.41802
Sindhi graffiti (single author)	891.418 +CD+02
Sindhi historical drama (multiple authors)	891.4120514*
Sindhi historical drama (multiple authors)- Collections	891.412051408**
Sindhi historical drama (multiple authors)- History and criticism	891.412051409**
Sindhi historical fiction (multiple authors)	891.413081*
Sindhi historical fiction (multiple authors)- Collections	891.41308108**
Sindhi historical fiction (multiple authors)- History and criticism	891.41308109**
Sindhi horror fiction (multiple authors)	891.41308738*
Sindhi horror fiction (multiple authors)- Collections	891.4130873808**
Sindhi horror fiction (multiple authors)- History and criticism	891.4130873809**
Sindhi humour and satire	891.417

Sindhi humour and satire (multiple authors) — to 1845	***See*** Main schedule
Sindhi humour and satire (multiple authors) -1845-1895	891.4174+
Sindhi humour and satire (multiple authors) -1895-1919	891.4175+
Sindhi humour and satire (multiple authors) -1920-1939	891.4176+
Sindhi humour and satire (multiple authors) -1940-	891.4177+
Sindhi humour and satire (multiple authors) -1940-1999	891.41771+
Sindhi humour and satire (multiple authors) -19th century	891.4174+
Sindhi humour and satire (multiple authors) –2000-	891.41772+
Sindhi humour and satire (multiple authors) -20th century	891.41771+
Sindhi humour and satire (multiple authors) -Collections	891.417008**
Sindhi humour and satire (multiple authors) -Dictionaries etc	891.417003
Sindhi humour and satire (multiple authors) -History and criticism	891.417009**
Sindhi humour and satire (multiple authors) -Periodicals	891.417005
Sindhi humour and satire (multiple authors) -Philosophy and theory	891.417001
Sindhi humour and satire (multiple authors) -Psychological aspects	891.4170019

Sindhi humour and satire (multiple authors) -Research	891.4170072
Sindhi humour and satire (multiple authors) -Study and teaching	891.417007
Sindhi humour and satire (multiple authors) -Value	891.4170013
Sindhi humourous and satirical poetry (multiple authors)	891.41107*
Sindhi humourous and satirical poetry (multiple authors)- Collections	891.4110708**
Sindhi humourous and satirical poetry (multiple authors)- History and criticism	891.4110709**
Sindhi jokes	***See*** Panjabi anecdotes ...
Sindhi language	491.41
Sindhi language - Applied linguistics	491.418
Sindhi language - Bilingual dictionaries	491.4132-39
Sindhi language - Bilingualism	491.41042
Sindhi language - Concordances	491.4103
Sindhi language - Content analysis	491.41014 1
Sindhi language - Dictionaries	491.413
Sindhi language - Discourse analysis	491.41014 1
Sindhi language - Education	491.41071
Sindhi language - Encyclopaedias	491.4103
Sindhi language - Etymology	491.412
Sindhi language - Functionalism	491.41018
Sindhi language - Grammar	491.415

Sindhi language - Specialized dictionaries	491.4131
Sindhi language - Spelling	491.41152
Sindhi language - Stress	491.4116
Sindhi language - Structural linguistics	491.41018
Sindhi language - Suprasegmental features	491.4116
Sindhi language - Terminology	491.41014
Sindhi language - Usage	491.418
Sindhi language - Variations (Dialects etc)	491.417
Sindhi language - Writing systems	491.4111
Sindhi language- Readers	491.418 6
Sindhi letters	891.416
Sindhi letters (multiple authors) - - to 1845	***See*** Main schedule
Sindhi letters (multiple authors) -1845-1895	891.4164+
Sindhi letters (multiple authors) -1895-1919	891.4165+
Sindhi letters (multiple authors) -1920-1939	891.4166+
Sindhi letters (multiple authors) -1940-	891.4167+
Sindhi letters (multiple authors) -1940-1999	891.41671+
Sindhi letters (multiple authors) -19th century	891.4164+
Sindhi letters (multiple authors) –2000-	891.41672+
Sindhi letters (multiple authors) -20th century	891.41671+
Sindhi letters (multiple authors) -Collections	891.416008**
Sindhi letters (multiple authors) - Dictionaries etc	891.416003
Sindhi letters (multiple authors) - History and criticism	891.416009**

Sindhi letters (multiple authors) - Periodicals	891.416005
Sindhi letters (multiple authors) - Philosophy and theory	891.416001
Sindhi letters (multiple authors) - Psychological aspects	891.4160019
Sindhi letters (multiple authors) -Research	891.4160072
Sindhi letters (multiple authors) - Study and teaching	891.416007
Sindhi letters (multiple authors) -Value	891.4160013
Sindhi letters (single author)- - to 1845	***See*** Main schedule
Sindhi letters (single author)- 1845 -1895	891.416 4
Sindhi letters (single author)- 1895 - 1919	891.416 5
Sindhi letters (single author)- 1920 1939	891.416 6
Sindhi letters (single author)- 1940 -	891.416 7
Sindhi letters (single author)- 1940-1999	891.416 71
Sindhi letters (single author)- 19th century	891.416 4
Sindhi letters (single author)- 2000-	891.416 72
Sindhi letters (single author)- 20th century	891.416 71
Sindhi light verse	***See*** Sindhi ephemeral...verse
Sindhi limericks (multiple authors)	891.411075*
Sindhi limericks (multiple authors)- Collections	891.41107508**
Sindhi limericks (multiple authors)- History and criticism	891.41107509**
Sindhi literature	891.41

Sindhi literature (collections of multiple forms)	891.4108
Sindhi literature (collections of multiple forms) - 19th century	891.410804
Sindhi literature (collections of multiple forms) - 20th century	891.4108071
Sindhi literature (collections of multiple forms) – 21st century	891.4108072
Sindhi literature (collections of multiple forms) - Allegory	891.4108015
Sindhi literature (collections of multiple forms) - Animals	891.41080362++
Sindhi literature (collections of multiple forms) - Artistic themes	891.41080357
Sindhi literature (collections of multiple forms) - Atmosphere	891.4108032161
Sindhi literature (collections of multiple forms) - Characters	891.4108027
Sindhi literature (collections of multiple forms) - Comedy	891.4108017
Sindhi literature (collections of multiple forms) - Evening	891.4108033
Sindhi literature (collections of multiple forms) - Fantasy	891.4108015
Sindhi literature (collections of multiple forms) - Forests	891.4108032152
Sindhi literature (collections of multiple forms) - Historical themes	891.41080358
Sindhi literature (collections of multiple forms) - Horror	891.41080164

Sindhi literature (collections of multiple forms) - Human characteristics (Biological, moral, psychological)	891.41080353
Sindhi literature (collections of multiple forms) - Legendary objects/themes	891.4108037
Sindhi literature (collections of multiple forms) - Literary themes	891.41080357
Sindhi literature (collections of multiple forms) - Love	891.410803543
Sindhi literature (collections of multiple forms) - Marriage	891.410803543
Sindhi literature (collections of multiple forms) - Morning	891.4108033
Sindhi literature (collections of multiple forms) - Mountains	891.4108032143
Sindhi literature (collections of multiple forms) - Myth	891.4108015
Sindhi literature (collections of multiple forms) - Mythological objects/themes	891.4108037
Sindhi literature (collections of multiple forms) - Philosophic themes	891.41080384
Sindhi literature (collections of multiple forms) - Places	891.4108032++
Sindhi literature (collections of multiple forms) - Plants	891.41080364
Sindhi literature (collections of multiple forms) - Political themes	891.41080358
Sindhi literature (collections of multiple forms) - Religious themes	891.41080382++
Sindhi literature (collections of multiple forms) - Rivers	891.41080321693

Sindhi literature (collections of multiple forms) - Romanticism	891.41080145
Sindhi literature (collections of multiple forms) - Scientific themes	891.41080356
Sindhi literature (collections of multiple forms) - Sea	891.4108032162
Sindhi literature (collections of multiple forms) - Seasons	891.4108033
Sindhi literature (collections of multiple forms) - Sex	891.410803538
Sindhi literature (collections of multiple forms) - Social themes	891.41080355
Sindhi literature (collections of multiple forms) - Space	891.410803219
Sindhi literature (collections of multiple forms) - Specific kinds of persons, e.g. heroes	891.41080352++
Sindhi literature (collections of multiple forms) - Specific persons (real or imaginary)	891.41080351
Sindhi literature (collections of multiple forms) - Stream of consciousness	891.4108025
Sindhi literature (collections of multiple forms) - Supernatural objects/themes	891.4108037
Sindhi literature (collections of multiple forms) - Symbolism	891.4108015
Sindhi literature (collections of multiple forms) - Technical themes	891.41080356
Sindhi literature (collections of multiple forms) - Times (seasons, parts of day, etc)	891.4108033
Sindhi literature (collections of multiple forms) - Towns	891.41080321732

Sindhi literature (collections of multiple forms) - Tragedy	891.41080162
Sindhi literature (collections of multiple forms) - Villages	891.41080321734
Sindhi literature (collections of multiple forms) - Weather	891.4108036
Sindhi literature (collections of multiple forms) emphasizing subjects	891.410804++
Sindhi literature (collections of multiple forms) for/by children	891.410809282
Sindhi literature (collections of multiple forms) for/by persons of racial, ethnic and national groups	891.410808++
Sindhi literature (collections of multiple forms) for/by persons of specific classes	891.4108092++
Sindhi literature (collections of multiple forms) for/by persons resident in specific regions	891.4108091++
Sindhi literature (collections of multiple forms) for/by women	891.410809287
Sindhi literature (multiple authors) - Concordances	891.4103
Sindhi literature (multiple authors) - Dictionaries	891.4103
Sindhi literature (multiple authors) - Education	891.41071
Sindhi literature (multiple authors) - Encyclopaedias	891.4103
Sindhi literature (multiple authors) - Organizations	891.4106

Sindhi literature (multiple authors) - Periodicals	891.4105
Sindhi literature (multiple authors) - Philosophy and theory	891.4101
Sindhi literature (multiple authors) - Research	891.41072
Sindhi literature (multiple authors) - Research in India	891.41072054
Sindhi literature (multiple authors) - Study and teaching	891.4107
Sindhi literature (multiple forms) - 19th century	891.4109004
Sindhi literature (multiple forms) – 2000-	891.41090072
Sindhi literature (multiple forms) - 20th century	891.41090071
Sindhi literature (multiple forms) - Allegory – History and criticism	891.410915
Sindhi literature (multiple forms) - Animals - History and criticism	891.4109362++
Sindhi literature (multiple forms) - Artistic themes - History and criticism	891.4109357
Sindhi literature (multiple forms) - Atmosphere - History and criticism	891.410932161
Sindhi literature (multiple forms) - Characters - History and criticism	891.410927
Sindhi literature (multiple forms) - Comedy - History and criticism	891.410917
Sindhi literature (multiple forms) - Evening - History and criticism	891.410933
Sindhi literature (multiple forms) - Fantasy - History, description, criticism	891.410915

Sindhi literature (multiple forms) - Forests - History and criticism	891.410932152
Sindhi literature (multiple forms) - Historical themes - History and criticism	891.4109358
Sindhi literature (multiple forms) - History and criticism	891.4109
Sindhi literature (multiple forms) - Horror - History and criticism	891.4109164
Sindhi literature (multiple forms) - Human characteristics (Biological, moral, psychological) - History and criticism	891.4109353
Sindhi literature (multiple forms) - Legendary objects/themes - History and criticism	891.410937
Sindhi literature (multiple forms) - Literary themes - History and criticism	891.4109357
Sindhi literature (multiple forms) - Love - History and criticism	891.41093543
Sindhi literature (multiple forms) - Marriage - History and criticism	891.41093543
Sindhi literature (multiple forms) - Morning - History and criticism	891.410933
Sindhi literature (multiple forms) - Mountains - History and criticism	891.410932143
Sindhi literature (multiple forms) - Myth - History and criticism	891.410915
Sindhi literature (multiple forms) - Mythological objects/themes - History and criticism	891.410937
Sindhi literature (multiple forms) - Persons of racial, ethnic and national groups - History and criticism	891.41098++

Sindhi literature (multiple forms) - Persons of specific classes - History and criticism	891.410992++
Sindhi literature (multiple forms) - Persons resident in specific regions - History and criticism	891.410991++
Sindhi literature (multiple forms) - Philosophic themes - History and criticism	891.4109384
Sindhi literature (multiple forms) - Places - History and criticism	891.410932++
Sindhi literature (multiple forms) - Plants - History and criticism	891.4109364
Sindhi literature (multiple forms) - Political themes - History and criticism	891.4109358
Sindhi literature (multiple forms) - Religious themes - History and criticism	891.4109382++
Sindhi literature (multiple forms) - Rivers - History and criticism	891.4109321693
Sindhi literature (multiple forms) - Romanticism - History and criticism	891.4109145
Sindhi literature (multiple forms) - Scientific themes - History and criticism	891.4109356
Sindhi literature (multiple forms) - Sea - History and criticism	891.410932162
Sindhi literature (multiple forms) - Seasons - History and criticism	891.410933
Sindhi literature (multiple forms) - Sex - History and criticism	891.41093538
Sindhi literature (multiple forms) - Social themes - History and criticism	891.4109355

Sindhi literature (multiple forms) - Space - History and criticism	891.41093219
Sindhi literature (multiple forms) - Specific kinds of persons, e.g. heroes - History and criticism	891.4109352++
Sindhi literature (multiple forms) - Specific persons - History and criticism	891.4109351
Sindhi literature (multiple forms) - Stream of consciousness - History and criticism	891.410925
Sindhi literature (multiple forms) - Subjects - History and criticism	891.41094++
Sindhi literature (multiple forms) - Supernatural objects/themes - History and criticism	891.410937
Sindhi literature (multiple forms) - Symbolism- History , description, criticism	891.410915
Sindhi literature (multiple forms) - Technical themes - History and criticism	891.4109356
Sindhi literature (multiple forms) - Times - History and criticism	891.410933
Sindhi literature (multiple forms) - Towns - History and criticism	891.4109321732
Sindhi literature (multiple forms) - Tragedy - History and criticism	891.4109162
Sindhi literature (multiple forms) - Villages - History and criticism	891.4109321734
Sindhi literature (multiple forms) - Weather - History and criticism	891.410936
Sindhi literature (single author)- - to 1845- Biography, collections, criticism	***See*** Main schedule

Sindhi literature (single author)- 1845 - 1895- Biography, collections, criticism	891.418 409
Sindhi literature (single author)- 1895 - 1919- Biography, collections, criticism	891.418 509
Sindhi literature (single author)- 1920 - 1939- Biography, collections, criticism	891.418 609
Sindhi literature (single author)- 1940 - Biography, collections, criticism	891.418 709
Sindhi literature (single author)- 1940- 2000- Biography, collections, criticism	891.418 7109
Sindhi literature (single author)- 19th century- Biography, collections, criticism	891.418 409
Sindhi literature (single author)- 2000- Biography, collections, criticism	891.418 7209
Sindhi literature (single author)- 20th century- Biography, collections, criticism	891.418 7109
Sindhi literature (single author)- Criticism, description, collections - - to 1845	***See*** Main schedule
Sindhi literature (single author)- Criticism, description, collections - 1845 - 1895	891.418 409
Sindhi literature (single author)- Criticism, description, collections - 1895 - 1919	891.418 509
Sindhi literature (single author)- Criticism, description, collections - 1920 - 1939	891.418 609
Sindhi literature (single author)- Criticism, description, collections - 1940- 2000	891.418 7109
Sindhi literature (single author)- Criticism, description, collections - 1940 -	891.418 709
Sindhi literature (single author)- Criticism, description, collections - 19th century	891.418 409

Sindhi literature (single author)- Criticism, description, collections - 2000-	891.418 7209
Sindhi literature (single author)- Criticism, description, collections - 20th century	891.418 7109
Sindhi literature for/by children - History and criticism	891.41099282
Sindhi literature for/by women - History and criticism	891.41099287
Sindhi love fiction (multiple authors)	891.413085*
Sindhi love fiction (multiple authors)- Collections	891.41308508**
Sindhi love fiction (multiple authors)- History and criticism	891.41308509**
Sindhi melodrama (multiple authors)	891.4120527*
Sindhi melodrama (multiple authors) - Collections	891.412052708**
Sindhi melodrama (multiple authors)- History and criticism	891.412052709**
Sindhi miscellaneous writings	891.418
Sindhi miscellaneous writings (multiple authors) - to 1845	***See*** Main schedule
Sindhi miscellaneous writings (multiple authors) -1845-1895	891.4184++
Sindhi miscellaneous writings (multiple authors) -1895-1919	891.4185++
Sindhi miscellaneous writings (multiple authors) -1920-1939	891.4186++
Sindhi miscellaneous writings (multiple authors) -1940-	891.4187++

Sindhi miscellaneous writings (multiple authors) -1940-1999	891.41871++
Sindhi miscellaneous writings (multiple authors) -19th century	891.4184++
Sindhi miscellaneous writings (multiple authors) –2000-	891.41872++
Sindhi miscellaneous writings (multiple authors) -20th century	891.41871++
Sindhi miscellaneous writings (multiple authors) -Collections	891.418008**
Sindhi miscellaneous writings (multiple authors) -Dictionaries etc	891.418003
Sindhi miscellaneous writings (multiple authors) -History and criticism	891.418009**
Sindhi miscellaneous writings (multiple authors) -Periodicals	891.418005
Sindhi miscellaneous writings (multiple authors) -Philosophy and theory	891.418001
Sindhi miscellaneous writings (multiple authors) -Psychological aspects	891.4180019
Sindhi miscellaneous writings (multiple authors) -Research	891.4180072
Sindhi miscellaneous writings (multiple authors) -Study and teaching	891.418007
Sindhi miscellaneous writings (multiple authors) -Value	891.4180013
Sindhi miscellaneous writings (single author)	891.418
Sindhi miscellaneous writings (single author)- - to 1845	***See*** Main schedule

Sindhi miscellaneous writings (single author)- 1845 -1895	891.418 4
Sindhi miscellaneous writings (single author)- 1895 - 1919	891.418 5
Sindhi miscellaneous writings (single author)- 1920 - 1939	891.418 6
Sindhi miscellaneous writings (single author)- 1940 -	891.418 7
Sindhi miscellaneous writings (single author)- 1940-1999	891.418 71
Sindhi miscellaneous writings (single author)- 19th century	891.418 4
Sindhi miscellaneous writings (single author)- 2000-	891.418 72
Sindhi miscellaneous writings (single author)- 20th century	891.418 71
Sindhi monologues (multiple authors)	891.412045*
Sindhi monologues (multiple authors)- Collections	891.41204508**
Sindhi monologues (multiple authors)- History and criticism	891.41204509**
Sindhi morality plays	***See*** Sindhi religious ... plays
Sindhi mystery fiction (multiple authors)	891.4130872*
Sindhi mystery fiction (multiple authors)- Collections	891.413087208**
Sindhi mystery fiction (multiple authors)- History and criticism	891.413087209**
Sindhi narrative poetry (multiple authors)	891.41103*

Sindhi narrative poetry (multiple authors)- Collections	891.4110308**
Sindhi narrative poetry (multiple authors)- History and criticism	891.4110309**
Sindhi notebooks	***See*** Sindhi diaries...
Sindhi odes (multiple authors)	891.411043*
Sindhi odes (multiple authors)- Collections	891.41104308**
Sindhi odes (multiple authors)- History and criticism	891.41104309**
Sindhi one act plays (multiple authors)	891.412.041*
Sindhi one act plays (multiple authors)- Collections	891.412.041 08**
Sindhi one act plays (multiple authors)- History and criticism	891.412.041 09**
Sindhi oratory (multiple authors)	***See*** Sindhi public speeches
Sindhi periodicals	059.9141
Sindhi poetry	891.411
Sindhi poetry (multiple authors) - - to 1845	***See*** Main schedule
Sindhi poetry (multiple authors) - 1845-1895	891.4114+
Sindhi poetry (multiple authors) - 1895-1919	891.4115+
Sindhi poetry (multiple authors) - 1920-1939	891.4116+
Sindhi poetry (multiple authors) - 1940-	891.4117+
Sindhi poetry (multiple authors) - 1940-1999	891.41171+
Sindhi poetry (multiple authors) - 19th century	891.4114+
Sindhi poetry (multiple authors) – 2000-	891.41172+

Sindhi poetry (multiple authors) - 20th century	891.41171+
Sindhi poetry (multiple authors)- Collections	891.411008**
Sindhi poetry (multiple authors)- Dictionaries etc	891.411003
Sindhi poetry (multiple authors)- History and criticism	891.411009**
Sindhi poetry (multiple authors)- Periodicals	891.411005
Sindhi poetry (multiple authors)- Philosophy and theory	891.411001
Sindhi poetry (multiple authors)- Psychological aspects	891.4110019
Sindhi poetry (multiple authors)- Research	891.4110072
Sindhi poetry (multiple authors)- Study and teaching	891.411007
Sindhi poetry (multiple authors)- Value	891.4110013
Sindhi poetry (single author)- - to 1845	***See*** Main schedule
Sindhi poetry (single author)- 1845 -1895	891.411 4
Sindhi poetry (single author)- 1895 - 1919	891.411 5
Sindhi poetry (single author)- 1920 - 1939	891.411 6
Sindhi poetry (single author)- 1940 -	891.411 7
Sindhi poetry (single author)- 1940-1999	891.411 71
Sindhi poetry (single author)- 19th century	891.411 4
Sindhi poetry (single author)- 2000-	891.411 72
Sindhi poetry (single author)- 20th century	891.411 71
Sindhi prose (single author)- - to 1845	***See*** Main schedule
Sindhi prose (single author)- 1845 -1895	891.418 408

Sindhi prose (single author)- 1895 - 1919	891.418 508
Sindhi prose (single author)- 1920 1939	891.418 608
Sindhi prose (single author)- 1940 -	891.418 708
Sindhi prose (single author)- 1940-1999	891.418 7108
Sindhi prose (single author)- 19th century	891.418 408
Sindhi prose (single author)- 2000-	891.418 7208
Sindhi prose (single author)- 20th century	891.418 7108
Sindhi prose literature (multiple authors)	891.41808
Sindhi psychological fiction (multiple authors)	891.413083+
Sindhi public discussions	***See*** Sindhi debates ...
Sindhi public speeches (multiple authors)	891.41501+
Sindhi quotations	***See*** Sindhi anecdotes ...
Sindhi quotations (single author)	891.418 +CD+02
Sindhi realistic fiction (multiple authors)	891.413083+
Sindhi recitations (multiple authors)	891.41504+
Sindhi religious and morality plays (multiple authors)	891.4120516+
Sindhi reminiscences	***See*** Sindhi diaries...
Sindhi romantic fiction (multiple authors)	891.413085*
Sindhi romantic fiction (multiple authors)- Collections	891.41308508**
Sindhi romantic fiction (multiple authors)- History and criticism	891.41308509**

Sindhi satire	***See*** Sindhi humour …
Sindhi satirical poetry	***See*** Sindhi humourous … poetry
Sindhi science fiction (multiple authors)	891.41308762*
Sindhi science fiction (multiple authors)-Collections	891.4130876208*
Sindhi science fiction (multiple authors)-History and criticism	891.4130876209*
Sindhi serious drama (multiple authors)	891.412051+
Sindhi short stories (multiple authors)	891.41301+
Sindhi sociological fiction (multiple authors)	891.413083+
Sindhi sonnets (multiple authors)	891.411042*
Sindhi sonnets (multiple authors)-Collections	891.41104208**
Sindhi sonnets (multiple authors)-History and criticism	891.41104209**
Sindhi speaking people	305.791 411
Sindhi speeches	891.415
Sindhi speeches (multiple authors) — to 1845	***See*** Main schedule
Sindhi speeches (multiple authors) - 1845-1895	891.4154+
Sindhi speeches (multiple authors) - 1895-1919	891.4155+
Sindhi speeches (multiple authors) - 1920-1939	891.4156+
Sindhi speeches (multiple authors) -1940-	891.4157+

Sindhi speeches (multiple authors) - 1940-1999	891.41571+
Sindhi speeches (multiple authors) - 19th century	891.4154+
Sindhi speeches (multiple authors) - 20th century	891.41571+
Sindhi speeches (multiple authors) – 21st century	891.41572+
Sindhi speeches (multiple authors) - Collections	891.415008**
Sindhi speeches (multiple authors) - Dictionaries etc	891.415003
Sindhi speeches (multiple authors) - History and criticism	891.415009**
Sindhi speeches (multiple authors) - Periodicals	891.415005
Sindhi speeches (multiple authors) - Philosophy and theory	891.415001
Sindhi speeches (multiple authors) - Psychological aspects	891.4150019
Sindhi speeches (multiple authors) - Research	891.4150072
Sindhi speeches (multiple authors) - Study and teaching	891.415007
Sindhi speeches (multiple authors) -Value	891.4150013
Sindhi speeches (single author)	891.415
Sindhi speeches (single author)- - to 1845	***See*** Main schedule
Sindhi speeches (single author)- 1845 -1895	891.415 4
Sindhi speeches (single author)- 1895 - 1919	891.415 5

Sindhi speeches (single author)- 1920 - 1939	891.415 6
Sindhi speeches (single author)- 1940 -	891.415 7
Sindhi speeches (single author)- 1940-1999	891.415 71
Sindhi speeches (single author)- 19th century	891.415 4
Sindhi speeches (single author)- 2000-	891.415 72
Sindhi speeches (single author)- 20th century	891.415 71
Sindhi suspense fiction (multiple authors)	891.4130872*
Sindhi suspense fiction (multiple authors)- Collections	891.413087208**
Sindhi suspense fiction (multiple authors)- History and criticism	891.413087209**
Sindhi tragedy (multiple authors)	891.4120512*
Sindhi tragedy (multiple authors)- Collections	891.412051208**
Sindhi tragedy (multiple authors)- History and criticism	891.412051209**
Sindhi variety drama (multiple authors)	891.412057*
Sindhi variety drama (multiple authors)- Collections	891.41205708**
Sindhi variety drama (multiple authors)- History and criticism	891.41205709**
Sindhi works of non-identifiable literary form	891.418+CD+ 07
Sindhis	305.894 8
Sinhalese - English dictionary	491.48321
Sinhalese adventure fiction (multiple authors)	891.483087*

Sinhalese adventure fiction (multiple authors) -Collections	891.48308708**
Sinhalese adventure fiction (multiple authors)- History and criticism	891.48308709**
Sinhalese anecdotes, epigrams, graffiti, jokes, quotations (multiple authors)	891.48802
Sinhalese anecdotes, epigrams, graffiti, jokes, quotations (single author)	891.488+CD+02
Sinhalese ballads (multiple authors)	891.481044*
Sinhalese ballads (multiple authors)- Collections	891.48104408**
Sinhalese ballads (multiple authors)- History and criticism	891.48104409**
Sinhalese comedy (multiple authors)	891.4820523*
Sinhalese comedy (multiple authors) - Collections	891.482052308**
Sinhalese comedy (multiple authors) - History and criticism	891.482052309**
Sinhalese conversations (multiple authors)	891.48506*
Sinhalese conversations (multiple authors) - Collections	891.4850608**
Sinhalese conversations (multiple authors) - History and criticism	891.4850609**
Sinhalese debates and public discussions (multiple authors)	891.48503*
Sinhalese debates and public discussions (multiple authors)- Collections	891.4850308**
Sinhalese debates and public discussions (multiple authors)- History and criticism	891.4850309**

Sinhalese detective fiction (multiple authors)	891.4830872*
Sinhalese detective fiction (multiple authors) - Collections	891.483087208**
Sinhalese detective fiction (multiple authors) - History and criticism	891.483087209**
Sinhalese diaries, notebooks, reminiscences (multiple authors)	891.48803
Sinhalese diaries, notebooks, reminiscences (single author)	891.488@
Sinhalese didactic poetry (multiple authors)	891.48105*
Sinhalese didactic poetry (multiple authors)- Collections	891.4810508**
Sinhalese didactic poetry (multiple authors)- History and criticism	891.4810509**
Sinhalese drama	891.482
Sinhalese drama (multiple authors) - - to 1845	***See*** Main schedule
Sinhalese drama (multiple authors) - 1845-1895	891.4824+
Sinhalese drama (multiple authors) - 1895-1919	891.4825+
Sinhalese drama (multiple authors) - 1920-1939	891.4826+
Sinhalese drama (multiple authors) - 1940-	891.4827+
Sinhalese drama (multiple authors) - 1940-1999	891.48271+
Sinhalese drama (multiple authors) - 19th century	891.4824+
Sinhalese drama (multiple authors) – 2000-	891.48272+

Sinhalese drama (multiple authors) - 20th century	891.48271+
Sinhalese drama (multiple authors) - Collections	891.482008**
Sinhalese drama (multiple authors) - Dictionaries etc	891.482003
Sinhalese drama (multiple authors) - History and criticism	891.482009**
Sinhalese drama (multiple authors) - Periodicals	891.482005
Sinhalese drama (multiple authors) - Philosophy and theory	891.482001
Sinhalese drama (multiple authors) - Psychological aspects	891.4820019
Sinhalese drama (multiple authors) - Research	891.4820072
Sinhalese drama (multiple authors) - Study and teaching	891.482007
Sinhalese drama (multiple authors) - Value	891.4820013
Sinhalese drama (single author) - to 1845	***See*** Main schedule
Sinhalese drama (single author)- 1845 -1895	891.482 4
Sinhalese drama (single author)- 1895 - 1919	891.482 5
Sinhalese drama (single author)- 1920 - 1939	891.482 6
Sinhalese drama (single author)- 1940 -	891.482 7
Sinhalese drama (single author)- 1940-1999	891.482 71
Sinhalese drama (single author)- 19th century	891.482 4

Sinhalese drama (single author)- 2000-	891.482 72
Sinhalese drama (single author)- 20th century	891.482 71
Sinhalese drama for cinema (multiple authors)	891.48203*
Sinhalese drama for cinema (multiple authors) - Collections	891.4820308**
Sinhalese drama for cinema (multiple authors) - History and criticism	891.4820309**
Sinhalese drama for radio (multiple authors)	891.482022*
Sinhalese drama for radio (multiple authors) - Collections	891.48202208**
Sinhalese drama for radio (multiple authors) - History and criticism	891.48202209**
Sinhalese drama for television (multiple authors)	891.482025*
Sinhalese drama for television (multiple authors) - Collections	891.48202508**
Sinhalese drama for television (multiple authors) - History and criticism	891.48202509**
Sinhalese dramatic poetry (multiple authors)	891.48102*
Sinhalese dramatic poetry (multiple authors)- Collections	891.4810208**
Sinhalese dramatic poetry (multiple authors)- History and criticism	891.4810209**
Sinhalese ephemeral and light verse (multiple authors)	891.48108*
Sinhalese ephemeral and light verse (multiple authors)- Collections	891.4810808**

Sinhalese ephemeral and light verse (multiple authors) - History and criticism	891.4810809**
Sinhalese epic poetry (multiple authors)	891.481032*
Sinhalese epic poetry (multiple authors)- Collections	891.48103208**
Sinhalese epic poetry (multiple authors)- History and criticism	891.48103209**
Sinhalese epigrams	***See*** Sinhalese anecdotes ...
Sinhalese essays	891.484
Sinhalese essays (multiple authors) - to 1845	***See*** Main schedule
Sinhalese essays (multiple authors) - 1845-1895	891.4844+
Sinhalese essays (multiple authors) - 1895-1919	891.4845+
Sinhalese essays (multiple authors) - 1920-1939	891.4846+
Sinhalese essays (multiple authors) -1940-	891.4847+
Sinhalese essays (multiple authors) - 1940-1999	891.48471+
Sinhalese essays (multiple authors) - 19th century	891.4844+
Sinhalese essays (multiple authors) –2000-	891.48472+
Sinhalese essays (multiple authors) - 20th century	891.48471+
Sinhalese essays (multiple authors) - Collections	891.484008**
Sinhalese essays (multiple authors) - Dictionaries etc	891.484003

Sinhalese essays (multiple authors) - History and criticism	891.484009**
Sinhalese essays (multiple authors) - Periodicals	891.484005
Sinhalese essays (multiple authors) - Philosophy and theory	891.484001
Sinhalese essays (multiple authors) - Psychological aspects	891.4840019
Sinhalese essays (multiple authors) - Research	891.4840072
Sinhalese essays (multiple authors) - Study and teaching	891.484007
Sinhalese essays (multiple authors) -Value	891.4840013
Sinhalese essays (single author)- - to 1845	***See*** Main schedule
Sinhalese essays (single author)- 1845 -1895	891.484 4
Sinhalese essays (single author)- 1895 - 1919	891.484 5
Sinhalese essays (single author)- 1920 - 1939	891.484 6
Sinhalese essays (single author)- 1940 -	891.484 7
Sinhalese essays (single author)- 1940-1999	891.484 71
Sinhalese essays (single author)- 19th century	891.484 4
Sinhalese essays (single author)- 2000-	891.484 72
Sinhalese essays (single author)- 20th century	891.484 71
Sinhalese fantasy fiction (multiple authors)	891.48308766*

Sinhalese fantasy fiction (multiple authors)- Collections	891.4830876608**
Sinhalese fantasy fiction (multiple authors)- History and criticism	891.4830876609**
Sinhalese farce (multiple authors)	891.48205232*
Sinhalese farce (multiple authors)- Collections	891.4820523208**
Sinhalese farce (multiple authors)- History and criticism	891.4820523209**
Sinhalese fiction	891.483
Sinhalese fiction (multiple authors) - - to 1845	***See*** Main schedule
Sinhalese fiction (multiple authors) - 1845-1895	891.4834+
Sinhalese fiction (multiple authors) - 1895-1919	891.4835+
Sinhalese fiction (multiple authors) - 1920-1939	891.4836+
Sinhalese fiction (multiple authors) - 1940-	891.4837+
Sinhalese fiction (multiple authors) - 1940-1999	891.48371+
Sinhalese fiction (multiple authors) - 19th century	891.4834+
Sinhalese fiction (multiple authors) – 2000-	891.48372+
Sinhalese fiction (multiple authors) - 20th century	891.48371+
Sinhalese fiction (multiple authors) - Collections	891.483008**
Sinhalese fiction (multiple authors) - Dictionaries etc	891.483003

Sinhalese fiction (multiple authors) - History and criticism	891.483009**
Sinhalese fiction (multiple authors) - Periodicals	891.483005
Sinhalese fiction (multiple authors) - Philosophy and theory	891.483001
Sinhalese fiction (multiple authors) - Psychological aspects	891.4830019
Sinhalese fiction (multiple authors) - Research	891.4830072
Sinhalese fiction (multiple authors) - Study and teaching	891.483007
Sinhalese fiction (multiple authors) - Value	891.4830013
Sinhalese fiction (single author)- - to 1845 schedule	***See*** Main
Sinhalese fiction (single author)- 1845 -1895	891.483 4
Sinhalese fiction (single author)- 1895 - 1919	891.483 5
Sinhalese fiction (single author)- 1920 - 1939	891.483 6
Sinhalese fiction (single author)- 1940 -	891.483 7
Sinhalese fiction (single author)- 1940-1999	891.483 71
Sinhalese fiction (single author)- 19th century	891.483 4
Sinhalese fiction (single author)- 2000-	891.483 72
Sinhalese fiction (single author)- 20th century	891.483 71
Sinhalese ghost fiction (multiple authors)	891.48308733*

Sinhalese ghost fiction (multiple authors) - Collections	891.4830873308**
Sinhalese ghost fiction (multiple authors)- History and criticism	891.4830873309**
Sinhalese graffiti	***See*** Sinhalese anecdotes ...
Sinhalese historical drama (multiple authors)	891.4820514*
Sinhalese historical drama (multiple authors)- Collections	891.482051408**
Sinhalese historical drama (multiple authors)- History and criticism	891.482051409**
Sinhalese historical fiction (multiple authors)	891.483081*
Sinhalese historical fiction (multiple authors)- Collections	891.48308108**
Sinhalese historical fiction (multiple authors)- History and criticism	891.48308109**
Sinhalese horror fiction (multiple authors)	891.48308738*
Sinhalese horror fiction (multiple authors)- Collections	891.4830873808**
Sinhalese horror fiction (multiple authors)- History and criticism	891.4830873809**
Sinhalese humour and satire	891.487
Sinhalese humour and satire (multiple authors) — to 1845	***See*** Main schedule
Sinhalese humour and satire (multiple authors) -1845-1895	891.4874+
Sinhalese humour and satire (multiple authors) -1895-1919	891.4875+

Sinhalese humour and satire (multiple authors) -1920-1939	891.4876+
Sinhalese humour and satire (multiple authors) -1940-	891.4877+
Sinhalese humour and satire (multiple authors) -1940-1999	891.48771+
Sinhalese humour and satire (multiple authors) -19th century	891.4874+
Sinhalese humour and satire (multiple authors) –2000-	891.48772+
Sinhalese humour and satire (multiple authors) -20th century	891.48771+
Sinhalese humour and satire (multiple authors) -Collections	891.487008**
Sinhalese humour and satire (multiple authors) -Dictionaries etc	891.487003
Sinhalese humour and satire (multiple authors) -History and criticism	891.487009**
Sinhalese humour and satire (multiple authors) -Periodicals	891.487005
Sinhalese humour and satire (multiple authors) -Philosophy and theory	891.487001
Sinhalese humour and satire (multiple authors) -Psychological aspects	891.4870019
Sinhalese humour and satire (multiple authors) -Research	891.4870072
Sinhalese humour and satire (multiple authors) -Study and teaching	891.487007
Sinhalese humour and satire (multiple authors) -Value	891.4870013

Sinhalese humourous and satirical poetry (multiple authors)	891.48107*
Sinhalese humourous and satirical poetry (multiple authors)- Collections	891.4810708**
Sinhalese humourous and satirical poetry (multiple authors)- History and criticism	891.4810709**
Sinhalese jokes	***See*** Sinhalese anecdotes ...
Sinhalese language	491.48
Sinhalese language - Applied linguistics	491.488
Sinhalese language - Bilingual dictionaries	491.48 32-39
Sinhalese language - Bilingualism	491.48 042
Sinhalese language - Concordances	491.48 03
Sinhalese language - Content analysis	491.48 014 1
Sinhalese language - Dictionaries	491.48 3
Sinhalese language - Discourse analysis	491.48 014 1
Sinhalese language - Education	491.48 071
Sinhalese language - Encyclopaedias	491.48 03
Sinhalese language - Etymology	491.48 2
Sinhalese language - Functionalism	491.48 018
Sinhalese language - Grammar	491.48 5
Sinhalese language - History	491.48 09
Sinhalese language - Intonation	491.48 16
Sinhalese language - Lexicography	491.48 302 8
Sinhalese language - Lexicology	491.48 014
Sinhalese language - Miscellany	491.48 02

Sinhalese language - Terminology	491.48 014
Sinhalese language - Usage	491.48 8
Sinhalese language - Variations (Dialects)	491.48 7
Sinhalese language - Writing systems	491.48 11
Sinhalese language- Readers	491.488 6
Sinhalese letters	891.486
Sinhalese letters (multiple authors) - - to 1845	***See*** Main schedule
Sinhalese letters (multiple authors) - 1845-1895	891.4864+
Sinhalese letters (multiple authors) - 1895-1919	891.4865+
Sinhalese letters (multiple authors) - 1920-1939	891.4866+
Sinhalese letters (multiple authors) -1940-	891.4867+
Sinhalese letters (multiple authors) - 1940-1999	891.48671+
Sinhalese letters (multiple authors) - 19th century	891.4864+
Sinhalese letters (multiple authors) – 2000-	891.48672+
Sinhalese letters (multiple authors) - 20th century	891.48671+
Sinhalese letters (multiple authors) - Collections	891.486008**
Sinhalese letters (multiple authors) - Dictionaries etc	891.486003
Sinhalese letters (multiple authors) - History and criticism	891.486009**

Sinhalese letters (multiple authors) - Periodicals	891.486005
Sinhalese letters (multiple authors) - Philosophy and theory	891.486001
Sinhalese letters (multiple authors) - Psychological aspects	891.4860019
Sinhalese letters (multiple authors) - Research	891.4860072
Sinhalese letters (multiple authors) - Study and teaching	891.486007
Sinhalese letters (multiple authors) -Value	891.4860013
Sinhalese letters (single author)- - to 1845	***See*** Main schedule
Sinhalese letters (single author)- 1845 -1895	891.486 4
Sinhalese letters (single author)- 1895 - 1919	891.486 5
Sinhalese letters (single author)- 1920 - 1939	891.486 6
Sinhalese letters (single author)- 1940 -	891.486 7
Sinhalese letters (single author)- 1940 - 1999	891.486 71
Sinhalese letters (single author)- 19th century	891.486 4
Sinhalese letters (single author)- 2000-	891.486 72
Sinhalese letters (single author)- 20th century	891.486 71
Sinhalese light verse	***See*** Sinhalese ephemeral...verse
Sinhalese limericks (multiple authors)	891.481075*

Sinhalese limericks (multiple authors)-Collections	891.48107508**
Sinhalese limericks (multiple authors)-History and criticism	891.48107509**
Sinhalese literature	891.48
Sinhalese literature (collections of multiple forms)	891.4808
Sinhalese literature (collections of multiple forms) - Allegory	891.4808015
Sinhalese literature (collections of multiple forms) - Animals	891.48080362++
Sinhalese literature (collections of multiple forms) - Artistic themes	891.48080357
Sinhalese literature (collections of multiple forms) - Atmosphere	891.4808032161
Sinhalese literature (collections of multiple forms) - Characters	891.4808027
Sinhalese literature (collections of multiple forms) - Comedy	891.4808017
Sinhalese literature (collections of multiple forms) - Evening	891.4808033
Sinhalese literature (collections of multiple forms) - Fantasy	891.4808015
Sinhalese literature (collections of multiple forms) - Forests	891.4808032152
Sinhalese literature (collections of multiple forms) - Historical themes	891.48080358
Sinhalese literature (collections of multiple forms) - Horror	891.48080164

Sinhalese literature (collections of multiple forms) - Human characteristics (Biological, moral, psychological)	891.48080353
Sinhalese literature (collections of multiple forms) - Legendary objects/themes	891.4808037
Sinhalese literature (collections of multiple forms) - Literary themes	891.48080357
Sinhalese literature (collections of multiple forms) - Love	891.480803543
Sinhalese literature (collections of multiple forms) - Marriage	891.480803543
Sinhalese literature (collections of multiple forms) - Morning	891.4808033
Sinhalese literature (collections of multiple forms) - Mountains	891.4808032143
Sinhalese literature (collections of multiple forms) - Myth	891.4808015
Sinhalese literature (collections of multiple forms) - Mythological objects/themes	891.4808037
Sinhalese literature (collections of multiple forms) - Philosophic themes	891.48080384
Sinhalese literature (collections of multiple forms) - Places	891.4808032++
Sinhalese literature (collections of multiple forms) - Plants	891.48080364
Sinhalese literature (collections of multiple forms) - Political themes	891.48080358
Sinhalese literature (collections of multiple forms) - Religious themes	891.48080382++
Sinhalese literature (collections of multiple forms) - Rivers	891.48080321693

Sinhalese literature (collections of multiple forms) - Romanticism	891.48080145
Sinhalese literature (collections of multiple forms) - Scientific themes	891.48080356
Sinhalese literature (collections of multiple forms) - Sea	891.4808032162
Sinhalese literature (collections of multiple forms) - Seasons	891.4808033
Sinhalese literature (collections of multiple forms) - Sex	891.480803538
Sinhalese literature (collections of multiple forms) - Social themes	891.48080355
Sinhalese literature (collections of multiple forms) - Space	891.480803219
Sinhalese literature (collections of multiple forms) - Specific kinds of persons, e.g. heroes	891.48080352++
Sinhalese literature (collections of multiple forms) - Specific persons (real or imaginary)	891.48080351
Sinhalese literature (collections of multiple forms) - Stream of consciousness	891.4808025
Sinhalese literature (collections of multiple forms) - Supernatural objects/themes	891.4808037
Sinhalese literature (collections of multiple forms) - Symbolism	891.4808015
Sinhalese literature (collections of multiple forms) - Technical themes	891.48080356
Sinhalese literature (collections of multiple forms) - Times (seasons, parts of day, etc)	891.4808033
Sinhalese literature (collections of multiple forms) - Towns	891.48080321732

Sinhalese literature (collections of multiple forms) - Tragedy	891.48080162
Sinhalese literature (collections of multiple forms) - Villages	891.48080321734
Sinhalese literature (collections of multiple forms) - Weather	891.4808036
Sinhalese literature (collections of multiple forms) -19th century	891.480804
Sinhalese literature (collections of multiple forms) -20th century	891.4808071
Sinhalese literature (collections of multiple forms) –21st century	891.4808072
Sinhalese literature (collections of multiple forms) emphasizing subjects	891.480804++
Sinhalese literature (collections of multiple forms) for/by children	891.480809282
Sinhalese literature (collections of multiple forms) for/by persons of racial, ethnic and national groups	891.480808++
Sinhalese literature (collections of multiple forms) for/by persons of specific classes	891.4808092++
Sinhalese literature (collections of multiple forms) for/by persons resident in specific regions	891.4808091++
Sinhalese literature (collections of multiple forms) for/by women	891.480809287
Sinhalese literature (multiple authors) - Concordances	891.4803
Sinhalese literature (multiple authors) - Dictionaries	891.4803

Sinhalese literature (multiple authors) - Education	891.48071
Sinhalese literature (multiple authors) - Encyclopaedias	891.4803
Sinhalese literature (multiple authors) - Organizations	891.4806
Sinhalese literature (multiple authors) - Periodicals	891.4805
Sinhalese literature (multiple authors) - Philosophy and theory	891.4801
Sinhalese literature (multiple authors) - Research	891.48072
Sinhalese literature (multiple authors) - Research in India	891.48072054
Sinhalese literature (multiple authors) - Study and teaching	891.4807
Sinhalese literature (multiple forms) - 19th century	891.4809004
Sinhalese literature (multiple forms) – 2000-	891.48090072
Sinhalese literature (multiple forms) - 20th century	891.48090071
Sinhalese literature (multiple forms) - Allegory – History and criticism	891.480915
Sinhalese literature (multiple forms) - Animals - History and criticism	891.4809362++
Sinhalese literature (multiple forms) - Artistic themes - History and criticism	891.4809357
Sinhalese literature (multiple forms) - Atmosphere - History and criticism	891.480932161

Sinhalese literature (multiple forms) - Characters - History and criticism	891.480927
Sinhalese literature (multiple forms) - Comedy - History and criticism	891.480917
Sinhalese literature (multiple forms) - Evening - History and criticism	891.480933
Sinhalese literature (multiple forms) - Fantasy - History , description, criticism	891.480915
Sinhalese literature (multiple forms) - Forests- History and criticism	891.480932152
Sinhalese literature (multiple forms) - Historical themes - History and criticism	891.4809358
Sinhalese literature (multiple forms) - History and criticism	891.4809
Sinhalese literature (multiple forms) - Horror - History and criticism	891.4809164
Sinhalese literature (multiple forms) - Human characteristics (Biological, moral, psychological) - History and criticism	891.4809353
Sinhalese literature (multiple forms) - Legendary objects/themes - History and criticism	891.480937
Sinhalese literature (multiple forms) - Literary themes - History and criticism	891.4809357
Sinhalese literature (multiple forms) - Love - History and criticism	891.48093543
Sinhalese literature (multiple forms) - Marriage - History and criticism	891.48093543
Sinhalese literature (multiple forms) - Morning - History and criticism	891.480933

Sinhalese literature (multiple forms) - Mountains - History and criticism	891.480932143
Sinhalese literature (multiple forms) - Myth - History and criticism	891.480915
Sinhalese literature (multiple forms) - Mythological objects/themes - History and criticism	891.480937
Sinhalese literature (multiple forms) - Persons of racial, ethnic and national groups - History and criticism	891.48098++
Sinhalese literature (multiple forms) - Persons of specific classes - History and criticism	891.480992++
Sinhalese literature (multiple forms) - Persons resident in specific regions - History and criticism	891.480991++
Sinhalese literature (multiple forms) - Philosophic themes - History and criticism	891.4809384
Sinhalese literature (multiple forms) - Places - History and criticism	891.480932++
Sinhalese literature (multiple forms) - Plants - History and criticism	891.4809364
Sinhalese literature (multiple forms) - Political themes - History and criticism	891.4809358
Sinhalese literature (multiple forms) - Religious themes - History and criticism	891.4809382++
Sinhalese literature (multiple forms) - Rivers - History and criticism	891.4809321693
Sinhalese literature (multiple forms) - Romanticism - History and criticism	891.4809145
Sinhalese literature (multiple forms) - Scientific themes - History and criticism	891.4809356

Sinhalese literature (multiple forms) - Sea - History and criticism	891.480932162
Sinhalese literature (multiple forms) - Seasons - History and criticism	891.480933
Sinhalese literature (multiple forms) - Sex - History and criticism	891.48093538
Sinhalese literature (multiple forms) - Social themes - History and criticism	891.4809355
Sinhalese literature (multiple forms) - Space - History and criticism	891.48093219
Sinhalese literature (multiple forms) - Specific kinds of persons, e.g. heroes, - History and criticism	891.4809352++
Sinhalese literature (multiple forms) - Specific persons - History and criticism	891.4809351
Sinhalese literature (multiple forms) - Stream of consciousness - History and criticism	891.480925
Sinhalese literature (multiple forms) - Subjects - History and criticism	891.48094++
Sinhalese literature (multiple forms) - Supernatural objects/themes - History and criticism	891.480937
Sinhalese literature (multiple forms) - Symbolism- History , description, criticism	891.480915
Sinhalese literature (multiple forms) - Technical themes - History and criticism	891.4809356
Sinhalese literature (multiple forms) - Times - History and criticism	891.480933
Sinhalese literature (multiple forms) - Towns - History and criticism	891.4809321732

Sinhalese literature (multiple forms) - Tragedy - History and criticism	891.4809162
Sinhalese literature (multiple forms) - Villages - History and criticism	891.4809321734
Sinhalese literature (multiple forms) - Weather - History and criticism	891.480936
Sinhalese literature (single author)- - to 1845 - Biography, collections, criticism	***See*** Main schedule
Sinhalese literature (single author)- 1845 - 1895 - Biography, collections, criticism	891.488 409
Sinhalese literature (single author)- 1895 - 1919 - Biography, collections, criticism	891.488 509
Sinhalese literature (single author)- 1920 - 1939 - Biography, collections, criticism	891.488 609
Sinhalese literature (single author)- 1940 - Biography, collections, criticism	891.488 709
Sinhalese literature (single author)- 1940-1999 - Biography, collections, criticism	891.488 7109
Sinhalese literature (single author)- 2000- Biography, collections, criticism	891.488 7209
Sinhalese literature for/by children - History and criticism	891.48099282
Sinhalese literature for/by women - History and criticism	891.48099287
Sinhalese love fiction (multiple authors)	891.483085*
Sinhalese love fiction (multiple authors)- Collections	891.48308508**
Sinhalese love fiction (multiple authors)- History and criticism	891.48308509**
Sinhalese melodrama (multiple authors)	891.4820527*

Sinhalese melodrama (multiple authors)-Collections	891.482052708**
Sinhalese melodrama (multiple authors)-History and criticism	891.482052709**
Sinhalese miscellaneous writings	891.488
Sinhalese miscellaneous writings (multiple authors) - to 1845	***See*** Main schedule
Sinhalese miscellaneous writings (multiple authors) -1845-1895	891.4884++
Sinhalese miscellaneous writings (multiple authors) -1895-1919	891.4885++
Sinhalese miscellaneous writings (multiple authors) -1920-1939	891.4886++
Sinhalese miscellaneous writings (multiple authors) -1940-	891.4887++
Sinhalese miscellaneous writings (multiple authors) -1940-1999	891.48871++
Sinhalese miscellaneous writings (multiple authors) -19th century	891.4884++
Sinhalese miscellaneous writings (multiple authors) –2000-	891.48872++
Sinhalese miscellaneous writings (multiple authors) -20th century	891.48871++
Sinhalese miscellaneous writings (multiple authors) -Collections	891.488008**
Sinhalese miscellaneous writings (multiple authors) -Dictionaries etc	891.488003
Sinhalese miscellaneous writings (multiple authors) -History and criticism	891.488009**
Sinhalese miscellaneous writings (multiple authors) -Periodicals	891.488005

Sinhalese miscellaneous writings (multiple authors) -Philosophy and theory	891.488001
Sinhalese miscellaneous writings (multiple authors) -Psychological aspects	891.4880019
Sinhalese miscellaneous writings (multiple authors) -Research	891.4880072
Sinhalese miscellaneous writings (multiple authors) -Study and teaching	891.488007
Sinhalese miscellaneous writings (multiple authors) -Value	891.4880013
Sinhalese miscellaneous writings (single author)- - to 1845	***See*** Main schedule
Sinhalese miscellaneous writings (single author)- 1845 -1895	891.488 4
Sinhalese miscellaneous writings (single author)- 1895 - 1919	891.488 5
Sinhalese miscellaneous writings (single author)- 1920 - 1939	891.488 6
Sinhalese miscellaneous writings (single author)- 1940 -	891.488 7
Sinhalese miscellaneous writings (single author)- 1940-1999	891.488 71
Sinhalese miscellaneous writings (single author)- 19th century	891.488 4
Sinhalese miscellaneous writings (single author)- 2000-	891.488 72
Sinhalese miscellaneous writings (single author)- 20th century	891.488 71
Sinhalese monologues (multiple authors)	891.482045*
Sinhalese monologues (multiple authors)-Collections	891.48204508**

Sinhalese monologues (multiple authors)- History and criticism	891.48204509**
Sinhalese morality plays	***See*** Sinhalese religious ... plays
Sinhalese mystery fiction (multiple authors)	891.4830872*
Sinhalese mystery fiction (multiple authors)- Collections	891.483087208**
Sinhalese mystery fiction (multiple authors)- History and criticism	891.483087209**
Sinhalese narrative poetry (multiple authors)	891.48103*
Sinhalese narrative poetry (multiple authors)- Collections	891.4810308**
Sinhalese narrative poetry (multiple authors)- History and criticism	891.4810309**
Sinhalese notebooks	***See*** Sinhalese diaries...
Sinhalese odes (multiple authors)	891.481043*
Sinhalese odes (multiple authors)- Collections	891.48104308**
Sinhalese odes (multiple authors)- History and criticism	891.48104309**
Sinhalese one act plays (multiple authors)	891.482.041*
Sinhalese one act plays (multiple authors)- Collections	891.482.041 08**
Sinhalese one act plays (multiple authors)- History and criticism	891.482.041 09**
Sinhalese oratory (multiple authors)	***See*** Sinhalese public speeches
Sinhalese poetry	891.481

Sinhalese poetry (multiple authors) - - to 1845	***See*** Main schedule
Sinhalese poetry (multiple authors) - 1845-1895	891.4814+
Sinhalese poetry (multiple authors) - 1895-1919	891.4815+
Sinhalese poetry (multiple authors) - 1920-1939	891.4816+
Sinhalese poetry (multiple authors) - 1940-	891.4817+
Sinhalese poetry (multiple authors) - 1940-1999	891.48171+
Sinhalese poetry (multiple authors) - 19th century	891.4814+
Sinhalese poetry (multiple authors) – 2000-	891.48172+
Sinhalese poetry (multiple authors) - 20th century	891.48171+
Sinhalese poetry (multiple authors)- Collections	891.481008**
Sinhalese poetry (multiple authors)- Dictionaries etc	891.481003
Sinhalese poetry (multiple authors)- History and criticism	891.481009**
Sinhalese poetry (multiple authors)- Periodicals	891.481005
Sinhalese poetry (multiple authors)- Philosophy and theory	891.481001
Sinhalese poetry (multiple authors)- Psychological aspects	891.4810019
Sinhalese poetry (multiple authors)- Research	891.4810072

Sinhalese poetry (multiple authors)- Study and teaching	891.481007
Sinhalese poetry (multiple authors)- Value	891.4810013
Sinhalese poetry (single author)- - to 1845	***See*** Main schedule
Sinhalese poetry (single author)- 1845 -1895	891.481 4
Sinhalese poetry (single author)- 1895 - 1919	891.481 5
Sinhalese poetry (single author)- 1920 - 1939	891.481 6
Sinhalese poetry (single author)- 1940 -	891.481 7
Sinhalese poetry (single author)- 1940-1999	891.481 71
Sinhalese poetry (single author)- 19th century	891.481 4
Sinhalese poetry (single author)- 2000—	891.481 72
Sinhalese poetry (single author)-20th century	891.481 71
Sinhalese prose (single author)- - to 1845	***See*** Main schedule
Sinhalese prose (single author)- 1845 -1895	891.488 408
Sinhalese prose (single author)- 1895 - 1919	891.488 508
Sinhalese prose (single author)- 1920 - 1939	891.488 608
Sinhalese prose (single author)- 1940 -	891.488 708
Sinhalese prose (single author)- 1940-1999	891.488 7108
Sinhalese prose (single author)- 19th century	891.488 408
Sinhalese prose (single author)- 2000—	891.488 7208
Sinhalese prose (single author)- 20th century	891.488 7108
Sinhalese prose literature (multiple authors)	891.48808

Sinhalese psychological fiction (multiple authors) - History and criticism	891.483083+
Sinhalese public discussions	***See*** Sinhalese debates ... discussions
Sinhalese public speeches (multiple authors)	891.48501
Sinhalese public speeches (multiple authors)- Collections	891.4850108
Sinhalese public speeches (multiple authors)- History and criticism	891.4850109
Sinhalese quotations	***See*** Sinhalese anecdotes ...
Sinhalese realistic fiction (multiple authors)- Collections	891.483083+
Sinhalese recitations (multiple authors)	891.48504+
Sinhalese religious and morality plays (multiple authors)	891.4820516+
Sinhalese reminiscences	***See*** Sinhalese diaries...
Sinhalese romantic fiction (multiple authors)	891.483085*
Sinhalese romantic fiction (multiple authors)- Collections	891.48308508**
Sinhalese romantic fiction (multiple authors)- History and criticism	891.48308509**
Sinhalese satire	***See*** Sinhalese humour ...
Sinhalese satirical poetry	***See*** Sinhalese humourous ... poetry
Sinhalese science fiction (multiple authors)	891.48308762*

Sinhalese science fiction (multiple authors)-Collections	891.4830876208**
Sinhalese science fiction (multiple authors)-History and criticism	891.4830876209**
Sinhalese serious drama (multiple authors)	891.482051+
Sinhalese short stories (multiple authors)	891.48301+
Sinhalese sociological fiction (multiple authors)	891.483083+
Sinhalese sonnets (multiple authors)	891.481042*
Sinhalese sonnets (multiple authors)-Collections	891.48104208**
Sinhalese sonnets (multiple authors)-History and criticism	891.48104209**
Sinhalese speeches	891.485
Sinhalese speeches (multiple authors) — to 1845	***See*** Main schedule
Sinhalese speeches (multiple authors) -1845-1895	891.4854+
Sinhalese speeches (multiple authors) -1895-1919	891.4855+
Sinhalese speeches (multiple authors) -1920-1939	891.4856+
Sinhalese speeches (multiple authors) -1940-	891.4857+
Sinhalese speeches (multiple authors) -1940-1999	891.48571+
Sinhalese speeches (multiple authors) –2000-	891.48572+
Sinhalese speeches (multiple authors) -Collections	891.485008**

Sinhalese speeches (multiple authors) -Dictionaries etc	891.485003
Sinhalese speeches (multiple authors) -History and criticism	891.485009**
Sinhalese speeches (multiple authors) - Periodicals	891.485005
Sinhalese speeches (multiple authors) - Philosophy and theory	891.485001
Sinhalese speeches (multiple authors) - Psychological aspects	891.4850019
Sinhalese speeches (multiple authors) - Research	891.4850072
Sinhalese speeches (multiple authors) - Study and teaching	891.485007
Sinhalese speeches (multiple authors) - Value	891.4850013
Sinhalese speeches (single author)- - to 1845	***See*** Main schedule
Sinhalese speeches (single author)- 1845 -1895	891.485 4
Sinhalese speeches (single author)- 1895 - 1919	891.485 5
Sinhalese speeches (single author)- 1920 - 1939	891.485 6
Sinhalese speeches (single author)- 1940 -	891.485 7
Sinhalese speeches (single author)- 1940-1999	891.485 71
Sinhalese speeches (single author)- 19th century	891.485 4
Sinhalese speeches (single author)- 2000-	891.485 72

Sinhalese speeches (single author)- 20th century	891.485 71
Sinhalese suspense fiction (multiple authors)	891.4830872*
Sinhalese suspense fiction (multiple authors)- Collections	891.483087208**
Sinhalese suspense fiction (multiple authors)- History and criticism	891.483087209**
Sinhalese tragedy (multiple authors)	891.4820512*
Sinhalese tragedy (multiple authors)- Collections	891.482051208**
Sinhalese tragedy (multiple authors)- History and criticism	891.482051209**
Sinhalese variety drama (multiple authors)	891.482057*
Sinhalese variety drama (multiple authors)- Collections	891.48205708**
Sinhalese variety drama (multiple authors)- History and criticism	891.48205709**
Sinhalese works of non-identifiable literary form	891.488+CD+07
Sinhalese-Maldivian languages	491.48
Sinhalese-Maldivian literatures	891.48
Social clubs - India	367.954
Social problems (Buddhism)	294.337 83
Social problems (Hinduism)	294.517 83
Social problems (Jainism)	294.417 83
Social problems (Sikhism)	294.617 83
Social problems. Social welfare- Andaman and Nicobar Islands	361.954 88

Social problems. Social welfare- Karnataka	361.954 87
Social problems. Social welfare- Kerala	361.954 83
Social problems. Social welfare- Lakshwadweep	361.954 81
Social problems. Social welfare- Madhya Pradesh	361.954 3
Social problems. Social welfare- Madras	361.954 82
Social problems. Social welfare- Maharashtra	361.954 792
Social problems. Social welfare- Manipur	361.954 17
Social problems. Social welfare- Meghalaya	361.954 164
Social problems. Social welfare- Mizoram	361.954 166
Social problems. Social welfare- Nagaland	361.954 165
Social problems. Social welfare- Northeast India	361.954 1
Social problems. Social welfare- Orissa	361.954 13
Social problems. Social welfare- Pondicherry	361.954 86
Social problems. Social welfare- Punjab	361.954 55 2
Social problems. Social welfare- Rajasthan	361.954 4
Social problems. Social welfare- Sikkim	361.954 167
Social problems. Social welfare- South Asia	361.954
Social problems. Social welfare- Southern India	361.954 8
Social problems. Social welfare- Tamil Nadu	361.954 82
Social problems. Social welfare- Tripura	361.954 15
Social problems. Social welfare- Uttar Pradesh	361.954 2

Social problems. Social welfare- Uttaranchal	361.954 51
Social problems. Social welfare- West Bengal	361.954 14
Social problems. Social welfare- Western India	361.954 7
Social service law- India	344.54
Social theology (Buddhism)	294.337
Social theology (Hinduism)	294.517
Social theology (Jainism)	294.417
Social theology (Sikhism)	294.617
Social welfare problems (Buddhism)	294.337 832
Social welfare problems (Hinduism)	294.517 832
Social welfare problems (Jainism)	294.417 832
Social welfare problems (Sikhism)	294.617 832
Social welfare problems and services	361
Social welfare problems and services- Andaman and Nicobar Islands	362.954 88
Social welfare problems and services- Andhra Pradesh	362.954 84
Social welfare problems and services- Arunachal Pradesh	362.954 163
Social welfare problems and services- Assam	362.954 162
Social welfare problems and services- Bengal	362.954 14
Social welfare problems and services- Bhopal	362.954 3

Social welfare problems and services- Bihar	362.954 12
Social welfare problems and services- Bombay	362.954 792 3
Social welfare problems and services- Buddhism	294.337 832
Social welfare problems and services- Calcutta	362.954 147
Social welfare problems and services- Chandigarh	362.954 525 2
Social welfare problems and services- Chhattisgarh	362.954 137
Social welfare problems and services- Dadra and Nagar Haveli	362.954 796
Social welfare problems and services- Delhi	362.954 526
Social welfare problems and services- Goa, Daman and Diu	362.954 799
Social welfare problems and services- Gujarat	362.954 75
Social welfare problems and services- Haryana	362.954 525 8
Social welfare problems and services- Himachal Pradesh	362.954 522
Social welfare problems and services- Hyderabad state	362.954 84
Social welfare problems and services- India	362.954
Social welfare problems and services- Jammu and Kashmir	362.954 6
Social welfare problems and services- Jharkhand	362.954 127

Social welfare problems and services-Karnataka	362.954 87
Social welfare problems and services-Kerala	362.954 83
Social welfare problems and services-Lakshwadweep	362.954 81
Social welfare problems and services-Madhya Pradesh	362.954 3
Social welfare problems and services-Madras	362.954 82
Social welfare problems and services-Maharashtra	362.954 792
Social welfare problems and services-Manipur	362.954 17
Social welfare problems and services-Meghalaya	362.954 164
Social welfare problems and services-Mizoram	362.954 166
Social welfare problems and services-Nagaland	362.954 165
Social welfare problems and services-Northeast India	362.954 1
Social welfare problems and services-Orissa	362.954 13
Social welfare problems and services-Pondicherry	362.954 86
Social welfare problems and services-Punjab	362.954 525 2
Social welfare problems and services-Rajasthan	362.954 4

Social welfare problems and services-Sikkim	362.954 167
Social welfare problems and services-South Asia	362.954
Social welfare problems and services-Southern India	362.954 8
Social welfare problems and services-Tamil Nadu	362.954 82
Social welfare problems and services-Tripura	362.954 15
Social welfare problems and services-Uttar Pradesh	362.954 2
Social welfare problems and services-Uttaranchal	362.954 51
Social welfare problems and services-West Bengal	362.954 14
Social welfare problems and services-Western India	362.954 7
Social welfare services (Buddhism)	294.337 832
Social welfare services (Hinduism)	294.517 832
Social welfare services (Jainism)	294.417 832
Social welfare services (Sikhism)	294.617 832
Socioeconomic problems (Buddhism)	294.337 8
Socioeconomic problems (Hinduism)	294.517 8
Socioeconomic problems (Jainism)	294.417 8
Socioeconomic problems (Sikhism)	294.617 8
Soka Gakkai	294.392 8
Soto	294.392 7

Soto doctrines	294.342 042 7
Soto Buddhism- Doctrines	294.342 042 7
Soul (Buddhism)	294.342 2
Soul (Hinduism)	294.522
Soul (Jainism)	294.422
Soul (Sikhism)	294.6 22
Sounds (Buddhism)	294.343 7
Sounds (Hinduism)	294.537
Sounds (Jainism)	294.437
Sounds (Sikhism)	294.637
Sources (Buddhism)	294.38
Sources (Hinduism)	294.58
Sources (Jainism)	294.48
Sources (Sikhism)	294.68
Sources of reform movements (Buddhism)	294.385
Sources of sects (Buddhism)	294.385
Sources of sects (Hinduism)	294.585
Sources of sects (Jainism)	294.485
Sources of sects (Sikhism)	294.685
South Asia- Architecture	720.954
South Asia- Budget	352.495 4
South Asia- Economic development	338.954
South Asia- Economic geography	330.954
South Asia- Education	370.954
South Asia- Fauna	591.954

South Asia- Flora	581.954
South Asia- Folk dancing	793.319 54
South Asia- Geography	915.4
South Asia- Geology	555.4
South Asia- History	954
South Asia- Painting and paintings	759.954
South Asia- Public administration	351.54
South Asia- Public finance	336.54
South Asia- Sculpture	730.954
South Asian folk music.	781 629 14
South Asians	305.891 4
South Dravidian folk music	781 629 481
South Dravidians	305.894 81
Southern India- Architecture	720.954 8
Southern India- Budget	352.495 48
Southern India- Economic development	338.954 8
Southern India- Economic geography	330.954 8
Southern India- Education	370.954 8
Southern India- Fauna	591.954 8
Southern India- Flora	581.954 8
Southern India- Folk dancing	793.319 548
Southern India- Geography	915.48
Southern India- Geology	555.48
Southern India- History	954.8
Southern India- Painting and paintings	759.954 8

Southern India- Public administration	351.548
Southern India- Public finance	336.548
Southern India- Sculpture	730.954 8
Specific moral issues (Buddhism)	294.356
Specific moral issues (Hinduism)	294.5486
Specific moral issues (Jainism)	294.456
Specific moral issues (Sikhism)	294.656
Specific sins (Buddhism)	294.356
Specific sins (Hinduism)	294.5486
Specific sins (Jainism)	294.456
Specific sins (Sikhism)	294.656
Specific vices (Buddhism)	294.356
Specific vices (Hinduism)	294.5486
Specific vices (Jainism)	294.456
Specific vices (Sikhism)	294.656
Specific virtues (Buddhism)	294.356
Specific virtues (Hinduism)	294.5486
Specific virtues (Jainism)	294.456
Specific virtues (Sikhism)	294.656
Spiritism (Buddhism)	294.3421
Spiritism (Hinduism)	294.521
Spiritism (Jainism)	294.421
Spiritism (Sikhism)	294.621
Stained, painted, leaded, mosaic glass and glass makers- India	748.59954

Standard English usage	428
Standard Hindi speaking people	305.791 431
State and provincial taxes	336.201 3
State taxes- Andaman and Nicobar Islands	336.201 354 88
State taxes- Andhra Pradesh	336.201 354 84
State taxes- Arunachal Pradesh	336.201 354 163
State taxes- Assam	336.201 354 162
State taxes- Bengal	336.201 354 14
State taxes- Bihar	336.201 354 12
State taxes- Chandigarh	336.201 354 55 2
State taxes- Chhattisgarh	336.201 354 137
State taxes- Dadra and Nagar Haveli	336.201 354 796
State taxes- Delhi	336.201 354 56
State taxes- Goa, Daman and Diu	336.201 354 79
State taxes- Gujarat	336.201 354 75
State taxes- Haryana	336.201 354 55 8
State taxes- Himachal Pradesh	336.201 354 52
State taxes- Hyderabad state	336.201 354 84
State taxes- Jammu and Kashmir	336.201 354 6
State taxes- Jharkhand	336.201 354 127
State taxes- Karnataka	336.201 354 87
State taxes- Kerala	336.201 354 83
State taxes- Lakshwadweep	336.201 354 81
State taxes- Madhya Pradesh	336.201 354 3
State taxes- Madras	336.201 354 82

State taxes- Maharashtra	336.201 354 792
State taxes- Manipur	336.201 354 17
State taxes- Meghalaya	336.201 354 164
State taxes- Mizoram	336.201 354 166
State taxes- Nagaland	336.201 354 165
State taxes- Orissa	336.201 354 13
State taxes- Pondicherry	336.201 354 86
State taxes- Punjab	336.201 354 55 2
State taxes- Rajasthan	336.201 354 4
State taxes- Sikkim	336.201 354 167
State taxes- Tamil Nadu	336.201 354 82
State taxes- Tripura	336.201 354 15
State taxes- Uttar Pradesh	336.201 354 2
State taxes- Uttaranchal	336.201 354 51
State taxes- West Bengal	336.201 354 14
Statistics- India	315.4
Statistics-Andaman and Nicobar Islands	315.488
Statistics-Andhra Pradesh	315.484
Statistics-Arunachal Pradesh	315.416 3
Statistics-Assam	315.416 2
Statistics-Bengal	315.414
Statistics-Bhopal	315.43
Statistics-Bihar	315.412
Statistics-Bombay	315.479 23
Statistics-Calcutta	315.414 7

Statistics-Chandigarh	315.452 52
Statistics-Chhattisgarh	315.413 7
Statistics-Dadra and Nagar Haveli	315.479 6
Statistics-Delhi	315.452 6
Statistics-Goa, Daman and Diu	315.479 9
Statistics-Gujarat	315.475
Statistics-Haryana	315.45 58
Statistics-Himachal Pradesh	315.452
Statistics-Hyderabad state	315.484
Statistics-Jammu and Kashmir	315.46
Statistics-Jharkhand	315.412 7
Statistics-Karnataka	315.487
Statistics-Kerala	315.483
Statistics-Lakshwadweep	315.481
Statistics-Madhya Pradesh	315.43
Statistics-Madras	315.482
Statistics-Maharashtra	315.479 2
Statistics-Manipur	315.417
Statistics-Meghalaya	315.416 4
Statistics-Mizoram	315.416 6
Statistics-Nagaland	315.416 5
Statistics-Northeast India	315.41
Statistics-Orissa	315.413
Statistics-Pondicherry	315.486
Statistics-Punjab	315.45 52

Statistics-Rajasthan	315.44
Statistics-Sikkim	315.416 7
Statistics-South Asia	315.4
Statistics-Southern India	315.48
Statistics-Tamil Nadu	315.482
Statistics-Tripura	315.415
Statistics-Uttar Pradesh	315.42
Statistics-Uttaranchal	315.451
Statistics-Vindhya Pradesh	315.43
Statistics-West Bengal	315.414
Statistics-Western India	315.47
Strikes- Andaman and Nicobar Islands	331.892 954 88
Strikes- Andhra Pradesh	331.892 954 84
Strikes- Arunachal Pradesh	331.892 954 163
Strikes- Assam	331.892 954 162
Strikes- Bengal	331.892 954 14
Strikes- Bhopal	331.892 954 3
Strikes- Bihar	331.892 954 12
Strikes- Bombay	331.892 954 7923
Strikes- Calcutta	331.892 954 147
Strikes- Chandigarh	331.892 954 55 2
Strikes- Chhattisgarh	331.892 954 137
Strikes- Dadra and Nagar Haveli	331.892 954 796
Strikes- Delhi	331.892 954 56
Strikes- Goa, Daman and Diu	331.892 954 79

Strikes- Gujarat	331.892 954 75
Strikes- Haryana	331.892 954 55 8
Strikes- Himachal Pradesh	331.892 954 52
Strikes- Hyderabad state	331.892 954 84
Strikes- India	331.892 954
Strikes- Jammu and Kashmir	331.892 954 6
Strikes- Jharkhand	331.892 954 127
Strikes- Karnataka	331.892 954 87
Strikes- Kerala	331.892 954 83
Strikes- Lakshwadweep	331.892 954 81
Strikes- Madhya Pradesh	331.892 954 3
Strikes- Madras	331.892 954 82
Strikes- Maharashtra	331.892 954 792
Strikes- Manipur	331.892 954 17
Strikes- Meghalaya	331.892 954 164
Strikes- Mizoram	331.892 954 166
Strikes- Nagaland	331.892 954 165
Strikes- Northeast India	331.892 954 1
Strikes- Orissa	331.892 954 13
Strikes- Pondicherry	331.892 954 86
Strikes- Punjab	331.892 954 55 2
Strikes- Rajasthan	331.892 954 4
Strikes- Sikkim	331.892 954 167
Strikes- South Asia	331.892 954
Strikes- Southern India	331.892 954 8

T

Tamil - English dictionary	494.811 321
Tamil adventure fiction (multiple authors)	894.8113087*
Tamil adventure fiction (multiple authors) - Collections	894.811308708**
Tamil adventure fiction (multiple authors)- History and criticism	894.811308709**
Tamil anecdotes, epigrams, graffiti, jokes, quotations (multiple authors)	894.811802
Tamil anecdotes, epigrams, graffiti, jokes, quotations (single author)	894.8118+CD+02
Tamil as second language in elementary education	372.659 481 1
Tamil ballads (multiple authors)	894.8111044*
Tamil ballads (multiple authors)- Collections	894.811104408**
Tamil ballads (multiple authors)- History and criticism	894.811104409**
Tamil comedy (multiple authors)	894.81120523*
Tamil comedy (multiple authors) - Collections	894.8112052308**
Tamil comedy (multiple authors) - History and criticism	894.8112052309**

Tamil conversations (multiple authors)	894.811506*
Tamil conversations (multiple authors) - Collections	894.81150608**
Tamil conversations (multiple authors) - History and criticism	894.81150609**
Tamil debates and public discussions (multiple authors)	894.811503*
Tamil debates and public discussions (multiple authors)- Collections	894.81150308**
Tamil debates and public discussions (multiple authors)- History and criticism	894.81150309**
Tamil detective fiction (multiple authors)	894.81130872*
Tamil detective fiction (multiple authors) - Collections	894.8113087208**
Tamil detective fiction (multiple authors) - History and criticism	894.8113087209**
Tamil diaries, notebooks, reminiscences (multiple authors)	894.811803
Tamil diaries, notebooks, reminiscences (single author)	894.8118@
Tamil didactic poetry (multiple authors)	894.811105*
Tamil didactic poetry (multiple authors)- Collections	894.81110508**
Tamil didactic poetry (multiple authors)- History and criticism	894.81110509**
Tamil drama	894.8112
Tamil drama (multiple authors) - - to 1845	***See*** Main schedule
Tamil drama (multiple authors) - 1845-1895	894.81124+
Tamil drama (multiple authors) - 1895-1919	894.81125+

Tamil drama (multiple authors) - 1920-1939	894.81126+
Tamil drama (multiple authors) - 1940-	894.81127+
Tamil drama (multiple authors) - 1940-1999	894.811271+
Tamil drama (multiple authors) - 19th century	894.81124+
Tamil drama (multiple authors) – 2000-	894.811272+
Tamil drama (multiple authors) - 20th century	894.811271+
Tamil drama (multiple authors) - Collections	894.8112008**
Tamil drama (multiple authors) - Dictionaries etc	894.8112003
Tamil drama (multiple authors) - History and criticism	894.8112009**
Tamil drama (multiple authors) - Periodicals	894.8112005
Tamil drama (multiple authors) - Philosophy and theory	894.8112001
Tamil drama (multiple authors) - Psychological aspects	894.81120019
Tamil drama (multiple authors) - Research	894.81120072
Tamil drama (multiple authors) - Study and teaching	894.8112007
Tamil drama (multiple authors) - Value	894.81120013
Tamil drama (single author) - to 1845	***See*** Main schedule
Tamil drama (single author)- 1845 -1895	894.8112 4
Tamil drama (single author)- 1895 - 1919	894.8112 5
Tamil drama (single author)- 1920 - 1939	894.8112 6
Tamil drama (single author)- 1940 -	894.8112 7
Tamil drama (single author)- 1940-1999	894.8112 71

Tamil drama (single author)- 19th century	894.8112 4
Tamil drama (single author)- 2000-	894.8112 72
Tamil drama (single author)- 20th century	894.8112 71
Tamil drama for cinema (multiple authors)	894.811203*
Tamil drama for cinema (multiple authors) - Collections	894.81120308**
Tamil drama for cinema (multiple authors) - History and criticism	894.81120309**
Tamil drama for radio (multiple authors)	894.8112022*
Tamil drama for radio (multiple authors) - Collections	894.811202208**
Tamil drama for radio (multiple authors) - History and criticism	894.811202209**
Tamil drama for television (multiple authors)	894.8112025*
Tamil drama for television (multiple authors) - Collections	894.811202508**
Tamil drama for television (multiple authors) - History and criticism	894.811202509**
Tamil dramatic poetry (multiple authors)	894.811102*
Tamil dramatic poetry (multiple authors)- Collections	894.81110208**
Tamil dramatic poetry (multiple authors)- History and criticism	894.81110209**
Tamil encyclopaedias	039.94811
Tamil ephemeral and light verse (multiple authors)	894.811108*
Tamil ephemeral and light verse (multiple authors)- Collections	894.81110808**

Tamil ephemeral and light verse (multiple authors) - History and criticism	894.81110809**
Tamil epic poetry (multiple authors)	894.8111032*
Tamil epic poetry (multiple authors)- Collections	894.811103208**
Tamil epic poetry (multiple authors)- History and criticism	894.811103209**
Tamil epigrams	***See*** Tamil anecdotes ...
Tamil essays	894.8114
Tamil essays (multiple authors) - to 1845	***See*** Main schedule
Tamil essays (multiple authors) -1845-1895	894.81144+
Tamil essays (multiple authors) -1895-1919	894.81145+
Tamil essays (multiple authors) -1920-1939	894.81146+
Tamil essays (multiple authors) -1940-	894.81147+
Tamil essays (multiple authors) -1940-1999	894.811471+
Tamil essays (multiple authors) -19th century	894.81144+
Tamil essays (multiple authors) –2000-	894.811472+
Tamil essays (multiple authors) -20th century	894.811471+
Tamil essays (multiple authors) -Collections	894.8114008**
Tamil essays (multiple authors) - Dictionaries etc	894.8114003
Tamil essays (multiple authors) - History and criticism	894.8114009**
Tamil essays (multiple authors) - Periodicals	894.8114005
Tamil essays (multiple authors) - Philosophy and theory	894.8114001

Tamil essays (multiple authors) - Psychological aspects	894.81140019
Tamil essays (multiple authors) -Research	894.81140072
Tamil essays (multiple authors) - Study and teaching	894.8114007
Tamil essays (multiple authors) -Value	894.81140013
Tamil essays (single author)- - to 1845	***See*** Main schedule
Tamil essays (single author)- 1845 -1895	894.8114 4
Tamil essays (single author)- 1895 - 1919	894.8114 5
Tamil essays (single author)- 1920 - 1939	894.8114 6
Tamil essays (single author)- 1940 -	894.8114 7
Tamil essays (single author)- 1940-1999	894.8114 71
Tamil essays (single author)- 19th century	894.8114 4
Tamil essays (single author)- 2000-	894.8114 72
Tamil essays (single author)- 20th century	894.8114 71
Tamil experimental and non-formalized works (single author)	894.8118+CD+07
Tamil experimental and non-formalized works (multiple authors)	894.811807
Tamil fantasy fiction (multiple authors)	894.811308766*
Tamil fantasy fiction (multiple authors)- Collections	894.81130876608**
Tamil fantasy fiction (multiple authors)- History and criticism	894.81130876609**
Tamil farce (multiple authors)	894.811205232*
Tamil farce (multiple authors)- Collections	894.81120523208**

Tamil farce (multiple authors)- History and criticism	894.81120523209**
Tamil fiction	894.8113
Tamil fiction (multiple authors)– - to 1845	***See*** Main schedule
Tamil fiction (multiple authors) - 1845-1895	894.81134+
Tamil fiction (multiple authors) - 1895-1919	894.81135+
Tamil fiction (multiple authors) - 1920-1939	894.81136+
Tamil fiction (multiple authors) - 1940-	894.81137+
Tamil fiction (multiple authors) - 1940-1999	894.811371+
Tamil fiction (multiple authors) - 19th century	894.81134+
Tamil fiction (multiple authors) – 2000-	894.811372+
Tamil fiction (multiple authors) - 20th century	894.811371+
Tamil fiction (multiple authors) - Collections	894.8113008**
Tamil fiction (multiple authors) - Dictionaries etc	894.8113003
Tamil fiction (multiple authors) - History and criticism	894.8113009**
Tamil fiction (multiple authors) - Periodicals	894.8113005
Tamil fiction (multiple authors) - Philosophy and theory	894.8113001
Tamil fiction (multiple authors) - Psychological aspects	894.81130019
Tamil fiction (multiple authors) - Research	894.81130072
Tamil fiction (multiple authors) - Study and teaching	894.8113007
Tamil fiction (multiple authors) - Value	894.81130013
Tamil fiction (single author)- - to 1845	***See*** Main schedule

Tamil fiction (single author)- 1845 -1895	894.8113 4
Tamil fiction (single author)- 1895 - 1919	894.8113 5
Tamil fiction (single author)- 1920 - 1939	894.8113 6
Tamil fiction (single author)- 1940 -	894.8113 7
Tamil fiction (single author)- 1940-1999	894.8113 71
Tamil fiction (single author)- 19th century	894.8113 4
Tamil fiction (single author)- 2000-	894.8113 72
Tamil fiction (single author)- 20th century	894.8113 71
Tamil folk music	781 629 4811
Tamil ghost fiction (multiple authors)	894.811308733*
Tamil ghost fiction (multiple authors) - Collections	894.81130873308**
Tamil ghost fiction (multiple authors)- History and criticism	894.81130873309**
Tamil graffiti	***See*** Tamil anecdotes ...
Tamil historical drama (multiple authors)	894.81120514*
Tamil historical drama (multiple authors)- Collections	894.8112051408**
Tamil historical drama (multiple authors)- History and criticism	894.8112051409**
Tamil historical fiction (multiple authors)	894.8113081*
Tamil historical fiction (multiple authors)- Collections	894.811308108**
Tamil historical fiction (multiple authors)- History and criticism	894.811308109**
Tamil horror fiction (multiple authors)	894.811308738*

Tamil horror fiction (multiple authors)-Collections	894.81130873808**
Tamil horror fiction (multiple authors)-History and criticism	894.81130873809**
Tamil humour and satire	894. 811 7
Tamil humour and satire (multiple authors) — to 1845	***See*** Main schedule
Tamil humour and satire (multiple authors) -1845-1895	894.81174+
Tamil humour and satire (multiple authors) -1895-1919	894.81175+
Tamil humour and satire (multiple authors) -1920-1939	894.81176+
Tamil humour and satire (multiple authors) -1940-	894.81177+
Tamil humour and satire (multiple authors) -1940-1999	894.811771+
Tamil humour and satire (multiple authors) -19th century	894.81174+
Tamil humour and satire (multiple authors) –2000-	894.811772+
Tamil humour and satire (multiple authors) -20th century	894.811771+
Tamil humour and satire (multiple authors) -Collections	894.8117008**
Tamil humour and satire (multiple authors) -Dictionaries etc	894.8117003
Tamil humour and satire (multiple authors) -History and criticism	894.8117009**

Tamil humour and satire (multiple authors) -Periodicals	894.8117005
Tamil humour and satire (multiple authors) -Philosophy and theory	894.8117001
Tamil humour and satire (multiple authors) -Psychological aspects	894.81170019
Tamil humour and satire (multiple authors) -Research	894.81170072
Tamil humour and satire (multiple authors) -Study and teaching	894.8117007
Tamil humour and satire (multiple authors) -Value	894.81170013
Tamil humour and satire (multiple authors)	894.8117
Tamil humourous and satirical poetry (multiple authors)	894.811107*
Tamil humourous and satirical poetry (multiple authors)- Collections	894.81110708**
Tamil humourous and satirical poetry (multiple authors)- History and criticism	894.81110709**
Tamil jokes	***See*** Tamil anecdotes ...
Tamil language	494.811
Tamil language- Applied linguistics	494.8118
Tamil language- Bilingual dictionaries	494.81132-39
Tamil language- Bilingualism	494.811042
Tamil language- Concordances	494.81103
Tamil language- Content analysis	494.811014 1
Tamil language- Dictionaries	494.8113

Tamil language- Discourse analysis	494.811014 1
Tamil language- Education	494.811071
Tamil language- Encyclopaedias	494.81103
Tamil language- Etymology	494.8112
Tamil language- Functionalism	494.811018
Tamil language- Grammar	494.8115
Tamil language- History	494.81109
Tamil language- Intonation	494.81116
Tamil language- Lexicography	494.811302 8
Tamil language- Lexicology	494.811014
Tamil language- Miscellany	494.81102
Tamil language- Multilingualism	494.811042
Tamil language- Organizations	494.81106
Tamil language- Orthography	494.811152
Tamil language- Pauses	494.81116
Tamil language- Periodicals	494.81105
Tamil language- Persons (men, women, etc)	494.81108
Tamil language- Philosophy and theory	494.81101
Tamil language- Phonetics	494.811158
Tamil language- Phonology	494.81115
Tamil language- Pitch	494.81116
Tamil language- Pronunciation	494.811152
Tamil language- Research	494.811072
Tamil language- Rhetoric	808.049 4811
Tamil language- Schools and theories of linguistics	494.811018

Tamil language- Semantics	494.811014 3
Tamil language- Semiotics	494.811014 1
Tamil language- Slang	494.8117
Tamil language- Special topics	494.81104
Tamil language- Specialized dictionaries	494.81131
Tamil language- Spelling	494.811152
Tamil language- Stress	494.81116
Tamil language- Structural linguistics	494.811018
Tamil language- Suprasegmental features	494.81116
Tamil language- Terminology	494.811014
Tamil language- Usage	494.8118
Tamil language- Variations (Dialects etc)	494.8117
Tamil language- Writing systems	494.81111
Tamil letters	894.8116
Tamil letters (multiple authors) - - to 1845	***See*** Main schedule
Tamil letters (multiple authors) -1845-1895	894.81164+
Tamil letters (multiple authors) -1895-1919	894.81165+
Tamil letters (multiple authors) -1920-1939	894.81166+
Tamil letters (multiple authors) -1940-	894.81167+
Tamil letters (multiple authors) -1940-1999	894.811671+
Tamil letters (multiple authors) -19th century	894.81164+
Tamil letters (multiple authors) –2000-	894.811672+
Tamil letters (multiple authors) -20th century	894.811671+
Tamil letters (multiple authors) -Collections	894.8116008**
Tamil letters (multiple authors) - Dictionaries etc	894.8116003

Tamil letters (multiple authors) - History and criticism	894.8116009**
Tamil letters (multiple authors) -Periodicals	894.8116005
Tamil letters (multiple authors) - Philosophy and theory	894.8116001
Tamil letters (multiple authors) - Psychological aspects	894.81160019
Tamil letters (multiple authors) -Research	894.81160072
Tamil letters (multiple authors) - Study and teaching	894.8116007
Tamil letters (multiple authors) -Value	894.81160013
Tamil letters (single author)- - to 1845	***See*** Main schedule
Tamil letters (single author)- 1845 -1895	894.8116 4
Tamil letters (single author)- 1895 - 1919	894.8116 5
Tamil letters (single author)- 1920 - 1939	894.8116 6
Tamil letters (single author)- 1940 -	894.8116 7
Tamil letters (single author)- 1940-1999	894.8116 71
Tamil letters (single author)- 19th century	894.8116 4
Tamil letters (single author)- 2000-	894.8116 72
Tamil letters (single author)- 20th century	894.8116 71
Tamil light verse	***See*** Tamil ephemeral and light verse
Tamil limericks (multiple authors)	894.8111075*
Tamil limericks (multiple authors)- Collections	894.811107508**
Tamil limericks (multiple authors)- History and criticism	894.811107509**

Tamil literature	894.811
Tamil literature (collections of multiple forms) - 19th century	894.8110804
Tamil literature (collections of multiple forms) - 20th century	894.81108071
Tamil literature (collections of multiple forms) – 21st century	894.81108072
Tamil literature (collections of multiple forms) - Allegory	894.81108015
Tamil literature (collections of multiple forms) - Animals	894.811080362++
Tamil literature (collections of multiple forms) - Artistic themes	894.811080357
Tamil literature (collections of multiple forms) - Atmosphere	894.81108032161
Tamil literature (collections of multiple forms) - Characters	894.81108027
Tamil literature (collections of multiple forms) - Comedy	894.81108017
Tamil literature (collections of multiple forms) - Evening	894.81108033
Tamil literature (collections of multiple forms) - Fantasy	894.81108015
Tamil literature (collections of multiple forms) - Forests	894.81108032152
Tamil literature (collections of multiple forms) - Historical themes	894.811080358
Tamil literature (collections of multiple forms) - Horror	894.811080164

Tamil literature (collections of multiple forms) - Human characteristics (Biological, moral, psychological)	894.811080353
Tamil literature (collections of multiple forms) - Legendary objects/themes	894.81108037
Tamil literature (collections of multiple forms) - Literary themes	894.811080357
Tamil literature (collections of multiple forms) - Love	894.8110803543
Tamil literature (collections of multiple forms) - Marriage	894.8110803543
Tamil literature (collections of multiple forms) - Morning	894.81108033
Tamil literature (collections of multiple forms) - Mountains	894.81108032143
Tamil literature (collections of multiple forms) - Myth	894.81108015
Tamil literature (collections of multiple forms) - Mythological objects/themes	894.81108037
Tamil literature (collections of multiple forms) - Philosophic themes	894.811080384
Tamil literature (collections of multiple forms) - Places	894.81108032++
Tamil literature (collections of multiple forms) - Plants	894.811080364
Tamil literature (collections of multiple forms) - Political themes	894.811080358
Tamil literature (collections of multiple forms) - Religious themes	894.811080382++
Tamil literature (collections of multiple forms) - Rivers	894.811080321693

Tamil literature (collections of multiple forms) - Romanticism	894.811080145
Tamil literature (collections of multiple forms) - Scientific themes	894.811080356
Tamil literature (collections of multiple forms) - Sea	894.81108032162
Tamil literature (collections of multiple forms) - Seasons	894.81108033
Tamil literature (collections of multiple forms) - Sex	894.8110803538
Tamil literature (collections of multiple forms) - Social themes	894.811080355
Tamil literature (collections of multiple forms) - Space	894.8110803219
Tamil literature (collections of multiple forms) - Specific kinds of persons, e.g. heroes	894.811080352++
Tamil literature (collections of multiple forms) - Specific persons (real or imaginary)	894.811080351
Tamil literature (collections of multiple forms) - Stream of consciousness	894.81108025
Tamil literature (collections of multiple forms) - Supernatural objects/themes	894.81108037
Tamil literature (collections of multiple forms) - Symbolism	894.81108015
Tamil literature (collections of multiple forms) - Technical themes	894.811080356
Tamil literature (collections of multiple forms) - Times (seasons, parts of day, etc)	894.81108033
Tamil literature (collections of multiple forms) - Towns	894.811080321732

Tamil literature (collections of multiple forms) - Tragedy	894.811080162
Tamil literature (collections of multiple forms) - Villages	894.811080321734
Tamil literature (collections of multiple forms) - Weather	894.81108036
Tamil literature (collections of multiple forms) emphasizing subjects	894.8110804++
Tamil literature (collections of multiple forms) for/by children	894.8110809282
Tamil literature (collections of multiple forms) for/by persons of racial, ethnic and national groups	894.8110808++
Tamil literature (collections of multiple forms) for/by persons of specific classes	894.81108092++
Tamil literature (collections of multiple forms) for/by persons resident in specific regions	894.81108091++
Tamil literature (collections of multiple forms) for/by women	894.8110809287
Tamil literature (multiple authors) - Concordances	894.81103
Tamil literature (multiple authors) - Dictionaries	894.81103
Tamil literature (multiple authors) - Education	894.811071
Tamil literature (multiple authors) - Encyclopaedias	894.81103
Tamil literature (multiple authors) - Organizations	894.81106

Tamil literature (multiple authors) - Periodicals	894.81105
Tamil literature (multiple authors) - Philosophy and theory	894.81101
Tamil literature (multiple authors) - Research	894.811072
Tamil literature (multiple authors) - Research in India	894.811072054
Tamil literature (multiple authors) - Study and teaching	894.81107
Tamil literature (multiple forms) - 19th century	894.81109004
Tamil literature (multiple forms) – 2000-	894.811090072
Tamil literature (multiple forms) - 20th century	894.811090071
Tamil literature (multiple forms) - Allegory – History and criticism	894.8110915
Tamil literature (multiple forms) - Animals - History and criticism	894.81109362++
Tamil literature (multiple forms) - Artistic themes - History and criticism	894.81109357
Tamil literature (multiple forms) - Atmosphere - History and criticism	894.8110932161
Tamil literature (multiple forms) - Characters - History and criticism	894.8110927
Tamil literature (multiple forms) - Comedy - History and criticism	894.8110917
Tamil literature (multiple forms) - Evening - History and criticism	894.8110933
Tamil literature (multiple forms) - Fantasy - History , description, criticism	894.8110915

Tamil literature (multiple forms) - Forests - History and criticism	894.8110932152
Tamil literature (multiple forms) - Historical themes - History and criticism	894.81109358
Tamil literature (multiple forms) - History and criticism	894.81109
Tamil literature (multiple forms) - Horror - History and criticism	894.81109164
Tamil literature (multiple forms) - Human characteristics (Biological, moral, psychological) - History and criticism	894.81109353
Tamil literature (multiple forms) - Legendary objects/themes - History and criticism	894.8110937
Tamil literature (multiple forms) - Literary themes - History and criticism	894.81109357
Tamil literature (multiple forms) - Love - History and criticism	894.811093543
Tamil literature (multiple forms) - Marriage - History and criticism	894.811093543
Tamil literature (multiple forms) - Morning - History and criticism	894.8110933
Tamil literature (multiple forms) - Mountains - History and criticism	894.8110932143
Tamil literature (multiple forms) - Myth - History and criticism	894.8110915
Tamil literature (multiple forms) - Mythological objects/themes - History and criticism	894.8110937
Tamil literature (multiple forms) - Persons of racial, ethnic and national groups - History and criticism	894.811098++

Tamil literature (multiple forms) - Persons of specific classes - History and criticism	894.8110992++
Tamil literature (multiple forms) - Persons resident in specific regions -History and criticism	894.8110991++
Tamil literature (multiple forms) - Philosophic themes - History and criticism	894.81109384
Tamil literature (multiple forms) - Places - History and criticism	894.8110932++
Tamil literature (multiple forms) - Plants - History and criticism	894.81109364
Tamil literature (multiple forms) - Political themes - History and criticism	894.81109358
Tamil literature (multiple forms) - Religious themes - History and criticism	894.81109382++
Tamil literature (multiple forms) - Rivers - History and criticism	894.81109321693
Tamil literature (multiple forms) - Romanticism - History and criticism	894.81109145
Tamil literature (multiple forms) - Scientific themes - History and criticism	894.81109356
Tamil literature (multiple forms) - Sea - History and criticism	894.8110932162
Tamil literature (multiple forms) - Seasons - History and criticism	894.8110933
Tamil literature (multiple forms) - Sex - History and criticism	894.811093538
Tamil literature (multiple forms) - Social themes - History and criticism	894.81109355
Tamil literature (multiple forms) - Space - History and criticism	894.811093219

Tamil literature (multiple forms) - Specific kinds of persons, e.g. heroes, - History and criticism	894.81109352++
Tamil literature (multiple forms) - Specific persons - History and criticism	894.81109351
Tamil literature (multiple forms) - Stream of consciousness - History and criticism	894.8110925
Tamil literature (multiple forms) - Subjects - History and criticism	894.811094++
Tamil literature (multiple forms) - Supernatural objects/themes - History and criticism	894.8110937
Tamil literature (multiple forms) - Symbolism- History , description, criticism	894.8110915
Tamil literature (multiple forms) - Technical themes - History and criticism	894.81109356
Tamil literature (multiple forms) - Times - History and criticism	894.8110933
Tamil literature (multiple forms) - Towns - History and criticism	894.81109321732
Tamil literature (multiple forms) - Tragedy - History and criticism	894.81109162
Tamil literature (multiple forms) - Villages - History and criticism	894.81109321734
Tamil literature (multiple forms) - Weather - History and criticism	894.8110936
Tamil literature (single author) - - to 1845 - Biography, collections, criticism	***See*** Main schedule
Tamil literature (single author)- 1845 - 1895 - Biography, collections, criticism	894.8118 409

Tamil literature (single author)- 1895 - 1919 - Biography, collections, criticism	894.8118 509
Tamil literature (single author)- 1920 - 1939 - Biography, collections, criticism	894.8118 609
Tamil literature (single author)- 1940 - Biography, collections, criticism	894.8118 709
Tamil literature (single author)- 1940- 1999 - Biography, collections, criticism	894.8118 7109
Tamil literature (single author)- 19th century- Biography, collections, criticism	894.8118 409
Tamil literature (single author)- 2000- Biography, collections, criticism	894.8118 7209
Tamil literature (single author)- 20th century - Biography, collections, criticism	894.8118 7109
Tamil literature for/by children - History and criticism	894.811099282
Tamil literature for/by women - History and criticism	894.811099287
Tamil love fiction (multiple authors)	894.8113085*
Tamil love fiction (multiple authors)- Collections	894.811308508**
Tamil love fiction (multiple authors)- History and criticism	894.811308509**
Tamil melodrama (multiple authors)	894.81120527*
Tamil melodrama (multiple authors)- Collections	894.8112052708**
Tamil melodrama (multiple authors)- History and criticism	894.8112052709**
Tamil miscellaneous writings	894.8118

Tamil miscellaneous writings (multiple authors) - to 1845	***See*** Main schedule
Tamil miscellaneous writings (multiple authors) -1845-1895	894.81184++
Tamil miscellaneous writings (multiple authors) -1895-1919	894.81185++
Tamil miscellaneous writings (multiple authors) -1920-1939	894.81186++
Tamil miscellaneous writings (multiple authors) -1940-	894.81187++
Tamil miscellaneous writings (multiple authors) -1940-1999	894.811871++
Tamil miscellaneous writings (multiple authors) -19th century	894.81184++
Tamil miscellaneous writings (multiple authors) –2000-	894.811872++
Tamil miscellaneous writings (multiple authors) -20th century	894.811871++
Tamil miscellaneous writings (multiple authors) -Collections	894.8118008**
Tamil miscellaneous writings (multiple authors) -Dictionaries etc	894.8118003
Tamil miscellaneous writings (multiple authors) -History and criticism	894.8118009**
Tamil miscellaneous writings (multiple authors) -Periodicals	894.8118005
Tamil miscellaneous writings (multiple authors) -Philosophy and theory	894.8118001
Tamil miscellaneous writings (multiple authors) -Psychological aspects	894.81180019

Tamil miscellaneous writings (multiple authors) -Research	894.81180072
Tamil miscellaneous writings (multiple authors) -Study and teaching	894.8118007
Tamil miscellaneous writings (multiple authors) -Value	894.81180013
Tamil miscellaneous writings (single author)- - to 1845	***See*** Main schedule
Tamil miscellaneous writings (single author)- 1845 -1895	894.8118 4
Tamil miscellaneous writings (single author)- 1895 - 1919	894.8118 5
Tamil miscellaneous writings (single author)- 1920 - 1939	894.8118 6
Tamil miscellaneous writings (single author)- 1940 -	894.8118 7
Tamil miscellaneous writings (single author)- 1940-1999	894.8118 71
Tamil miscellaneous writings (single author)- 19th century	894.8118 4
Tamil miscellaneous writings (single author)- 2000-	894.8118 72
Tamil miscellaneous writings (single author)- 20th century	894.8118 71
Tamil monologues (multiple authors)	894.8112045*
Tamil monologues (multiple authors)- Collections	894.811204508**
Tamil monologues (multiple authors)- History and criticism	894.811204509**

Tamil morality plays	***See*** Tamil religious ... plays
Tamil mystery fiction (multiple authors)	894.81130872*
Tamil mystery fiction (multiple authors)- Collections	894.8113087208**
Tamil mystery fiction (multiple authors)- History and criticism	894.8113087209**
Tamil Nadu- Architecture	720.954 82
Tamil Nadu- Budget	352.495 482
Tamil Nadu- Economic development	338.954 82
Tamil Nadu- Economic geography	330.954 82
Tamil Nadu- Education	370.954 82
Tamil Nadu- Fauna	591.954 82
Tamil Nadu- Flora	581.954 82
Tamil Nadu- Folk dancing	793.319 5482
Tamil Nadu- Geography	915.482
Tamil Nadu- Geology	555.482
Tamil Nadu- History	954.82
Tamil Nadu- Painting and paintings	759.954 82
Tamil Nadu- Public administration	351.548 2
Tamil Nadu- Public finance	336.548 2
Tamil Nadu- Sculpture	730.954 82
Tamil narrative poetry (multiple authors)	894.811103*
Tamil narrative poetry (multiple authors)- Collections	894.81110308**
Tamil narrative poetry (multiple authors)- History and criticism	894.81110309**

Tamil notebooks	***See*** Tamil diaries …
Tamil odes (multiple authors)	894.8111043*
Tamil odes (multiple authors)- Collections	894.811104308**
Tamil odes (multiple authors)- History and criticism	894.811104309**
Tamil one act plays (multiple authors)	894.811 204 1*
Tamil one act plays (multiple authors)- Collections	894.811 204 108**
Tamil one act plays (multiple authors)- History and criticism	894.811 204 109**
Tamil oratory (multiple authors)	***See*** Tamil public speeches
Tamil periodicals	059.94811
Tamil poetry	894.8111
Tamil poetry (multiple authors) - - to 1845 schedule	***See*** Main
Tamil poetry (multiple authors) - 1845-1895	894.81114+
Tamil poetry (multiple authors) - 1895-1919	894.81115+
Tamil poetry (multiple authors) - 1920-1939	894.81116+
Tamil poetry (multiple authors) - 1940-	894.81117+
Tamil poetry (multiple authors) - 1940-1999	894.811171+
Tamil poetry (multiple authors) - 19th century	894.81114+
Tamil poetry (multiple authors) – 2000-	894.811172+
Tamil poetry (multiple authors) - 20th century	894.811171+
Tamil poetry (multiple authors)- Collections	894.8111008**
Tamil poetry (multiple authors)- Dictionaries etc	894.8111003

Tamil poetry (multiple authors)- History and criticism	894.8111009**
Tamil poetry (multiple authors)- Periodicals	894.8111005
Tamil poetry (multiple authors)- Philosophy and theory	894.8111001
Tamil poetry (multiple authors)- Psychological aspects	894.81110019
Tamil poetry (multiple authors)- Research	894.81110072
Tamil poetry (multiple authors)- Study and teaching	894.8111007
Tamil poetry (multiple authors)- Value	894.81110013
Tamil poetry (single author)- - to 1845	***See*** Main schedule
Tamil poetry (single author)- 1845 -1895	894.8111 4
Tamil poetry (single author)- 1895 - 1919	894.8111 5
Tamil poetry (single author)- 1920 - 1939	894.8111 6
Tamil poetry (single author)- 1940 -	894.8111 7
Tamil poetry (single author)- 1940-1999	894.8111 71
Tamil poetry (single author)- 19th century	894.8111 4
Tamil poetry (single author)- 2000-	894.8111 72
Tamil poetry (single author)- 20th century	894.8111 71
Tamil prose (single author)- - to 1845	***See*** Main schedule
Tamil prose (single author)- 1845 -1895	894.8118 408
Tamil prose (single author)- 1895 - 1919	894.8118 508
Tamil prose (single author)- 1920 - 1939	894.8118 608
Tamil prose (single author)- 1940 -	894.8118 708
Tamil prose (single author)- 1940-1999	894.8118 7108

Tamil prose (single author)- 19th century	894.8118 408
Tamil prose (single author)- 2000-	894.8118 7208
Tamil prose (single author)- 20th century	894.8118 7108
Tamil prose literature (multiple authors)	894.811808
Tamil psychological, realistic, sociological fiction (multiple authors)	894.8113083*
Tamil psychological, realistic, sociological fiction (multiple authors)- Collections	894.811308308**
Tamil psychological, realistic, sociological fiction (multiple authors)- History and criticism	894.811308309**
Tamil public discussions	***See*** Tamil debates ...
Tamil public speeches (multiple authors)	894.811501
Tamil public speeches (multiple authors)- Collections	894.81150108*
Tamil public speeches (multiple authors)- History and criticism	894.81150109*
Tamil quotations	***See*** Tamil anecdotes ...
Tamil realistic fiction	***See*** Tamil psychological... fiction
Tamil recitations (multiple authors)	894.811504+
Tamil religious and morality plays (multiple authors)	894.81120516+
Tamil reminiscences	***See*** Tamil diaries...
Tamil romantic fiction (multiple authors)	894.8113085*

Tamil romantic fiction (multiple authors)- Collections	894.811308508**
Tamil romantic fiction (multiple authors)- History and criticism	894.811308509**
Tamil satire	***See*** Tamil humour ...
Tamil satirical poetry	***See*** Tamil humourous ... poetry
Tamil science fiction (multiple authors)	894.811308762*
Tamil science fiction (multiple authors)	894.81130876208**
Tamil science fiction (multiple authors)	894.81130876209**
Tamil serious drama (multiple authors)	894.8112051+
Tamil short stories (multiple authors)	894.811301*
Tamil short stories (multiple authors)- Collections	894.81130108**
Tamil short stories (multiple authors)- History and criticism	894.81130109**
Tamil sociological fiction (multiple authors)	***See*** Tamil psychological... fiction
Tamil sonnets (multiple authors)	894.8111042*
Tamil sonnets (multiple authors)- Collections	894.811104208**
Tamil sonnets (multiple authors)- History and criticism	894.811104209**
Tamil speaking people	305.794 811
Tamil speeches	894.8115
Tamil speeches (multiple authors) — to 1845	***See*** Main schedule

Tamil speeches (multiple authors) - 1845-1895	894.81154+
Tamil speeches (multiple authors) - 1895-1919	894.81155+
Tamil speeches (multiple authors) - 1920-1939	894.81156+
Tamil speeches (multiple authors) -1940-	894.81157+
Tamil speeches (multiple authors) - 1940-1999	894.811571+
Tamil speeches (multiple authors) - 19th century	894.81154+
Tamil speeches (multiple authors) –2000-	894.811572+
Tamil speeches (multiple authors) - 20th century	894.811571+
Tamil speeches (multiple authors) - Collections	894.8115008**
Tamil speeches (multiple authors) - Dictionaries etc	894.8115003
Tamil speeches (multiple authors) - History and criticism	894.8115009**
Tamil speeches (multiple authors) - Periodicals	894.8115005
Tamil speeches (multiple authors) - Philosophy and theory	894.8115001
Tamil speeches (multiple authors) - Psychological aspects	894.81150019
Tamil speeches (multiple authors) - Research	894.81150072
Tamil speeches (multiple authors) - Study and teaching	894.8115007

Tamil speeches (multiple authors) -Value	894.81150013
Tamil speeches (single author)- - to 1845	***See*** Main schedule
Tamil speeches (single author)- 1845 -1895	894.8115 4
Tamil speeches (single author)- 1895 - 1919	894.8115 5
Tamil speeches (single author)- 1920 - 1939	894.8115 6
Tamil speeches (single author)- 1940 -	894.8115 7
Tamil speeches (single author)- 1940-1999	894.8115 71
Tamil speeches (single author)- 19th century	894.8115 4
Tamil speeches (single author)- 2000-	894.8115 72
Tamil speeches (single author)- 20th century	894.8115 71
Tamil suspense fiction (multiple authors)	894.81130872*
Tamil suspense fiction (multiple authors)- Collections	894.8113087208**
Tamil suspense fiction (multiple authors)- History and criticism	894.8113087209**
Tamil tragedy (multiple authors)	894.81120512*
Tamil tragedy (multiple authors)- Collections	894.8112051208**
Tamil tragedy (multiple authors)- History and criticism	894.8112051209**
Tamil variety drama (multiple authors)	894.8112057*
Tamil variety drama (multiple authors)- Collections	894.811205708**
Tamil variety drama (multiple authors)- History and criticism	894.811205709**
Tamils	305.894 811
Tantric Buddhism	294.392 5

Tantric Buddhism- Doctrines	294.342 0425
Tantric Hinduism	294.551 4
Technology and Buddhism	294.337 5
Technology and Hinduism	294.517 5
Technology and Jainism	294.417 5
Technology and Sikhism	294.617 5
Telugu (people)	305.894 827
Telugu adventure fiction (multiple authors)	894.8273087*
Telugu adventure fiction (multiple authors) - Collections	894.827308708**
Telugu adventure fiction (multiple authors)- History and criticism	894.827308709**
Telugu anecdotes, epigrams, graffiti, jokes, quotations (multiple authors)	894.827802
Telugu anecdotes, epigrams, graffiti, jokes, quotations (single author)	894.8278+CD+02
Telugu as second language in elementary education in elementary education	372.659 482 7
Telugu ballads (multiple authors)	894.8271044*
Telugu ballads (multiple authors)- Collections	894.827104408**
Telugu ballads (multiple authors)- History and criticism	894.827104409**
Telugu comedy (multiple authors)	894.82720523*
Telugu comedy (multiple authors) - Collections	894.8272052308**
Telugu comedy (multiple authors) - History and criticism	894.8272052309**

Telugu conversations (multiple authors)	894.827506*
Telugu conversations (multiple authors) - Collections	894.82750608**
Telugu conversations (multiple authors) - History and criticism	894.82750609**
Telugu debates and public discussions (multiple authors)	894.827503*
Telugu debates and public discussions (multiple authors)- Collections	894.82750308**
Telugu debates and public discussions (multiple authors)- History and criticism	894.82750309**
Telugu detective fiction (multiple authors)	894.82730872*
Telugu detective fiction (multiple authors) - Collections	894.8273087208**
Telugu detective fiction (multiple authors) - History and criticism	894.8273087209**
Telugu diaries, notebooks, reminiscences (multiple authors)	894.827803
Telugu diaries, notebooks, reminiscences (single author)	894.8278@
Telugu didactic poetry (multiple authors)	894.827105*
Telugu didactic poetry (multiple authors)- Collections	894.82710508**
Telugu didactic poetry (multiple authors)- History and criticism	894.82710509**
Telugu drama	894.8272
Telugu drama (multiple authors) - - to 1845	***See*** Main schedule
Telugu drama (multiple authors) - 1845-1895	894.82724+
Telugu drama (multiple authors) - 1895-1919	894.82725+

Telugu drama (multiple authors) - 1920-1939	894.82726+
Telugu drama (multiple authors) - 1940-	894.82727+
Telugu drama (multiple authors) - 1940-1999	894.827271+
Telugu drama (multiple authors) - 19th century	894.82724+
Telugu drama (multiple authors) – 2000-	894.827272+
Telugu drama (multiple authors) - 20th century	894.827271+
Telugu drama (multiple authors) - Collections	894.8272008**
Telugu drama (multiple authors) - Dictionaries etc	894.8272003
Telugu drama (multiple authors) - History and criticism	894.8272009**
Telugu drama (multiple authors) - Periodicals	894.8272005
Telugu drama (multiple authors) - Philosophy and theory	894.8272001
Telugu drama (multiple authors) - Psychological aspects	894.82720019
Telugu drama (multiple authors) - Research	894.82720072
Telugu drama (multiple authors) - Study and teaching	894.8272007
Telugu drama (multiple authors) - Value	894.82720013
Telugu drama (single author) - to 1845 schedule	***See*** Main
Telugu drama (single author)- 1845 -1895	894.8272 4
Telugu drama (single author)- 1895 - 1919	894.8272 5

Telugu drama (single author)- 1920 1939	894.8272 6
Telugu drama (single author)- 1940 -	894.8272 7
Telugu drama (single author)- 1940-1999	894.8272 71
Telugu drama (single author)- 19th century	894.8272 4
Telugu drama (single author)- 2000-	894.8272 72
Telugu drama (single author)- 20th century	894.8272 71
Telugu drama for cinema (multiple authors)	894.827203*
Telugu drama for cinema (multiple authors) - Collections	894.82720308**
Telugu drama for cinema (multiple authors) - History and criticism	894.82720309**
Telugu drama for radio (multiple authors)	894.8272022*
Telugu drama for radio (multiple authors) - Collections	894.827202208**
Telugu drama for radio (multiple authors) - History and criticism	894.827202209**
Telugu drama for television (multiple authors)	894.8272025*
Telugu drama for television (multiple authors) - Collections	894.827202508**
Telugu drama for television (multiple authors) - History and criticism	894.827202509**
Telugu dramatic poetry (multiple authors)	894.827102*
Telugu dramatic poetry (multiple authors)- Collections	894.82710208**
Telugu dramatic poetry (multiple authors)- History and criticism	894.82710209**
Telugu encyclopaedias	039.94827

Telugu- English dictionary	494.827 321
Telugu ephemeral and light verse (multiple authors)	894.827108*
Telugu ephemeral and light verse (multiple authors)- Collections	894.82710808**
Telugu ephemeral and light verse (multiple authors) - History and criticism	894.82710809**
Telugu epic poetry (multiple authors)	894.8271032*
Telugu epic poetry (multiple authors)- Collections	894.827103208**
Telugu epic poetry (multiple authors)- History and criticism	894.827103209**
Telugu epigrams	***See*** Telugu anecdotes ...
Telugu essays	894.8274
Telugu essays (multiple authors) - to 1845	***See*** Main schedule
Telugu essays (multiple authors) - 1845-1895	894.82744+
Telugu essays (multiple authors) - 1895-1919	894.82745+
Telugu essays (multiple authors) - 1920-1939	894.82746+
Telugu essays (multiple authors) -1940-	894.82747+
Telugu essays (multiple authors) - 1940-1999	894.827471+
Telugu essays (multiple authors) - 19th century	894.82744+
Telugu essays (multiple authors) –2000-	894.827472+
Telugu essays (multiple authors) - 20th century	894.827471+

Telugu essays (multiple authors) - Collections	894.8274008**
Telugu essays (multiple authors) - Dictionaries etc	894.8274003
Telugu essays (multiple authors) - History and criticism	894.8274009**
Telugu essays (multiple authors) - Periodicals	894.8274005
Telugu essays (multiple authors) - Philosophy and theory	894.8274001
Telugu essays (multiple authors) - Psychological aspects	894.82740019
Telugu essays (multiple authors) -Research	894.82740072
Telugu essays (multiple authors) - Study and teaching	894.8274007
Telugu essays (multiple authors) -Value	894.82740013
Telugu essays (single author)- - to 1845	***See*** Main schedule
Telugu essays (single author)- 1845 -1895	894.8274 4
Telugu essays (single author)- 1895 - 1919	894.8274 5
Telugu essays (single author)- 1920 - 1939	894.8274 6
Telugu essays (single author)- 1940 -	894.8274 7
Telugu essays (single author)- 1940-1999	894.8274 71
Telugu essays (single author)- 19th century	894.8274 4
Telugu essays (single author)- 2000-	894.8274 72
Telugu essays (single author)- 20th century	894.8274 71
Telugu experimental and non-formalized works (single author) - 19th century	894.8278 407

Telugu experimental and non-formalized works (single author) - 20th century	894.8278 7107
Telugu experimental and non-formalized works (single author) – 21st century	894.8278 7207
Telugu experimental and non-formalized works (multiple authors)	894.827807
Telugu fantasy fiction (multiple authors)	894.827308766*
Telugu fantasy fiction (multiple authors)-Collections	894.82730876608**
Telugu fantasy fiction (multiple authors)-History and criticism	894.82730876609**
Telugu farce (multiple authors)	894.827205232*
Telugu farce (multiple authors)-Collections	894.82720523208**
Telugu farce (multiple authors)-History and criticism	894.82720523209**
Telugu fiction	894.8273
Telugu fiction (multiple authors) - - to 1845	***See*** Main schedule
Telugu fiction (multiple authors) - 1845-1895	894.82734+
Telugu fiction (multiple authors) - 1895-1919	894.82735+
Telugu fiction (multiple authors) - 1920-1939	894.82736+
Telugu fiction (multiple authors) - 1940-	894.82737+
Telugu fiction (multiple authors) - 1940-1999	894.827371+
Telugu fiction (multiple authors) - 19th century	894.82734+
Telugu fiction (multiple authors) – 2000-	894.827372+
Telugu fiction (multiple authors) - 20th century	894.827371+

Telugu fiction (multiple authors) - Collections	894.8273008**
Telugu fiction (multiple authors) - Dictionaries etc	894.8273003
Telugu fiction (multiple authors) - History and criticism	894.8273009**
Telugu fiction (multiple authors) - Periodicals	894.8273005
Telugu fiction (multiple authors) - Philosophy and theory	894.8273001
Telugu fiction (multiple authors) - Psychological aspects	894.82730019
Telugu fiction (multiple authors) - Research	894.82730072
Telugu fiction (multiple authors) - Study and teaching	894.8273007
Telugu fiction (multiple authors) - Value	894.82730013
Telugu fiction (single author)- - to 1845	***See*** Main schedule
Telugu fiction (single author)- 1845 -1895	894.8273 4
Telugu fiction (single author)- 1895 - 1919	894.8273 5
Telugu fiction (single author)- 1920 - 1939	894.8273 6
Telugu fiction (single author)- 1940 -	894.8273 7
Telugu fiction (single author)- 1940-1999	894.8273 71
Telugu fiction (single author)- 19th century	894.8273 4
Telugu fiction (single author)- 2000-	894.8273 72
Telugu fiction (single author)- 20th century	894.8273 71
Telugu folk music	781 629 4827
Telugu ghost fiction (multiple authors)	894.827308733*
Telugu ghost fiction (multiple authors) - Collections	894.82730873308**

Telugu ghost fiction (multiple authors)-History and criticism	894.82730873309**
Telugu graffiti	***See*** Telugu anecdotes ...
Telugu historical drama (multiple authors)	894.82720514*
Telugu historical drama (multiple authors)-Collections	894.8272051408**
Telugu historical drama (multiple authors)-History and criticism	894.8272051409**
Telugu historical fiction (multiple authors)	894.8273081*
Telugu historical fiction (multiple authors)-Collections	894.827308108**
Telugu historical fiction (multiple authors)-History and criticism	894.827308109**
Telugu horror fiction (multiple authors)	894.827308738*
Telugu horror fiction (multiple authors)-Collections	894.82730873808**
Telugu horror fiction (multiple authors)-History and criticism	894.82730873809**
Telugu humour and satire	894.8277
Telugu humour and satire (multiple authors) - - to 1845	***See*** Main schedule
Telugu humour and satire (multiple authors) -1845-1895	894.82774+
Telugu humour and satire (multiple authors) -1895-1919	894.82775+
Telugu humour and satire (multiple authors) -1920-1939	894.82776+
Telugu humour and satire (multiple authors) -1940-	894.82777+

Telugu humour and satire (multiple authors) -1940-1999	894.827771+
Telugu humour and satire (multiple authors) -19th century	894.82774+
Telugu humour and satire (multiple authors) –2000-	894.827772+
Telugu humour and satire (multiple authors) -20th century	894.827771+
Telugu humour and satire (multiple authors) -Collections	894.8277008**
Telugu humour and satire (multiple authors) -Dictionaries etc	894.8277003
Telugu humour and satire (multiple authors) -History and criticism	894.8277009**
Telugu humour and satire (multiple authors) -Periodicals	894.8277005
Telugu humour and satire (multiple authors) -Philosophy and theory	894.8277001
Telugu humour and satire (multiple authors) -Psychological aspects	894.82770019
Telugu humour and satire (multiple authors) -Research	894.82770072
Telugu humour and satire (multiple authors) -Study and teaching	894.8277007
Telugu humour and satire (multiple authors) -Value	894.82770013
Telugu humourous and satirical poetry (multiple authors)	894.827107*
Telugu humourous and satirical poetry (multiple authors)- Collections	894.82710708**

Telugu humourous and satirical poetry (multiple authors)- History and criticism	894.82710709**
Telugu jokes	***See*** Telugu anecdotes ...
Telugu language	494.827
Telugu language- Applied linguistics	494.8278
Telugu language- Bilingual dictionaries	494.82732-39
Telugu language- Bilingualism	494.827042
Telugu language- Concordances	494.82703
Telugu language- Content analysis	494.827014 1
Telugu language- Dictionaries	494.8273
Telugu language- Discourse analysis	494.827014 1
Telugu language- Education	494.827071
Telugu language- Encyclopaedias	494.82703
Telugu language- Etymology	494.8272
Telugu language- Functionalism	494.827018
Telugu language- Grammar	494.8275
Telugu language- History	494.82709
Telugu language- Intonation	494.82716
Telugu language- Lexicography	494.827302 8
Telugu language- Lexicology	494.827014
Telugu language- Miscellany	494.82702
Telugu language- Multilingualism	494.827042
Telugu language- Organizations	494.82706
Telugu language- Orthography	494.827152

Telugu language- Pauses	494.82716
Telugu language- Periodicals	494.82705
Telugu language- Persons (men, women, etc)	494.82708
Telugu language- Philosophy and theory	494.82701
Telugu language- Phonetics	494.827158
Telugu language- Phonology	494.82715
Telugu language- Pitch	494.82716
Telugu language- Pronunciation	494.827152
Telugu language- Readers	494.827 86
Telugu language- Research	494.827072
Telugu language- Rhetoric	808.049 4827
Telugu language- Schools and theories of linguistics	494.827018
Telugu language- Semantics	494.827014 3
Telugu language- Semiotics	494.827014 1
Telugu language- Slang	494.8277
Telugu language- Special topics	494.82704
Telugu language- Specialized dictionaries	494.82731
Telugu language- Spelling	494.827152
Telugu language- Stress	494.82716
Telugu language- Structural linguistics	494.827018
Telugu language- Suprasegmental features	494.82716
Telugu language- Terminology	494.827014
Telugu language- Usage	494.8278

Telugu language- Variations (Dialects etc)	494.8277
Telugu language- Writing systems	494.82711
Telugu letters	894.8276
Telugu letters (multiple authors) - - to 1845	***See*** Main schedule
Telugu letters (multiple authors) -1845-1895	894.82764+
Telugu letters (multiple authors) -1895-1919	894.82765+
Telugu letters (multiple authors) -1920-1939	894.82766+
Telugu letters (multiple authors) -1940-	894.82767+
Telugu letters (multiple authors) -1940-1999	894.827671+
Telugu letters (multiple authors) - 19th century	894.82764+
Telugu letters (multiple authors) –2000-	894.827672+
Telugu letters (multiple authors) - 20th century	894.827671+
Telugu letters (multiple authors) -Collections	894.8276008**
Telugu letters (multiple authors) - Dictionaries etc	894.8276003
Telugu letters (multiple authors) - History and criticism	894.8276009**
Telugu letters (multiple authors) -Periodicals	894.8276005
Telugu letters (multiple authors) - Philosophy and theory	894.8276001
Telugu letters (multiple authors) - Psychological aspects	894.82760019
Telugu letters (multiple authors) -Research	894.82760072
Telugu letters (multiple authors) - Study and teaching	894.8276007

Telugu letters (multiple authors) -Value	894.82760013
Telugu letters (single author)- - to 1845	***See*** Main schedule
Telugu letters (single author)- 1845 - 1895	894.8276 4
Telugu letters (single author)- 1895 - 1919	894.8276 5
Telugu letters (single author)- 1920 - 1939	894.8276 6
Telugu letters (single author)- 1940 -	894.8276 7
Telugu letters (single author)- 1940-1999	894.8276 71
Telugu letters (single author)- 19th century	894.8276 4
Telugu letters (single author)- 2000-	894.8276 72
Telugu letters (single author)- 20th century	894.8276 71
Telugu light verse	***See*** Telugu ephemeral ... verse
Telugu limericks (multiple authors)	894.8271075*
Telugu limericks (multiple authors)- Collections	894.827107508**
Telugu limericks (multiple authors)- History and criticism	894.827107509**
Telugu literature	894.827
Telugu literature (collections of multiple forms)	894.82708
Telugu literature (collections of multiple forms) - 19th century	894.8270804
Telugu literature (collections of multiple forms) - 20th century	894.82708071
Telugu literature (collections of multiple forms) – 21st century	894.82708072
Telugu literature (collections of multiple forms) - Allegory	894.82708015

Telugu literature (collections of multiple forms) - Animals	894.827080362++
Telugu literature (collections of multiple forms) - Artistic themes	894.827080357
Telugu literature (collections of multiple forms) - Atmosphere	894.82708032161
Telugu literature (collections of multiple forms) - Characters	894.82708027
Telugu literature (collections of multiple forms) - Comedy	894.82708017
Telugu literature (collections of multiple forms) - Evening	894.82708033
Telugu literature (collections of multiple forms) - Fantasy	894.82708015
Telugu literature (collections of multiple forms) - Forests	894.82708032152
Telugu literature (collections of multiple forms) - Historical themes	894.827080358
Telugu literature (collections of multiple forms) - Horror	894.827080164
Telugu literature (collections of multiple forms) - Human characteristics (Biological, moral, psychological)	894.827080353
Telugu literature (collections of multiple forms) - Legendary objects/themes	894.82708037
Telugu literature (collections of multiple forms) - Literary themes	894.827080357
Telugu literature (collections of multiple forms) - Love	894.8270803543
Telugu literature (collections of multiple forms) - Marriage	894.8270803543

Telugu literature (collections of multiple forms) - Morning	894.82708033
Telugu literature (collections of multiple forms) - Mountains	894.82708032143
Telugu literature (collections of multiple forms) - Myth	894.82708015
Telugu literature (collections of multiple forms) - Mythological objects/themes	894.82708037
Telugu literature (collections of multiple forms) - Philosophic themes	894.827080384
Telugu literature (collections of multiple forms) - Places	894.82708032++
Telugu literature (collections of multiple forms) - Plants	894.827080364
Telugu literature (collections of multiple forms) - Political themes	894.827080358
Telugu literature (collections of multiple forms) - Religious themes	894.827080382++
Telugu literature (collections of multiple forms) - Rivers	894.827080321693
Telugu literature (collections of multiple forms) - Romanticism	894.827080145
Telugu literature (collections of multiple forms) - Scientific themes	894.827080356
Telugu literature (collections of multiple forms) - Sea	894.82708032162
Telugu literature (collections of multiple forms) - Seasons	894.82708033
Telugu literature (collections of multiple forms) - Sex	894.8270803538

Telugu literature (collections of multiple forms) - Social themes	894.827080355
Telugu literature (collections of multiple forms) - Space	894.8270803219
Telugu literature (collections of multiple forms) - Specific kinds of persons, e.g. heroes	894.827080352++
Telugu literature (collections of multiple forms) - Specific persons (real or imaginary)	894.827080351
Telugu literature (collections of multiple forms) - Stream of consciousness	894.82708025
Telugu literature (collections of multiple forms) - Supernatural objects/themes	894.82708037
Telugu literature (collections of multiple forms) - Symbolism	894.82708015
Telugu literature (collections of multiple forms) - Technical themes	894.827080356
Telugu literature (collections of multiple forms) - Times (seasons, parts of day, etc)	894.82708033
Telugu literature (collections of multiple forms) - Towns	894.827080321732
Telugu literature (collections of multiple forms) - Tragedy	894.827080162
Telugu literature (collections of multiple forms) - Villages	894.827080321734
Telugu literature (collections of multiple forms) - Weather	894.82708036
Telugu literature (collections of multiple forms) emphasizing subjects	894.8270804++
Telugu literature (collections of multiple forms) for/by children	894.8270809282

Telugu literature (collections of multiple forms) for/by persons of racial, ethnic and national groups	894.8270808++
Telugu literature (collections of multiple forms) for/by persons of specific classes	894.82708092++
Telugu literature (collections of multiple forms) for/by persons resident in specific regions	894.82708091++
Telugu literature (collections of multiple forms) for/by women	894.8270809287
Telugu literature (multiple authors) - Concordances	894.82703
Telugu literature (multiple authors) - Dictionaries	894.82703
Telugu literature (multiple authors) - Education	894.827071
Telugu literature (multiple authors) - Encyclopaedias	894.82703
Telugu literature (multiple authors) - Organizations	894.82706
Telugu literature (multiple authors) - Periodicals	894.82705
Telugu literature (multiple authors) - Philosophy and theory	894.82701
Telugu literature (multiple authors) - Research	894.827072
Telugu literature (multiple authors) - Research in India	894.827072054
Telugu literature (multiple authors) - Study and teaching	894.82707

Telugu literature (multiple forms) - 19th century	894.82709004
Telugu literature (multiple forms) – 2000-	894.827090072
Telugu literature (multiple forms) - 20th century	894.827090071
Telugu literature (multiple forms) - Allegory – History and criticism	894.8270915
Telugu literature (multiple forms) - Animals - History and criticism	894.82709362++
Telugu literature (multiple forms) - Artistic themes - History and criticism	894.82709357
Telugu literature (multiple forms) - Atmosphere - History and criticism	894.8270932161
Telugu literature (multiple forms) - Characters - History and criticism	894.8270927
Telugu literature (multiple forms) - Comedy - History and criticism	894.8270917
Telugu literature (multiple forms) - Evening - History and criticism	894.8270933
Telugu literature (multiple forms) - Fantasy - History , description, criticism	894.8270915
Telugu literature (multiple forms) - Forests - History and criticism	894.8270932152
Telugu literature (multiple forms) - Historical themes - History and criticism	894.82709358
Telugu literature (multiple forms) - History and criticism	894.82709
Telugu literature (multiple forms) - Horror - History and criticism	894.82709164

Telugu literature (multiple forms) - Human characteristics (Biological, moral, psychological) - History and criticism	894.82709353
Telugu literature (multiple forms) - Legendary objects/themes - History and criticism	894.8270937
Telugu literature (multiple forms) - Literary themes - History and criticism	894.82709357
Telugu literature (multiple forms) - Love - History and criticism	894.827093543
Telugu literature (multiple forms) - Marriage - History and criticism	894.827093543
Telugu literature (multiple forms) - Morning - History and criticism	894.8270933
Telugu literature (multiple forms) - Mountains - History and criticism	894.8270932143
Telugu literature (multiple forms) - Myth - History and criticism	894.8270915
Telugu literature (multiple forms) - Mythological objects/themes - History and criticism	894.8270937
Telugu literature (multiple forms) - Persons of racial, ethnic and national groups - History and criticism	894.827098++
Telugu literature (multiple forms) - Persons of specific classes - History and criticism	894.8270992++
Telugu literature (multiple forms) - Persons resident in specific regions - History and criticism	894.8270991++
Telugu literature (multiple forms) - Philosophic themes - History and criticism	894.82709384

Telugu literature (multiple forms) - Places - History and criticism	894.8270932++
Telugu literature (multiple forms) - Plants - History and criticism	894.82709364
Telugu literature (multiple forms) - Political themes - History and criticism	894.82709358
Telugu literature (multiple forms) - Religious themes - History and criticism	894.82709382++
Telugu literature (multiple forms) - Rivers - History and criticism	894.82709321693
Telugu literature (multiple forms) - Romanticism - History and criticism	894.82709145
Telugu literature (multiple forms) - Scientific themes - History and criticism	894.82709356
Telugu literature (multiple forms) - Sea - History and criticism	894.8270932162
Telugu literature (multiple forms) - Seasons - History and criticism	894.8270933
Telugu literature (multiple forms) - Sex - History and criticism	894.827093538
Telugu literature (multiple forms) - Social themes - History and criticism	894.82709355
Telugu literature (multiple forms) - Space - History and criticism	894.827093219
Telugu literature (multiple forms) - Specific kinds of persons, e.g. heroes, - History and criticism	894.82709352++
Telugu literature (multiple forms) - Specific persons - History and criticism	894.82709351
Telugu literature (multiple forms) - Stream of consciousness - History and criticism	894.8270925

Telugu literature (multiple forms) - Subjects - History and criticism	894.827094++
Telugu literature (multiple forms) - Supernatural objects/themes - History and criticism	894.8270937
Telugu literature (multiple forms) - Symbolism- History and criticism	894.8270915
Telugu literature (multiple forms) - Technical themes - History and criticism	894.82709356
Telugu literature (multiple forms) - Times - History and criticism	894.8270933
Telugu literature (multiple forms) - Towns - History and criticism	894.82709321732
Telugu literature (multiple forms) - Tragedy - History and criticism	894.82709162
Telugu literature (multiple forms) - Villages - History and criticism	894.82709321734
Telugu literature (multiple forms) - Weather - History and criticism	894.8270936
Telugu literature (single author)- - to 1845 - Biography, collections, criticism schedule	***See*** Main
Telugu literature (single author)- 1845 - 1895 - Biography, collections, criticism	894.8278 409
Telugu literature (single author)- 1895 - 1919 - Biography, collections, criticism	894.8278 509
Telugu literature (single author)- 1920 - 1939 - Biography, collections, criticism	894.8278 609
Telugu literature (single author)- 1940 - Biography, collections, criticism	894.8278 709

Telugu literature (single author)- 1940-1999 - Biography, collections, criticism	894.8278 7109
Telugu literature (single author)- 19th century - Biography, collections, criticism	894.8278 409
Telugu literature (single author)- 2000- Biography, collections, criticism	894.8278 7209
Telugu literature (single author)- 20th century - Biography, collections, criticism	894.8278 7109
Telugu literature for/by children - History and criticism	894.827099282
Telugu literature for/by women - History and criticism	894.827099287
Telugu love fiction (multiple authors)	894.8273085*
Telugu love fiction (multiple authors)- Collections	894.827308508**
Telugu love fiction (multiple authors)- History and criticism	894.827308509**
Telugu melodrama (multiple authors)	894.82720527*
Telugu melodrama (multiple authors)- Collections	894.8272052708**
Telugu melodrama (multiple authors)- History and criticism	894.8272052709**
Telugu miscellaneous writings	894.8278
Telugu miscellaneous writings (multiple authors) - to 1845	***See*** Main schedule
Telugu miscellaneous writings (multiple authors) -1845-1895	894.82784++
Telugu miscellaneous writings (multiple authors) -1895-1919	894.82785++

Telugu miscellaneous writings (multiple authors) -1920-1939	894.82786++
Telugu miscellaneous writings (multiple authors) -1940-	894.82787++
Telugu miscellaneous writings (multiple authors) -1940-1999	894.827871++
Telugu miscellaneous writings (multiple authors) -19th century	894.82784++
Telugu miscellaneous writings (multiple authors) –2000-	894.827872++
Telugu miscellaneous writings (multiple authors) -20th century	894.827871++
Telugu miscellaneous writings (multiple authors) -Collections	894.8278008**
Telugu miscellaneous writings (multiple authors) -Dictionaries etc	894.8278003
Telugu miscellaneous writings (multiple authors) -History and criticism	894.8278009**
Telugu miscellaneous writings (multiple authors) -Periodicals	894.8278005
Telugu miscellaneous writings (multiple authors) -Philosophy and theory	894.8278001
Telugu miscellaneous writings (multiple authors) -Psychological aspects	894.82780019
Telugu miscellaneous writings (multiple authors) -Research	894.82780072
Telugu miscellaneous writings (multiple authors) -Study and teaching	894.8278007
Telugu miscellaneous writings (multiple authors) -Value	894.82780013

Telugu miscellaneous writings (single author)- - to 1845	***See*** Main schedule
Telugu miscellaneous writings (single author)- 1845 -1895	894.8278 4
Telugu miscellaneous writings (single author)- 1895 - 1919	894.8278 5
Telugu miscellaneous writings (single author)- 1920 - 1939	894.8278 6
Telugu miscellaneous writings (single author)- 1940 -	894.8278 7
Telugu miscellaneous writings (single author)- 1940-1999	894.8278 71
Telugu miscellaneous writings (single author)- 19th century	894.8278 4
Telugu miscellaneous writings (single author)- 2000-	894.8278 72
Telugu miscellaneous writings (single author)- 20th century	894.8278 71
Telugu monologues (multiple authors)	894.8272045*
Telugu monologues (multiple authors)- Collections	894.827204508**
Telugu monologues (multiple authors)- History and criticism	894.827204509**
Telugu morality plays	***See*** Telugu religious … plays
Telugu mystery fiction (multiple authors)	894.82730872*
Telugu mystery fiction (multiple authors)- Collections	894.8273087208**
Telugu mystery fiction (multiple authors)- History and criticism	894.8273087209**

Telugu narrative poetry (multiple authors)	894.827103*
Telugu narrative poetry (multiple authors)- Collections	894.82710308**
Telugu narrative poetry (multiple authors)- History and criticism	894.82710309**
Telugu notebooks	***See*** Telugu diaries...
Telugu odes (multiple authors)	894.8271043*
Telugu odes (multiple authors)- Collections	894.827104308**
Telugu odes (multiple authors)- History and criticism	894.827104309**
Telugu one act plays (multiple authors)	894.827 204 1*
Telugu one act plays (multiple authors)- Collections	894.827 204 108**
Telugu one act plays (multiple authors)- History and criticism	894.827 204 109**
Telugu oratory (multiple authors)	***See*** Telugu public speeches
Telugu periodicals	059.94827
Telugu poetry	894.8271
Telugu poetry (multiple authors) - - to 1845	***See*** Main schedule
Telugu poetry (multiple authors) - 1845-1895	894.82714+
Telugu poetry (multiple authors) - 1895-1919	894.82715+
Telugu poetry (multiple authors) - 1920-1939	894.82716+
Telugu poetry (multiple authors) - 1940-	894.82717+

Telugu poetry (multiple authors) - 1940-1999	894.827171+
Telugu poetry (multiple authors) - 19th century	894.82714+
Telugu poetry (multiple authors) – 2000-	894.827172+
Telugu poetry (multiple authors) - 20th century	894.827171+
Telugu poetry (multiple authors)- Collections	894.8271008**
Telugu poetry (multiple authors)- Dictionaries etc	894.8271003
Telugu poetry (multiple authors)- History and criticism	894.8271009**
Telugu poetry (multiple authors)- Periodicals	894.8271005
Telugu poetry (multiple authors)- Philosophy and theory	894.8271001
Telugu poetry (multiple authors)- Psychological aspects	894.82710019
Telugu poetry (multiple authors)- Research	894.82710072
Telugu poetry (multiple authors)- Study and teaching	894.8271007
Telugu poetry (multiple authors)- Value	894.82710013
Telugu poetry (single author)- - to 1845	***See*** Main schedule
Telugu poetry (single author)- 1845 -1895	894.8271 4
Telugu poetry (single author)- 1895 - 1919	894.8271 5
Telugu poetry (single author)- 1920 - 1939	894.8271 6
Telugu poetry (single author)- 1940 -	894.8271 7
Telugu poetry (single author)- 1940-1999	894.8271 71

Telugu poetry (single author)- 19th century	894.8271 4
Telugu poetry (single author)- 2000-	894.8271 72
Telugu poetry (single author)- 20th century	894.8271 71
Telugu prose (single author)- - to 1845	***See*** Main schedule
Telugu prose (single author)- 1845 -1895	894.8278 408
Telugu prose (single author)- 1895 - 1919	894.8278 508
Telugu prose (single author)- 1920 - 1939	894.8278 608
Telugu prose (single author)- 1940 -	894.8278 708
Telugu prose (single author)- 1940-1999	894.8278 7108
Telugu prose (single author)- 19th century	894.8278 408
Telugu prose (single author)- 2000-	894.8278 7208
Telugu prose (single author)- 20th century	894.8278 7108
Telugu prose literature (multiple authors)	894.827808
Telugu psychological, realistic, sociological fiction (multiple authors)	894.8273083*
Telugu psychological, realistic, sociological fiction (multiple authors)- Collections	894.827308308**
Telugu psychological, realistic, sociological fiction (multiple authors) - History and criticism	894.827308309**
Telugu public discussions	***See*** Telugu debates ...
Telugu public speeches (multiple authors)	894.827501*
Telugu public speeches (multiple authors)- Collections	894.82750108**
Telugu public speeches (multiple authors)- History and criticism	894.82750109**

Telugu quotations	***See*** Telugu anecdotes ...
Telugu realistic fiction	***See*** Telugu psychological... fiction
Telugu recitations (multiple authors)	894.827504+
Telugu religious and morality plays (multiple authors)	894.82720516+
Telugu reminiscences	***See*** Telugu diaries
Telugu romantic fiction (multiple authors)	894.8273085*
Telugu romantic fiction (multiple authors)-Collections	894.827308508**
Telugu romantic fiction (multiple authors)-History and criticism	894.827308509**
Telugu satire humour	***See*** Telugu ...
Telugu satirical poetry	***See*** Telugu humourous ... poetry
Telugu science fiction (multiple authors)	894.827308762*
Telugu science fiction (multiple authors)-Collections	894.82730876208**
Telugu science fiction (multiple authors)-History and criticism	894.82730876209**
Telugu serious drama (multiple authors)	894.8272051+
Telugu short stories (multiple authors)	894.827301*
Telugu short stories (multiple authors)-Collections	894.82730108**
Telugu short stories (multiple authors)-History and criticism	894.82730109**

Telugu sociological fiction (multiple authors)	***See*** Telugu psychological... fiction
Telugu sonnets (multiple authors)	894.8271042*
Telugu sonnets (multiple authors)-Collections	894.827104208**
Telugu sonnets (multiple authors)-History and criticism	894.827104209**
Telugu speaking people	305.794 827
Telugu speeches	894.8275
Telugu speeches (multiple authors) — to 1845	***See*** Main schedule
Telugu speeches (multiple authors) - 1845-1895	894.82754+
Telugu speeches (multiple authors) - 1895-1919	894.82755+
Telugu speeches (multiple authors) - 1920-1939	894.82756+
Telugu speeches (multiple authors) -1940-	894.82757+
Telugu speeches (multiple authors) - 1940-1999	894.827571+
Telugu speeches (multiple authors) - 19th century	894.82754+
Telugu speeches (multiple authors) –2000-	894.827572+
Telugu speeches (multiple authors) - 20th century	894.827571+
Telugu speeches (multiple authors) - Collections	894.8275008**
Telugu speeches (multiple authors) - Dictionaries etc	894.8275003

Telugu speeches (multiple authors) - History and criticism	894.8275009**
Telugu speeches (multiple authors) - Periodicals	894.8275005
Telugu speeches (multiple authors) - Philosophy and theory	894.8275001
Telugu speeches (multiple authors) - Psychological aspects	894.82750019
Telugu speeches (multiple authors) - Research	894.82750072
Telugu speeches (multiple authors) - Study and teaching	894.8275007
Telugu speeches (multiple authors) -Value	894.82750013
Telugu speeches (single author)- - to 1845	***See*** Main schedule
Telugu speeches (single author)- 1845 -1895	894.8275 4
Telugu speeches (single author)- 1895 - 1919	894.8275 5
Telugu speeches (single author)- 1920-1939	894.8275 6
Telugu speeches (single author)- 1940 -	894.8275 7
Telugu speeches (single author)- 1940-1999	894.8275 71
Telugu speeches (single author)- 19th century	894.8275 4
Telugu speeches (single author)- 2000-	894.8275 72
Telugu speeches (single author)- 20th century	894.8275 71
Telugu suspense fiction (multiple authors)	894.82730872*
Telugu suspense fiction (multiple authors)- Collections	894.8273087208**

Telugu suspense fiction (multiple authors)- History and criticism	894.8273087209**
Telugu tragedy (multiple authors)	894.82720512*
Telugu tragedy (multiple authors)- Collections	894.8272051208**
Telugu tragedy (multiple authors)- History and criticism	894.8272051209**
Telugu variety drama (multiple authors)	894.8272057*
Telugu variety drama (multiple authors)- Collections	894.827205708**
Telugu variety drama (multiple authors)- History and criticism	894.827205709**
Thedavada (Southern, Hinayana) Buddhism- Doctrines	294.342 041
Theocracy (Buddhism)	294.337 73
Theocracy (Hinduism)	294.517 73
Theocracy (Jainism)	294.417 73
Theocracy (Sikhism)	294.617 73
Theodicy (Buddhism)	294.342 118
Theodicy (Hinduism)	294.521 18
Theodicy (Jainism)	294.421 18
Theodicy (Sikhism)	294.621 18
Theravada (Southern, Hinayana) Buddhism	294.391
Theravadin sacred texts	294.382
Tibetan Buddhism	294.392 3
Tibetan Buddhism- Doctrines	294.342 0423
Tipitaka	294.382
Toda (People)	305.894 81
Toda folk music	781 629 481

Toda language	494.81
Toda literature	894.81
Trees (Buddhism)	294.342 12
Trees (Hinduism)	294.521 2
Trees (Jainism)	294.421 2
Trees (Sikhism)	294.621 2
Tripitaka.	294.382
Tripura- Architecture	720.954 15
Tripura- Budget	352.495 415
Tripura- Economic development	338.954 15
Tripura- Economic geography	330.954 15
Tripura- Education	370.954 15
Tripura- Fauna	591.954 15
Tripura- Flora	581.954 15
Tripura- Folk dancing	793.319 5415
Tripura- Geography	915.415
Tripura- Geology	555.415
Tripura- History	954.15
Tripura- Painting and paintings	759.954 15
Tripura- Public administration	351.541 5
Tripura- Public finance	336.541 5
Tripura- Sculpture	730.954 15
Troubled persons (Buddhism)	294.344 42
Troubled persons (Hinduism)	294.5442
Troubled persons (Jainism)	294.4442
Troubled persons (Sikhism)	294.6442

U

Unemployment -Andaman & Nicobar Islands	331.137 954 88
Unemployment -Andhra Pradesh	331.137 954 84
Unemployment -Arunachal Pradesh	331.137 954 163
Unemployment -Assam	331.137 954 162
Unemployment -Bengal	331.137 954 14
Unemployment -Bihar	331.137 954 12
Unemployment -Bombay	331.137 954 792 3
Unemployment -Calcutta	331.137 954 147
Unemployment -Chandigarh	331.137 954 55 2
Unemployment -Chhattisgarh	331.137 954 137
Unemployment -Dadra and Nagar Haveli	331.137 954 796
Unemployment -Delhi	331.137 954 56
Unemployment -Goa, Daman and Diu	331.137 954 799
Unemployment -Gujarat	331.137 954 75
Unemployment -Haryana	331.137 954 55 8
Unemployment -Himachal Pradesh	331.137 954 52
Unemployment -Hyderabad state	331.137 954 84
Unemployment -India	331.137 954

Unemployment -Jammu and Kashmir	331.137 954 6
Unemployment -Jharkhand	331.137 954 127
Unemployment -Karnataka	331.137 954 87
Unemployment -Kerala	331.137 954 83
Unemployment -Lakshwadweep	331.137 954 81
Unemployment -Madhya Pradesh	331.137 954 3
Unemployment -Madras	331.137 954 82
Unemployment -Maharashtra	331.137 954 792
Unemployment -Manipur	331.137 954 17
Unemployment -Meghalaya	331.137 954 164
Unemployment -Mizoram	331.137 954 166
Unemployment -Nagaland	331.137 954 165
Unemployment -Northeast India	331.137 954 1
Unemployment -Orissa	331.137 954 13
Unemployment -Pondicherry	331.137 954 86
Unemployment -Punjab	331.137 954 55 2
Unemployment -Rajasthan	331.137 954 4
Unemployment -Sikkim	331.137 954 167
Unemployment -South Asia	331.137 954
Unemployment -Southern India	331.137 954 8
Unemployment -Tamil Nadu	331.137 954 82
Unemployment -Tripura	331.137 954 15
Unemployment -Uttar Pradesh	331.137 954 2
Unemployment -Uttaranchal	331.137 954 51
Unemployment -West Bengal	331.137 954 14

Unemployment -Western India	331.137 954 7
University libraries - India.	027.754
Upanishads	294.5921 8++
Urdu - English dictionary	491.439 321
Urdu adventure fiction (multiple authors)	891.4393087*
Urdu adventure fiction (multiple authors) - Collections	891.439308708**
Urdu adventure fiction (multiple authors)- History and criticism	891.439308709**
Urdu anecdotes, epigrams, graffiti, jokes, quotations (multiple authors)	891.439802
Urdu anecdotes, epigrams, graffiti, jokes, quotations (single author)	891.4398+CD+02
Urdu as second language in elementary education	372.659 143 9
Urdu ballads (multiple authors)	891.4391044*
Urdu ballads (multiple authors)- Collections	891.439104408**
Urdu ballads (multiple authors)- History and criticism	891.439104409**
Urdu comedy (multiple authors)	891.43920523*
Urdu comedy (multiple authors) - Collections	891.4392052308**
Urdu comedy (multiple authors) - History and criticism	891.4392052309**
Urdu conversations (multiple authors)	891.439506*
Urdu conversations (multiple authors) - Collections	891.43950608**
Urdu conversations (multiple authors) - History and criticism	891.43950609**

Urdu debates and public discussions (multiple authors)	891.439503*
Urdu debates and public discussions (multiple authors)- Collections	891.43950308**
Urdu debates and public discussions (multiple authors)- History and criticism	891.43950309**
Urdu detective fiction (multiple authors)	891.43930872*
Urdu detective fiction (multiple authors) - Collections	891.4393087208**
Urdu detective fiction (multiple authors) - History and criticism	891.4393087209**
Urdu diaries, notebooks, reminiscences (multiple authors)	891.439803
Urdu diaries, notebooks, reminiscences (single author)	891.4398@
Urdu didactic poetry (multiple authors)	891.439105*
Urdu didactic poetry (multiple authors)- Collections	891.43910508**
Urdu didactic poetry (multiple authors)- History and criticism	891.43910509**
Urdu drama	891.439 2
Urdu drama (multiple authors) - - to 1845	***See*** Main schedule
Urdu drama (multiple authors) - 1845-1895	891.43924+
Urdu drama (multiple authors) - 1895-1919	891.43925+
Urdu drama (multiple authors) - 1920-1939	891.43926+
Urdu drama (multiple authors) - 1940-	891.43927+
Urdu drama (multiple authors) - 1940-1999	891.439271+
Urdu drama (multiple authors) - 19th century	891.43924+

Urdu drama (multiple authors) – 2000-	891.439272+
Urdu drama (multiple authors) - 20th century	891.439271+
Urdu drama (multiple authors) - Collections	891.4392008**
Urdu drama (multiple authors) - Dictionaries etc	891.4392003
Urdu drama (multiple authors) - History and criticism	891.4392009**
Urdu drama (multiple authors) - Periodicals	891.4392005
Urdu drama (multiple authors) - Philosophy and theory	891.4392001
Urdu drama (multiple authors) - Psychological aspects	891.43920019
Urdu drama (multiple authors) - Research	891.43920072
Urdu drama (multiple authors) - Study and teaching	891.4392007
Urdu drama (multiple authors) - Value	891.43920013
Urdu drama (single author) - to 1845	***See*** Main schedule
Urdu drama (single author)- 1845 -1895	891.4392 4
Urdu drama (single author)- 1895 - 1919	891.4392 5
Urdu drama (single author)- 1920 - 1939	891.4392 6
Urdu drama (single author)- 1940 -	891.4392 7
Urdu drama (single author)- 1940-1999	891.4392 71
Urdu drama (single author)- 19th century	891.4392 4
Urdu drama (single author)- 2000-	891.4392 72
Urdu drama (single author)- 20th century	891.4392 71
Urdu drama for cinema (multiple authors)	891.439203*

Urdu drama for cinema (multiple authors) - Collections	891.43920308**
Urdu drama for cinema (multiple authors) - History and criticism	891.43920309**
Urdu drama for radio (multiple authors)	891.4392022*
Urdu drama for radio (multiple authors) - Collections	891.439202208**
Urdu drama for radio (multiple authors) - History and criticism	891.439202209**
Urdu drama for television (multiple authors)	891.4392025*
Urdu drama for television (multiple authors) - Collections	891.439202508**
Urdu drama for television (multiple authors) - History and criticism	891.439202509**
Urdu dramatic poetry (multiple authors)	891.439102*
Urdu dramatic poetry (multiple authors)- Collections	891.43910208**
Urdu dramatic poetry (multiple authors)- History and criticism	891.43910209**
Urdu encyclopaedias	039.91439
Urdu ephemeral and light verse (multiple authors)	891.439108*
Urdu ephemeral and light verse (multiple authors)- Collections	891.43910808**
Urdu ephemeral and light verse (multiple authors) - History and criticism	891.43910809**
Urdu epic poetry (multiple authors)	891.4391032*
Urdu epic poetry (multiple authors)- Collections	891.439103208**

Urdu epic poetry (multiple authors)- History and criticism	891.439103209**
Urdu epigrams	***See*** Urdu anecdotes …
Urdu essays	891.439 4
Urdu essays (multiple authors) - to 1845	***See*** Main schedule
Urdu essays (multiple authors) -1845-1895	891.43944+
Urdu essays (multiple authors) -1895-1919	891.43945+
Urdu essays (multiple authors) -1920-1939	891.43946+
Urdu essays (multiple authors) -1940-	891.43947+
Urdu essays (multiple authors) -1940-1999	891.439471+
Urdu essays (multiple authors) -19th century	891.43944+
Urdu essays (multiple authors) –2000-	891.439472+
Urdu essays (multiple authors) -20th century	891.439471+
Urdu essays (multiple authors) -Collections	891.4394008**
Urdu essays (multiple authors) - Dictionaries etc	891.4394003
Urdu essays (multiple authors) - History and criticism	891.4394009**
Urdu essays (multiple authors) -Periodicals	891.4394005
Urdu essays (multiple authors) - Philosophy and theory	891.4394001
Urdu essays (multiple authors) - Psychological aspects	891.43940019
Urdu essays (multiple authors) -Research	891.43940072
Urdu essays (multiple authors) - Study and teaching	891.4394007

Urdu essays (multiple authors) -Value	891.43940013
Urdu essays (single author)- - to 1845	***See*** Main schedule
Urdu essays (single author)- 1845 -1895	891.4394 4
Urdu essays (single author)- 1895 - 1919	891.4394 5
Urdu essays (single author)- 1920 - 1939	891.4394 6
Urdu essays (single author)- 1940 -	891.4394 7
Urdu essays (single author)- 1940-1999	891.4394 71
Urdu essays (single author)- 19th century	891.4394 4
Urdu essays (single author)- 2000-	891.4394 72
Urdu essays (single author)- 20th century	891.4394 71
Urdu experimental and non-formalized works (single author) - 19th century	891.4398 407
Urdu experimental and non-formalized works (single author) – 2000-	891.4398 7207
Urdu experimental and non-formalized works (single author) - 20th century	891.4398 7107
Urdu experimental and non-formalized works (multiple authors)	891.439807
Urdu fantasy fiction (multiple authors)	891.439308766*
Urdu fantasy fiction (multiple authors)- Collections	891.43930876608**
Urdu fantasy fiction (multiple authors)- History and criticism	891.43930876609**
Urdu farce (multiple authors)	891.439205232*
Urdu farce (multiple authors)- Collections	891.43920523208**
Urdu farce (multiple authors)- History and criticism	891.43920523209**

Urdu fiction	891.439 3
Urdu fiction (multiple authors) - - to 1845	***See*** Main schedule
Urdu fiction (multiple authors) - 1845-1895	891.43934+
Urdu fiction (multiple authors) - 1895-1919	891.43935+
Urdu fiction (multiple authors) - 1920-1939	891.43936+
Urdu fiction (multiple authors) - 1940-	891.43937+
Urdu fiction (multiple authors) - 1940-1999	891.439371+
Urdu fiction (multiple authors) - 19th century	891.43934+
Urdu fiction (multiple authors) - 20th century	891.439371+
Urdu fiction (multiple authors) – 21st century	891.439372+
Urdu fiction (multiple authors) - Collections	891.4393008**
Urdu fiction (multiple authors) - Dictionaries etc	891.4393003
Urdu fiction (multiple authors) - History and criticism	891.4393009**
Urdu fiction (multiple authors) - Periodicals	891.4393005
Urdu fiction (multiple authors) - Philosophy and theory	891.4393001
Urdu fiction (multiple authors) - Psychological aspects	891.43930019
Urdu fiction (multiple authors) - Research	891.43930072
Urdu fiction (multiple authors) - Study and teaching	891.4393007
Urdu fiction (multiple authors) - Value	891.43930013
Urdu fiction (single author)- - to 1845	***See*** Main schedule
Urdu fiction (single author)- 1845 -1895	891.4393 4

Urdu fiction (single author)- 1895 - 1919	891.4393 5
Urdu fiction (single author)- 1920 - 1939	891.4393 6
Urdu fiction (single author)- 1940 -	891.4393 7
Urdu fiction (single author)- 1940-1999	891.4393 71
Urdu fiction (single author)- 19th century	891.4393 4
Urdu fiction (single author)- 2000-	891.4393 72
Urdu fiction (single author)- 20th century	891.4393 71
Urdu ghost fiction (multiple authors)	891.439308733*
Urdu ghost fiction (multiple authors) - Collections	891.43930873308**
Urdu ghost fiction (multiple authors)- History and criticism	891.43930873309**
Urdu graffiti	***See*** Urdu anecdotes ...
Urdu historical drama (multiple authors)	891.43920514*
Urdu historical drama (multiple authors)- Collections	891.4392051408**
Urdu historical drama (multiple authors)- History and criticism	891.4392051409**
Urdu historical fiction (multiple authors)	891.4393081*
Urdu historical fiction (multiple authors)- Collections	891.439308108**
Urdu historical fiction (multiple authors)- History and criticism	891.439308109**
Urdu horror fiction (multiple authors)	891.439308738*
Urdu horror fiction (multiple authors)- Collections	891.43930873808**

Urdu horror fiction (multiple authors)-History and criticism	891.43930873809**
Urdu humour and satire	891.439 7
Urdu humour and satire (multiple authors) - to 1845	***See*** Main schedule
Urdu humour and satire (multiple authors) -1845-1895	891.43974+
Urdu humour and satire (multiple authors) -1895-1919	891.43975+
Urdu humour and satire (multiple authors) -1920-1939	891.43976+
Urdu humour and satire (multiple authors) -1940-	891.43977+
Urdu humour and satire (multiple authors) -1940-1999	891.439771+
Urdu humour and satire (multiple authors) -19th century	891.43974+
Urdu humour and satire (multiple authors) –2000-	891.439772+
Urdu humour and satire (multiple authors) -20th century	891.439771+
Urdu humour and satire (multiple authors) -Collections	891.4397008**
Urdu humour and satire (multiple authors) -Dictionaries etc	891.4397003
Urdu humour and satire (multiple authors) -History and criticism	891.4397009**
Urdu humour and satire (multiple authors) -Periodicals	891.4397005
Urdu humour and satire (multiple authors) -Philosophy and theory	891.4397001

Urdu humour and satire (multiple authors) -Psychological aspects	891.43970019
Urdu humour and satire (multiple authors) -Research	891.43970072
Urdu humour and satire (multiple authors) -Study and teaching	891.4397007
Urdu humour and satire (multiple authors) -Value	891.43970013
Urdu humour and satire (multiple authors)	891.4397
Urdu humourous and satirical poetry (multiple authors)	891.439107*
Urdu humourous and satirical poetry (multiple authors)- Collections	891.43910708**
Urdu humourous and satirical poetry (multiple authors)- History and criticism	891.43910709**
Urdu jokes	***See*** Urdu anecdotes ...
Urdu language	491.439
Urdu language- Applied linguistics	491.4398
Urdu language- Bilingual dictionaries	491.4393 2-39
Urdu language- Bilingualism	491.439042
Urdu language- Concordances	491.43903
Urdu language- Content analysis	491.439014 1
Urdu language- Dictionaries	491.4393
Urdu language- Discourse analysis	491.439014 1
Urdu language- Education	491.439071
Urdu language- Encyclopaedias	491.43903
Urdu language- Etymology	491.4392

Urdu language- Functionalism	491.439018
Urdu language- Grammar	491.4395
Urdu language- History	491.43909
Urdu language- Intonation	491.43916
Urdu language- Lexicography	491.439302 8
Urdu language- Lexicology	491.439014
Urdu language- Miscellany	491.43902
Urdu language- Multilingualism	491.439042
Urdu language- Organizations	491.43906
Urdu language- Orthography	491.439152
Urdu language- Pauses	491.43916
Urdu language- Periodicals	491.43905
Urdu language- Persons (men, women, etc)	491.43908
Urdu language- Philosophy and theory	491.43901
Urdu language- Phonetics	491.439158
Urdu language- Phonology	491.43915
Urdu language- Pitch	491.43916
Urdu language- Pronunciation	491.439152
Urdu language- Readers	491.439 86
Urdu language- Research	491.439072
Urdu language- Rhetoric	808.049 1439++
Urdu language- Schools and theories of linguistics	491.439018
Urdu language- Semantics	491.439014 3
Urdu language- Semiotics	491.439014 1

Urdu language- Slang	491.4397
Urdu language- Special topics	491.43904
Urdu language- Specialized dictionaries	491.43931
Urdu language- Spelling	491.439152
Urdu language- Stress	491.43916
Urdu language- Structural linguistics	491.439018
Urdu language- Suprasegmental features	491.43916
Urdu language- Terminology	491.439014
Urdu language- Usage	491.4398
Urdu language- Variations (Dialects etc)	491.4397
Urdu language- Writing systems	491.43911
Urdu letters	891.439 6
Urdu letters (multiple authors) - -to 1845	***See*** Main schedule
Urdu letters (multiple authors) -1845-1895	891.43964+
Urdu letters (multiple authors) -1895-1919	891.43965+
Urdu letters (multiple authors) -1920-1939	891.43966+
Urdu letters (multiple authors) -1940-	891.43967+
Urdu letters (multiple authors) -1940-1999	891.439671+
Urdu letters (multiple authors) -19th century	891.43964+
Urdu letters (multiple authors) –2000-	891.439672+
Urdu letters (multiple authors) -20th century	891.439671+
Urdu letters (multiple authors) -Collections	891.4396008**
Urdu letters (multiple authors) - Dictionaries etc	891.4396003
Urdu letters (multiple authors) - History and criticism	891.4396009**

Urdu letters (multiple authors) -Periodicals	891.4396005
Urdu letters (multiple authors) - Philosophy and theory	891.4396001
Urdu letters (multiple authors) - Psychological aspects	891.43960019
Urdu letters (multiple authors) -Research	891.43960072
Urdu letters (multiple authors) - Study and teaching	891.4396007
Urdu letters (multiple authors) -Value	891.43960013
Urdu letters (multiple authors)	891.4396
Urdu letters (single author)- - to 1845	891.4396 1
Urdu letters (single author)- 1845 -1895	891.4396 4
Urdu letters (single author)- 1895 - 1919	891.4396 5
Urdu letters (single author)- 1920 - 1939	891.4396 6
Urdu letters (single author)- 1940 -	891.4396 7
Urdu letters (single author)- 1940-1999	891.4396 71
Urdu letters (single author)- 19th century	891.4396 4
Urdu letters (single author)- 2000-	891.4396 72
Urdu letters (single author)- 20th century	891.4396 71
Urdu light verse	***See*** Urdu ephemeral ... verse
Urdu limericks (multiple authors)	891.4391075*
Urdu limericks (multiple authors)- Collections	891.439107508**
Urdu limericks (multiple authors)- History and criticism	891.439107509**
Urdu literature	891.439

Urdu literature (collections of multiple forms)	891.43908
Urdu literature (collections of multiple forms) - 19th century	891.4390804
Urdu literature (collections of multiple forms) - 20th century	891.43908071
Urdu literature (collections of multiple forms) – 21st century	891.43908072
Urdu literature (collections of multiple forms) - Allegory	891.43908015
Urdu literature (collections of multiple forms) - Animals	891.439080362++
Urdu literature (collections of multiple forms) - Artistic themes	891.439080357
Urdu literature (collections of multiple forms) - Atmosphere	891.43908032161
Urdu literature (collections of multiple forms) - Characters	891.43908027
Urdu literature (collections of multiple forms) - Comedy	891.43908017
Urdu literature (collections of multiple forms) - Evening	891.43908033
Urdu literature (collections of multiple forms) - Fantasy	891.43908015
Urdu literature (collections of multiple forms) - Forests	891.43908032152
Urdu literature (collections of multiple forms) - Historical themes	891.439080358
Urdu literature (collections of multiple forms) - Horror	891.439080164

Urdu literature (collections of multiple forms) - Human characteristics (Biological, moral, psychological)	891.439080353
Urdu literature (collections of multiple forms) - Legendary objects/themes	891.43908037
Urdu literature (collections of multiple forms) - Literary themes	891.439080357
Urdu literature (collections of multiple forms) - Love	891.4390803543
Urdu literature (collections of multiple forms) - Marriage	891.4390803543
Urdu literature (collections of multiple forms) - Morning	891.43908033
Urdu literature (collections of multiple forms) - Mountains	891.43908032143
Urdu literature (collections of multiple forms) - Myth	891.43908015
Urdu literature (collections of multiple forms) - Mythological objects/themes	891.43908037
Urdu literature (collections of multiple forms) - Philosophic themes	891.439080384
Urdu literature (collections of multiple forms) - Places	891.43908032++
Urdu literature (collections of multiple forms) - Plants	891.439080364
Urdu literature (collections of multiple forms) - Political themes	891.439080358
Urdu literature (collections of multiple forms) - Religious themes	891.439080382++
Urdu literature (collections of multiple forms) - Rivers	891.439080321693

Urdu literature (collections of multiple forms) - Romanticism	891.439080145
Urdu literature (collections of multiple forms) - Scientific themes	891.439080356
Urdu literature (collections of multiple forms) - Sea	891.43908032162
Urdu literature (collections of multiple forms) - Seasons	891.43908033
Urdu literature (collections of multiple forms) - Sex	891.4390803538
Urdu literature (collections of multiple forms) - Social themes	891.439080355
Urdu literature (collections of multiple forms) - Space	891.4390803219
Urdu literature (collections of multiple forms) - Specific kinds of persons, e.g. heroes	891.439080352++
Urdu literature (collections of multiple forms) - Specific persons (real or imaginary)	891.439080351
Urdu literature (collections of multiple forms) - Stream of consciousness	891.43908025
Urdu literature (collections of multiple forms) - Supernatural objects/themes	891.43908037
Urdu literature (collections of multiple forms) - Symbolism	891.43908015
Urdu literature (collections of multiple forms) - Technical themes	891.439080356
Urdu literature (collections of multiple forms) - Times (seasons, parts of day, etc)	891.43908033
Urdu literature (collections of multiple forms) - Towns	891.439080321732

Urdu literature (collections of multiple forms) - Tragedy	891.439080162
Urdu literature (collections of multiple forms) - Villages	891.439080321734
Urdu literature (collections of multiple forms) - Weather	891.43908036
Urdu literature (collections of multiple forms) emphasizing subjects	891.4390804++
Urdu literature (collections of multiple forms) for/by children	891.4390809282
Urdu literature (collections of multiple forms) for/by persons of racial, ethnic and national groups	891.4390808++
Urdu literature (collections of multiple forms) for/by persons of specific classes	891.43908092++
Urdu literature (collections of multiple forms) for/by persons resident in specific regions	891.43908091++
Urdu literature (collections of multiple forms) for/by women	891.4390809287
Urdu literature (multiple authors) - Concordances	891.43903
Urdu literature (multiple authors) - Dictionaries	891.43903
Urdu literature (multiple authors) - Education	891.439071
Urdu literature (multiple authors) - Encyclopaedias	891.43903
Urdu literature (multiple authors) - Organizations	891.43906

Urdu literature (multiple authors) - Periodicals	891.43905
Urdu literature (multiple authors) - Philosophy and theory	891.43901
Urdu literature (multiple authors) - Research	891.439072
Urdu literature (multiple authors) - Research in India	891.439072054
Urdu literature (multiple authors) - Study and teaching	891.43907
Urdu literature (multiple forms) - Supernatural objects/themes - History and criticism	891.4390937
Urdu literature (multiple forms) - 19th century	891.43909004
Urdu literature (multiple forms) – 2000-	891.439090072
Urdu literature (multiple forms) - 20th century	891.439090071
Urdu literature (multiple forms) - Allegory – History and criticism	891.4390915
Urdu literature (multiple forms) - Animals - History and criticism	891.43909362++
Urdu literature (multiple forms) - Artistic themes - History and criticism	891.43909357
Urdu literature (multiple forms) - Atmosphere - History and criticism	891.4390932161
Urdu literature (multiple forms) - Characters - History and criticism	891.4390927
Urdu literature (multiple forms) - Comedy - History and criticism	891.4390917
Urdu literature (multiple forms) - Evening - History and criticism	891.4390933

Urdu literature (multiple forms) - Fantasy - History , description, criticism	891.4390915
Urdu literature (multiple forms) - Forests - History and criticism	891.4390932152
Urdu literature (multiple forms) - Historical themes - History and criticism	891.43909358
Urdu literature (multiple forms) - History and criticism	891.43909
Urdu literature (multiple forms) - Horror - History and criticism	891.43909164
Urdu literature (multiple forms) - Human characteristics (Biological , moral, psychological) - History and criticism	891.43909353
Urdu literature (multiple forms) - Legendary objects/themes - History and criticism	891.4390937
Urdu literature (multiple forms) - Literary themes - History and criticism	891.43909357
Urdu literature (multiple forms) - Love - History and criticism	891.439093543
Urdu literature (multiple forms) - Marriage - History and criticism	891.439093543
Urdu literature (multiple forms) - Morning - History and criticism	891.4390933
Urdu literature (multiple forms) - Mountains - History and criticism	891.4390932143
Urdu literature (multiple forms) - Myth - History and criticism	891.4390915
Urdu literature (multiple forms) - Mythological objects/themes - History and criticism	891.4390937

Urdu literature (multiple forms) - Persons of racial, ethnic and national groups - History and criticism	891.439098++
Urdu literature (multiple forms) - Persons of specific classes - History and criticism	891.4390992++
Urdu literature (multiple forms) - Persons resident in specific regions - History and criticism	891.4390991++
Urdu literature (multiple forms) - Philosophic themes - History and criticism	891.43909384
Urdu literature (multiple forms) - Places - History and criticism	891.4390932++
Urdu literature (multiple forms) - Plants - History and criticism	891.43909364
Urdu literature (multiple forms) - Political themes - History and criticism	891.43909358
Urdu literature (multiple forms) - Religious themes - History and criticism	891.43909382++
Urdu literature (multiple forms) - Rivers - History and criticism	891.43909321693
Urdu literature (multiple forms) - Romanticism - History and criticism	891.43909145
Urdu literature (multiple forms) - Scientific themes - History and criticism	891.43909356
Urdu literature (multiple forms) - Sea - History and criticism	891.4390932162
Urdu literature (multiple forms) - Seasons - History and criticism	891.4390933
Urdu literature (multiple forms) - Sex - History and criticism	891.439093538

Urdu literature (multiple forms) - Social themes - History and criticism	891.43909355
Urdu literature (multiple forms) - Space - History and criticism	891.439093219
Urdu literature (multiple forms) - Specific kinds of persons, e.g. heroes, - History and criticism	891.43909352++
Urdu literature (multiple forms) - Specific persons - History and criticism	891.43909351
Urdu literature (multiple forms) - Stream of consciousness - History and criticism	891.4390925
Urdu literature (multiple forms) - Subjects - History and criticism	891.439094++
Urdu literature (multiple forms) - Symbolism- History and criticism	891.4390915
Urdu literature (multiple forms) - Technical themes - History and criticism	891.43909356
Urdu literature (multiple forms) - Times - History and criticism	891.4390933
Urdu literature (multiple forms) - Towns - History and criticism	891.43909321732
Urdu literature (multiple forms) - Tragedy - History and criticism	891.43909162
Urdu literature (multiple forms) - Villages - History and criticism	891.43909321734
Urdu literature (multiple forms) - Weather - History and criticism	891.4390936
Urdu literature (single author)- - to 1845 - Biography, collections, criticism	***See*** Main schedule

Urdu literature (single author)- 1845 – 1895- Biography, collections, criticism	891.4398 409
Urdu literature (single author)- 1895 - 1919 - Biography, collections, criticism	891.4398 509
Urdu literature (single author)- 1920 - 1939 - Biography, collections, criticism	891.4398 609
Urdu literature (single author)- 1940 - Biography, collections, criticism	891.4398 709
Urdu literature (single author)- 1940- 1999 - Biography, collections, criticism	891.4398 7109
Urdu literature (single author)- 19th century- Biography, collections, criticism	891.4398 409
Urdu literature (single author)- 2000- Biography, collections, criticism	891.4398 7209
Urdu literature (single author)-20th century - Biography, collections, criticism	891.4398 7109
Urdu literature for/by children - History and criticism	891.439099282
Urdu literature for/by women - History and criticism	891.439099287
Urdu love fiction (multiple authors)	891.4393085*
Urdu love fiction (multiple authors)- Collections	891.439308508**
Urdu love fiction (multiple authors)- History and criticism	891.439308509**
Urdu melodrama (multiple authors)	891.43920527*
Urdu melodrama (multiple authors)- Collections	891.4392052708**
Urdu melodrama (multiple authors)- History and criticism	891.4392052709**

Urdu miscellaneous writings (multiple authors)	891.4398
Urdu miscellaneous writings (multiple authors) - to 1845	***See*** Main schedule
Urdu miscellaneous writings (multiple authors) -1845-1895	891.43984++
Urdu miscellaneous writings (multiple authors) -1895-1919	891.43985++
Urdu miscellaneous writings (multiple authors) -1920-1939	891.43986++
Urdu miscellaneous writings (multiple authors) -1940-	891.43987++
Urdu miscellaneous writings (multiple authors) -1940-1999	891.439871++
Urdu miscellaneous writings (multiple authors) -19th century	891.43984++
Urdu miscellaneous writings (multiple authors) –2000-	891.439872++
Urdu miscellaneous writings (multiple authors) -20th century	891.439871++
Urdu miscellaneous writings (multiple authors) -Collections	891.4398008**
Urdu miscellaneous writings (multiple authors) -Dictionaries etc	891.4398003
Urdu miscellaneous writings (multiple authors) -History and criticism	891.4398009**
Urdu miscellaneous writings (multiple authors) -Periodicals	891.4398005
Urdu miscellaneous writings (multiple authors) -Philosophy and theory	891.4398001

Urdu miscellaneous writings (multiple authors) -Psychological aspects	891.43980019
Urdu miscellaneous writings (multiple authors) -Research	891.43980072
Urdu miscellaneous writings (multiple authors) -Study and teaching	891.4398007
Urdu miscellaneous writings (multiple authors) -Value	891.43980013
Urdu miscellaneous writings (single author)- - to 1845	***See*** Main schedule
Urdu miscellaneous writings (single author)- 1845 -1895	891.4398 4
Urdu miscellaneous writings (single author)- 1895 - 1919	891.4398 5
Urdu miscellaneous writings (single author)- 1920 - 1939	891.4398 6
Urdu miscellaneous writings (single author)- 1940 -	891.4398 7
Urdu miscellaneous writings (single author)- 1940-1999	891.4398 71
Urdu miscellaneous writings (single author)- 19th century	891.4398 4
Urdu miscellaneous writings (single author)- 2000-	891.4398 72
Urdu miscellaneous writings (single author)- 20th century	891.4398 71
Urdu monologues (multiple authors)	891.4392045*
Urdu monologues (multiple authors)- Collections	891.439204508**
Urdu monologues (multiple authors)- History and criticism	891.439204509**

Urdu morality plays	***See*** Urdu religious ... plays
Urdu mystery fiction (multiple authors)	891.43930872*
Urdu mystery fiction (multiple authors)- Collections	891.4393087208**
Urdu mystery fiction (multiple authors)- History and criticism	891.4393087209**
Urdu narrative poetry (multiple authors)	891.439103*
Urdu narrative poetry (multiple authors)- Collections	891.43910308**
Urdu narrative poetry (multiple authors)- History and criticism	891.43910309**
Urdu notebooks	***See*** Urdu diaries...
Urdu odes (multiple authors)	891.4391043*
Urdu odes (multiple authors)- Collections	891.439104308**
Urdu odes (multiple authors)- History and criticism	891.439104309**
Urdu one act plays (multiple authors)	891.439 204 1*
Urdu one act plays (multiple authors)- Collections	891.439 204 108**
Urdu one act plays (multiple authors)- History and criticism	891.439 204 109**
Urdu oratory (multiple authors)	***See*** Urdu public speeches
Urdu periodicals	059.91439
Urdu poetry	891.439 1
Urdu poetry (multiple authors) - - to 1845	***See*** Main schedule

Urdu poetry (multiple authors) - 1845-1895	891.43914+
Urdu poetry (multiple authors) - 1895-1919	891.43915+
Urdu poetry (multiple authors) - 1920-1939	891.43916+
Urdu poetry (multiple authors) - 1940-	891.43917+
Urdu poetry (multiple authors) - 1940-1999	891.439171+
Urdu poetry (multiple authors) - 19th century	891.43914+
Urdu poetry (multiple authors) – 2000-	891.439172+
Urdu poetry (multiple authors) - 20th century	891.439171+
Urdu poetry (multiple authors)- Collections	891.4391008**
Urdu poetry (multiple authors)- Dictionaries etc	891.4391003
Urdu poetry (multiple authors)- History and criticism	891.4391009**
Urdu poetry (multiple authors)- Periodicals	891.4391005
Urdu poetry (multiple authors)- Philosophy and theory	891.4391001
Urdu poetry (multiple authors)- Psychological aspects	891.43910019
Urdu poetry (multiple authors)- Research	891.43910072
Urdu poetry (multiple authors)- Study and teaching	891.4391007
Urdu poetry (multiple authors)- Value	891.43910013
Urdu poetry (single author)- - to 1845	***See*** Main schedule
Urdu poetry (single author)- 1845 -1895	891.4391 4
Urdu poetry (single author)- 1895 - 1919	891.4391 5
Urdu poetry (single author)- 1920 - 1939	891.4391 6
Urdu poetry (single author)- 1940 -	891.4391 7

Urdu poetry (single author)- 1940-1999	891.4391 71
Urdu poetry (single author)- 19th century	891.4391 4
Urdu poetry (single author)- 2000-	891.4391 72
Urdu poetry (single author)- 20th century	891.4391 71
Urdu prose (single author)- - to 1845	***See*** Main schedule
Urdu prose (single author)- 1845 -1895	891.4398 408
Urdu prose (single author)- 1895 - 1919	891.4398 508
Urdu prose (single author)- 1920 - 1939	891.4398 608
Urdu prose (single author)- 1940 -	891.4398 708
Urdu prose (single author)- 1940-1999	891.4398 7108
Urdu prose (single author)- 19th century	891.4398 408
Urdu prose (single author)- 2000-	891.4398 7208
Urdu prose (single author)- 20th century	891.4398 7108
Urdu prose literature (multiple authors)	891.439808
Urdu psychological, realistic, sociological fiction (multiple authors)	891.4393083*
Urdu psychological, realistic, sociological fiction (multiple authors)- Collections	891.439308308**
Urdu psychological, realistic, sociological fiction (multiple authors)- History and criticism	891.439308309**
Urdu public discussions	***See*** Urdu debates ...
Urdu public speeches (multiple authors)	891.439501**
Urdu public speeches (multiple authors)- Collections	891.43950108**
Urdu public speeches (multiple authors)- History and criticism	891.43950109**

Urdu quotations	***See*** Urdu anecdotes ...
Urdu realistic fiction	***See*** Urdu psychological... fiction
Urdu recitations (multiple authors)	891.439504+
Urdu religious and morality plays (multiple authors)	891.43920516+
Urdu reminiscences	***See*** Urdu diaries
Urdu romantic fiction (multiple authors)	891.4393085*
Urdu romantic fiction (multiple authors)-Collections	891.439308508**
Urdu romantic fiction (multiple authors)-History and criticism	891.439308509**
Urdu satire	***See*** Urdu humour ...
Urdu satirical poetry	***See*** Urdu humourous ... poetry
Urdu science fiction (multiple authors)	891.439308762*
Urdu science fiction (multiple authors) - Collection	891.43930876208**
Urdu science fiction (multiple authors) - History and criticism	891.43930876209**
Urdu serious drama (multiple authors)	891.4392051+
Urdu short stories (multiple authors)	891.439301*
Urdu short stories (multiple authors)-Collections	891.43930108**
Urdu short stories (multiple authors)-History and criticism	891.43930109**

Urdu sociological fiction (multiple authors)	***See*** Urdu psychological... fiction
Urdu sonnets (multiple authors)	891.4391042*
Urdu sonnets (multiple authors)- Collections	891.439104208**
Urdu sonnets (multiple authors)- History and criticism	891.439104209**
Urdu speaking people	305.791 439
Urdu speeches	891.439 5
Urdu speeches (multiple authors) - to 1845	***See*** Main schedule
Urdu speeches (multiple authors) - 1845-1895	891.43954+
Urdu speeches (multiple authors) - 1895-1919	891.43955+
Urdu speeches (multiple authors) - 1920-1939	891.43956+
Urdu speeches (multiple authors) -1940-	891.43957+
Urdu speeches (multiple authors) - 1940-1999	891.439571+
Urdu speeches (multiple authors) - 19th century	891.43954+
Urdu speeches (multiple authors) - 20th century	891.439571+
Urdu speeches (multiple authors) – 21st century	891.439572+
Urdu speeches (multiple authors) - Collections	891.4395008**
Urdu speeches (multiple authors) - Dictionaries etc	891.4395003

Urdu speeches (multiple authors) - History and criticism	891.4395009**
Urdu speeches (multiple authors) - Periodicals	891.4395005
Urdu speeches (multiple authors) - Philosophy and theory	891.4395001
Urdu speeches (multiple authors) - Psychological aspects	891.43950019
Urdu speeches (multiple authors) - Research	891.43950072
Urdu speeches (multiple authors) - Study and teaching	891.4395007
Urdu speeches (multiple authors) -Value	891.43950013
Urdu speeches (single author)- - to 1845	***See*** Main schedule
Urdu speeches (single author)- 1845 -1895	891.4395 4
Urdu speeches (single author)- 1895 - 1919	891.4395 5
Urdu speeches (single author)- 1920 - 1939	891.4395 6
Urdu speeches (single author)- 1940 -	891.4395 7
Urdu speeches (single author)- 1940-1999	891.4395 71
Urdu speeches (single author)- 19th century	891.4395 4
Urdu speeches (single author)- 2000-	891.4395 72
Urdu speeches (single author)- 20th century	891.4395 71
Urdu suspense fiction (multiple authors)	891.43930872*
Urdu suspense fiction (multiple authors)- Collections	891.4393087208**
Urdu suspense fiction (multiple authors)- History and criticism	891.4393087209**
Urdu tragedy (multiple authors)	891.43920512*

Urdu tragedy (multiple authors)- Collections	891.4392051208**
Urdu tragedy (multiple authors)- History and criticism	891.4392051209**
Urdu variety drama (multiple authors)	891.4392057*
Urdu variety drama (multiple authors)- Collections	891.439205708**
Urdu variety drama (multiple authors)- History and criticism	891.439205709**
Uttar Pradesh- Architecture	720.954 2
Uttar Pradesh- Budget	352.495 42
Uttar Pradesh- Economic development	338.954 2
Uttar Pradesh- Economic geography	330.954 2
Uttar Pradesh- Education	370.954 2
Uttar Pradesh- Fauna	591.954 2
Uttar Pradesh- Flora	581.954 2
Uttar Pradesh- Folk dancing	793.319 542
Uttar Pradesh- Geography	915.42
Uttar Pradesh- Geology	555.42
Uttar Pradesh- History	954.2
Uttar Pradesh- Painting and paintings	759.954 2
Uttar Pradesh- Public administration	351.542
Uttar Pradesh- Public finance	336.542
Uttar Pradesh- Sculpture	730.954 2
Uttarakhand	***See*** Uttaranchal
Uttaranchal- Architecture	720.954 51
Uttaranchal- Budget	352.495 451

Uttaranchal- Economic development	338.954 51
Uttaranchal- Economic geography	330.954 51
Uttaranchal- Education	370.954 51
Uttaranchal- Fauna	591.954 51
Uttaranchal- Flora	581.954 51
Uttaranchal- Folk dancing	793.319 545 1
Uttaranchal- Geography	915.451
Uttaranchal- Geology	555.451
Uttaranchal- History	954.51
Uttaranchal- Painting and paintings	759.954 51
Uttaranchal- Public administration	351.5451
Uttaranchal- Public finance	336.5451
Uttaranchal- Sculpture	730.954 51

V

W

Y

Z

Zen Doctrines	294.342 042 7
Zen (Ch'an)	294.392 7
Zen Buddhism- Doctrines	294.342 042 7
Zoogeography	***See*** Fauna